CHIANTI
AND THE WINES OF TUSCANY

CHIANTI

AND THE WINES OF TUSCANY

Rosemary George

THE WINE APPRECIATION GUILD

in association with

SOTHEBY'S PUBLICATIONS

© 1990 Rosemary George

First published 1990 for Sotheby's Publications by
Philip Wilson Publishers Limited
26 Litchfield Street
London WC2H 9NJ

Available to the USA book trade from
Rizzoli International Publications, Inc
300 Park Avenue South
New York
NY 10010

Exclusive distribution to the wine trade in the USA:
THE WINE APPRECIATION GUILD
155 Connecticut Street
San Francisco
California 94107
(415) 864 1202

ISBN 0 85667 379 X
LCC 90 060779

Designed by Liz Jobling
Printed and bound by Singapore National Printers Ltd,
Singapore

Contents

Foreword

Che un competente italiano scriva sulla Toscana viticola e enologica è una grande soddisfazione per i produttori di questa meravigliosa regione, ma essere apprezzati e descritti da una sapiente penna inglese, non è solo soddisfazione, ma anche molto onore! E in Toscana ci sentiamo davvero gratificati per il puntuale e dotto studio descrittivo di Rosemary George su quanto è di più attuale della nostra vite e del nostro vino.

Gli Inglesi sono proprio dei raffinati conoscitori dell' arte enologica: basta pensare che i vini più importanti non solo in Italia, ma in tutta Europa e direi nel mondo intero, li hanno identificati loro...

Rosemary ha inoltre avuto una sensibilità particolare: direi 'sensibilità di momento storico' per quanto riguarda non solo il Chianti nelle sue varie zone, ma per tutta la vitienologia Toscana. Infatti l'epoca attuale rappresenta davvero un tempo nuovo nella storia della viticoltura e dell' enologia Toscana.

Parlo infatti di vigna, perchè da qualche anno i nostri produttori, incoraggiati dalle prime sperimentazioni innovatrici da parte di coraggiosi e avveduti operatori vitivinicoli, hanno iniziato una fase innovatrice del vigneto; una trasformazione che, senza mortificare la tradizione, è riuscita a modificare in meglio e in più attuale i caratteri della vigna e quindi del vino.

Il viticoltore del Chianti ha perfezionato la pianta di Sangiovese nella sua selezione massale e clonale, nella forma di allevamento e quindi di capacità produttiva, vo candola essenzialmente alla qualità del frutto anzichè alla quantità di esso. Ha separato dalle uve rosse, in vendemmia, la più parte dell'uva bianca di Trebbiano e Malvasia, destinandola ad altre produzioni enologiche diversificate: ne sono nati cosi vini bianchi di nuova concezione ed è rinato il gusto di produrre del buon Vin Santo.

In più il viticoltore Toscano ha sperimentato con successo anche la coltivazione di piccolissime aree di vitigni stranieri adatti a produrre vini da grande invecchiamento in barrique, riuscendoci piuttosto bene e con molta soddisfazione.

Rosemary George, con la sua sensibilità enologica e giornalistica ha 'captato' tutti questi movimenti, tutti questi 'fermenti' e li ha trasformati in un'opera sapiente e ricca al tempo stesso; un'opera che non solo ci onora, ma utile anche a noi stessi che operiamo in questa terra amica di chi è appassionato e colto di vigna, di vino e di tutta l'arte del bello.

Giacomo Tachis

Foreword

It is always a great satisfaction for the producers of Tuscany when a competent Italian writes about the viticulture and oenology of this wonderful region – but to be appreciated and described by such a knowledgeable English hand is not only a great satisfaction, but also a very great honour! We in Tuscany feel flattered by the precise and highly detailed research that Rosemary George has undertaken to produce this most up to date study of our vines and wines.

The English are perceptive connoisseurs when it comes to the appreciation of fine wine. One needs only to reflect that the most important wines of Italy, of Europe and indeed of the whole world, have been identified by them...

Rosemary has shown a particular sensitivity, I would call it a special historical awareness, in realising the right moment to describe the various regions of Chianti. This is a new age for Tuscan viticulture and winemaking.

I am referring in particular to the vine. Some years ago our producers, encouraged by the first experiments carried out by a few courageous and determined predecessors, began an innovative.phase in the vineyard; a transformation that has in no way gone against tradition, but which has improved the condition of the vineyard, and therefore of the wines themselves.

The grower in Chianti has improved the Sangiovese plant through clonal selection, concentrating essentially on the quality of the fruit rather than on quantity. At the harvest he has separated the red grapes from most of the white Trebbiano and Malvasia grapes, which are now destined for other use. This has given birth to new white wines and has also meant the rebirth of good Vin Santo.

In addition the grower has made successful experiments in the cultivation of very small areas of 'foreign' vines, suitable for the production of wines with long *barrique* ageing.

Rosemary George's oenological sensitivity and journalistic skills have enabled her to capture all these movements and trends, which she has transformed into an authoritative book. This not only does us a great honour, but is also of great value to all who work the Tuscan soil – a companion to those who have a passion for and a knowledge of the vineyard, of wine and of art.

Giacomo Tachis

Acknowledgments

Many people have contributed to this book. It is a great honour that Dott. Giacomo Tachis should have written the Foreword, for few have played as great a part in the recent development of Tuscan winemaking. My thanks go also particularly to friends at the Italian Trade Centre, both in London and Italy, especially Giorgio Lulli, Leonardo Montemiglio, Joanne Dougherty, Luciano Mori and Gaetano Gallo. Their help in arranging visits and putting me in touch with the various growers' associations has been invaluable. Amongst those I must thank in particular are the Consorzio di Brunello di Montalcino, the Consorzio di Vernaccia di San Gimignano, Antonella Abeti of the Consorzio del Chianti Putto, Maddalena Mazzeschi of the Consorzio del Vino Nobile di Montepulciano, and last but certainly not least the Consorzio del Gallo Nero, both in Florence and in London. Katharina Trauttmansdorff, Ursula Thurner, Geoffrey Frankcom and Paul Dwyer deserve special mention for all their assistance. Help has come too from Maureen Ashley, Luciana Lynch, Helena Harwood, Renato Trestini, Charles Carey, Bette Anne Scaveta, not to mention my husband, Christopher Galleymore.

Wine books are above all about the people who make wine. So it goes without saying that all those featured in this exploration of Tuscany contributed in their own way. Italian hospitality can be wonderfully overwhelming. Bottles were opened for me and questions answered in the most convivial surroundings; and friendships were made.

The photograph on the front of the jacket is by Janet Price. The colour illustrations opposite pp. 73 and 169 are by Patrick Eagar Photography (Jan Traylen and Mike Newton). Sara Matthews deserves a special thank you for the photographs opposite pp. 84, 168. The endpaper and black and white illustrations on pp. 19, 21, 33, 59 and 61 are reproduced courtesy of Archivi Alinari. I am also very grateful to the many growers who have supplied photographs of their estates, their wines and themselves.

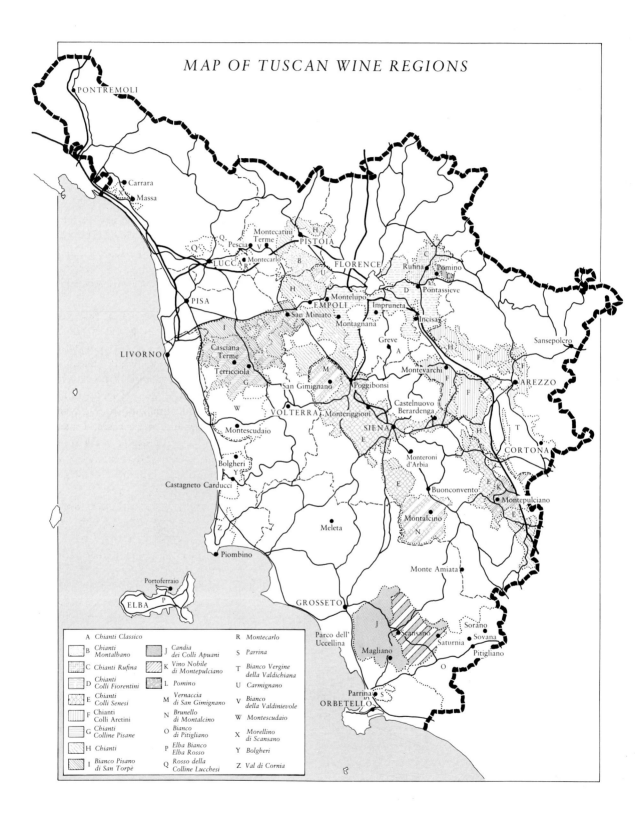

MAP OF TUSCAN WINE REGIONS

PONTREMOLI

Carrara
Massa

Montecatini Terme
Q.
Q.
Q Pescia
V
Montecarlo
LUCCA
R

PISTOIA
B
U
FLORENCE
Rufina
Pomino
C
D
Pontassieve

Montelupo
PISA
EMPOLI
Montagnana
Impruneta
Incisa
San Miniato
H

I
Casciana Terme
L
Greve
A
H
Sansepolcro
F
Montevarchi
F
AREZZO
Terricciola
LIVORNO
G
San Gimignano
M
Poggibonsi
F
F

W
VOLTERRA
Monteriggioni
Castelnuovo
Berardenga
H
T
Montescudaio
E
SIENA
CORTONA

Monteroni
d'Arbia
Bolgheri
Y
E
K
Castagneto Carducci
E
Buonconvento
Montepulciano

Z
Meleta
Montalcino
N

Piombino

Portoferraio
P
ELBA
Monte Amiata

GROSSETO
Parco dell'
Uccellina
J
Sorano
Scansano
Sovana
Magliano
Saturnia
Pitigliano
O

Parrina
S
ORBETELLO

A	Chianti Classico	J	Candia dei Colli Apuani	R	Montecarlo
B	Chianti Montalbano	K	Vino Nobile di Montepulciano	S	Parrina
C	Chianti Rufina	L	Pomino	T	Bianco Vergine della Valdichiana
D	Chianti Colli Fiorentini	M	Vernaccia di San Gimignano	U	Carmignano
E	Chianti Colli Senesi	N	Brunello di Montalcino	V	Bianco della Valdinievole
F	Chianti Colli Aretini	O	Bianco di Pitigliano	W	Montescudaio
G	Chianti Colline Pisane	P	Elba Bianco Elba Rosso	X	Morellino di Scansano
H	Chianti	Q	Rosso della Colline Lucchesi	Y	Bolgheri
I	Bianco Pisano di San Torpè			Z	Val di Cornia

Setting the Scene

I have never forgotten the first time I saw the countryside of Tuscany. I was on a train travelling from Florence to Perugia to attend Italian classes at the Università per i Stranieri. A new course was beginning and the train was filled with students, and their luggage. I was squeezed between another body and a rucksack in the corridor. It was hot and airless and, to say the least, uncomfortable. Then suddenly the Tuscan landscape unfolded before my eyes. I was instantly enchanted. This was the scenery of Renaissance paintings, the backdrop to countless Madonnas. There were cypress trees and olive trees, vineyards and woods, on hillsides that seemed not to have changed for centuries. It was breathtakingly beautiful and I forgot the discomfort of the train.

This was long before I knew anything of Chianti. If memory serves me right, the only Chianti that came my way during that month in Perugia was a bottle to celebrate by room-mate's exam results. The label described the contents as Chianti Bianco, such was the sorry state of Italian wine law at the time. What I drank as Chianti Bianco would probably today be a simple *vino da tavola* Toscano Bianco.

Any survey of the wines of Tuscany must centre upon Chianti. Chianti is the name that everyone knows. On first meeting, it is a friendly and unassuming wine, but on better acquaintance you begin to realise that it has hidden depths and many facets to its character. Chianti is made over a large part of Tuscany, with seven different sub-zones recognised in the regulations for DOCG (Denominazione di Origine Controllata e Garantita), which give the wine a legal guarantee of origin. Chianti Classico comes from the heart of Tuscany, from the hills between Florence and Siena, where there are medieval castles and Renaissance villas. This is where one finds most of the best Chiantis, wines with depth and complexity. Rufina too makes some long-lived wines, but Chianti from the other outlying zones, from the Colli Fiorentini, Colli Aretini, Colli Senesi, Colline Pisane and Montalbano tends to be lighter.

Chianti has undergone an enormous transition in the last twenty, or even ten years. Its reputation had been sadly tarnished. The Sangiovese grape is the mainstay of Chianti, and indeed of all the red wines of Tuscany, but the DOC (Denominazione di Origine Controllata) regulations of 1967 allowed as much as 30 per cent of white grapes, for what was supposed to be a red wine. The 1960s also saw the dismantling of the *mezzadria* or sharecropping system, a system of landholding and agriculture which had been part of Tuscan life since the Middle Ages. This brought radical changes in landownership and the abandonment of the *cultura promiscua*, the growing of mixed crops, which had provided the traditional framework of the countryside. Specialised vineyards were then planted, often without thought and with the wrong grape varieties. The market was awash with bad Chianti. There was a crisis of confidence among consumers and Chianti lost many friends.

The thinking wine grower realised that something needed to be done. The introduction of the tighter DOCG regulations in 1984 has certainly helped to eliminate bad wines and given producers a much needed boost of confidence. More exciting, however, is the wave of revolutionary winemaking outside the regulations that has swept through Tuscany in the last ten years. The pace was set initially by Sassicaia from the Tenuta San Guido, near Bolgheri, and quickly followed by Antinori's Tignanello, a wine with Tuscan flavours but designed for the international market. It combined the Sangiovese of Tuscany with Cabernet Sauvignon, the grape variety of Bordeaux, which has also now spread to most of the New World. The success of Tignanello surprised even Antinori and many others have followed the company's example.

Over the last ten years Tuscany has seen the creation of an astonishing number of new wines. More attention has been paid to Sangiovese, which is now recognised as a fine grape in its own right and varieties from outside Tuscany have been planted. This has been accompanied by an enormous improvement in winemaking techniques, not least in the maturing of the wine. Few are the serious estates, particularly in Chianti Classico, that have neither Cabernet Sauvignon nor French *barriques*. These *vini da tavola*, sometimes called Supertuscans or alternative wines, are by no means all super. Some are over-oaked and over-priced to match, but the best show just what superb wines Tuscany can produce. The quality of Chianti has improved in their wake.

This new wave of winemaking has spread throughout Tuscany. In nearly every DOC there are winemakers who are questioning established ideas and trying to improve upon accepted practices. They have provided the backbone of this book, making it possible by contributing their ideas and offering their wines for tasting.

Writing it has taken me to every corner of the Tuscan vineyards. I began my researches in May 1986, spending a happy month in a villa outside Tavarnelle discovering Chianti Classico. In 1987 another book intervened, but 1988 brought me three times to Tuscany and 1989 four times, amounting to over four months exploring what was already my favourite part of Italy. Inevitably I spent much time in Chianti Classico, for that is the heart of Tuscany, where much has happened in a very short time; but other fine wines merited attention: Brunello di Montalcino, Vino Nobile di Montepulciano, Carmignano and Vernaccia di San Gimignano.

I have tried also not to neglect the lesser known wines, which are off the beaten track and rarely seen outside their own locality. I spent a day with the growers of the Candia dei Colli Apuani, whose enthusiasm at their very first encounter with a foreign wine writer can only be described as overwhelming. I explored the hills behind Lucca to find Montecarlo, one of the most individual of white wines. Bolgheri, close to the coast, is the home of Sassicaia and of other new wines too. Further south lies the Maremma, which covers the coastal lowlands and the wild hills inland from Grosseto. Here the two principal wines are the complementary pair, Morellino di Scansano and Bianco di Pitigliano, from hilltop towns that date back to the Etruscans. La Parrina is one of the smallest DOCs of Tuscany, while the Val di Cornia is the newest. The island of Elba also has its own flavours.

Finally no book on the wines of Tuscany would be complete without that most individual of Tuscan wines, Vin Santo. The olive trees demand a mention too, for they are an as essential part of the Tuscan landscape as the vineyards, and olive oil as intrinsic to Tuscan cooking as the wine that accompanies it.

The vineyards are rich in history and art, as well as wine and the welcome has always been friendly and the hospitality warm; such is the nature of Tuscany. The flavours of the region are epitomised by a glass of Chianti and a piece of *bruschetta*, the delicious baked bread that is generously moistened with the best olive oil; or on a sweeter note, some rich Vin Santo with *biscotti di Prato*.

I could be sitting in the sunshine in that most magical of Tuscan squares, the Piazza del Campo in Siena, watching the theatre of the street pass by; or on the terrace of the house where I stayed at the top of a very steep hill outside Greve, with views across the valley of olive groves and vineyards, to the tiny village of Montefioralle. But Chianti, not to mention Brunello, Vino Nobile, Carmignano and others is now acquiring a reputation that extends far beyond the boundaries of Tuscany. I could equally well enjoy a bottle at home with friends in London. The wines of Tuscany have taken on such stature that they can compete without shame in the world marketplace, rivalling the finest of France, California or Australia.

Chianti from the Etruscans

It was the Etruscans who gave their name to Tuscany. They occupied much of central Italy, from some time in the eighth century BC, until they were ousted by the Romans during the course of the third century BC. Evidence remains of their attachment to the fruits of the vine, in the form of a wine cup found in an Etruscan tomb at Castellina-in-Chianti, now exhibited in the archaeological museum in Florence, and surviving Etruscan frescos depict scenes that relate to Bacchus. The fossilised vines that have been found at San Miniato, however, indicate that vines were here long before man, which, as Raymond Flower says in *Chianti, the Land, the People and the Wine*, is not a bad start for a wine-producing region.

There is no doubt that very early on in the history of Tuscany, the vine became an essential part of the region's agriculture, along with olives and grain, providing one of the three staples in the Tuscan diet, which are wine, oil and bread. The name Chianti came much later. There are various theories as to its origins, but most are purely speculative. One idea, put forward by Emmanuele Repetti in his *Dizionario Geografico Fisico Storico della Toscana* (1833–48), is that it comes from the Latin *clangor*, meaning the high-pitched sound of a trumpet, or the cry of a bird; and that it alludes to the wild, uncultivated state of the country, which was used for hunting rather than agriculture. Other placenames, too, have strong associations with hunting.

A document dated 790 refers to a donation to the Abbey of San Bartolomeo in Ripoli, of some land situated 'in clanti cum integro salingo'. There is speculation as to whether the scribe really meant to write *chianti*, or even *campi*. It has also been suggested that the word Chianti derives from an Etruscan family who lived in the area: or even that it was the name of a wine grower, who used to come down from the hills into Florence with his produce.

The place is certainly identified by name in the thirteenth century. A document dated 14th July 1211, 'actum in Clanti apud canonicam Santi Reguli', refers to sales of property by Ugo Ranieri and Bernardino, sons of Ugo Fortibraccio della Val Curiale, to the priest Pietro of San Giusto a Rentennano (still a Chianti estate today). By 1260 the name Chianti was current usage in the Book of Montaperti, a record book of the Florentine commune which includes information about the agricultural activities of the region.

Vermiglio, Vernacchia and Florence

The word is first found describing a wine at the end of the fourteenth century. This is in the papers of the Prato merchant, Francesco di Marco Datini, best known as the inventor of the bill of exchange or cheque: in the *Campagnia del Banco*, written in December 1398, Francesco Datini and Bartolomeo Cambioni describe Francesco di Marco and Stoldo di Lorenzo as being in debt to Piero di Tino Riccio for 'three florins, twenty-six soldi and eight denari, the price of six casks of white Chianti wine'. In correspondence with the same Datini, Amedeo Gherardini of Vignamaggio (still an important estate today) wrote on 26th October 1404 that he was sending half a barrel of his own personal stock from Vignamaggio, one of the choicest wines of Chianti. Thus it seems that the very first references describe it as a white wine. Indeed, during the Middle Ages, the red wines of Florence were more often called Vino Vermiglio and the white wines Vernaccia.

The medieval history of the vineyards of Chianti is very much tied up with the struggles between the Florentines and the Sienese, and the wars of the Guelphs and the Ghibellines. This is not the place to embark upon an account of this long drawn-out power struggle between, not only the city states of central Italy, but also the papacy and the Holy Roman Emperor; in brief, the Guelphs of Florence supported the Hohenstaufen Emperors against the Ghibellines of Siena and the papacy. Viticulture was an essential part of country life in the hills between Florence and Siena, and it must on occasions have been severely disrupted by the warring factions. One response to this was the creation in the middle of the thirteenth century of the Lega del Chianti, an organisation comprising the principal landowners of Chianti, with the prime object of protecting their property. In this century the old league was recalled with the creation of a white wine called Bianco della Lega.

As elsewhere in medieval Europe, the monasteries played a part in the establishment of successful viticulture. The Vallombrosan monasteries of Badia a Passignano, Badia a Coltibuono and Badia a Monte Scalari were no exception. Today Badia a Coltibuono is still an important wine estate and Badia a Passignano is about to take on new impetus, with its recent purchase by the house of Antinori. Viticulture must also have extended into the city of Florence. Some street names indicate the presence of vineyards, Via della Vigna Vecchia and Via della Vigna Nuova, as do such church names as Sancta Maria inter Vineas and Sant' Jacopo tra le Vigne. Even the square of Santa Maria Novella, in the heart of city, is reputed to have been made by uprooting a vineyard. The end of the thirteenth century saw the creation of the Guild of the Vinattieri (1282), in the heyday of the guild system, with their crest of a red octagonal drinking bowl on a white background. This was the organisation that Giovanni di Piero Antinori joined in 1385, justifying the claim of his family to be one of the oldest wine-producing dynasties in Europe.

Viticulture flourished and the wine trade prospered, paying taxes on its commercial success. Ruffino's history of Chianti suggests that taxes were levied on in excess of 300,000 hectolitres of wine in Florence during the fourteenth century. In 1364 a list of the contents of the cellars of the Palazzo Vecchio included Vermiglio, Vernaccia, Vino Bianco Trebbiano, Verdea and Vernacciola, confirming that the reputation of Tuscan wines was based on Vino Vermiglio, rather than Chianti. Vino Vermiglio was sent home by ambassadors in Florence to their kings and princes. As we shall see, it became popular in England.

There are numerous references to wine by Florentine writers throughout the medieval and Renaissance period. Dante does not mention Vino Vermiglio by name, but it is not unreasonable to assume that he is thinking of his native wine when he writes in the 25th Canto of *Purgatory*: 'Watch the heat from the sun which turns to wine as it mixes with the humour flowing from the vine'. Boccaccio too makes frequent references to wine in the *Decameron*.

The title page of Francesco Redi's poem
Bacchus in Tuscany, *Florence 1685.*

On a more frivolous note, Antonio Pucci, town-crier of Florence in the fourteenth century, wrote numerous songs, of which the following is a typical example:

Just as wine is good for man if drunk in modest quantities.
Just so can Vermiglio or Trebbiano in excess bring him many an ague.

Chianti is named in the miracle play of Sant' Antonio, performed during the latter half of the fifteenth century.

I have some Chianti and wine of San Losino
Sweet Trebbiano, Vernaccia and Malvasia.

Two centuries later, a famous poem by Francesco Redi called *Bacchus in Tuscany* is a survey of all the best wines of the year 1685 (see illustration). Chianti is mentioned by name:

Tongue of mine, now shrewd and discerning in these things
Taste this other wine, robust and strong: it boasts of birth
Among the wines of Chianti, and was made on stony ground,
For those who know to tell good wine from a poor,
By a thick, low vine, but not on the Broncone.

The stony soil is still the same today; 'Broncone' was a method of pruning.

Andrea Bacci, the doctor of Pope Sixtus V, relates observations made on a journey through Tuscany in the year 1596 in his *De Naturali Vinorum Historia*. He talks of the vines of Moscatelli around Florence, the exquisite Trebbiano of San Giovanni Valdarno, the generous wines of San Gimignano, the ruby-red elixirs of the hills of San Casciano and the potent brews produced in the southern Sienese, in and around

Montepulciano. The wines grown on the hills of Florence and Fiesole, however, are by far the best.

The vine features in art too, most strikingly in Giorgio Vasari's *Vision of Chianti* on the ceiling of the Sala dei Cinquecento in the Palazzo Vecchio. A young Bacchus, with vine shoots, is laden down with large ripe bunches of grapes, in a rich and fertile countryside.

The red wine of the Chianti region had acquired a reputation abroad. In England it was known as 'Florence'. Records of trade with Italy in the mid-fourteenth century mention 'vernage' or 'vernacchia' from the neighbourhood of Florence. A. D. Francis notes in *The Wine Trade* that in the sixteenth century the wines of Florence were well regarded, but inclined to go off quickly, so that they needed to be shipped promptly through the Straits of Gibraltar before the autumn winds held them up.

The same problem is identified by Charles Longland, writing from Leghorn in January 1653, who informs his suppliers that owing to the sea voyage some types of *vino di Firenze* are not successful in England. According to Mr. Longland, shipping wine in casks is only possible in the cold months from January to March. It is also noted that wines from Tuscany are subject to heavy duty in London, whereas French and Spanish wines are not.

Samuel Pepys records in his diary on 9th January 1661 a gift of two bottles of Florence from Lady Sandwich, wife of his chief at the Admiralty, to take home to his wife. W. Salmon in the *Compleat English Physician* (1693), writes that 'Florence white and red are both good stomach wines, but the red is something binding'!

Imports of Florence wine rose rapidly at the end of the seventeenth century. It was apparently exported in uncorked flasks, sealed with olive oil, stoppered and packed in chests. From 29th October 1682 to 1st February 1683, only thirty-three chests were imported in London, while in February 1683 seventy-three arrived and from 30th October 1698 to 23rd August 1699 2,000 tuns.

Florence was on sale in the London taverns and Richard Ames in 'The Search After Claret', written in 1691, describes how he combed them in vain for claret:

At the Head of old jolly gruff great cod-piec'd Harry
We expected to find out a glass to be merry;
But the name of Puntack was forgotten and dead,
And strange Barcelona now reign'd in his stead;
Withal such a noise was still made at the bar,
Of Florentine flasks and full quarts of Navar;
Let me dye of the pip, or my mistress scorn,
If I did not suppose that I was at Leghorn.

At the Shepherd when boldly for claret we askt.
He told us he'd very good Florence was flaskt
At the Greyhound...Sir, we've Florence...

He assur'd us of Claret he had not a gill,
But of delicate Florence we might have our fill.

Cyril Ray notes in his history of the firm of Ruffino that there were periods in the eighteenth century when Florence was open to criticism, with complaints that wines 'when genuine and well made probably had a certain degree of delicacy but carelessness or malculture diminished their fineness', and some that began with

The Bando, or Edict, of Cosimo III de' Medici, Grand Duke of Tuscany, issued in 1716.

'freshness and a beautiful deep colour', developed 'a disagreeable roughness'. The satirist Dean Swift was particularly vehement in his complaints, going in 1711 to a tavern, 'after a scurvy dinner', to drink Florence 'at four-and-sixpence a flask, damned wine'. He also wrote of the wine sent by the Grand Duke to the Secretary of State, Bolingbroke, which had begun to spoil within a fortnight: 'Do you know that I fear that my whole chest of Florence is turned sour, at least the first two bottles were, and hardly drinkable. How plaguy unfortunate am I! And the Secretary's own is the best I ever tasted!'

The Edict of Cosimo III 1716

The Grand Duke of Tuscany Cosimo III produced wine at his villa at Poggio a Caiano, which adjoins Carmignano, and sent some as a gift to Queen Anne, who apparently much appreciated it. His greatest contribution to the viticultural development of the region was an edict issued in 1716, which defined the boundaries of Chianti, along with those of Pomino, Carmignano and the Val d'Arno di Sopra, now part of the Colli Fiorentini (see illustration). The area of Chianti was determined to extend from Spedaluzzo to Greve, and from there to Panzano, including Radda, Gaiole and Castellina up to the boundary with Siena. This, of course, still constitutes the heart of Chianti Classico today.

The imposing Castello di Brolio, in a photograph of 1878. Note the vineyards below, planted with mixed vines and olive trees.

If the seventeenth century saw the expansion of the foreign reputation of the wine of Florence, the eighteenth century brought an improvement in viticulture and, above all, in vinification techniques. Cosimo Trinici, in *L'Agricoltore Sperimentato*, published in Lucca in 1738, mentions the various grape varieties, commenting particularly upon Canaiolo Nero, Canaiolo Rosso, Malvasia, Trebbiano and Sangiovese or S. Zoveto. He had experimented with various proportions of them and confirms that the best Chianti is undoubtedly a blend.

Another oenologist of the period Gian Cosimo Villifranchi classifies the best wines of the region, in his *Oenologia Toscana* (1773), namely red and white Montepulciano, and Chianti, particularly that from Castellina, Panzano and Brolio. For Villifranchi, the wines that keep the best are those that are made the most simply. He considers that the best Chianti is made from a lot of Canaiolo and a small quantity of Sangiovese, and that it should be a full ruby-red colour. He also describes the *governo* method, entailing the use of must that has been concentrated and then filtered; made from grapes picked at the same time as the others, but left to dry until they are needed. He recommends the keeping of Chianti in flasks, in which it will last easily for three or four years, and withstand journeys, even by sea.

Baron Bettino Ricasoli (1807–1880)

Baron Bettino Ricasoli must take much of the credit for making Chianti the wine that we know today. The Ricasolis are an old Tuscan family, whose seat is the austere and imposing castle of Brolio, near Gaiole-in-Chianti (see illustration). Romantic rumour has it that the Iron Baron, so called for his inflexibility of character, took his young wife Anna to a ball in Florence, where she danced with another young nobleman more times than her husband deemed proper; leading her from the ballroom, the Baron instructed his coachman to drive them to Brolio, which had been uninhabited for many years; and there they lived virtually for the rest of their lives. Bettino Ricasoli devoted himself to the estate, going on to play a part in Italian politics as the second Prime Minister of the recently united kingdom of Italy, while Anna looked after their numerous children.

Tuscan vineyards had always included a mixture of grape varieties and the *governo* method was long established, having developed from peasant traditions. What Bettino Ricasoli did was to experiment with different blends of grapes and with winemaking techniques. He kept an extensive diary from 1851 to 1877 about his cellar at Brolio, which is full of observations on viticulture and oenology. A letter to Professor Studiati of the University of Pisa sums up his thoughts on the blend of grape varieties that gives the best Chianti: 'I was convinced by the results of the first experiments, that the wine receives from the Sangioveto grape most part of its bouquet (for which I particularly aim) and some vigour of sensation; from Canajuolo it gets the sweetness which moderates the roughness without taking away any bouquet. Malvasia which could be left out of wines due for long maturation, has a tendency to dilute the products of the first two grapes. It increases the taste and by making it lighter, makes the wine ready for everyday consumption.'

It is significant that there is no mention at all of the ubiquitous Trebbiano, and Malvasia is needed only if a wine is intended for early drinking. A Chianti that is destined for some ageing should only be made from red grapes, principally Sangiovese, with some Canaiolo. This is how many of the modern winemakers of Chianti Classico would like to make their wine today.

In the latter half of the nineteenth century Chianti began to feature at the various international exhibitions. Visiting Vienna in 1873 Henry Vizetelly judged Chianti to be a wine 'with great finesse and a pleasant acidity not dissimilar to the wines of Beaujolais but with more colour and strength'. At the Paris Exhibition of 1879 there were numerous samples of Chianti. A certain Briosi wrote in the *Esame chimico-comparativo dei vini italiani inviati all Esposizione di Parigi del 1878* that it reminded him of Barolo, 'as its components appear in the right proportions; a more appealing red wine, less substantial than Barolo but more delicate and homogeneous'. It was declared at the presentation of medals that 'Chianti vecchio' could compete with the best wines of France.

Chianti now appears under its own name in literature. Domenico Gnoli (1838–1915) wrote:

O flask of Chianti, I need
your help: I drink, I want
to drown my past in you:
I want to laugh, laugh for
everything I have loved!

Giuseppina Strepponi, Verdi's wife wrote in a letter in 1873: 'Verdi is very well, he eats, runs in the garden, sleeps and drinks Chianti, nothing but Chianti and more Chianti. Long live Chianti then and he who has provided such a good one!'

A cart loaded with fiaschi *of Chianti, belonging to the firm of Fratelli Marinelli, a photograph of around 1930.*

Flasks and Bottling

At this time there was a significant development in the presentation of the wine. The flask had long been traditional to Tuscany. The first references occur in documents of the twelfth century, about the same time as the name Chianti itself. The town of San Gimignano authorised in 1265 an artisan by the name of Cheronimo to open 'a kiln for the art of glass-working', and other kilns followed in the Val d'Elsa and Val d'Arno, especially around Empoli. It was in these kilns that the Tuscan flask was produced. The vessel seems initially to have formed part of a set, including wine glasses, for the dinner tables of the well-to-do. Flasks were divided into two categories, the normal *fiaschi alla fiorentina*, and bottle flasks, or *fiaschi strapesi*, meaning literally 'overweight flasks'.

Some attribute to Leonardo da Vinci the idea of covering the fragile bodies with straw to protect them, but straw-covered examples were certainly in use by the second half of the fifteenth century. A fresco by Domenico Ghirlandaio in the church of Santa Maria Novella in Florence includes a figure holding two straw-covered flasks. Michelangelo complained to his relations in Tuscany, while he was painting the Sistine Chapel, that he would much rather that they had sent him two flasks of Trebbiano than eight shirts.

Flasks were given strong handles so that they could be carried by hand, or alternatively hung from a pole. If a large quantity needed to be transported, they might be piled, carefully balanced, on a cart (see illustration). One problem of the flask was its uncertain capacity. A Florentine decree issued in 1574 laid down that the contents should be 'half a quarter', which equalled 2.28 litres. Later glassworks were issued with dies and ordered to stamp an impression on the neck of each bottle as a guarantee of the measure. The die showed the lily, the medieval emblem of Florence. Flasks normally had a stopper and a layer of oil to protect the wine, but no airtight cork, as the flask was not strong enough to take it.

Adolfo Laborel Melini was responsible for the next stage in their development in the mid-nineteenth century. Here are his thoughts on the problem: 'Tuscan wine abroad does not seem to be successful if bottled in flasks with oil because our foreign customers do not understand about the necessity of the oil and inconvenience is caused by it. Tuscan wine is not appreciated in bottles because the overseas' consumer now demands the Tuscan flask. In conclusion: we need a container that has the appeal of the flask and at the same time the strength of the bottle!'

With the help of the director of the glass factory at Pontassieve, he tried to design a flask that was strong enough to resist the pressure of a cork applied by machine. Eventually they were successful; so successful that Melini was awarded a diploma by the Chamber of Commerce in 1877 for establishing a market for Tuscan wine abroad.

Towards a Legal Guarantee of Quality

At the beginning of the 1900s two qualities of Chianti were recognised, Chianti *di prima qualità* and Chianti *di seconda qualità*, sometimes called *mezzo* Chianti. The better wines could not be sold until the July after the vintage, while the inferior ones might be offered for sale in February. What was now needed was some form of legal recognition for the provenance of Chianti. As things stood, there was no guarantee that the wine came from Tuscany, let alone the vineyards between Florence and Siena. The popularity of the name led to its use for wines from other parts of Italy, and parts of Tuscany where similar wine was produced. White wines were even described as 'Chianti Bianco'.

An association of producers was formed in Siena in 1902 for the 'difesa dei vini del vero Chianti', which took the name of the Sindicato Enologico Cooperativo Chiantigiano. Its members came from Greve, Radda, Castellina, Gaiole and Castelnuovo Berardenga, but there was uncertainty as to the precise limits of the area, resulting in an outcry from neighbours who felt excluded. There was talk of legislation, but nothing very concrete was achieved before the First World War. More discussion followed on the need for a law on the *denominazione di origine dei vini*, but the one that was actually passed in 1924 achieved very little. It recognised that *vino tipico* should be produced under specified conditions, but no consideration at all was given to provenance. In other words, a 'Chianti' could still be made in any part of Italy, with the help of chemistry and technology.

The Gallo Nero and the Putto

The same year, however, saw the creation of the Consorzio per la difesa del vino tipico del Chianti, with thirty-three founder members from Castellina, Gaiole, Greve and Radda. The producers took the black cockerel, or Gallo Nero, as their trade mark. This harks back to a boundary dispute between the Florentines and the Sienese, which was settled by the treaty of Fonterutoli of 1208. It had been agreed that the border should be drawn where a horseman each from Florence and Siena met on the road, having set out at cock-crow. The Florentines starved their cockerels, who crowed early, giving their man a headstart.

This Consorzio was and still is a purely voluntary organisation, with the objective of promoting and defending the reputation of Chianti Classico. Members from the neighbouring areas of San Casciano, Tavarnelle and Barberino were included in 1925, with the expansion of the zone to incorporate some vineyards in these villages. Then in 1927 a second Consorzio was created, to cover the larger area of Chianti vineyards beyond Chianti Classico. This took the emblem of the putto, or chubby baby cherub.

In 1932 came the first legal recognition of the zones where 'un vino denominato del Chianti' could be produced, namely Chianti Classico, Montalbano, Rufina, Colli Fiorentini, Colli Senesi, Colli Aretini and Colline Pisane. The area recognised as Chianti Classico was almost identical to that laid down by the Grand Duke in his edict of 1716. There were no precise regulations, but this law was considered a declaration of intent. A decree of the Minister of Agriculture determined in October 1941 that the best Chianti came from Chianti Classico, while wines from the other zones of Chianti were to be considered of secondary quality; but there was no legal recognition of the different zones. They were called simply Chianti, as opposed to Chianti Classico.

The DOC Regulations

No precise regulations regarding methods of production came into effect until the creation of the DOC, or Denominazione di Origine Controllata, for Chianti in 1967. The framework for this had been laid by the Italian Wine Law of 1963. Italy had finally caught up with France, which had introduced the *appellation contrôlée* system over thirty years earlier, in 1936. The DOC regulations defined the areas of Chianti and Chianti Classico as those already agreed in 1932. The use of the following grape varieties was accepted:

Sangiovese   50–80 per cent
Canaiolo Nero   10–30 per cent
Trebbiano Toscano and Malvasia del Chianti   10–30 per cent
Complementary grape varieties   5 per cent, of which Colorino was particularly recommended, especially for the *governo* method

These percentages were the proportions in the vineyard, not in the vat of fermenting juice, so that in practice there could be even more than a third of white grapes in this red wine, for Trebbiano vines are much more prolific than those of Sangiovese.

Yields were set at 125 quintals per hectare for specialised vines, with a 70 per cent yield of juice, equating to 87 hectolitres per hectare. For Chianti Classico the permitted yield was 115 quintals, again with a 70 per cent yield in juice equating to 80 hectolitres per hectare. Traditional techniques in vineyard and cellar such as the *governo all'uso toscano* were upheld and it was not possible to offer Chianti for sale until 1st March following the vintage. Alcohol levels were determined, at a minimum of 11.5° for Chianti and 12° for Chianti Classico. It was also permitted to add a corrective 15 per cent of wine or must from outside the defined area of Chianti. This regulation recognised a common practice, but ran completely contrary to the concept of authenticity in the origin of a wine. It gave legal recognition to the fact that a red wine containing so many white grapes, needed boosting with deeper coloured and more alcoholic wines from the south. The category of *riserva* was recognised for wines aged for three years from the January following the vintage, in either cask or bottle. This replaced the former usage of *vecchio*, which is no longer found, except on very old labels.

It is easy to see the inadequacy of these regulations, notably in the excessive amount of white grapes and the possibility of using wine or grapes from outside the region. Nor were the permitted yields in keeping with a red wine of quality.

The DOCG Regulations

The institution in 1984 of the stricter DOCG, or Denominazione di Origine Controllata e Garantita, has gone some way to correct these deficiences, but as discussed in subsequent chapters, there is still much scope for improvement. The percentages of grape varieties have been amended, and in particular the allowable amount of white grapes has been reduced; but unfortunately not eliminated. The permitted percentages are now as follows:

Sangiovese   70–90 per cent
Canaiolo   5–10 per cent
Trebbiano and Malvasia   2–5 per cent for Chianti Classico
⠀⠀⠀⠀⠀⠀⠀⠀⠀⠀⠀⠀⠀⠀⠀⠀⠀⠀⠀⠀5–10 per for the other areas
Complementary grape varieties   10 per cent

This still allows plenty of room for manoeuvre. Yields have been reduced, to 100 quintals per hectare, giving 70 hectolitres of juice, except for Chianti Classico and what are considered to be the two better zones of Chianti, Rufina and Colli Fiorentini. Chianti Classico is restricted to 75 quintals, making 53 hectolitres per hectare, and Rufina and Colli Fiorentini to 80 quintals, making 56 hectolitres per hectare. The 15 per cent corrective of wine or must from elsewhere has also been eliminated from these regions. A vine in these areas may not produce more than three kilos of grapes, whereas elsewhere in Chianti five kilos per vine is allowed. The guarantee of authenticity entails stricter controls on production and bottling, supported by analysis and tasting. If the permitted production is exceeded by more than 20 per cent, the entire crop is automatically declassified into anonymous *vino da tavola*.

The implementation of DOCG has resulted in a fairly drastic and desirable reduction in the production of Chianti. By reducing the amount of white grapes and the introduction of tasting and analysis, the overall production has dropped from 1,417,336 hectolitres in 1983 to a more manageable 847,104 hectolitres in 1988. In Chianti Classico alone the production fell from 378,469 hectolitres in 1983, to 301,499 hectolitres in 1988 (see Appendix I).

Although there is much muttering about the bureaucracy entailed in obtaining the seal for DOCG, there is a consensus that the controls have gone some way towards eliminating the inferior Chianti that was spoiling the market for more reputable producers. Chianti is certainly a better wine than it was before DOCG, but there is still scope for improvement. The new law of DOCG has really only implemented what serious producers were already doing.

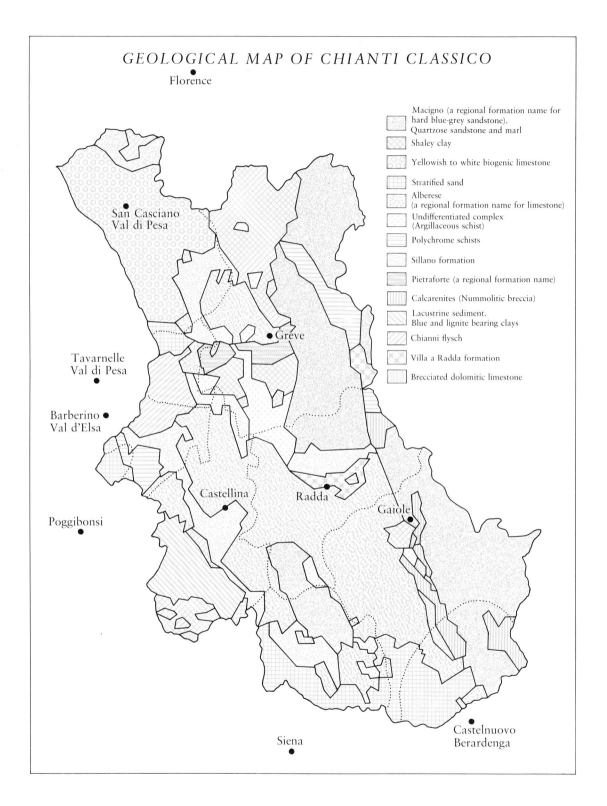

GEOLOGICAL MAP OF CHIANTI CLASSICO

Florence

San Casciano
Val di Pesa

Tavarnelle
Val di Pesa

Barberino
Val d'Elsa

Poggibonsi

Greve

Castellina

Radda

Gaiole

Siena

Castelnuovo
Berardenga

Macigno (a regional formation name for hard blue-grey sandstone). Quartzose sandstone and marl

Shaley clay

Yellowish to white biogenic limestone

Stratified sand

Alberese (a regional formation name for limestone)

Undifferentiated complex (Argillaceous schist)

Polychrome schists

Sillano formation

Pietraforte (a regional formation name)

Calcarenites (Nummolitic breccia)

Lacustrine sediment. Blue and lignite bearing clays

Chianni flysch

Villa a Radda formation

Brecciated dolomitic limestone

Viticulture: Working towards Chianti 2000

Chianti covers an enormous area of Tuscany, in seven different zones. The heart of the region is Chianti Classico in the beautiful hills between the cities of Florence and Siena. For the rest, the Colli Fiorentini, the Colli Senesi, Colline Pisane, Colli Aretini, Rufina and Montalbano together cover a large part of central Tuscany. In some ways the different areas are quite distinct, but there is a common thread running between them. The same grape varieties are grown, although in varying proportions. It is a common but well-founded cliché that Italians are individualists, and maybe none more so than Italian winemakers. They may accept a fundamental legal outline of what constitutes Chianti, but each producer worth his salt wants to add his own stamp of character to his wine. The variations, therefore, are infinite.

The Soil and Climate in Chianti Classico

The following general analysis of viticulture and vinification concentrates on Chianti Classico, which is the heart of the region. The differences within other zones are discussed in the chapters devoted to them. There are enormous soil variations even within Chianti Classico, as the geological map opposite shows. The best for wine growing is generally considered to be *galestro*, a poor stony soil, typical of the area, which also gives its name to a white wine. The region is made up of several large valleys, in turn divided by numerous smaller ones. With so many hills, the permutations of microclimate are considerable, with variations almost in adjoining vineyards.

The vineyards at Greve are at a relatively low altitude, around 250–350 metres. This tends to make for soft perfumed wines, especially when they are young, but which will tend to age quite quickly. Further south around Panzano, the vineyards are higher. The soil is predominantly *galestro*, with some sand and chalk, and the wines are more robust, with deeper colour. The highest parts of Chianti Classico are in the south, around Radda and Gaiole. The soil of Gaiole is poor, with limestone, which gives wines that are quite high in acidity with good tannins. They are long-lasting and elegant, with good structure. In Radda too, the soil is very stony, *galestro* and limestone, again giving wines that will age slowly with tannin and acidity. Lamole on the other hand has a mixture of *galestro* and sand, its vineyards lying at an altitude between 400 and 500 metres. Here the wines never have very deep colour and the taste is quite hard at the beginning. They need ageing to develop more fruit after the second year. Around Monti, where Badia a Coltibuono have their vineyards, the wines are big with good ageing potential, but generally with softer tannins than those from Greve and Panzano. The soil is quite rich, but varied in content, with clay, rock and some chalk. At Castelnuovo Berardenga, also in the south, the soil is very mixed, with *galestro*, limestone, sand and a little clay.

A high percentage of clay in the soil may mean that extra drainage is required in the vineyard. At La Madonnina, drainage channels had to be built before they could even plant the vines. At Castel Ruggero, also on the northern edge of Chianti, there is as much as 80 per cent clay. They have artificial drainage, for without it the vines could well asphyxiate. Stony soil makes for good drainage, but the vines may suffer from drought in very dry years.

The Apennines protect Chianti, and Chianti Classico in particular, on the east and from the damper valley of the Arno, while sea breezes blow over the Maremma from the west. Winters are not especially cold and harsh. Spring and autumn may bring rain and the summer is usually warm and dry, with little or no rainfall from the beginning of June until October. Drought can be a problem, although some areas, such as that around the Castello di Querceto, have supplies of underground water for the vines to tap. Hail too, can cause damage in the summer. If there is rain, this sometimes leads to rot and disease. Certainly the weather varies enough from year to year for vintages to matter. Spring frost is not a danger, but winter frosts have occasionally caused damage, although more often to olive trees than to vines.

The weather varies too within each area. Gaiole is one of the dryer parts of Chianti Classico, so that there is little humidity and therefore small risk of disease. More rain falls in Panzano. The ventilation of the vineyards can be significant. Those of Fontodi in Panzano, for example, are open to the west and so to the influence of sea breezes. Temperatures are milder in Greve than on the higher slopes of Radda; at Vignale, where they have vineyards at 550 metres, the winters are cold, so that there is a late budbreak. The harvest will also be late, often not beginning until about 20th October, some twenty days later than Greve.

The higher the vineyard, the cooler the average temperature, with less danger of the grapes over-ripening. In very hot years they have had problems at La Madonnina, where the vineyards are at only 300 metres; the wines can be too ripe and alcoholic. Elegant wines with a firm robust structure are obtained from higher altitudes, and softer, fuller wines from lower down.

Variation in temperature also plays a part. At a high altitude there can be significant differences between day and night-time temperatures, from 37°C at midday to 15°C at night, in summer. These variations make for wines with more aroma and less body than, say, those of Montalcino, where they do not have these differences and obtain much riper, more concentrated grapes.

The different characteristics of soil and microclimate can be used as an argument for distinguishing between the different villages of Chianti Classico, rather in the same way that the Médoc of Bordeaux is divided into appellations, each with its own character. A suggested list of smaller zones could perhaps include Castellina, Radda, Gaiole, the bottom of the Val d'Arbia, the Val di Pesa, the Val di Greve, the Val d'Ema, Panzano and Lamole. However, many other factors come into play in determining a wine's character.

Grape Varieties

The variety of soil allows a number of different grapes to be grown with some success. The DOCG regulations lay down the grape varieties for Chianti, but within these there are variations, both authorised and otherwise. The composition of the vineyards has also changed radically over the last ten or twenty years, with considerable investment. Originally they were planted to make a completely different style of Chianti. The elimination of most of the white grapes has been a first step towards the production of a red wine of quality. Italy has generally been considered to lag way behind France in the field of viticultural research, notably on clonal selection, which accounts for the mistakes of the 1970s. Today there is a concentration on the quality of the raw material, on the need to produce good grapes, from the right clones, and in small quantity, to demonstrate the characteristics of the region.

The principal grape variety is the Sangiovese, a variety that is found all over central Italy, from Emilia Romagna down to the Abruzzi. To quote Piero Antinori, 'the Sangiovese is to Chianti, what Cabernet Sauvignon is to Bordeaux.' However Sangiovese does not have the same structure as Cabernet Sauvignon. The variations in flavour are vast, from the insipid and feeble Sangiovese di Romagna, to hefty, mouth-filling Brunello di Montalcino. The name derives from *sanguis Jovis*, or the blood of Jove, implying an ability to produce deep red, powerful wines, which is certainly not necessarily the case today. Sangiovese is also more subject to the vagaries of clonal selection than virtually any other grape variety. In broad terms it seems that there are two sub-varieties, Sangiovese Grosso and Sangiovese Piccolo. Sangiovese Grosso, so called because the grapes are bigger than those of Sangiovese Piccolo, although still not particularly large, grows notably in Montalcino and Montepulciano, where it answers to the synonyms of Brunello and Prugnolo respectively; Brunello, for its dusky, almost brown hue and Prugnolo, for its plum-like form. Sangiovese Piccolo, for which the common synonym in Chianti is Sangioveto, is grown extensively in Chianti, and also in Emilia Romagna. There is a difference between the Sangiovese di Romagna and that of Tuscany. The principal characteristic of the Sangiovese di Romagna is its large yields, of soft-skinned juicy grapes. There can be enormous variations in flavour, with the right clones giving rich flavoured wine and the wrong ones, pale watery tastes.

In some ways it is difficult to generalise about the characteristics of Sangiovese as, with the exception of Brunello di Montalcino, it is relatively unusual to find it as a varietal wine. Throughout the rest of Tuscany, the wine laws dictate the blending of Sangiovese with other grape varieties, both red and white. However an increasing number of producers are making *vino da tavola* from pure Sangiovese, with fascinating results. If broad generalisations are to be made, it seems that Sangiovese can give wines with a lot of colour. There is a tendency for it to oxidise, so that a Chianti of any age is likely to be showing orange hints around the rim, although this may be heightened by the percentage of white grapes. Astringency is another characteristic, with quite high acidity and tannin. In other works it is a grape variety that does benefit from blending with others. If it is made as a pure varietal, it needs to come from particularly successful clones, from grapes chosen from the best part of a vineyard.

Sangiovese is very much a grape variety of Central Italy. It is not found anywhere else, except Corsica, California and Australia; and there only in insignificant quantity. In Corsica it is known as Nielluccio and was brought to the island by the Pisans and Genoese in the Middle Ages. It is the mainstay of the island's principal appellation, Patrimonio. As for Australia, I am told that there is a vineyard of

Sangiovese at the Montrose Winery in the Mudgee area of New South Wales, where there is a large Italian population.

In California Sangiovese is playing a part in a combined project, funded mainly by Whitbread, but with contributions from Bollinger and Antinori. They have planted just seven acres (17.5 hectares) of it in the Napa valley, in the hills to the east of the town of Napa itself at about 1,200 feet in altitude. The clone is Sangiovese Grosso and Piero Antinori is optimistic about the results, as he sees climate similarities to Montalcino. The first harvest was in 1988, but of only a tiny amount, so it is still too soon to say what will be done with it. Maybe it could be blended with Cabernet Sauvignon to make a Californian Tignanello.

Following Antinori's example, there are some signs of a growing interest in Sangiovese. Sam Sebastiani at Vianusa in Carneros is planning to plant twenty-five acres and a few other wineries are beginning to experiment. However, the fact is that the reputation of Chianti is not such as to inspire imitations in the New World; so we wait to see what Antinori will achieve.

Some estates in Tuscany have identified the characteristics of their own strongest clones of Sangiovese. The most notable of these is Biondi Santi in Montalcino (see p. 130). At Badia a Coltibuono they always take cuttings from the best of their existing vineyards, from vines that are over twenty-five years old, which are then grafted on to American rootstock in a nursery. At Nipozzano in Rufina, they have identified their own clones, not only of Sangiovese, but also of Canaiolo.

It is Canaiolo that is most commonly blended with Sangiovese. Canaiolo Nero – there is also a very rare Canaiolo Bianco – has adapted badly to the necessity of grafting after phylloxera and seems to perform less satisfactorily in the specialised vineyards of Tuscany than in *cultura promiscua*. It is also very susceptible to *coulure*. Canaiolo gives colour to the Sangiovese, but otherwise has less tannin, acidity and indeed character, so it can tone down some of the rough edges of the more dominant grape variety. It is useful in a Chianti *normale*, to soften the Sangiovese and make a wine suitable for early drinking.

Trebbiano and Malvasia are the most common white grapes. It seems an anathema that white grapes should be allowed in a red wine, especially in a red wine that may already be deficient in colour. Another example of the use of white grapes in a red wine is Côte Rôtie from the Rhône valley, where it is possible to tone down the heavy full-bodied Syrah with the softer Viognier; but this is an option that many growers prefer not to use. In central Tuscany the law dictates a minimum of 2 per cent of white grapes for Chianti Classico and a minimum of 5 per cent for the other regions of Chianti; with a maximum of 5 per cent for Chianti Classico, and 10 per cent for the other zones. It is true that this represents an improvement on the DOC regulations, which dictated between 10 and 30 per cent, but it is to be hoped that the minimum percentage will soon be removed.

The reasons for this adherence to the white grapes are both historical and political. Traditionally, white grapes were grown mixed up with the red and everything was thrown into the fermenting vat together. If we look back to the words of Baron Ricasoli, however, he recommended the inclusion of white grapes only if you were making a Chianti for early consumption; and he mentioned only Malvasia, not Trebbiano. Nevertheless, there is Trebbiano in Tuscany and indeed, all over Italy. In her informative book *Vines, Grapes and Wines* Jancis Robinson names it as the world's most prolific wine-producer. Much is grown in France, as Ugni Blanc or St. Emilion, where it is often destined for the still; or makes uninspiring whites in the Midi. In Italy it forms the mainstay of a large number of white wines from Soave to Sicily, with regional subvarieties all over the country, including Trebbiano Toscano.

The origins of Trebbiano are undoubtedly central Italian. What is less certain is the origin of the name. Jancis Robinson suggests various theories. It may even be the *trebulanum* mentioned by Pliny in his natural history. Andrea Bacci, the doctor of Pope Sixtus V and an eminent botanist, attributed the vines to the village of the same name in Tuscany. There is a river Trebbia in Emilia Romagna, which may alternatively have had something to do with it. The Bolognese agronomist Pier de' Cresenzi was the first to describe Trebbiano by name in 1303.

Trebbiano is a late ripener, with a high degree of acidity, a reliable grape variety that is resistant to disease and produces large juicy bunches. For the simple grape growers and peasant farmers a good vintage was a large harvest, so a grape variety that gave quantity was infinitely more important than one that contributed quality; hence the adherence to the white grapes and to Trebbiano. The powers that be were therefore reluctant to eliminate Trebbiano and Malvasia altogether from the blend of Chianti. They say that they wanted to maintain tradition, that historically Chianti has always included a sprinkling of white grapes and that 2 per cent makes virtually no difference to the taste of a wine. For that reason, ironically, it is perfectly possible for more questioning producers to omit the white grapes without legal repercussions, for it is impossible to prove that they have done so.

Malvasia is a very old grape variety, which probably originated in Asia Minor before spreading to most of the Mediterranean vineyards. It has a strong presence in Italy, again with numerous subvarieties and although it is often twinned with Trebbiano, it has much more to offer by way of flavour. Baron Ricasoli favoured its presence in young Chianti, to add a little fruit and flavour, considering that it improved upon the finesse of the Sangiovese and contributed extra body. However as far as grape growers are concerned, it is much more susceptible to rot and disease than the sturdy thick-skinned Trebbiano. It also oxidises more easily. In any case to modern thinking, its presence in Chianti at all is questionable. It is at its best in Tuscany as a vital component of Vin Santo.

The DOCG regulations also allow for a complementary 10 per cent of other grapes. These may include varieties as diverse as Colorino, Mammolo, Ciliegiolo, Malvasia Nera and Cabernet Sauvignon; in fact anything that you are allowed to grow in Tuscany may be added to Chianti under this umbrella. Colorino was valued because it gave colour, hence its name, to the wine, balancing the large amount of white grapes; but this is now tending to disappear. It is also low in alcohol. Mammolo is found most often around Montepulciano. Malvasia Nera is grown at Castellare, but not for their Chianti Classico, while at Castello di Ama it is part of the Bellavista vineyard. Otherwise it is now rarely found in Chianti, although it was once quite typical.

Most significant today is Cabernet Sauvignon, which is an easy grape variety to grow as it is resistant to disease. There are two school of thought regarding the role of Cabernet Sauvignon in Tuscan winemaking. The protagonists in Chianti are led by Dott. Giacomo Tachis and Piero Antinori, who were inspired by the success of Sassicaia, made by Piero Antinori's cousin the Marchese Incisa della Rocchetta. As will be seen in a discussion of the town of Carmignano, however, the presence of Cabernet Sauvignon in Tuscany dates back much further than this century; a fact recognised in the DOC regulations for Carmignano. There is no doubt that the combination of Sangiovese and Cabernet Sauvignon is a very happy marriage, for in some respects there are similarities between the two grape varieties. For those aiming at a well structured Chianti with some aspirations to longevity, a hint of Cabernet Sauvignon may add something. But it should not dominate the flavour; like garlic in cooking, you should hardly be aware of its presence. Although Piero Antinori has favoured the planting of Cabernet Sauvignon, he firmly believes that, if they can get Sangiovese right, Cabernet Sauvignon will no longer be necessary in Chianti.

Opponents argue strongly that it has no place at all in a traditional wine of Tuscany, and that it will deform the flavours of Sangiovese, camouflaging any defects that may result from overcropping or the wrong clones – an invitation to laziness. With Cabernet Sauvignon being planted all over the world, they maintain that wines will taste the same everywhere. Rather, it would be better to concentrate on the intrinsic quality of Sangiovese. They argue that not enough people are cultivating Sangiovese properly, or reducing yields with correct pruning. On the contrary, bad winemaking and unsatisfactory clones have led to excessive yields.

The Sharecropping System and Cultura Promiscua

The face of Tuscan viticulture has changed dramatically since the Second World War, when the time-honoured system of sharecropping began to be dismantled. Since the sixteenth century every large estate had been divided up into several small farms, each of which supported a family. The landowner provided the necessary capital expenditure, bought seed, tools and so on, while the peasant farmers or *contadini* contributed their manual labour. All the crops, olives, wheat and wine, were divided, usually equally, between the landowner and his farmers, who could then sell any that was surplus to their needs. There would be a villa, several houses and a chapel, making for a self-contained community. The estate was frequently run in the landowner's absence by his *fattore*, or manager, a position which often passed from father to son. A Tuscan estate at the beginning of this century was an example of self-sufficient subsistence agriculture.

The Italian government was partly responsible for the disintegration of the system. It encouraged the breaking up of large estates and in some cases helped the *contadini* to buy their own land. At the same time, many succumbed to the lure of the city. Life on the land was hard and the attraction of the towns, offering, they thought, easy wages, created a rural exodus. As a result, landowners were often left without the manpower to farm their properties and the cost of labour became of great significance. The inefficiency of many estates was brought to light.

A later element promoting change was the mechanisation of agriculture. Tractors did not arrive in any number in the vineyards of Chianti until the 1960s, but then suddenly there was not the same demand for manual labour. This undoubtedly hastened the depopulation. In the last century the tiny village of La Lecce in the hills outside Castellina supported fifty people; today five people live there and there are eight tractors.

A view of Radda in Chianti Classico, showing vineyards planted in cultura promiscua, *in a photograph of 1915–20.*

Those who suffered initially were the large landowners. They found themselves without the means, either in terms of money or manpower, to run their estates in the traditional way. Where once it had been a sign of wealth and prosperity to have *un podere in Chianti*, that farm became a millstone. Many estates changed hands during the 1960s and early 1970s. It was possible to buy land in Chianti for a song, but enormous amounts of money often needed to be spent on the renovation of buildings and the improvement of vineyards.

The charms of Tuscany have always attracted people from outside the province and indeed from outside Italy. The new landowners came and are still coming from northern Italy, from the industrial cities of Milan or Turin, or from the capital. The new men had money and often worked as high-powered industrialists or lawyers during the week. Many have applied their expertise in other fields to their land and to winemaking. Instead of a *fattore* to run the estate in their absence, they may employ a consultant oenologist to make their wine.

Traditional Tuscan agriculture, based on the sharecropping system, encouraged what is known as *cultura promiscua*, with crops all mixed up together. There might be an olive tree or two in the middle of a row of vines, and other crops or vegetables between two rows (see illustration). Everything was delightfully disorganised. With *cultura promiscua* there would be only about 500 vines per hectare, so that the vines had a lot of root space and were also well ventilated. Methods in the vineyard were natural; the vines were hoed by hand, or with oxen, and fertilised only with manure. Signora Fabbri at Savignola Paolina says firmly that she preferred *cultura promiscua*;

it provided better aeration for the vines. With the decline of the sharecropping system came the move towards what are called *specializzato*, or specialised vineyards, unbroken parcels of vines; but the change has not been uniform and you can still see odd parcels of *cultura promiscua*, where a *mezzadria* or sharecropping farm survives.

The new landownership brought with it a great planting of these specialised vineyards (see Appendix I). Growth in specialised vineyards rose dramatically in the early 1970s, reaching a peak in 1982. The cultivation of *promiscua* vineyards declined with the introduction of DOCG.

Unfortunately in the rush to create vineyards, the right grape varieties, or more significantly the right clones were not always planted. There was a failure to appreciate the finer points of Sangiovese Grosso and Sangiovese Piccolo. Cuttings of vines were bought in Emilia Romagna, where the worst type of Sangiovese proliferates, and brought to Chianti. Vineyards were planted with high yields rather than fine quality in mind, without knowledge of how a specialised vineyard should work and with too many white grapes.

Until about 1960 wine in Tuscany had been made mainly for family and friends. With the investment from outside, more people were making wine for sale and expecting a return: whereas in 1960 there were only twenty bottlers of Chianti Classico, by 1975 there were 292. This brought enormous problems in its wake. There was a gross overproduction, not just in Chianti Classico, but all over Chianti. Prices fell to the extent that it was impossible for a grape farmer to make a living. Some of the large merchants had contracts with grape owners, whose crops they were obliged to buy and they are the prime culprits for the flooding of the market with inferior wine. The reputation of Chianti as a whole suffered accordingly.

Chianti 2000 and Clonal Selection

Since then a better understanding of the intricacies of clonal selection has been developed and many inferior vines have either been grafted with a better grape variety, or pulled up. There will be an important phase of replanting in Chianti Classico towards the end of the century, as most of the vineyards planted between 1965 and 1974 come to the end of their useful lives. This time, the Consorzio for Chianti Classico is determined not to repeat the mistakes of the past and they are conducting extensive experiments in the vineyards, under the name of Chianti 2000, with the help of several of their members.

The Consorzio of the Gallo Nero is masterminding fifteen experimental vineyards, on different estates, such as San Felice and Montagliari. In particular they are examining clones of Sangiovese and Canaiolo, but they are also looking at grafting and pruning, and the possibility of increasing the number of plants per hectare. As Piero Antinori has said, the Italians have been behind the rest of Europe in their understanding of viticulture, and now they are trying hard to catch up.

At San Felice there is a vineyard planted with 165 different grape varieties, all of them growing in Chianti Classico. Sometimes it is a case of one producer having a different clone from his neighbour. They want to ensure that these old vines are not lost and forgotten, and also to see if any of them would give better results under different conditions. The vineyard was only planted in May 1987, with sixteen plants of each variety, and the 1990 harvest will be the first from which they are able to make wine. They have already been able to examine the vigour of different plants, and how they react to water, or the lack of it. Some non-Tuscan grape varieties are present, such as Arneis, Chardonnay and Pinot Bianco for white wine, and Nebbiolo, Barbera, Gamay and Cabernet Sauvignon for red, to see how they perform in the same soil and microclimate. Cuttings have also been taken from a few pre-phylloxera vines that have survived in sandy soil near Grosseto. Studies of grafting are aimed at identifying the right combination of grape varieties and also studying how the vines react.

Experiments with Foreign Grape Varieties

Cabernet Sauvignon is not the only foreign red grape variety in Tuscany and experimentation with others is another aspect of the current spirit of enquiry. There are plantings of Cabernet Franc and Merlot, not to mention Pinot Noir or Nero, and Syrah. The protagonist of Syrah is Paolo de Marchi at Isole e Olena, where he has planted just one and half hectares, which first came into production in 1985. His intention is not to blend it with Sangiovese, but possibly with Cabernet, or maybe to make a varietal wine. However a little was incorporated into his 1987 Chianti, with some success. Syrah produces quite large yields, which de Marchi is learning to control. It also ripens early.

Pinot Noir is potentially much more problematic, for it is a temperamental grape, of more elusive character than either Cabernet Sauvignon or Syrah. Ruffino are growing it; so are Castello di Volpaia and Castello di Ama. Pinot Noir was planted at Volpaia in 1986 and will not really come into production until 1992. Maurizio Castelli hopes that the exchange of night and daytime temperatures will give good results there, on sandy, chalky soil, mixed with a little clay. The vineyards are at 200 metres, with 6,600 plants per hectare, which is dense for Chianti Classico. It is too early to draw any conclusions, although Ruffino are pleased with their Nero del Tondo, which was made for the first time in 1985. The vines grow in cooler vineyards at 500 metres.

The same quest for experimentation extends to white grapes, in a search to improve upon the flavours of Trebbiano. Many of the white wines of Tuscany now contain a percentage of Chardonnay, Sauvignon, Gewürztraminer, Pinot Grigio and so on. Sometimes Chardonnay is fermented and aged in oak, or sometimes it is kept just in stainless steel. Both can be equally successful. Sauvignon is more problematic. Quite the best Sauvignon I have tasted in Tuscany, came not from the heart of Chianti Classico, but from Ornellaia at Bolgheri. Maurizio Castelli is convinced that good things can be achieved with Sauvignon at Volpaia. Meriggio from Fontodi is a blend of Pinot Bianco, with some Gewürztraminer and Sauvignon.

The Vineyard

Many of the vineyards of the 1960s have only about 2,500 vines per hectare, which is now considered far too few, making for vines that are over vigorous. For the moment, 2,800 to 3,000 or 3,300 plants per hectare is the norm in Chianti Classico, on a grid system of 1.2 metres between the vines in the rows, with 2.8 metres between the rows, or alternatively one metre in the rows with rows three metres wide. Experimental vineyards have been planted with vines at different densities, 3,000, 6,000 and 9,000 plants. Any more would lead to problems with tractors and other machinery. The ideal will probably turn out to be about 5,000 plants per hectare, in which case the DOCG regulations should be altered accordingly to allow a smaller yield per vine. At the moment, in Chianti Classico each vine is allowed to produce three kilos of grapes. If there is competition between the vines, they produce less vegetation, and consequently better grapes. As a broad generalisation, it seems that the plantings with an increased number of vines and a reduced yield give better results, with more structure in the wine, better acidity and softer tannins, while the plantings with fewer vines give wines with a more accentuated perfume, but less body and staying power.

Paolo de Marchi at Isole e Olena firmly believes that it is not so much clonal selection that is important in determining the quality of Sangiovese, as the conditions of the *terreno*, notably of soil. He maintains that you need to control, above all, the vigour of Sangiovese. He has observed a considerable variation in style within the same vineyard, where the conditions for the nutrition of the vines are different, irrespective of the type of clones. Differences in humidity also have an effect and a heavy soil will result in unbalanced flavours. De Marchi reckons that whereas most people want to use weak rootstock and increase the number of plants per hectare, it would be better to have strong rootstock, which can find its way through the poor stony soil. A vine on weak rootstock is also much more susceptible to disease.

Nevertheless poor clonal selection has been a major problem in Chianti, along with the excess of white grapes. The best clones are gradually being identified and there is optimism among growers that by the year 2000 70 per cent of the vineyards of Chianti will have been replanted with the right clones of Sangiovese. If so, they will have become yet more specialised, and there should be a significant decline in the amount of white vines.

When the sharecropping system was at its height, different grape varieties were planted all mixed up together. Today with the well regulated specialised vineyards, everything is very organised, with each variety planted in defined vineyards, according to the required percentages of grapes required in the finished wine.

Pruning and Grafting

The customary method of pruning is the double *guyot*, leaving twelve eyes, six per branch and trained rather higher than the double *guyot* in France, on four wires. There is less need for the grapes to benefit from the reflection of heat from the stones in the soil here, which is the principal reason for the low vines of northern France. Occasionally you find *cordone speronata*, or the cordon spur system, with more shoots, as at Castello di Querceto. They find that this method reduces the amount of work necessary in the vineyards, as it is suitable for mechanical work. Also the grapes are not hidden in the foliage, as they can be with double *guyot*, and so are well exposed to both sun and air.

At Castello di Ama they are experimenting with a new method of pruning, called *alire*, like a lyre. The vines are planted 1.2 metres apart in the rows, with 3.5 metres between the rows, and each trained in the form of a 'V', 2.5 metres high. The aim is to distribute the foliage more evenly, so that there is better aeration, and therefore less problem with disease and rot resulting from excess humidity. It seems that with better exposure to light and sunshine the grapes may also ripen earlier, so that the harvest can take place before autumn rain spoils them.

Pruning is one of the ways in which yields can be reduced. Another is to limit the amount of fertiliser added to the soil. At Isole e Olena, Paolo de Marchi has succeeded in reducing his production from 2,600 hectolitres to 1,400 hectolitres, with more severe pruning and less fertiliser. He practises a type of *gobelet* system, with four or five spurs, which he finds helps the grapes to ripen earlier, with better sugar and acidity levels.

To replant a vineyard takes time, for you lose at least three if not four years' crop, and even then it will be several more years before the vines and their root systems reach full maturity. A much quicker way to change the contents of a vineyard, when the vines themselves are relatively young and healthy, is to graft a different grape variety on to the trunk of the established vine, so that you lose only one or two harvests (see illustration). This process has become very popular in Chianti, as an easy way of eliminating Trebbiano and Malvasia vines; of introducing Cabernet Sauvignon or other experimental grape varieties; and even of increasing the proportion of Sangiovese. Quite often a hectare or two of Cabernet Sauvignon may be grafted, to see how it adapts to the particular vineyard; then if it is successful, more will be planted in the normal way. Grafting provides a quick method of assessing the potential of a grape variety, and the risk of the plant dying is 10 per

Grafting: inserting the bud into the trunk of the vine, at Capezzana.

cent at most. The disadvantage is that it reduces the lifespan of a vine, as it has quite a violent impact on the plant.

More usual in Tuscany than the T-budding method, which entails the insertion of a young bud into the trunk of the vine, is *sparco inglese*, whereby the wood of the new grape variety is grafted into the trunk of the established vine. You take a cane, or even two canes, to give you a double chance of success. These are tapered and forced into the trunk, which has been split where the old vine has been cut off. The canes are held in place with raffia and the join is protected with special wax.

The work in a vineyard in Tuscany is not so different from that in other parts of the world. Treatments are necessary against disease and rot, although the Italians may be more ecologically minded than those in climates where rot and disease are more problematic. Numerous growers say that they avoid chemical sprays, weedkiller and chemical fertilisers, preferring to use natural treatments, such as the traditional copper sulphate sprays. Sometimes the grass between the vines is left and sometimes a bean crop is planted to increase the nitrogen content of the soil. Other natural fertilisers include animal manure. Drip irrigation is allowed for young vines, so that they do not suffer from drought before their root system is fully developed. Another hazard can be thirsty wild boar, who find ripe grapes positively delicious. At Castello di Ama they have wire fences to deter them.

The Vintage

One important criterion of quality is limitation of the yield. In the years before the introduction of DOCG, yields tended to be inappropriately high. A way to reduce the yield of over-vigorous vines is to practise what is called *vendemmia verde*, or a green harvest; that is, to cut off excess grapes in July, after the bunches have set and you can estimate the potential crop. At the same time, excess foliage may be removed. To the peasant mentality, however, this is to refuse a gift of God and waste the fruits of Nature. At the cooperative of Castelgreve, where they have compared wine produced with and without the *vendemmia verde*, they find that the remaining grapes ripen better after a green harvest, so that the wine has more flavour.

The vintage in Chianti takes place over several weeks, generally from mid-September until mid-October. There can be considerable differences between the ripening times of one vineyard and another. At Castello di Ama they have noticed that two adjoining parcels of Sangiovese ripen a week apart, as the soil, aspect and altitude of each are different. White grapes, like Chardonnay and Sauvignon ripen very early, maybe at the end of August, while Trebbiano is best left until after the Sangiovese is picked. Tests are carried out in the vineyards for four weeks prior to the vintage, to follow the maturation of the grapes. At Ama they take a hundred grapes from each variety and from each plot, weigh them and analyse their sugar, acidity and pH, to determine which parcels will ripen first and how to order the harvest. They are particularly well organised, as they keep extensive records about their grape varieties and vineyards. Most people pick grape variety by grape variety.

The terrain does not allow for mechanical harvesters and few people have them. Rocca delle Macie is one of the exceptions. Usually there is no problem in finding labour for the harvest, although most people feel that the best results are obtained

Picking the grapes.

from experienced pickers, who know which are the best bunches of grapes, and which are rotten or unripe, to be left on the vines. Antinori pick the grapes for their *riserva* wines by hand and then harvest the remaining grapes by machine. They claim that the cost of the vintage would double otherwise. Others do two pickings, first of the better riper grapes for the *riserva* wines, and second for the *normale*.

Once the grapes are in the cellar, a Chianti maker has numerous choices. The next chapter proceeds from the grape to the finished wine, but the last word on the harvest should go to the Principessa Pignatelli at Castell'in Villa. 'The most exciting moment is picking the grapes. Then I really go wild. It's like something that is born, it's a creation!'

Vinification: Governo or No?

The flavours of Chianti have been developed enormously over the past twenty years or so. Until 1967 and the advent of DOC, it was common practice to ferment the grapes with their stalks on, and the blend might include as much as a third of white grapes. Today, the fruit is always destalked and the proportion of white grapes has been drastically reduced. Without the astringency and tannin from the stalks, the white grapes are not needed to soften the wine and make it drinkable sooner. The taste of Chianti has changed; and it must be said, for the better.

When I met Dott. Tachis, Antinori's talented oenologist, he had just completed twenty-eight years of winemaking with the company. He remembers how they used to vinify, in large oak or chestnut vats, and how they turned then to closed cement vats. There were no *remontagi*, the pumping of the fermenting juice over the cap of grape skins. You always used the *governo* method, the traditional Tuscan practice of adding dried grapes to the almost finished wine, to cause a second fermentation. At Antinori they gave up this practice ten years ago. Dott. Tachnis thinks it was valid when it was done in the traditional way with dried grapes, but that the method came into disrepute in the 1960s, when concentrated must of uncertain provenance was used. This was the nadir of Tuscan viticulture and winemaking. But now it is once again in the ascendant, for we are in the midst of a tremendously exciting period of development, in which the true potential of Tuscany may be realised.

Hugh Hamilton at Le Lodoline points out how the criteria for judging Chianti have changed over the last forty years, since he first arrived at Vagliagli. Now you aim to keep a wine young for longer, whereas you used to want to make it age quickly, for early consumption. Forty years ago Chianti was tough and astringent, so that it needed white grapes and the second fermentation of the *governo* method to reduce the tannin levels, making it ready to drink earlier. Today it is expected of the better Chianti *riservas* that they should have the structure and balance to last for several years.

The inclusion of what was once a substantial proportion of white grapes and the practice of the *governo all'uso toscano* have distinguished the vinification of Chianti from that of most other red wines. This has undergone considerable modification in the last ten years, as traditional methods have been questioned and new procedures implemented into the amended regulations of the DOCG. As we saw in the last chapter, much also depends upon the individual producers; how they age their wine and how much care they apply to its vinification. As with cooks, each has his own particular recipe, with variations in expertise, talent and equipment. At some estates the owner is also the winemaker, such as Paolo de Marchi at Isole e Olena, or John Dunkley at Riecine, but in many instances the proprietor employs the services of one of the several very capable and indeed talented oenologists in the area.

Stainless steel fermentation vats in a modern cellar.

Fermentation

Vinification methods have improved markedly all over the world in the last twenty years. Tuscany may have lagged behind at first, but in the past decade she has caught up with a vengeance, and is now overtaking some other areas, with a prolonged burst of questioning experimentation. We take the control of fermentation temperatures for granted and yet John Dunkley of Riecine remembers Maurizio Castelli, as the consultant oenologist of the Consorzio, giving him such fundamental advice for his first vintage, back in 1972, as that he should buy a thermometer. No one considered temperature control and nature was allowed to take its course. Today in large estates vats may be linked to computer programmes, ready to respond to the minutest fluctuations of temperature.

Open-topped wooden vats, usually made of chestnut have been replaced, either by cement vats lined with epoxy resin, or in the estates enjoying recent modernisation and extensive investment, by pristine stainless steel (see illustration). Powerful heat exchangers can cool or heat the fermenting juice. Less accurate, but also quite efficient, is the running of cold water over the outside of the vats. Usually the fermentation is controlled at a little below 30°C, down to about 26°–28°C, which is normal for any red wine vinification. A lower temperature will make for a wine that is quite perfumed, but with insufficient tannins. Paolo de Marchi's fermentation vats at Isole e Olena are outside, which means that he has no problems allowing the carbon dioxide to escape. The cool October nights are usually sufficient to keep the fermentation temperatures under control. If they are not, he can resort to cold water. Cement vats hold the heat more than stainless steel. Less sophisticated winemakers may just open the cellar door to let in the cold night air of late October.

The other mutable factor in a red-wine fermentation is the length of time that the juice spends on the skins. This will vary depending on the type of wine that is desired, and also on the quality and character of the vintage. Eight to twelve days on the skins is average, though it may be as long as three weeks if the grapes are healthy, with no rot to contaminate the flavour of the wine; and if the wine is destined to be a long-lived *riserva*. In 1988 less time was needed on the skins, as the grapes were so ripe and the skins so rich in concentrated extract that the juice was able easily to absorb colour and tannin. With quite lengthy contact, producers are looking for body and structure in their wine, something that was lacking when so many white grapes were used, and also with excessive yields of poor red grapes from the wrong clones of Sangiovese. At Volpaia, for instance, the Chianti Classico *normale* will spend about ten days on the skins, the *riserva* ten to fifteen days, and what they call the *crus*, of pure Sangiovese and Cabernet Sauvignon twenty days.

An old fashioned vertical grape press.

Whereas forty years ago Chianti was fermented with whole bunches of grapes, today everyone destalks them. The fruit is gently crushed before fermentation. For the best wines only the free-run juice will be used, unless a little extra tannin and backbone is needed, in which case the results of a gentle pressing may be included in the final blend.

Another permutation in the fermentation process is the practice of *remontagi*, the pumping of the juice over the cap of skins, which naturally rises to the top of the fermenting vat, looking in an open top vat, like a large cauldron of bubbling blackcurrant jam. Usually *remontagi* are carried out every day, at least once, if not twice, for five or ten minutes. This also has the effect of cooling the juice by a degree or two. At Volpaia, their consultant oenologist Maurizio Castelli prefers a longer period of skin contact, with fewer *remontagi*, as in this way he reckons to obtain sweeter, softer tannins in the wine. He feels that frequent *remontagi* result in too violent an extraction of tannins and that they can lead to undesirable oxidation. Instead, at San Polo in Rosso he practises what he calls a gentle irrigation, whereby the cap falls gently through the fermenting juice, rather like the filter in the jug type of coffee machine.

Most estates, especially those that are less methodical, ferment all the different grape varieties together, as they were often mixed up in the vineyard in the first place. Others, where the vines have been planted in separate plots, such as Castello di Ama, will ferment each grape variety on its own. They then decide what is to be blended with what, after the initial assessment of the young wine and before putting it into wood, as is the customary practice in Bordeaux.

Governo

Governo or no *governo* is one of the leading questions in the making of Chianti today. Some are firmly in its favour and others are equally fervently against it. Tuscany is the only part of Italy with this particular method of winemaking and it goes back a long way, forming one of the fundamental peasant traditions of winemaking, endorsed by Baron Ricasoli. Twenty years ago it was taken for granted as an intrinsic part of producing youthful fruity Chianti. Now that there is a demand for more long-lived wines, its use is being questioned.

Vittorio Fiore, the talented oenologist responsible for Vecchie Terre di Montefili, explained to me how and why he practises the *governo all'uso toscano*. A few days before starting the main harvest, you select the appropriate grapes. They must be absolutely free of rot, ripe and healthy, and preferably the best Sangiovese grapes' rather than Canaiolo. You should certainly never use inferior fruit. The bunches are laid out on plastic nets so that they are exposed to the air and are gradually *passiti*, that is dried so that they gently shrivel like raisins and the juice concentrates, which takes about six weeks. Then they are pressed and the juice is added to the wine that has just finished fermenting, in which no sugar is left, usually sometime in November. The fresh must that is rich in sugar sets off a second fermentation, which lasts until February or even March.

The objective of the *governo* is to enhance a wine that is intended for early drinking, for the *governo* method gives flavours that would not otherwise occur, making for a richer, fruitier Chianti. In the case of older wines, these flavours will come with wood and bottle ageing instead. However, Franco Bernabei, another successful and respected oenologist, argues that the *governo* is also appropriate for a wine that is to be aged. All the wines at Fontodi are *governato*, as are most of those at Felsina Berardenga. As much as 15 per cent of *governato* grapes is added to Felsina's Fontalloro, but that is an unusually high percentage of the total volume; something of the order of 5 to 10 per cent is more common. Bernabei believes that the *governo* adds freshness, retaining an element of youthfulness in a mature wine, as well as giving more concentration and flavour. Old fashioned Chianti was rather thin, without much colour, and the *governo* was also useful to give additional colour.

Those who are against the *governo* method, argue that it ages a wine too quickly. Contrary to the view of his great-great-grandfather, the present Baron Ricasoli does not use it, as he believes that it can affect the stability of a wine, resulting in excessive volatile acidity. He points out that it was in the economic interest of the peasant farmers to have wine that was ready for sale early, as it brought them some income early in the year; but if a wine is to be aged, the practice is no longer valid.

Maurizio Castelli is generally not in favour either, with one exception. At Castellare he makes a wine called Governo di Castellare, which as the name implies, is the result of the *governo* method. The object is to have a wine that can be sold in the spring following the vintage, rather than waiting for the release of the new Chianti in June or later. Castelli says that he does it for fun, but that otherwise he considers the *governo* method old fashioned.

Certainly the *governo* method was useful in that it helped the malolactic fermentation to take place, which was less certain before winemakers had the means of warming their cellars and when the process was not fully understood. It also added natural glycerine to the wine, making it smoother and more velvety. However, now that the malolactic fermentation is more completely comprehended, many consider that they have better control of their wine without injecting an extra element of instability. Those who do not practise the *governo* method believe it to be detrimental to wines for ageing. The other significant disadvantage of the *governo* is that, done properly, it is very expensive in terms of labour and time, as well as requiring the setting aside of a certain amount of space for drying the grapes.

Chaptalization and Concentrated Must

In some ways the *governo* can be seen as a form of chaptalization, as one of its purposes is to increase the sugar content and thereby the alcohol level of the finished wine. There is a potential confusion here with the addition of concentrated must. Chaptalization, the addition of sugar to the fermenting juice, is forbidden in Italy for DOC and DOCG wines. Instead, those wishing to increase the alcohol level can add concentrated must. If you are a producer of Chianti Classico, Colli Fiorentini or Rufina, this has to be the product of your own grapes. It is forbidden to buy in grapes from elsewhere. If you make Chianti in one of the other zones, however, you are still allowed to add a ridiculous 15 per cent of must or wine, not just from outside your own vineyard, but from outside the area of production, even from outside Tuscany, in other words from the south of Italy, Apulia, Calabria or Sicily. This part of the regulations throws the whole reputation of DOCG and Chianti into disrepute.

Although it is possible to enhance the colour of a wine with heady brews from the south, and to stretch production by adding concentrated must from elsewhere, no winemaker at all concerned with his reputation takes advantage of this loophole.

The production of good quality concentrated must is not easy. Stefano Farkas at Cafaggio is one of the few producers with his own machinery for this purpose, which he also uses for neighbouring producers. It is a very sophisticated piece of equipment, boiling the must under pressure to 40°C, causing the water content to evaporate. Originally concentrated must was made more simply by boiling to an even higher temperature. This reduced its volume, but in the process turned it to caramel, which caused the wine to which it was added to taste of caramel too. Concentrated must should be as pure as possible, so that it adds no foreign flavour to the wine. Dott. Tachis remembers with a grimace the cooked flavours, the *sapore di cotto*, obtained from the poor concentrated must used in the 1960s and 1970s. Happily things are better now and it is perfectly possible to obtain neutral concentrated must for boosting the alcohol content of a wine, if necessary.

The need for it depends very much upon the vintage. Like chaptalization, it should only be used as a remedial action, in poor vintages, such as 1984. In a ripe year such as 1988 it was certainly not necessary. A kilo of concentrated must will increase the alcohol level of one hectolitre of grapes by 6°. The trouble with concentrated must, even of the best quality, is that it intensifies every characteristic of the wine, acidity as well as sugar, so it can create unbalanced flavours. The concentrate is added during the tumultuous fermentation.

Once the fermentations, both alcoholic and malolactic are over and the finished wine is racked, it will need blending if the different grape varieties have been fermented separately. This will be done in the spring, before it is put into *botti*, the traditional large casks of Slavonic oak; or *barriques*, 225-litre barrels of French oak, for further ageing (see colour illustrations opposite p. 72). Here the maker of Chianti is presented with further choices.

Chianti Normale and Chianti Riserva

The DOCG regulations allow for two categories of Chianti, Chianti *normale* and Chianti *riserva*. These are differentiated by the amount of time that each has been aged. In the case of Chianti, rather than Chianti Classico, the *normale* cannot be released until 1st March following the vintage, while Chianti Classico *normale*, and that of Rufina and Colli Fiorentini have had to wait until 1st June. In an attempt to encourage longer ageing for Chianti Classico, however, the release date is gradually being delayed. While the 1987 vintage could be offered for sale on 1st June 1988, the 1988 vintage was not released until 1st September 1989. The 1989 vintage must remain in the cellars until 15th November 1990, and the 1990 vintage will not be sold until 1st January 1992, so that over four years the compulsory period for Chianti Classico *normale* has been extended by seven months. A *riserva* requires three years of ageing, from the 1st January following the vintage, so that the 1988 *riservas* will not be sold until the spring of 1992.

What the regulations do not lay down is the method of ageing. It can be in tank, barrel or bottle. A *riserva* quality implies first of all a wine made from the better grapes of the vineyard, those that were chosen at the time of the harvest as being the ripest and healthiest, which would make the wine most suitable for longer ageing, both in barrel and in bottle. The decision about a *riserva* will probably be made immediately after the harvest and the two wines, the *normale* and the *riserva* will be separated. Most estates make some *riserva* wine each year, but the amount varies, fluctuating in accordance with the quality of the vintage. You will not find a 1984 *riserva* and quantities of 1989 *riserva* will be limited, but of the excellent vintages of 1988 and 1985 there is no shortage. However, making too much *riserva* runs the risk of detracting from the quality of the *normale*. Essentially Chianti *normale* should be youthful and fruity, while a *riserva* is a more serious wine of some structure and stature, intended for a longer life.

In addition to a *riserva*, some estates make what they describe as a *cru*, a wine from a particular vineyard that consistently produces very fine wine. This may or may not conform to the Chianti Classico regulations. Examples that do include Prima Vigna at Castello di Vicchiomaggio, made as the name implies from the oldest vines of the estate, planted in the 1930s. Il Poggio at Monsanto comes from a particularly fine hilltop vineyard – *poggio* means a hill – where the grapes are regularly riper and richer than elsewhere on the property. Sometimes the so-called *cru* will instead come under the category of *vino da tavola*, of which more later. An example is Cepparello from Isole e Olena, which is made of pure Sangiovese. As such, Paolo de Manchi cannot legally call it Chianti. On the other hand, some producers admit that their wines are virtually pure Sangiovese, although they are labelled Chianti Classico *riserva*; no one can tell whether or not they contain Canaiolo and white grapes.

Barrels and Casks: Barriques and Botti

Chianti *normale* will usually be kept in large oak barrels for several months. The customary wood employed in Italy is Slavonic oak from Yugoslavia, and the traditional form is the large *botte*, as it is called. They vary in capacity from 70 hectolitres to 25 hectolitres. Sometimes you find barrels of chestnut, which was the traditional wood of Chianti and more neutral than oak, but today it is much less common. At Uzzano they have both chestnut and oak barrels. They consider that the oak yields finer results. In fact such large barrels do not give much wood influence to the wine, but rather provide a gentle oxidation, which would not be obtained if the wine were stored in a cement or stainless steel vat. Often these *botti* are very old, as much as a hundred years at Cafaggio. They are cleaned out regularly to remove the deposit of tartrates. For the moment it is virtually impossible to obtain new barrels of this size, as there is a shortage of Slavonic oak, with very strict limitations on the felling of trees.

A common proverb among Italian winemakers is 'la botte piccola fa buon vino', in other words, small barrels make good wine. What this means is that the large *botti* are really only regarded as storage containers. It is the small barrels that have some effect on the taste of the wine.

At Isole e Olena Paolo de Marchi is gradually replacing his *botti* with 500-litre barrels, still in Slavonic oak. He prefers them to the large *botti* and finds that they have a more neutral effect than the smaller *barriques*. Yugoslavian oak is softer than the French, giving less tannin to the wine, and allows the fruit to develop fully. It gives good results with Sangiovese, the flavours of which can be killed by the harsh tannic effect of French wood. De Marchi has *barriques* too and considers it very important to adapt the wood to the quality of the vintage, to obtain the right balance in a wine. A lighter vintage will not need so much wood ageing. Seven or eight months in wood is usual for his Chianti *normale*, while his Cepparello spends more time in new wood.

Barriques are more likely to be used for the so-called alternative wines than for Chianti; they were first used at Sassicaia and then by Antinori for Tignanello. Although the DOCG regulations do not specify as much, it is against the spirit of them to keep your *riservas* in *barriques*. They give tastes that are not 'typical of the region' and the wine may not pass the tasting commission. A number of the more

A medieval woodcut of barrel-making.

sophisticated estates are experimenting nevertheless. At Felsina, the *riserva* spends a little time in *barriques*, as well as in *botti*. In order to ensure that there is not too much wood influence, it will then go into stainless steel vats for a couple of months, before spending further time in wood. The aim is a very gradual maturation. At Vignamaggio, 15 per cent of the *riserva* wine is *barricata*, to use a new Italian word, while the rest alternates between *botti* and stainless steel, at six-monthly intervals. They also have chestnut barrels and Slavonic oak casks. At Fontodi, 20 per cent of the *riserva* spends nine months in *barriques*, the new oak giving it just a hint more structure. John Matta at Vicchiomaggio puts his Prima Vigna into new *barriques* for three to five months, which he sees as a concession to fashion. However he chooses the most neutral and the wine is put in large *botti* first.

Estates that are experimenting with *barriques* usually have a mixture of different oaks; Nevers, Vosges, Limousin, Allier and Tronçais *barriques* are all to be found in cellars in Chianti Classico. Although there are numerous oak trees in Tuscany, you never find barrels made from the local oak, as it is deemed to be unsuitable.

At most estates *barriques* are a recent innovation. At Castello di Querceto, the first were bought in 1982 and they say that they are still learning how to use them. For the moment, each is used for three or four wines, before it is cleaned out and used again for another three. Three years seems to be the accepted time for renewing *barriques*.

The cost is high. The price I was given in 1988 was 450,000 lire each, about £225, which if you were to use it for three years, would add 1,000 lire per bottle to the price of wine at the cellar door. For an estate like Volpaia to buy, as they do, 100 barriques a year represents an enormous investment. New *botti*, if you can obtain them, cost about 5 million lire apiece.

Many people are wary that the *barrique* may be only a passing fashion. If you put bad wine into a *barrique*, it does not get any better; you need wine of a certain structure to benefit from wood ageing in the first place. Furthermore, as Paolo de Marchi explains, the flavours of the Sangiovese grape can be overwhelmed by too much new wood and drowned by long oak ageing.

Ageing

The time set down for ageing *riservas* is only seen as a guideline by many estates, which may give their wine considerably more time in wood and bottle before they offer it for sale. At Vignale, where the wines have the rather tough character of Radda, the *riservas* spend four years in *botti*, and the *normale* two years; then both are given at least a year's bottle age. Their wines are high in tannin and they believe that the slow ageing in wood has the desired softening effect. At Montagliari, Minuccio Cappelli has a very traditional approach to ageing. While his *normale* spends twelve to eighteen months in *botti*, his *riservas* may spend anything between five and seven years in wood.

During the ageing period the wine is racked regularly, usually three times during the first year and then every six months, in order to remove the sediment. This generally makes it unnecessary to fine the wine, or even filter it before bottling, as there has been sufficient time for it to fall clear naturally. John Dunkley fines his wine with real egg white, rather than powdered albumen; the yolks are used for

The bottaia, *or ageing cellar for* botti, *at Villa Banfi.*

zabaglione. *Barriques* are topped up each week, unless the bungs are on the side, and both large and small barrels may have glass stoppers.

For lighter Chianti, wood is by no means essential. Many of the estates outside Chianti Classico have no oak at all, neither large nor small barrels. They consider that their wine is too light to benefit from it; and in any case they may quite simply not be able to afford new oak barrels.

Ageing in bottle is important. At Badia a Coltibuono the *riserva* wines may spend only two years in wood, but they have a total of five years ageing altogether, two more in cement vats, and a year in bottle before sale. At Castello di Ama, they have an insulated cellar for bottle ageing. The white and pink wines will spend three months there; the young Chianti nine months and the older wines two years before sale. This is considered an essential part of the process of finishing and refinement. The timing of bottling can be important too. Sometimes wines are bottled as and when there is an order for them. Signora Fabbri at Savignola Paolina only bottles during the last quarter of the moon, when the wine is calm. She considers the phases of the moon when she is racking too, and so does Alceo di Napoli at Rampolla.

The determining factors in the taste of Chianti are the use of the *governo* method and the ageing process, as well as the precise blend of grape varieties. In other words, there is plenty of scope for individuality and the next chapters give more details of who does what.

Chianti in the Doldrums and the Rise of Vino da Tavola

It is one of the contradictions of Italian wine law that the best wine of an estate may not conform to any legal requirements; nowhere is this more true than in Tuscany. Tuscany is known above all for its Chianti and yet more often than not, an estate bases its reputation and concentrates all its efforts on an upstart *vino da tavola*.

The *vini da tavola*, called in some circles the Supertuscans or alternative wines (*vini alternativi*), were born of the doldrums in which Chianti found itself during the 1970s. Chianti was seen as a cheap but far from cheerful wine, with no image of quality at all. Thinking producers saw the urgent need for action and responded. They tried to improve their Chianti, but worked even harder on alternatives. A plethora of table wines was born, often not made with Tuscan grape varieties. New white wines were created from the surplus of white grapes, following the amended regulations of the DOCG. Like many revolutions, for it was indeed a revolution in winemaking, this one has gone too far. You now need a special dictionary to decipher a Tuscan wine list – my attempt at compiling one is to be found on p. 224 and it makes no claim to be complete – such is the variety of fantasy names. There is no doubt, however, that all these new *vini da tavola* have made Tuscany one of the most exciting viticultural regions during the 1980s, no mean achievement in a world that is also discovering other European countries, as well as Australia, New Zealand and Chile.

Sassicaia and Tignanello

No one will dispute the leadership of the house of Antinori in this revolution, although the initial credit should go to a cousin, the Marchese Incisa della Rocchetta, at Sassicaia outside Bolgheri. As is explained in the chapter on Sassicaia and Bolgheri (see p. 190), the present Marchese's father planted Cabernet Sauvignon and Cabernet Franc on his estate soon after the Second World War. His motives were no more complicated than that he liked claret and wanted to see if he could make something similar of his own. At first Sassicaia was little more than a hobby. The first commercial vintage was not until 1968, when the Antinoris were responsible for bottling and selling it. But its popularity was immediate.

In the meanwhile Piero Antinori had been considering the possibility of making a wine with international character, in which Sangiovese would be the dominant grape variety. His father had also planted some Cabernet Sauvignon as an experiment, and for similar motives, but the vineyard had been abandoned. They tried again with Tignanello, which is the name of a particular vineyard on the Antinori estate of Santa Cristina, near San Casciano. In fact the first vintage of Tignanello, the

1971, was pure Sangiovese. It was not until the 1975 vintage that the Cabernet
Sauvignon which they had planted at the end of the 1960s came fully into production
for them to blend with it.

They had the luck and talent to find the right wine for the market at the right
time. Yet again, the impact was immediate. Antinori admit that they were surprised
by its success, but today it is an established part of their repertoire, incorporating
about 20 per cent Cabernet Sauvignon with 80 per cent Sangiovese. The popularity
of Tignanello has set the example for numerous imitators, inspiring people to plant
not only Cabernet Sauvignon, but other French red grape varieties too, such as
Merlot, Pinot Noir and Syrah (see p. 35); and for white wine, Chardonnay and
Sauvignon.

As well as blending Cabernet Sauvignon with Sangiovese, to give the Tuscan
grape variety a little more structure and balance, Piero Antinori and Giacomo Tachis
bought French *barriques* in which to age the wine, as was mentioned in the previous
chapter. They were following the Italian premise that small barrels make good wine,
and felt that the traditional large *botti* were inappropriate to their search for an
international flavour. So it can be said that Antinori also began the trend for what
is now called *vino barricato*. Virtually any wine estate worth its salt will today have
some Cabernet Sauvignon and a few *barriques*, even those which are firmly
traditional in their outlook.

The imitators of Antinori have been numerous and successful, but the plethora
of *vini da tavola* has brought problems of its own. The labels are confusing. How

is the consumer to know what Flaccianello or Cepparello will taste like? How can one tell whether the wine is made from Cabernet Sauvignon or Sangiovese, or both? Why too, is it more expensive than the Chianti Classico of Fontodi, or Isole e Olena? Why, in other words, are growers devoting so much energy, time and money to producing wine that can only ever be *vino da tavola*?

Predicato Wines

One attempt has been made to give some form of legality or official recognition to the increasing number of *vini da tavola*. The three largest merchants' houses, Ruffino, Antinori and Frescobaldi have joined forces to form an association for what are now called the Predicato wines. The aim was to create an image of quality, with an association for its promotion. There are four categories of Predicato, based on four grape varieties. Predicato di Cardisco, taking its name from the medieval word for Sangiovese, is based on that grape variety and allows up to 10 per cent of other grapes, but not Cabernet or Merlot. Predicato di Biturica comes from the Latin name for Cabernet Sauvignon and must include a minimum of 30 per cent of that grape variety, as well as some Sangiovese and up to 10 per cent of other varieties.

For white wine, there is Predicato del Selvante, a name intended to convey the wild aspect of the Sauvignon grape; this allows for up to 20 per cent of other white grapes, but is predominantly Sauvignon. Predicato del Muschio, coming from a synonym for Chardonnay, *blanc musqué*, is made from either Chardonnay or Pinot Bianco and allows for the addition of up to 20 per cent of Rhine or Italian Riesling, Pinot Grigio or Müller Thurgau. The members of the Predicato association impose their own standards of quality, including tasting checks and a minimum period of ageing before sale, almost a year for the white wines and eighteen months for the red. The emphasis with the use of the term Predicato is not so much on a varietal wine, as on the name of the vineyard, or *cru*.

There are now about eighty-five members of the association, but by no means all making a Predicato wine, as many are still at the aspirational and experimental stage. So far the producers of Predicato include the larger merchants such as Antinori, although they do not use the term on their labels, Frescobaldi, Ruffino, Melini and Cecchi, San Felice, the two cooperatives and, among the smaller growers, Gabbiano, Falchini in San Gimignano and Villa Cilnia in the Colli Aretini. Certainly not everyone who makes an alternative wine has joined the Predicato association, although the regulations would be sufficiently fluid to accommodate most of them. Numerous producers prefer not to join, as they feel that a wine should be sold on its own merits, not for being part of an association.

White wines too have been created out of the despair in Chianti. The radical decrease in the percentage of white grapes in the standard blend of Chianti has led to the creation of Galestro, a light neutral white wine, of little character (see p. 174). Bianco della Lega was also born of the excess production of Trebbiano and Malvasia, but more recently it has tended to disappear as these vines have either been grafted with more exciting grape varieties, or simply replaced. Alternatively the wine may have been improved with Chardonnay, Gewürztraminer or some other grape variety, and given a sophisticated fantasy name.

Vino Novello and Sarmento

There have been other innovations with red wines too. *Vino novello* has followed the example and success of Beaujolais Nouveau in France. There is no common brand name like Galestro. Instead each producer has his own, such as Antinori's San Giocondo or Villa Banfi's Santa Costanza. The Istituto di Vino Novello in Tuscany, of which the founder members were Antinori, Frescobaldi, Ruffino, Ricasoli and Villa Banfi, lays down some guidelines, which as yet have no legal backing. The members decide the release date amongst themselves, depending upon the conditions of the vintage. For instance, in 1988 22nd October was the date set for bottling and 10th November the release date, which allowed for at least fifteen days in bottle before sale.

Sarmento is a purely Tuscan development. Intended as an alternative to Chianti Classico, it is a light red wine for release in the May following the harvest and for consumption during that summer. Sarmento is made partially by carbonic maceration, with whole bunches of grapes added to a vat filled with carbon dioxide, so that it is light and fruity, ideal for summer drinking, especially when slightly chilled. The grape varieties are the same as for Chianti Classico, but it is a useful way to use up some of the lighter grapes which would otherwise detract from the quality of Chianti. The first vintage was 1988.

The Increase in Bottling

Another marked change in Chianti over the last thirty years has been the increase in the number of producers who put their wine in bottle. In 1960 only about twenty members of the Chianti Classico Consorzio actually bottled every year. Most wine was still produced by peasant farmers for their own consumption, or it was sold in cask for merchants to blend and bottle.

More often than not, the bottle was the traditional dumpy wicker-covered *fiasco*, with a straw handle. The growing shortage and rising cost of labour, however, made it increasingly impractical to employ people to cover these bottles and the traditional *fiasco* began to disappear. Today they cost 1,000 lire each to produce, which is often almost as much as the wine inside. It is no longer the symbol of the cheerful Italian *trattoria* in London or New York.

There are other reasons for its decline. The ubiquitous *fiasco* conjured up an image of rustic quaffing, which was all that Chianti had ever pretended to be. With the need to escape from the vinous doldrums of neglect, Chianti has needed a change of image. Some producers do still maintain the wicker bottle, adhering to tradition for a small part of their production. Truly appalling are the imitations in plastic, turning tradition into modern kitsch. The *fiasco* may have arisen as an easy means of transport, but for a wine that is to be kept and laid down in a cellar it has distinct disadvantages, which also partly account for its demise. Consequently most Chianti now comes in the tall-shouldered Bordeaux bottle, often with smart labels, designed with inimitable Italian style; bottles that can be laid down and kept for several years.

More estates began to bottle their wine as the price at which they could sell it in bulk declined. To put your wine in a bottle, with your signature on the label, proved to be a way of making money out of it; although even then it was not easy. Some bottled without putting any effort into marketing, while others just dumped quantities of indifferent Chianti on the market. There are now nearly 300 bottlers of Chianti Classico, and many more of Chianti. That is a lot of different labels. However, infinitely more care is now taken over the sale of wine in bottle and the market has developed accordingly. The number of those who bottle good wine and also know how to sell it is growing.

Profits and Costs

The increase in production during the 1960s and early 1970s brought a dramatic slump in price. There was greater supply than demand. In 1971 a hectolitre of Chianti sold for 40,000 lire, but by 1974 that figure had dropped to just 18,000 lire. The large merchants stopped buying from the smaller growers, whose livelihood was consequently in crisis. It was simply not feasible to earn a living from growing grapes. In 1985 Hugh Hamilton at Le Lodoline reckoned that it cost him 55,000 lire to produce a quintal of grapes, giving seventy litres of wine. This would have to be sold at 80,000 lire for him to break even, let alone make any profit. The wine was required to have an alcohol level of $12°$, which probably meant that you also had to buy concentrated must, another expense.

There was a big increase in the price of grapes in 1985, from 60,000 to 110,000 lire per quintal. This was prompted partly by the quality of the vintage and partly by the fact that this was the first year in which the effects of DOCG were really felt. By 1989 the price of a bottle of Chianti Classico had risen to 4,000 lire, as opposed to 1,000 lire in 1984. It is only now that prices are hardening, at a little above the cost of production, with a better balance between supply and demand.

The Consorzio of Chianti Classico has been examining production expenses and reckons that in 1987 it cost 3,000 lire to produce a bottle of Chianti Classico, including production, work in the vineyard and cellar, and bottling, but not transport or sales' costs. It worked out more expensive in 1988, as there was an increase in the price of raw materials. The Consorzio hopes to prevent the price from falling too low. They see the problem as lying with bottlers outside the area of production. Members of the Gallo Nero are not allowed to bottle outside, whereas companies that are not members, and there is no obligation to join, may bottle elsewhere; and indeed do so, such as the Swiss company Schenk, who have a bottling plant in Bolsena.

The Effects of DOCG in Chianti Classico

The introduction of DOCG must take some credit for this improvement in the fortunes of Chianti Classico, although sadly not yet of other Chianti. It entails the tasting and analysis of each wine. This does not necessarily mean a better quality of wine, of course, but rather a stricter regulation of its production and stringent controls on its origin.

Nevertheless DOCG has probably helped to sort out the good Chiantis from the bad. The tasting tests are conducted by the Chambers of Commerce that supervise the activities of each of the seven Chianti zones, but opinions vary as to how efficiently. The procedure is this. When you want to bottle your wine, you arrange for samples to be taken by the inspector of the appropriate Chamber. If the wine passes the tests, you receive the exact number of *bollini* or authenticating seals for the wine that is available for bottling; so there is no question of *bollini* being saved for another vat of wine. If your wine fails the first test, because it is suffering from a rectifiable fault, you are given a second chance. If it fails again, it is declassified into table wine.

The regulations have also stipulated reduced yields for both Chianti Classico and Chianti: from 115 to 75 quintals for Chianti Classico, and 125 to 100 quintals for Chianti, with no more than five kilos of grapes per vine for Chianti and three kilos for Chianto Classico. The grape farmer was initially reluctant to believe that by producing less, he could earn more; but it has paid off in Chianti Classico. Excess yields are penalised, so that up to twenty per cent more than the maximum yield is declassified into table wine; over twenty per cent above the permitted yield and the entire crop is declassified.

On DOCG John Dunkley of Riecine has the cynical view of the foreigner: 'Guaranteed,' he says, 'like the railways and the postal service', which are notoriously inefficient in Italy. André Verwoort at Quercetorta was equally sceptical, quoting that well known Italian proverb, 'fatto la legge, l'inganno trovato', meaning that no sooner is a law made, than someone finds the loophole. However he did concede that there was stricter quality control as a result of DOCG and that DOCG had achieved greater recognition for Chianti on the Italian market. Maurizio Castelli describes the bureaucracy as 'byzantine'.

For all that, DOCG has eliminated a considerable amount of poor Chianti, which is now turned into simple table wine. Production has dropped dramatically, as a result of the decrease in yields, the elimination of most of the white grapes and even the rejection of some wines by the tasting panels.

The Consorzio of Chianti Classico and the Consorzio del Gallo Nero

As has already been mentioned, the growers of Chianti are loosely grouped in a number of different organisations. These are playing a part in determining the future. The Consorzio of Chianti Classico does not have the support of all the producers in the area. Since 1987 there have been two separate organisations: the Consorzio of Chianti Classico, which has the legal control of the wine, administering the DOCG regulations, with 650 members; and the Consorzio del Gallo Nero, with 620 members, which plays a purely promotional role, with no legal authority. It concentrates at the moment on the export market, and is funded by a contribution of so many lire per *bollino*, the *bollino* being the seal of the black cockerel on the DOCG capsule. Of its 620 members, only 250 bottle their own wines, while the rest are either members of the cooperatives, or sell in bulk to merchants.

However it is not essential to be a member of either organisation, for as we have seen, the administration of the analysis and tasting tests for DOCG is conducted by the respective Chambers of Commerce in Florence and Siena. Antinori is a prime example of a company that does not belong to either; nor does Brolio. They consider that they are better equipped to promote their wines on their own. Notable smaller producers outside the organisations include Castello dei Rampolla and Castello di

The logo of the Consorzio del Gallo Nero on a bollino for DOCG.

San Polo in Rosso, who feel that the Consorzio has a stifling effect on possible improvements to the wine, and that they are overwhelmed by bureaucracy.

Other producers do not even feel the need to call their wine Chianti Classico, notably Montevertine and Capannelle. At Montevertine Klaus Reimitz says very firmly: 'We do not need the name Chianti, nor the classification of DOCG. We promote the wine of Montevertine and the geographical indication of Vino da tavola di Radda in Chianti is sufficient'. Raffaele Rossetti of Capannelle used to be a member of the Consorzio, but says that he is too much of a perfectionist to tolerate its inadequacies. The Consorzio del Gallo Nero is hamstrung by Italian bureaucracy and while some members feel that it works well for them, one can sympathise with others who prefer to go it alone.

The Fortunes of Chianti Putto

In the same way as in Chianti Classico, there are two separate associations representing the rest of Chianti, or Chianti Putto, one for controlling the legal administration of the DOCG and the other, which was created in 1984, with the principal aim of promoting the wines. The membership by no means coincides. The promotional organisation has a much smaller following than the equivalent organisation in Chianti Classico. There are only ninety-five members, while 250 belong to the administrative Consorzio. In fact, the promotional body of the Chianti Putto has its own stringent tests for the wine of its members, with its own inspectors. Few people are aware of this. The consumer certainly will not know why a bottle of Chianti does not carry the seal of the Putto: whether it is because the wine has failed to come up to their standards, or whether the producer simply does not choose to be a member of the association.

As a producer, you pay 120 lire per bottle for the *bollino* of the Putto and controls are even stricter than for the standard DOCG regulations. However the DOCG regulations for the Putto are less stringent than for Chianti Classico, allowing higher yields and worst of all, 15 per cent of wine from outside the area (except in Rufina and Colli Fiorentini). Traditionally wine from the south was used to boost alcohol levels and enhance the colour. Nowadays the 15 per cent tends to be in the form of concentrated must, rather than wine. Even so, its use is distinctly questionable.

While promotion is the main objective of the Consorzio of the Chianti Putto, it is also concerned with the improvement of quality and the maintenance of prices. Prices are still very much a problem, and the producer of simple Chianti has a hard time making a living. In 1989 Andrea Dzieduszycki of the Fattoria di Sammontana, near Montelupo, reckoned that it cost 1,700 lire to produce a bottle of Chianti at the estate, not allowing for transport, tax or any profit. In 1988 the minimum price was set at 800 lire a litre for sale in bulk, and at 3,000 lire a bottle for sale outside the area. Signor Dzieduszycki blames the merchants for setting a price that barely covers the cost of production. What happens is this. A producer with wine that may not even pass the DOCG tasting tests, will sell it off to a merchant. He then blends and 'improves' it, so that it does scrape through, and sells it cheaply as Chianti. There is a strong feeling that such inferior wine should be eliminated at source, but the power of the large merchants is such that the Consorzio feels unable to act against them.

*The three labels of
the promotional
body of the Chianti
Putto.*

Members of the Consorzio agree that Chianti should never be expensive, but that its production should nonetheless be profitable, allowing a producer to invest in his cellar and vineyards. In fact the area of production has fallen, by as much as 15 to 20 per cent since about 1985, and it will continue to decline. However there are not many agricultural alternatives to wine, except for olive oil. Some estates practise what is called *agriturismo*, which takes advantage of the popular appeal of Tuscany to the holidaymaker.

Chianti, as opposed to Chianti Classico, has been intended traditionally for young drinking. The Chianti Putto Consorzio is in favour of two separate DOCGs, one for them and one for Chianti Classico. This would help create the idea of two distinct styles of wine. It is therefore concentrating its promotional efforts on the lighter, fruitier style of Chianti and emphasising the differences between this and Chianti Classico. The sub-zones of the Putto region may each have their own identity, but in marketing terms they produce similar wines.

To help the consumer, the Consorzio has designed three different neck labels, each portraying the putto on a different coloured background: a black background indicates a wine for early drinking; a silver background a wine that should be drunk when it is about eighteen months old; and a beige background for *riserva* wines, which are not available until at least three years after the vintage (see illustrations). Unfortunately few people are aware as yet of the niceties of these distinctions. More consumer education is needed.

Two Steps towards a New DOCG

In retrospect the DOCG regulations probably came too early, at a time when Tuscany was overwhelmed by a wave of experimentation, but before there were clear results. Laws tend to fix what is fluctuating, crystallising what is really in a stage of transition. What is the next step?

It is now generally agreed that Chianti as a whole is too big and that so many zones should never have been grouped together in the first place. There is a strong demand for a separate DOCG for Chianti Classico, even from the Consorzio of Chianti Putto, as we have seen. A case can also be argued for Chianti Rufina and, to a lesser extent, for the Colli Fiorentini. Differences in the regulations for Chianti Classico, Rufina and Colli Fiorentini already single them out from the rest as areas of more distinctive quality.

A separate Chianti Classico has been agreed by the local government and a decision by the national government is awaited. When bureaucracy eventually takes its course, the new Chianti Classico will provide an ideal opportunity to amend the recognised shortcomings of the regulations in other ways. But before looking further into the future, another important change is already imminent.

The two earlier Tuscan DOCGs, namely Brunello di Montalcino and Vino Nobile di Montepulciano, brought in their wake the creation of parallel DOCs, namely Rosso di Montalcino and Rosso di Montepulciano. The same is happening for Chianti, with the creation for the 1989 vintage of a new DOC, Colli dell'Etruria Centrale, for red, white and pink wine, as well as Vin Santo. Dott. Tachis is the man behind this, for with his vast experience of Tuscan viticulture, he has been overseeing the regulations. The red wine will be called Vermiglio dei Colli dell'Etruria

Centrale, taking up the medieval name for Chianti. Numerous permutations of grape varieties are possible. Sangiovese is the principal, with a minimum of 75 per cent, but no maximum, so that the pure Sangiovese *vini da tavola* can be brought within the parameters of the law. Canaiolo Nero is limited to 10 per cent, likewise Malvasia and Trebbiano; and other complementary grape varieties are allowed up to 20 per cent. Cabernet and Merlot are specifically mentioned and are each limited to 10 per cent. Again this should bring yet more table wines within a legal framework.

For white wine, Trebbiano will inevitably remain the base, at between 50 and 90 per cent of the total. Malvasia is restricted to 5 per cent and Pinot Bianco and Pinot Grigio, Chardonnay and Sauvignon may contribute 40 per cent to the blend. Other grape varieties allowed in Tuscany are limited to 15 per cent. This will bring many of the experimental white wines into the fold of the law, but only those which still include a substantial proportion of Trebbiano, none of the pure varietals of Chardonnay or Sauvignon. Pink wine may come from 75–100 per cent Sangiovese and up to 25 per cent Canaiolo.

As is discussed in the chapter on Vin Santo (see p. 206), there is a need for regulations to control the production of this wine, for with the exception of a few of the later DOCs, Vin Santo is made according to the producer's whim. The new DOC will lay down guidelines for Vin Santo produced in Chianti, requiring a minimum of three years ageing, and a yield of no more than 200 to 250 litres per hectare.

It remains to be seen whether people will use this new DOC, or whether they will continue to make table wines with fancy names and prices to match; but the new DOC should give some element of control. Vermiglio dei Colli dell'Etruria Centrale should come to be seen as a second wine to Chianti, as Rosso di Montalcino and Rosso di Montepulciano are to Brunello and Vino Nobile. Will it allow for a new flexibility, and range of quality and price?

A New Chianti Classico

What changes might be made to the DOCG regulations themselves? Serious producers in Chianti Classico agree that the *vini da tavola* need to be brought back within the law. They decry the fact that the most expensive wine in their repertoire should be a table wine. John Dunkley, who was one of the last to produce a *vino da tavola*, says it is public suicide, for you are making a public statement that Chianti Classico is your second wine. It draws attention to 5 or 10 per cent of the estate's production at the cost of reducing the quality of the rest. Silvano Formigli of Castello di Ama is another who considers that the winemakers of central Tuscany should now concentrate their efforts on Chianti. Piero Antinori feels that the changes are slowing down, now that the table wines have shown just what can be done. Chianti has benefited from these experiments and the two should now be brought in to line. The Chianti Classico of tomorrow should be more substantial, more homogeneous in style, of *riserva* quality and produced in much smaller quantity.

Antinori and his oenologist Giacomo Tachis hope the DOCG regulations for a new Chianti Classico will allow Chianti to be made purely from Sangiovese and that the legal minimum percentage of white grapes will be removed. In other words that they should make legal what many producers are already doing. In Italy the wine law has always followed the people rather than the other way around.

Chianti comes traditionally from a blend of grape varieties and that possibility should always be maintained. On the other hand there is no reason why it should not also be made of pure Sangiovese. Canaiolo is sometimes capricious and does not always contribute much flavour, and the virtue of the white grapes is debatable. The answer might be a maximum, but no minimum percentage of the white, as in Vino Nobile, for the benefit of those who want them.

Should Cabernet Sauvignon be allowed in the blend for Chianti? If so, it will never be mentioned by name in any regulation. In fact most of the people who grow it do not include it in Chianti, but use it for table wine. There are exceptions, such as the Castello dei Rampolla, where they consider that a little, say 5 per cent improves the flavour. For all its advantages, however, the popularity of Cabernet arises to a considerable extent from an inferiority complex, a lack of confidence in the native grape varieties. Better Sangiovese is the answer for the purists.

If I were to stare into the crystal ball, I would confidently predict that the next few years will see the creation of a separate DOCG for Chianti Classico, and maybe for Rufina. Improvements will continue to take place in viticultural methods, with the planting of better clones in the vineyards. Many of the alternative wines will come back within the fold of the law. There will of course always be individualists who continue to experiment, but with the acceptance of a Chianti Classico made from pure Sangiovese and with no white grapes, the need will be less urgent.

The next step after that might be a definition of the different zones within the region, but this is still some way off. So too is any classification of the numerous estates, as in Bordeaux. John Dunkley has put forward the idea of a floating classification, rather like a football league table, with a tasting panel taking into account both price and performance each year. This would avoid the historical rigidity of the Bordeaux classification of 1855 and be a continuing spur to excellence.

What really counts of course is who makes the wine. As Giovanni Sacchet of Carpineto says: the merit is not in the laws, but in the people, that is, in the winemakers. They are the subject of the following chapters.

*The Strada
Chiantigiana at
Fonterutoli, around
1915–20.*

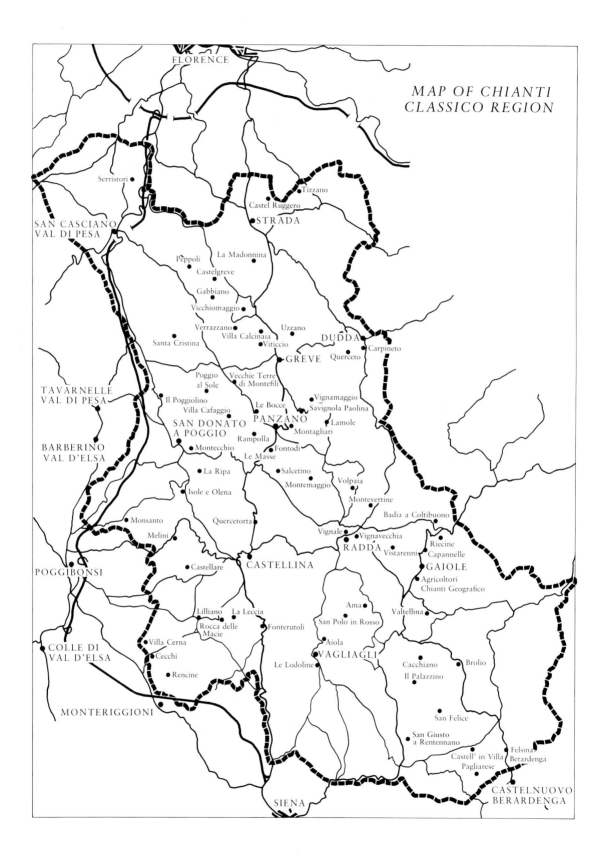

MAP OF CHIANTI
CLASSICO REGION

FLORENCE

Serristori

SAN CASCIANO
VAL DI PESA

Tizzano

Castel Ruggero

STRADA

Peppoli   La Madonnina

Castelgreve

Gabbiano

Vicchiomaggio

Verrazzano   Uzzano

Villa Calcinaia

Santa Cristina   Viticcio   DUDDA

GREVE   Carpineto

Querceto

Poggio   Vecchie Terre
al Sole   di Montefili

TAVARNELLE
VAL DI PESA   Il Poggiolino   Vignamaggio
Villa Cafaggio   Le Bocce   Savignola Paolina

SAN DONATO   PANZANO   Lamole
A POGGIO   Rampolla   Montagliari

BARBERINO   Montecchio   Fontodi
VAL D'ELSA   Le Masse

La Ripa   Salcetino   Volpaia

Isole e Olena   Montemaggio

Montevertine

Monsanto   Quercetorta   Badia a Coltibuono

Melini   Vignale   Vignavecchia

RADDA   Riecine
Vistarenni   Capannelle

POGGIBONSI   Castellare   CASTELLINA   GAIOLE

Agricoltori
Chianti Geografico

Ama

Lilliano   La Leccia   Valtellina

Rocca delle   San Polo in Rosso
Macie   Fonterutoli

COLLE DI   Villa Cerna   Aiola
VAL D'ELSA   Cecchi   VAGLIAGLI   Cacchiano   Brolio
Le Lodoline   Il Palazzino
Rencine

San Felice

MONTERIGGIONI   San Giusto
a Rentennano
Felsina
Castell' in Villa   Berardenga
Pagliarese

CASTELNUOVO
BERARDENGA

SIENA

WHO'S WHO IN *CHIANTI CLASSICO*

Chianti Classico is the historic heart of Chianti, including the vineyards between the two great cities of Florence and Siena. Early records refer to 'lo Chianti storico', by which they mean the area around the three small towns of Castellina-in-Chianti, Radda-in-Chianti and Gaiole-in-Chianti. Subsequently it was extended to cover Panzano, Greve and parts of other villages closer to Florence. Today the northern edge of Chianti Classico is Strada. The best way to approach it is to drive out of Florence, past the monastery of Galluzzo. Ignore the *superstrada* and take the Chiantigiana, the old road to Siena, which bends and turns with every hillside and valley (see illustration on p. 59).

The arcaded square in Greve, with the statue of Verrazzano.

You will soon reach Greve, today the largest town of the region. There is an attractive arcaded square, with a statue of Verrazzano, who discovered the mouth

of the Hudson river and gave his name to one of New York's bridges. Greve was his birthplace. On market day the square is full of colourful stalls and there are several wine shops. The one that is really worth a visit is the *enoteca* at the top of the square, where there are numerous old and dusty bottles, with vintages going back decades. They have the oldest known bottle of Chianti, dated 1885. Every September Greve hosts a wine fair for Chianti Classico, which is supported by many of the producers, providing a wonderful opportunity for tasting and comparison.

Panzano is a small hilltop village, and from there the road goes to Castellina, where there are the remains of an old defence tower and an Etruscan tomb. To the east is Radda, where the Consorzio has its official seat, a cheerful little town, with the vestiges of the fourteenth-century Palazzo del Podestà. Gaiole, in the south-east corner of Chianti Classico, lies quietly at the foot of the Monti del Chianti. Back on the Chiantigiana, from Castellina the road leads past the little village of Fonterutoli, towards Siena. A few kilometres further south the scenery changes and the hillsides flatten, so that you can see the evocative tower of the Palazzo Publico in the Piazza del Campo.

Chianti Classico is rich in history. It was the battleground of the Guelphs and Ghibellines, and there are still castles, Brolio, San Polo in Rosso, Gabbiano, to name but a few. They were succeeded by Renaissance villas, such as Vistarenni and Montecchio. The hillsides have hardly changed since the Renaissance painters first captured them, although inevitably the demise of *cultura promiscua* has altered the agricultural pattern. The variety of landscape is infinite, with appropriate complexities in the wines. Take the time to stand and stare, to sip the wine and savour the atmosphere. You will be richly rewarded.

Aiola

The thirteenth-century castle of Aiola, near Castellina, played a part in the wars between the Florentines and the Sienese, opposing in particular the Florentine castle of Brolio. Today it is the family residence of the Malagodi family, who have owned it for the last fifty years. Giovanni Malagodi is a prominent political figure in Italy; his daughter runs the estate in his absence. The castle is sombre and imposing, with the thick walls of an impregnable fortress. The furniture is heavy, and the shuttered rooms are gloomy. Tunnels that once provided escape routes still exist.

Methods here have remained very traditional. There is little evidence of renovation in the cellars, which are full of old *botti*, both oak and chestnut, in which the Chianti *normale* spends at least twelve to fifteen months and the *riserva* at least three years. As Signora Malagodi says, here the wine sleeps peacefully. The *governo* method is still used and this is one of the few Chianti

Classico estates that continues to bottle some of its wine in the traditional wicker-covered *fiaschi* – Cacchiano is another. These cost 1,000 lire a piece.

However traditional they may be, they too have a *vino alternativo*, Logaiolo, made from 70 per cent Sangiovese and 30 per cent Cabernet Sauvignon, aged in sixty-hectolitre chestnut casks for a year. The Sangiovese comes from a particularly good vineyard, among the thirty-six hectares of vines grown on the estate.

Aiola falls within the DOC of Bianco Val d'Arbia, which Signora Malagodi describes as 'a child of the DOCG' of Chianti. They also make Vin Santo under the same DOC, in the traditional way, drying the Malvasia grapes until after Christmas. The taste is delicately nutty, reminiscent of madeira cake.

Castello di Ama

Ama is a tiny hamlet in the southern part of Chianti Classico. The castle was destroyed in the fifteenth century, having formed part of the boundary line of Florentine castles against the Sienese. Subsequently a villa was built and the estate, with its eighty-five hectares of vines, is now owned by five shareholders and managed by Silvano Formigli. The welcome at Ama is instant. Dott. Formigli is friendly, enthusiastic and very well informed about the Chianti region in general and Ama in particular.

He talked at length about the history of the area, about his experiments in the vineyards and projects in the cellar. He believes fervently in Chianti Classico and considers it an aberration that the best wine of an estate should be a *vino da tavola*. While he and his oenologist are putting Ama among the most advanced estates of the whole region, they are concentrating their efforts on improving their Chianti, rather than any alternative red wine.

The eighty-five hectares of vines are divided up into four specific vineyards, Bellavista, San Lorenzo, La Casuccia and Bertinga. These are split in turn into small parcels, each planted with a specific grape variety chosen for its suitability to the particular soil and microclimate of that vineyard. The approach is very analytical. They are looking to improve upon the typical varieties of central Tuscany and are experimenting with some twenty different grapes, including Chardonnay, Sauvignon, Pinot Nero, Cabernet Sauvignon, Cabernet Franc, Merlot and so on. Their aim with the red varieties is to improve the structure of Sangiovese, without changing its essential character. With whites, they consider that you can only go so far using Trebbiano and Malvasia; they would like to make wines with more flavour and appeal to the international market.

Castello di Ama is one of the very few estates to ferment each grape variety for Chianti separately. The cellar is full of stainless steel vats of different sizes. This means that they pick the grapes at the optimum moment of ripeness, for the Sangiovese ripens before Canaiolo and the Canaiolo before the Malvasia Nera. The blending is done in January prior to putting the wine into barrel. They reckon that this method makes no

difference to the ultimate taste of the wine, but that you can really see what you are doing with each grape variety, thus achieving much greater control over the final taste. They never practise the *governo* method, as they make wines to age. The *normale* will go into *botti*, for nine to twelve months, but the *riserva* will spend time in *barriques*, following the Tuscan saying that 'the small barrel makes good wine'.

A comprehensive tasting at Ama included about a dozen wines. The highlights were several. A white Bianco delle Colline di Ama, made from 80 per cent Trebbiano and 20 per cent Malvasia had hints of grapefruit and a full, almond-flavoured palate. Rosato del Toson d'Oro, named after the Order of the Golden Fleece awarded to one of the Medici Grand Dukes of Tuscany, is an attractive pink wine, redolent of strawberries on the nose and raspberries on the palate, with fresh acidity, made from 80 per cent Sangiovese, 10 per cent Canaiolo and 10 per cent Malvasia Nera.

Sauvignon, which was first planted in 1982, did not show much varietal character, with flavours of apricots and peaches. The 1987 Chardonnay, the second vintage of production, which had been fermented in stainless steel vats, with eight days of skin contact, was rich and buttery with a good balance of acidity. They have experimented with Chardonnay in *barriques* too, but are not yet satisfied with the results, maybe because the vines are still very young. Pinot Grigio was their first atypical grape variety, planted back in 1978. It is fermented in barrel and spends six months in wood altogether. They have tried blending it with Trebbiano and Malvasia, but prefer it as a pure varietal. The wood apparently tones down any astringency, and the wine I tasted was fat and biscuity, with a slightly toasted character.

Chianti *normale* is made of 80 per cent Sangiovese, 10 per cent Malvasia Nera and 10 per cent Canaiolo. Malvasia Nera does not feature specifically in the Chianti regulations, but is acceptable as a complementary grape variety. Dott. Formigli believes that it enhances the Sangiovese, giving good structure to the wine, and from what I tasted at

Ama, I am inclined to agree. Sour cherries was the dominant flavour there.

The 1985 San Lorenzo from Sangiovese, softened with 20 per cent Canaiolo, had spent eight months in wood, mainly new wood, and needed some bottle age to soften the tannins. There was plenty of fruit, with oaky overtones. The 1985 Vigna Bellavista, which was Dott. Formigli's own personal favourite, as he considerd that it showed the Sangiovese at its best, comes from Sangiovese, with some Malvasia Nera. It was similar to the San Lorenzo, but softer and more accessible. Casuccia comes from Sangiovese and 20 per cent Merlot, which has spent a year mainly in new wood. It had good rounded fruit with a firm backbone. The Castello di Ama already has a fine reputation and will certainly be an estate to watch for the future.

L. & P. Antinori

In some ways the name Antinori is synonymous with Tuscany, for it represents the best of both its traditions and its innovations. The family's involvement in wine goes back over 600 years, for the city archives of Florence record that in 1385 Giovanni di Piero Antinori was registered as a novice winemaker member of the guild of *vinattieri*. However at that time wine was not the sole activity of the Antinoris. Men of many parts, they were bankers and silk merchants too. Affluent citizens they certainly were, for in the fifteenth century they built their Renaissance palace, the Palazzo Antinori, which to this day is the headquarters of the company.

Their reputation continued to flourish, for in the seventeenth century Francesco Redi sang their praises in his poem *Bacchus in Tuscany*:

There in Antinoro, in those noble hills,
That have, from the roses, received their
     name,
O, happy am I!
As from the darkest clusters
Of a mature Canaiuolo
I squeeze a juice so pure,
That, in the glass splashes,
Jumps, bubbles and sparkles!

And when in the fine company
Of every other wine, I taste it,
It stimulates in my breast
A certain something
That I cannot name
Joy, or pure Desire.
It is a young desire
A new desire to drink
Which grows the more
The more wine you pour.

This was enthusiasm indeed, in what may be considered equivalent to a review of the best cellars of the time.

The merchant house of Marchesi L. & P. Antinori was founded by two brothers Ludovico and Piero at the end of the nineteenth century. Four generations later, another Piero Antinori is the driving force behind the reputation of the company. His elder brother, another Ludovico, is creating an independent reputation with a new estate, Ornellaia in Bolgheri (see p. 190).

Marchese Piero Antinori is an immediately likeable man. He has the distinguished style of a cosmopolitan Italian nobleman, urbane, friendly, intelligent and very ready to give his views about Tuscany. His oenologist Dott. Giacomo Tachis must take the credit for many of the innovations discussed in the preceding pages. Again, modesty seems a dominant quality in Dott. Tachis' character. As an oenologist he ranks amongst the superstars, but as a man he is friendly and approachable, far from the awe-inspiring figure that I had expected. It is no exaggeration to say that these two men have done more than anyone to determine the present path of Tuscan winemaking.

The Antinori estates are several. Santa Cristina at Mercatale Val di Pesa is in Chianti Classico, as are two recent purchases, Pèppoli, which was formerly known as Villa Terciona, and the dramatically imposing Badia a Passignano (see colour illustration opposite p. 73). Outside Chianti Classico they have vineyards at Bolgheri for a pink *vino da tavola* and in Orvieto, in the heart of Umbria, they own the thirteenth-century Castello della Sala, where they concentrate their experiments on white wine and Pinot Noir. It is at Santa Cristina that Tignanello, and its successors Solaia and Seicentenario, were born.

The mainstay of the Antinori portfolio is Villa Antinori Chianti, which is mostly aged in large barrels for a couple of years. This is characteristic and reliable. Better are the wines sold under the Tenuta Marchese Antinori label, as these entail a stricter selection of grapes. The vineyards of Pèppoli, once a cell of Badia a Passignano, lie at 350 metres, overlooking the valley of the Greve. The soil is quite rich and fertile, making for soft fruity wines, without a great deal of acidity. The 1986 was the first vintage of Pèppoli, although Antinori had already been buying the grapes of Villa Terciona for several years.

At Badia a Passignano they are planning a pure Sangiovese *cru*, which will probably be aged in six-hectolitre *botti* for a couple of years, followed by some time in bottle. Maybe the 1988 vintage, the first under the Antinori regime, will be released in 1991, but at the time of writing nothing is definite. In the meanwhile the monks will remain at the abbey, while Antinori run the cellars and vineyards. At the moment these cover thirty-five hectares, but there are plans to extend them to seventy or eighty hectares.

With Tignanello, the object was to make a wine composed principally of Sangiovese, but with an international character. They were inspired to some extent by the success of the first commercial vintage of Sassicaia, the 1968, produced by Piero Antinóri's cousin, the Marchese Incisa della Rocchetta. The first attempt at Tignanello, the 1971 vintage, was pure Sangiovese and not sufficiently different from a good Chianti Classico. Meanwhile they had begun planting Cabernet Sauvignon. By 1975 they were able to include this in the blend. Tignanello has become so established, with such proven success, that it has set the example for the numerous *vini da tavola* that are blends of Sangiovese and Cabernet Sauvignon. Antinori was also the first Chianti house to use French *barriques*, which form an essential part of the vinification of Tignanello. While Tignanello usually contains about 20 per cent Cabernet Sauvignon, from a specific vineyard on the Santa Cristina estate, Solaia is made in an opposite proportion, with 20 per cent Sangiovese and the rest Cabernet Sauvignon.

Vinification methods are similar for both wines. Seicentenario was made especially for the 600th anniversary, as a 'super Tignanello' and the blend is roughly the same, coming from the very best wine available at the time.

Things do not stand still with Antinori. Santa Cristina was previously the label for their Chianti Classico, but since the 1986 vintage this wine has been transformed into a pure Sangiovese, which is currently sold as a *vino da tavola*. Eventually it will be incorporated into the proposed DOC of Colli dell'Etruria Centrale, but for the moment it represents a youthful fruity Sangiovese, very agreeable to drink, but without great staying power. In contrast, the Villa Antinori wines maintain a *riserva* style, as a more substantial Chianti Classico.

The vinification plant of Antinori is a modern establishment at San Casciano. There is the usual forest of fermentation vats, but most of the wines are aged in the more traditional cellars at Santa Cristina. Other wines include a pink wine from Bolgheri, sold as a *vino da tavola*, rather than as a DOC, and a sparkling wine, made by the champagne method from grapes bought in northern Italy. There is a *vino novello* too, called San Giocondo.

Antinori's interests stretch well beyond Tuscany, for the company has joined a project, funded mainly by the large brewers Whitbread and the champagne house Bollinger to plant 600 acres of vineyards in California's Napa Valley. The principal grape varieties for this venture are Chardonnay, Cabernet Sauvignon, Sauvignon and Merlot, but there are also eight acres of Sangiovese Grosso. Piero Antinori is very optimistic about the potential success of this Sangiovese, for the climate and conditions are similar to those of Montalcino. It is not yet in production, so he is undecided as to how it will be vinified and marketed; but maybe it will be blended with Cabernet Sauvignon, as a Californian Tignanello. The future offers many possibilities for the house of Antinori.

Badia a Coltibuono

The old *badia* or abbey of Coltibuono was one of the major Tuscan houses of the Vallombrosan Order, a sub-order of the Benedictines, along with Badia a Passignano and Badia a Monte Scalari. The foundation dates from the eleventh century and there are written records of monks planting vineyards here in 1080. The old bell tower still stands, but the rest of the abbey was rebuilt in the fifteenth century. The monks remained until Napoleon secularised the monasteries in Italy at the beginning of the nineteenth century; some monks returned to their abbeys later, but not here, as the community was already in decline at the time of the dissolution. Then in 1841 the property was bought by the Stucchi family, to whom it still belongs. Piero Stucchi is a Milanese industrialist, with an enthusiastic interest in his estate and his son Roberto is the first member of the family to become a winemaker. Roberto has spent two and half years at the University of California

at Davis, the leading American oenology school and a further year working for Chappellet, a California winery. He is assisted by Maurizio Castelli, as the consultant oenologist.

A visit to Badia a Coltibuono is always a delight. You are given a friendly welcome by the shaggy white Maremma sheepdog, cousin to the pair at Capezzana. There are beautiful gardens, with vine-shaded paths, and an attractive courtyard. The seventeenth-century frescos in the monks' former refectory have been restored, after being obliterated by whitewash. There is a rustic restaurant, serving typical Tuscan food, masterminded by Roberto's mother, Lorenza de' Medici, who also runs cookery classes at Badia a Coltibuono. *Botti* are housed in the crypt of the church and in a long series of cellars under the villa. There was a baby toad outside the cellar door, which brings you good luck in Italy. My good luck was to enjoy a very enlightening tasting of the various wines of Badia a Coltibuono.

Roberto and Maurizio together have been working hard for the reputation of Badia a Coltibuono, to make it one of the most exciting estates of Chianti Classico, with some very successful, innovative wines. As well as the traditional Tuscan grape varieties, they have Cabernet Sauvignon, Merlot, Cabernet Franc and Pinot Nero; and for white wine, Chardonnay, Sauvignon, Pinot Bianco and Müller Thurgau. However as far as red wine is concerned, their main interest is to improve the quality of the traditional grape varieties, above all of Sangiovese; for white wine, the new grape varieties are more interesting, as they see absolutely no potential in the Trebbiano or Malvasia that have been traditional to Chianti.

Coltibuono Bianco consists of one third each of Trebbiano, Malvasia and Chardonnay, fermented separately and blended together afterwards. They are considering experimenting with skin contact, and a small part of the wine undergoes a malolactic fermentation. It had the leafy character of Chardonnay on the nose and was quite full flavoured, with some firm acidity on the finish. The vineyards of Badia a Coltibuono come within the DOC of Bianco Val d'Arbia, but they see no advantage in the name and prefer not to use it. A pink wine is made from Sangiovese with a little Ciliegiolo, which is given four or five hours of skin contact and fermented very slowly at a cool temperature. The flavour is that of ripe strawberries. Coltibuono Rosso is a rounded fruity wine, intended for easy drinking, coming mainly from Sangiovese Grosso, with some Canaiolo and a little Cabernet Sauvignon added in the blending.

The very first bottlings at Badia were back in 1934 and they began more regular commercial bottling in the 1950s, which was quite innovative at the time. The wines here are made to last, coming from vineyards close to Monti, rather than by the abbey, which is generally too high in altitude. In 1988 they were still selling the particularly fine 1958 vintage. Today the *riserva* may spend only two years in wood, but it will have five years of ageing altogether before sale, including a year in bottle. The *normale* spends just a year in wood and the flavours are rich, powerful and spicy.

Even more exciting is the *vino da tavola*, Sangioveto, a wine made as the name implies from pure Sangiovese, which is otherwise called Sangioveto in Tuscany. It comes from the oldest vineyards, planted in 1947. These were the first specialised vineyards on the estate, with as many as 6,000 vines to the hectare. The wine is aged in cask for a year and for a further year in *barriques*, a quarter of which are new. However they do not want to overdo the new wood, as it can overwhelm the Sangiovese. The juice spends as long as three weeks in contact with the skins, as opposed to two weeks for the *riserva* and one week for the *normale*. The 1982 was redolent of cedarwood on the nose, with hints of blackberries and lots of lovely rich fruit on the palate. The 1983, which was less concentrated, from what they consider to be a marginally less exciting vintage, had some herbal eucalyptus flavours. Roberto Stucchi has no doubt that the future of Tuscany lies with Sangioveto and these wines demonstrate the reason why.

Le Bocce

Le Bocce, in the hills just outside Panzano, is an estate in transition. It was bought in 1986 by three brothers – Giancarlo, Gino and Bruno Farina – who also own an estate in Barolo. The oenologist Vittorio Fiore took over responsibility for the winemaking with the 1988 vintage. This explains why I liked the 1988 white table wine, even though it was made from Trebbiano and Malvasia, while I found the 1987 Chianti *normale* a little astringent, and the 1985 *riserva* rather soft but with a harsh finish. However, the potential is there, for the cellars are well equipped and spacious. There is refrigeration equipment for the efficient control of vinifications. *Barriques* have been bought for ageing part of the *riserva* and they are looking at alternative wines and planting other grape varieties. Some 1988 Sangiovese has been kept separately in *barriques*, to see how it develops. In other words, this is an estate to watch out for in the future.

Castello di Brolio

As has been explained in an earlier chapter, Brolio may be seen as the spiritual home of Chianti, for it was here that Baron Bettino Ricasoli, the great-great-grandfather of the present Baron, conducted his experiments with the *governo* method and with blends of different grape varieties, to create the forerunner of modern Chianti.

Brolio was the property of the Vallombrosan monks until the Ricasoli family arrived in 1141, following an exchange of land. However they are known to have been settled in Tuscany since 770, making them one of the very oldest recorded Tuscan families. They were powerful warriors supporting the Florentines against the Sienese, and the castle was destroyed on numerous occasions. It was rebuilt for the last time in 1486 by the city of Florence, in gratitude for services rendered during the wars. It is in sombre grey stone, with a red brick addition of the nineteenth century, and from the bottom of the hill it looks severe and imposing (see illustration on p. 19). It is no surprise that the Ricasoli family no longer live here, but prefer the comfort of Florence.

You can visit the chapel, with its crypt where various members of the Ricasoli family are buried. There is an air of sobriety about the place, enhanced by the clanging bell that must be rung by all visitors to gain entry into the grounds. The gardens, with views over the vineyards, are more cheerful.

At one time the Ricasoli family owned three other large estates in Chianti, Meleto, Castagnole and Montefiridolfi, but today, they concentrate their energies on the vineyards of Brolio. The Baron's sister-in-law is at nearby Castello di Cacchiano. The majority shareholding in the merchant company of Ricasoli was bought from Seagrams by a British businessman, Roger Lamberth of United Wine Producers. He, in turn, in February 1990 sold a controlling share to the large Australian wine company, Hardy's. Lamberth still retains a small interest in the merchant house, while the Ricasoli family control the estate of Brolio. To clarify any confusion between the two activities, the mention of Castello di Brolio on the label means that the wine comes from the vineyards of Brolio, but if the producer's name is the Casa Vinicola Ricasoli, the grapes have been bought from other growers, with whom there are often long term contracts, and vinified by the merchant house.

The present Baron Bettino Ricasoli firmly believes in the traditions of Tuscany. The introduction of foreign grape varieties may have a novelty value, but he wants to maintain the intrinsic character of Tuscan wines, especially the red; so there is no Cabernet Sauvignon at Brolio, nor does he make any Predicato wine. He does produce Galestro and includes 40 per cent Chardonnay with the Trebbiano. In 1988 they launched two new wines. Nebbiano, named after a vineyard on the estate, is two parts Sauvignon to one part Italian Riesling, which undergoes a cool fermentation to produce a light fruity wine, with a little more character and flavour than Galestro. The pink Tramonto is made from Sangiovese, which is left on the skins for a very short time before pressing. The result is a soft fruity pink wine.

There are three different soil types within the 250-hectare estate: sandstone on the higher hills yields lighter wine and is therefore better for the white and pink wines; *galestro* is the classic soil of Chianti; and there is also limestone, which gives rich, robust wines. The Chianti of Ricasoli is traditional in flavour, that is to say, quite warm and soft, without the structure of some of the newer estates. As well as the standard *normale* and *riserva*, they make a Riserva del Barone, described as a *riserva* of a *riserva*. This is aged for five years, instead of their usual four, which is already a year longer than the regulations demand.

Other wines include Citerno, a Pinot Bianco and Malvasia blend; Agrestino, a *vino novello*; a sparkling champagne-method wine and San Ripolo, made from the classic grape varieties of Chianti. Ten per cent of the wine is aged in *barriques* for eight months, while the rest spends twelve months in *botti*. Then there is Torricella, first produced in 1928, from Malvasia, which is aged in both *botti* and *barriques*. On the label it is a simple *vino da tavola*, but the taste is far from simple and quite unusual. It is deep golden in colour, very smooth and rounded on the palate, with hints of toffee and marmalade.

The cellars at Brolio are breathtaking. Not only is there one of the largest *vinsanteria* in the whole of Tuscany, but a cellar capacity of 230,000 hectolitres; the entire production of Chianti Classico is only 300,000 hectolitres. Of course, this is far too much for their needs. The creation of this vast cellarage and capacity originated in a scheme of Seagrams that has long since been abandoned. Brolio also have the largest cask in Chianti, which holds 225 hectolitres.

The tradition of the first Baron Bettino is being continued with experimental work on *barriques*, different types of French and Slavonic oak and selections of grape varieties, mainly of Sangiovese, but also of Vernaccia. My last visit to Brolio left me with the impression that this giant of an estate, with its distinguished history, was waking up. I suspect that the company was rather neglected by Seagrams after their considerable investment in the cellars during the 1960s and 1970s. Now with a fresh injection of energy and money, it is beginning to take a new look at the Tuscan winescape and may achieve some fine results in the next decade.

Castello di Cacchiano

The Castello di Cacchiano has belonged to the Ricasoli-Firidolfi family since the middle of the twelfth century. The castle was destroyed by the Aragonese in 1478, but rebuilt by the Florentine republic for the family, in recognition of their services. Today Elisabetta Ricasoli-Firidolfi runs the estate. Baron Bettino Ricasoli of the nearby Castello di Brolio is her brother-in-law.

Cacchiano is in the southern part of Chianti Classico, close to the sprawling village of Monti. You can see both Siena and Brolio from the terrace on a clear day. There are twenty-eight hectares of vines, planted with the traditional Tuscan grape varieties. The grapes are fermented together, with no Trebbiano and no *governo*, and the wine goes into wood the following summer. The traditional

oak *botti* are housed in what were once the dungeons of the castle. The *normale* will spend twelve months in wood and the *riserva* as much as three years, in both wood and cement vats. A third wine is made from the grapes of the best vineyard, from the same varieties as the Chianti. Labelled R.F., it spends twelve months in *barriques* of Allier oak, which have been gradually acquired over the past few years. After a further six months in stainless steel vats, it is bottled.

The Baroness is working towards a change in her wines. They used to be rather light and lacking in body. Now she wants a fuller flavour, with texture and perfume, and that is what she is achieving. The 1986, when it was two years old, was tough and concentrated, with some sweet berry fruit. The 1985 was quite meaty but more elegant, while the 1985 R.F. was very concentrated and perfumed, ripe and rich and quite different in taste from the Chianti, as a result of the different ageing process. The taste of *barriques* is not typical of Chianti, but the wine is good and indicative of the potential of this estate.

Villa Cafaggio

Villa Cafaggio was bought by the Farkas family in 1963 and has been run by Stefano Farkas since 1973. The estate is in the middle of nowhere. It is part of the parish of Panzano, a hamlet that dates back to the thirteenth century and which belonged to the Benedictine monks of Siena. Stefano Farkas works from new cellars, equipped with stainless steel fermentation vats and a refrigeration machine, and the traditional Slavonic oak barrels. Unlike most Chianti producers, he is equipped to make concentrated must, and even makes it for his neighbours, who bring him their own grape must. In years when the use of concentrated must is necessary, it is added during the alcoholic fermentation. He no longer uses the *governo* method and his Chianti spends about eighteen months in wood; not too long, he says, or the result would just be an infusion of oak. He believes that *barriques* have too violent an effect on the wine.

He is also sceptical about the current fashion for Cabernet Sauvignon, attributing it to Dott. Tachis, Antinori's oenologist, whose example everyone has followed 'like sheep'. An inferiority complex among Chianti producers has resulted in the fad for *barricato* Cabernet Sauvignon, when they should really be growing better Sangiovese. Consequently Signor Farkas makes his Chianti Classico *riserva* from pure Sangiovese, which gives an excellent concentration of flavour, while his *normale* contains a little white wine. He also has a little Canaiolo, but most of his thirty hectares of vines are planted with Sangiovese. In addition he produces what he calls a *cru*, Solatio Basilica, which translates literally as 'sunny basil'. Basilica is in fact the name of one of the farms on the estate. Again it is a pure Sangiovese, but from some of the oldest vines of Cafaggio and it is aged in smaller *botti* than the Chianti *riserva*. I tasted the 1983, which was a solid mouthful of fruit and tannin, and the 1981 which was very concentrated with fruit and depth. Cafaggio, in common with many other Tuscan estates, had an exceptional year in 1985, the wine that I tasted proving very concentrated, with fruit and tannin. The 1982 *riserva* was more elegant.

Villa Calcinaia

Calcinaia, just outside Greve, is approached along a driveway lined with imposing cypress trees. This rather old fashioned estate has belonged to the Capponi family since 1523. Calcinaia means chalk and refers to old chalk quarries nearby. Count Niccolò Capponi explains that in the Middle Ages it was a feudal village, but that as the feudal system died out at the end of the thirteenth century, with the abolition of serfdom in 1288, people moved to the towns. In later centuries the well-to-do from Florence, including his own family, began to invest in land, but did not want to stay there. *Un podere in Chianti*, or a farm in Chianti, was a symbol of success and wealth in the sixteenth century; the situation is not so dissimilar today.

Methods here are quite traditional. The thirty hectares of vineyards are planted with the usual grape varieties for Chianti, as well as a little Gewürztraminer for white wine, which is unusual; but there is no Cabernet Sauvignon and no *barriques*. They ferment the wine either in cement vats or in open chestnut vats, and sometimes crush the grapes with their feet. They no longer use the *governo* method, except for their alternative wine, which is really just a younger version of a Chianti and sold from the May following the vintage, like Sarmento. All the grapes are fermented together and they use concentrated must if necessary. They never fine the wine as it spends sufficient time in wood to fall clear naturally.

I tasted the 1982 *riserva* in May 1986. It was quite elegant with flavours of raspberries, lacking the weight of Chianti from further south. The 1983 *normale* had some peppery fruit. Bottles from Calcinaia are distinguished by the striking black and white label, based on the family coat of arms.

Capannelle

If there is a 'state of the art' winery in Chianti Classico, it is Capannelle, a tiny estate outside Gaiole-in-Chianti, owned by Raffaele Rossetti. The small, immaculately neat cellar is equipped to deal with the production of three hectares of specialised vines and two hectares of *promiscua* vines. Rossetti has an ascetic, almost fanatical approach to hygiene in the cellar. Stainless steel pipes connect up with every vat. He condemned the rubber hose pipes that you so often trip across on cellar floors, as the worst thing possible. They are unhygienic as they cannot be sterilised by steam. Every bottle is sterilised too and there is a tiny laboratory to control the development of the wine.

Rossetti works in plastics. He says that he does not pretend to understand anything about oenology, so he employs Andrea Mazzoni from the Institute of Oenology in Siena to make his wine. Instead of the modern Vaslin press they prefer to use the old fashioned vertical press, which is much softer than a horizontal one. *Barriques* are used only once and the ageing of the wine is carefully controlled, with no exposure to light or temperature changes. As Rossetti says, it sleeps in sterile peace.

They make three wines at Capannelle, a white wine from Chardonnay, a pure Sangiovese that is aged in *barriques* and a Sangiovese, blended with 10 per cent Canaiolo that is matured in *botti* for nine or ten months. For red wine they firmly believe in the value of Sangiovese, describing it as a 'splendid grape variety'. They are adamant that Tuscany does not need Cabernet Sauvignon. The *barriques* are changed every year and the *botti* every six or seven. The 1987 was the first vintage of Chardonnay, which I tasted in June 1989. It had been fermented in Tronçais *barriques* and kept in them for six months, with *bâtonnage*, as in the traditional manner of the Côte d'Or, in Burgundy. I found the wine rather heavy overall, both on nose and palate. The bouquet was quite nutty, while in the mouth the wine was rather clumsy, soft and rich with overtones of hay and almonds, and a curiously sweet finish.

It was the red wine of Capannelle that really excited me. I tasted the 1983 vintage of the Sangiovese and Canaiolo blend. The colour was just beginning to develop. It had some of the cedarwood character of mature Sangiovese, and was very elegant, harmonious and balanced with tannin, fruit and length, a delicious glass of wine, with the finesse of classed growth St. Julien.

Carpineto

Unlike so many Chianti estates with their long histories, Carpineto is a recent creation. Giovanni Sacchet and his associate Antonio Zaccheo bought land and planted vineyards here some twenty years ago. They started from scratch and now have fifteen hectares of vines and a functional warehouse, which houses barrels, tanks and bottles, outside Dudda on the eastern edge of Chianti Classico. Their first serious vintage was 1968. The vineyards are planted not only for Chianti, but also for sparkling wine. They have some Chardonnay, a small quantity of Pinot Nero and some other experimental grape varieties. Sacchet is an oenologist from the Veneto,

training at Conegliano, one of Italy's leading oenology schools, and was driven above all by the desire to make his own wine. You need both passion and courage to undertake such a venture.

Italians prefer to taste wine with a meal. They do not appreciate the clinical Anglo-Saxon approach to wine tasting and Sacchet is no exception. He took me into the hills to Badia a Monte Scalari, once a Vallombrosan monastery, but now a restaurant and hotel. The monks left as recently as 1940 and the place still retains a medieval atmosphere. Our aperitif was the sparkling wine, made by the Charmat method, with the wine spending between three and six months on the lees. They are experimenting with different grape varieties for their sparkling wine, including Chardonnay and Vernaccia. The wine we tasted, or rather drank, was based on Vernaccia. With the *antipasti* came the 1988 Chardonnay. The juice is given two days of skin contact and then vinified in oak *barriques* from the Allier, in which the wine stays for seven months. This was their first vintage. There were hints of marzipan on the nose, with full, rich, oaky flavours on the palate. It promised well.

Then with the pasta dishes came Sarmento. This was the right time to drink it, on a warm June day, eating outside under a large oak tree. Part of the wine is made by carbonic maceration and the rest by normal fermentation, though at a cooler temperature than is usual for red wine. It was fruity with fresh acidity and remarkably easy to drink. Finally there was a 1983 *riserva*, which had spent a year in *botti*. This was rounded soft and mature, with plenty of fruit, for the vineyards around Dudda give perfume, rather than body. I was left with the impression of a sound, serious estate, with a rational view towards experimentation and innovation.

Castellare

Castellare, in the hills near Castellina, is the property of Paolo Panerai and his wife Fioretta. He is a journalist from Milan and editor of the magazine *Class*. They first came here about 1980, although the vines had already been planted by the previous owner in 1972. There are now about eighteen hectares around the house, mainly of Sangiovese, although they have subsequently grafted Chardonnay, Sauvignon and Cabernet Sauvignon on to their Trebbiano and Malvasia vines, 'because the market wants them'. However they have no intention of using Cabernet Sauvignon to mask any defects in the Sangiovese, for Panerai is insistent that he has selected good Sangiovese clones. He is only too aware of the shortcomings of Sangiovese from Romagna, which was planted extensively in Chianti Classico during the 1970s.

His cellar is neat and well run. We were accompanied by the young daughter, who watched us while we tasted and earnestly enquired, 'Why are they spitting it out?!' The fermentation takes place in stainless steel vats and the *barriques* are only for ageing. Everything is carefully controlled by the oenologist Maurizio Castelli. New barrels are used for their alternative wine, called I Sodi di San Niccolò, after the remains of the twelfth-century monastic castle of San Niccolò on the site. The wine comes from a special selection of Sangiovese, or Sangioveto, with 10 to 20 per cent Malvasia Nera, which ripens well in the particular microclimate of Castellare. Their Chianti spends three to five months in *barriques* and is then aged in bottle. We tasted the 1985, which consisted of 90 per cent Sangiovese, with some Canaiolo and Colorino, but no white grapes. It was very intense, with concentrated fruit on nose and palate.

As well as a little white *vino da tavola* made from Trebbiano and Malvasia, there is a red wine for early drinking called Governo di Castellare. Here as the name implies, the *governo* method is used, with traditional Chianti grapes, for this is a wine that is destined for sale in the spring. It later proved a delicious picnic wine, with easy-to-drink fruit and the distinctive tell-tale prickle of the second fermentation of the dried grapes. The other grape varieties were not yet in production at the time of my visit. Castellare has particularly attractive wine labels, with a different wild bird for each vintage, and for the Governo di Castellare, the lily of Florence.

Castel Ruggero

Castel Ruggero on the northern edge of Chianti Classico, close to Florence, was fortified at the beginning of the eleventh century. In subsequent centuries it became a monastery, then a villa and was bought by Niccolò d'Afflitto's grandfather in 1921. Vines, including Gewürztraminer, were planted then, but the next generation took little interest in the estate, so that only three hectares of vineyards remain. Niccolò d'Afflitto is a young man with wide wine horizons, for he has spent six years in Bordeaux and a further year working for the Felton Empire winery in California. He criticises the Italian schools of oenology for their limited approach, for instructing their students how to make wine, but never giving the reasons why something should be done. Sadly he is handicapped by his father's lack of enthusiasm for Chianti, for there is more money to be made in *agriturismo*.

The cellars at Castel Ruggero are old fashioned with solid cement vats, and old oak *botti*. The chestnut ones are no longer used. Unusually the Sangiovese and Canaiolo are kept separately until they are blended in March. There is also some Cabernet Sauvignon, but planted across the rows and so mixed up with the other vines. However d'Afflitto reckons that there is too much clay in the soil of his vineyards for successful Cabernet Sauvignon.

He makes just one wine, for reasons of economy and practicality, as much as anything. A third of his Chianti will spend a year in wood and then be blended with the rest, which has stayed in vat for bottling eighteen months after the vintage. The result seemed quite austere, and there is the underlying feeling that d'Afflitto is hampered by his father's unwillingness to invest money in the cellars. There is also a little white, made from equal amounts of Trebbiano and Malvasia, together with 30 per cent Gewürztraminer, which makes for a fat spicy wine, full and rounded on the palate.

Castell'in Villa

Castell'in Villa is the property of the charming Principessa Carolia Pignatelli della

Botti *in the cellars at Castello di Nipozzano, in Rufina.*

Barriques *in the Frescobaldi cellars at Pomino.*

Leonessa. A Greek by birth, the Principessa has lived here since 1971, when she was first introduced to winemaking. Castell'in Villa belonged to the Counts of Berardenga in the twelfth century and is close to the town of Castelnuovo Berardenga. The present villa was built in the mid-seventeenth century and there are wonderful views towards Siena from the terrace.

Altogether the Principessa has sixty hectares of vines, including six of Cabernet Sauvignon, which are not yet in production. Sangiovese is the main grape variety in her Chianti, as she considers that Canaiolo oxidises too quickly and is therefore unsuitable for wines intended for ageing. Nor has she included any white grapes in her Chianti since 1975. Instead, she occasionally makes a Bianco Val d'Arbia.

We wandered round the cellars, accompanied by two very noisy spaniels, called Trebbiano and Ultimatum, whose barks seemed to ricochet off the vats. For the Principessa, the quality of her wine is very much determined in the vineyard. She ferments the grapes of the different vineyards separately, and blends them as necessary. Ultimately the wine of a particular vineyard may be sold as a *cru*. She does not believe in the *governo* method, for she does not consider that it contributes anything to a wine; it is just a means of making it ready to drink earlier. In any case it is an expensive procedure. Her Chianti *normale* is sold after three years of ageing, mainly in Slavonic oak, while her *riserva* wines will not be sold until they are five years old.

She also makes a 'fantasy wine', because 'everyone else does'. It comes from carefully selected Sangiovese that is aged in *barriques*. The first vintage, 1983, had not yet been bottled when I visited her in 1986. She has a somewhat sceptical view of the Tuscan alternative wines, considering that many are not yet worth the high price being asked for them. We tasted the Principessa's Chiantis in her elegant drawing-room. The flavours were traditional in the very best sense of the word, with warm fruit and the dry, astringent finish that complements olive oil so well.

Luigi Cecchi & Figli

The family company of Cecchi features amongst the big five Chianti producers, but compared to the Antinoris, Frescobaldis and Ricasolis does not have the same long antecedents, for the company was founded less than a hundred years ago, in 1893. It is now run by the third and fourth generations. First they worked as merchants, not acquiring any vineyards until the middle of this century. The flagship, upon which their pretensions to quality rest, is Villa Cerna, an old estate, with its origins in the eleventh century, outside Castellina, just on the edge of Chianti Classico, with a substantial 110 hectares of vines. It was bought in 1962. A much more recent purchase is Castello di Montauto in San Gimignano. Cecchi also have links with the Fattoria del Casello, rent ten hectares of vineyards in Montepulciano at the Fattoria della Seta, and rent a further forty hectares on the estate of San Giorgio in Orvieto. Finally there is their commercial activity. They buy in grapes for Galestro, Sarmento, Chianti and Chianti Classico.

A modern vinification plant and high-tech bottling line, with the very latest equipment for sterilisation processes the grapes, in the valley below Villa Cerna. Those from Villa Cerna itself are kept separate, and include four hectares of forty-year-old Sangiovese vines, which produce Spargolo, their Predicato di Cardisco. Spargolo is a Tuscan term describing a small, not very dense bunch of grapes. The wine was made for the first time in 1982. I tasted the 1983, of which a third of the wine had spent twelve months in *barriques*, and the rest had been aged in forty-hectolitre barrels. The taste was quite rich, reminiscent of soft ripe cherries and more approachable and drinkable, but with less stature, than many of the other alternative wines.

The Chianti from Villa Cerna is also aged in wood, for as much as two years for the *riserva*. I tasted the 1986 vintage, which in 1989 had the warm stony character of the Rhône valley, with plenty of ripe fruit. The taste was not classic Chianti Classico, but it compared very favourably with the run-of-

Opposite above
Vineyard at Pieve di Panzano in Chianti Classico.

Opposite below
Badia a Passignano in Chianti Classico, where Antinori run the cellars and vineyards.

the-mill Chianti that forms the bulk of Cecchi's business.

Agricoltori del Chianti Geografico

The cooperative of the Agricoltori del Chianti
Geografico is the Sienese counterpart to the
cooperative of Castelgreve. With cellars near
Gaiole, it receives grapes from its members
with vineyards in Radda, Castellina and
Gaiole. The cooperative was created in 1961,
starting with seventeen founding members
and has grown steadily, so that by 1989
some 135 members are farming about 350
hectares.

They have made an enormous investment
in modernising their cellars and buying new
equipment, with new stainless steel fermentation vats. The cellars give the impression of
an efficient well-run organisation. However
when I first visited them in 1984, I found
their wines disappointing, not in keeping with
the cellars nor with the ultramodern tasting
room, with individual spitoons looking like
upturned hairdryer casks. Vittorio Fiore
became their consultant oenologist in 1986
and things have definitely changed for the
better, with a marked improvement in quality
and flavour. They continue to use the *governo*
method, as they believe that it rounds out
the wine, and their ageing methods are traditional to Chianti Classico, with lots of large
casks.

Contessa di Radda is their *riserva* label,
made only of grapes from the vineyards of
Radda, and produced only in the better years.
They also sell the wine of four of their
larger estates under the individual labels
of Lucignano, Tenuta Montegiachi, Castello
Fagnano and Le Colonica. They follow the
Tuscan trend of Sarmento and Predicato.
One of their members planted Cabernet Sauvignon in 1983, so that since 1986 they have
made a Predicato di Biturica, which consists
of 30 per cent Cabernet Sauvignon, blended
with 70 per cent Sangiovese, aged in *barriques*
for six months. Sarmento is made by carbonic
maceration for early drinking. They make
Galestro too, and also have some sparkling
wine made for them, in an attempt to use
up the excess production of white grapes.

Certainly it now seems as if this cooperative
is working well for its members.

Felsina Berardenga

You always receive a warm, friendly welcome
from Giuseppe Mazzocolin. He used to teach
Dante, as a school teacher of Italian literature,
and came to wine through marriage; for
Felsina was the property of his wife Gloria's
parents, purchased in 1966. Mazzocolin
became involved in the estate in 1975 and
since 1981 he has devoted all his energy and
enthusiasm to making some of the best wine
of Chianti Classico, with the help of his
oenologist Franco Bernabei.

Felsina is on the southern edge of Chianti
Classico, just north of the town of Castelnuovo Berardenga. The earliest written mention of Felsina dates back to the beginning
of the twelfth century. The existing house
and cellars were built in the eighteenth. There
has been a considerable investment in the
cellars, with blanketed stainless steel fermentation vats and a powerful refrigeration
machine. Even more impressive is what in a
classed-growth château of Bordeaux would
be called a *chai d'élevage*, or barrel-ageing
cellar, and indeed that is what it looks like.
Transported there with eyes closed, you could
easily believe yourself to be in the heart of
the Médoc. The cunning aspect of the design
is that the entrance is through what were
once the old stables, with a gallery of *botti*,
narrower and more oblong than usual,
designed to fit each stable stall. Then you go
down a slope to the *chai*, which looks as
though it is a natural continuation of the
stables. In fact it was built 250 years later,
but from old materials. The divide between
the old and the new is imperceptible.

When I first met Giuseppe Mazzocolin in
1984, he was talking of Chardonnay and had
just grafted some. In 1989 we were able to
taste his first production of I Sistri from
the 1987 vintage. It had been made in the
traditional Burgundian way, fermented in
wood and kept in *barriques* for ten months,
on the fine lees, which were shaken up at
regular intervals. The *barriques* were medium-toasted Tronçais oak, and the toasted

character came out on both nose and palate, with some rich Chardonnay fruit and a good balance of acidity, finishing with a firm bite. For a first attempt it was very successful.

Mazzocolin considers it crazy that you should be able to include a foreign grape variety, Cabernet Sauvignon, in Chianti, but that officially you cannot make Chianti from that most Tuscan of grape varieties, Sangiovese, alone. His Chianti conforms more or less to the regulations, and has flavours of sour cherries with some dry spiciness. However he is building his reputation above all on two table wines, Rancia and Fontalloro. Rancia is a five-hectare vineyard, planted only with Sangiovese, from which he obtains very low yields of small concentrated berries. Unlike his other red wines, it is not *governato* and is aged in *barriques* for twelve months, and also in slightly larger 680-litre barrels. The 1985 still tasted very young when it was nearly four years old, with a good elegant structure, and plenty of tannin and fruit. It promised well. The 1985 Chianti *riserva* was similar yet different. This had been kept in *botti* rather than *barriques*, and alternated between wood and vat, so that the ageing was gradual. It tasted fuller in the mouth than the Rancia.

Fontalloro is another pure Sangiovese, from a different vineyard, of six hectares. Part of the wine spends twelve months in *barriques*, which are usually new. Unlike Rancia, Fontalloro is *governato*. Mazzocolin is one of the partisans of the *governo* method. I tasted the 1986 Fontalloro, which in 1989, had more obvious overtones of new wood with some vanilla and rich berry fruit. Finally we tried the 1988 Cabernet Sauvignon, which was the first vintage of that grape variety. In June 1989 it had not yet spent any time in wood, but Mazzocolin is anticipating giving it two years in wood and two years in bottle, so it may be drunk in about 1993. The colour was very deep and the flavour very concentrated, tannic blackcurrants; potentially delicious, but not yet.

The final experiment that Mazzocolin is considering is an alternative to Vin Santo. Just for fun, he is putting late harvested Chardonnay in a Limousin barrel. Maybe it will turn out like Sauternes. There was no noble rot on the Chardonnay, but he is optimistic about some vines near his lake!

Castello di Fonterutoli

The pretty little village of Fonterutoli nestles in the valley just below Castellina on the road to Siena. Fonterutoli played its part in the long struggle between the Florentines and the Sienese, for this is where the boundary between the two cities was fixed in 1208. It had been agreed that a horseman should leave each city when the cock crowed, and that the boundary would be drawn where they met on the road. Fonterutoli is much closer to Siena than to Florence, but this is less a reflection upon the prowess of the rider than upon the Florentine character. The sly Florentines, so the story goes, had starved their cockerels the previous night, so that they woke well before daylight and crowed from hunger. The Florentine horseman therefore had a headstart.

The Mazzei family, who own the Castello di Fonterutoli, have been there since 1435, when Lady Smeralda Mazzei married Piero di Aguseo di Fonterutoli. They had no sons and so the property passed to the Mazzei family. The present head of the family, Lapo Mazzei is the president of the Chianti Classico Consorzio and an influential banker. The Mazzei family were merchants before they were landowners, but they have produced wine since they first came to Fonterutoli. The house was built in the early 1500s. From the terrace there are views with the towers of Siena in the distance. The delightful formal gardens are Signora Mazzei's pride and joy.

Altogether there are thirty hectares of vines, from which they make not only Chianti, but also an alternative wine called Concerto, comprising approximately 80 per cent Sangiovese and 20 per cent Cabernet Sauvignon. The two grape varieties are blended after fermentation and aged in *barriques* for about seven or eight months. The first vintage of Concerto was in 1981, since when the blend has been gradually refined; they began with equal quantities of both grape varieties and have gradually increased the amount of Sangiovese. They are also considering a pure Cabernet Sauvignon. The first Cabernet Sauvignon vines were planted ten years ago, in the interests of experimentation and occasionally they put a drop of Cabernet in their *riserva* wine, called Ser Lapo. Normally however, their Chianti blend consists of 90 per cent Sangiovese, with 10 per cent Canaiolo and some Malvasia, but no Trebbiano. Franco Bernabei is their oenologist and consequently all their Chianti is made with the *governo* method. The cellars are scattered around the village, as building regulations are very strict. They are unable to build any new cellars to house their fermentation tanks, which are outside. In fact, this means that it is very easy to cool the vats with cold water.

Trebbiano is used for their white wine, and blended with a small amount of Chardonnay and Riesling, which were planted in the mid-1970s. There is no more than 10 per cent of both grape varieties, which are fermented together with the Trebbiano. The taste had a hint of honeyed Riesling, and was dry and fresh with some good fruit. The red wines of Fonterutoli are good too, with rich rounded flavours, robust, with body and weight, wines of good structure that will age well.

There is a little shop just off the Chiantigiana where you can stop and buy not only wine, but the other products of the estate, lavender soap and bath oil, honey and of course olive oil. Signora Mazzei is responsible for the lavender fields, and also for the cultivation of juniper berries for gin.

Fontodi

The estate of Fontodi is on a hill just south of Panzano, from where you can look across the valley towards Rampolla and Cafaggio. In May the cuckoos are noisy and the garden is full of irises and rosemary. The origins of Fontodi are Lombard and the name means *fonte di odo*, or a place rich with water. It has belonged to the Manetti family since 1968. I talked to young Giovanni Manetti, who explained how neglected the estate had been when they bought it. They now have thirty hectares of vines, not all in production

as yet, including some Cabernet Sauvignon, a little Pinot Nero, which was vinified for the first time in 1989, and a hectare and a half of Pinot Bianco, Gewürztraminer and Sauvignon for their white table wine.

Franco Bernabei is the consultant oenologist here and the wines have his distinctive touch. He believes in the value of the *governo* method and so all the Fontodi Chiantis are made in this way. Contrary to general belief, Bernabei considers that *governato* wines age well; and certainly the taste of those from Fontodi bears this out. Their Chianti is made principally from Sangiovese, with 5 per cent each of Canaiolo and white grapes, and spends seven or eight months in large Slavonic oak barrels before bottling. The structure is good, for the vines are at 450 metres, which tends to make for more robust wines, especially as the soil is the typical *galestro* of Chianti Classico.

Bernabei is an enthusiast of *barriques* and so the *riserva* at Fontodi, which contains 5 per cent of Cabernet Sauvignon, entails a little ageing in these barrels. Just 20 per cent of the wine spends nine months in *barriques* of Allier or Nevers oak, out of a total ageing in larger wood of two and a half years. Everything is then blended together a couple of months before bottling. I tasted the 1982 *riserva*, which was quite tough and certainly needed more bottle age to round out. They began with ten *barriques* and at the last count had 130, from Tronçais, Allier and Nevers oak, as well as *botti* of Slavonic oak. The wine in *barriques* is followed meticulously, so that the barrels are topped up each week and regularly racked, three times in the course of nine months. They are adamant that these do not overdo the wood effect.

Their third red wine is Flaccianello della Pieve, the *pieve* or chapel referring to the nearby Pieve di San Leolino, while Flaccianello is the old name of a vineyard on the estate. They made this wine for the first time in 1981 and it is produced only in the best years. It is pure Sangiovese, aged in *barriques* for nine to twelve months, depending on the development of the wine. The 1982, which I tasted in May 1986, was deep in colour, with a rich nose, showing some oak character,

Giovanni Manetti of Fontodi.

while the palate was rich and concentrated too. It needed time in bottle, but its quality was apparent. Giovanni Manetti calls it a *vino da meditazione*, that delightful Italian expression to describe a wine that demands contemplation and consideration. He does not see it as a competitor to his Chianti, but rather in a class of its own, as his flagship, or what the Italians would describe as the buttonhole in his jacket.

The final red wine in the Fontodi repertoire is called Vigna del Sorbo, after a vineyard with 25-year-old Sangiovese vines, to which 10 per cent of Cabernet Sauvignon is added. Half the Sangiovese is aged in *barriques* for twelve months, while the Cabernet Sauvignon is kept separately, and everything is blended together just before bottling. Only 5,000 bottles are produced altogether. The 1985 vintage was firm and elegant and still very youthful in September 1989. If one were to make comparisons with Bordeaux, this would be a St. Julien, while the Flaccianello would be a St. Emilion.

Their white wine is given a fantasy name, Meriggio, which is a Tuscan word to describe a patch of shade in the heat of the midday sun. Pinot Bianco makes up the bulk of the wine, with 10 per cent each of Gewürztraminer and Sauvignon. They are all vinified together in a slow, well controlled fermentation that takes about twenty days, after which the wine spends three months in Tronçais oak barrels. The taste was quite full and dry, slightly honeyed on the nose and almost oily on the palate. The first vintage of Meriggio was 1984; before that their white wine was sold under the now virtually defunct label of Bianco della Lega.

Castello di Gabbiano

The Castello di Gabbiano is one of the more northerly estates of Chianti Classico, with Nozzole on the other side of the valley and Pèppoli also nearby. Unlike many of the so-called castles of Chianti, this one is real. The first glimpse is of an imposing medieval tower, built in 1250 by the Bardi family. The property belonged later to Francesco Solderini, a patron of Leonardo, and remained in his family until they were exiled by the Medicis. In 1980 Gabbiano was bought by the Alcaini family. Raino Alcaini is a chemical engineer from Milan, who has turned green, as he puts it, with his new interest in viticulture and winemaking. Franco Bernabei makes the wine for him, while Alcaini has provided the considerable investment necessary to turn Gabbiano into a significant estate, with innovative ideas and some serious wines.

Twenty-seven hectares of vineyards have been expanded to fifty, including twelve of Chardonnay, and there are plans to plant another ten hectares of Merlot and Cabernet Sauvignon. Thus there is scope for a considerable variety of wines, characteristic of the experimental attitude in Tuscany today. Vinifications are carried out in stainless steel vats outside. The old cellars under the castle house chestnut and oak *botti*, and *barriques* of Tronçais oak for the Chardonnay, as well as Vosges, Nevers, Limousin and Allier *barriques* for the various reds.

We tasted our way through the range of wines. The Galestro had more character than most, with some fruity acidity and the gentle almond flavour of Trebbiano, enlivened with some Chardonnay and Pinot Grigio. They make Sarmento too. Bianco del Castello consists mainly of Trebbiano and Malvasia, with one third Pinot Bianco and a drop of Gewürztraminer. It was fuller flavoured than the Galestro, with a hint of apples and a touch of butter. The Chardonnay, called Ariella after a daughter, spends about four months in medium-toasted Tronçais barrels. It was very good, with some attractive toasted character on the nose, and rich but elegant fruit on the palate, making a good balance of oak and fruit; and with a long, dry finish.

Three qualities of Chianti are made, *normale*, *riserva* and *riserva oro*, which they describe as a *riserva* of a *riserva*. The *normale* spends six months in wood and the ordinary *riserva* two years. A third of the *riserva oro* will spend eight to nine months in *barriques*, as well as two years in *botti*. We tasted the 1987 *normale*, which was a full meaty wine, with some acidity and rounded, with good backbone. The 1982 *riserva oro*, which usually comes from the same vineyard as the *riserva*, had an attractive cedarwood quality. This was the first year that they removed all the white grapes and it was also the first year that Bernabei masterminded the winemaking

at Gabbiano. You could taste the effect of the *barriques* in the wine, but not too much.

Even more outstanding was Ania, after another daughter, a wine made purely of Sangiovese Grosso, as in Montalcino. We tasted the 1983, which had spent ten to twelve months in *botti*. It was rich and long, with a very good balance of fruit and wood, and a lovely rich smoky character. It is wines such as this that support the argument for pure Sangiovese within the legal framework of DOCG. Although they make a Predicato di Biturica, more interesting is R. e R., so called for Raynella and Raino Alcaini. The blend is 60 per cent Cabernet Sauvignon, 10 per cent Merlot and 30 per cent Sangiovese, with each grape variety spending fourteen months in *barriques* before blending. The 1985 vintage, which was the first year of production for Cabernet Sauvignon, was rather austere on the nose, with more fruit on the palate. The immediate impression in 1989 was of austerity combined with richness. It was one of those wines that you admire in the tasting glass, but do not want to drink at the dinner table; in twenty years time it may be delicious.

The Cooperative of Castelli del Grevepesa

This cooperative, with large cellars outside Greve, covers the vineyards of Chianti Classico in the province of Florence, while the Agricoltori del Chianti Geografico is its counterpart in the province of Siena. With 160 members, it is responsible for 800 hectares of vineyards altogether, including 650 of Chianti Classico. The remaining 150 hectares are for *vino da tavola*, mainly from the Colli della Toscana Centrale. The cooperative was founded in 1965 and the first vintage was in 1968. Since 1987 the members have leased the abbey of Sant'Angiolo Vico l'Abate from the Archbishop of Florence on a twenty-year contract. This old abbey stands on a hill above the cooperative buildings and here they have their *vinsantaia*. Methods of vinification are quite traditional, with a spacious cool underground cellar full of large oak casks for ageing, giving a capacity of some 17,000 hectolitres.

The cooperative has tried to play a part in the wave of improvements sweeping through the vineyards of Chianti. As it covers such a large area, it makes several different sorts of Chianti Classico, based upon a selection of grapes from specific areas, each with its own particular characteristics. There is Panzano, Lamole and Montefiridolfi, as well as two individual vineyards, or *crus*, to use the Italian term, called Sant'Angiolo and Vigna Elisa. If a generalisation can be made, the wines of the province of Siena have more bones or structure than those of Florence, while the Florentine wines are fuller with more body. Within this broad outline the cooperative has identified further differences.

Lamole is one of the highest parts of Chianti Classico, with vineyards at 600 to 650 metres, on very poor soil, giving low yields. The aspect is good; the vineyards are protected on all sides, but still have a good air circulation. In contrast the village of Panzano, which is on the opposite side of the valley from Lamole, is lower in altitude with vineyards at 350 metres and therefore a warmer microclimate. The wine is fuller, fatter and ages better. It has been described as 'a wine that sings in the mouth'. Finally Montefiridolfi in the north-west part of Chianti Classico is at the lowest altitude of all, producing wines that are ready to drink earlier. The vineyard of Sant'Angiolo, around the abbey, has its own particular microclimate. The soil is *galestro*, with particularly good drainage.

As well as Chianti Classico, the cooperative also makes several *vini da tavola*. Valgreve is a white wine from the Alta Valle della Greve, made from ripe Trebbiano with a drop of Malvasia, in other words the white grapes surplus to Chianti. A Vino da Tavola di Mercatale Val di Pesa is suggested as an alternative to Sarmento. It is made partly by carbonic maceration, while the rest consists of Sangiovese and Trebbiano, which spend just forty-eight hours on the skins. It is fresh and fruity with sufficient acidity; very easy to drink when lightly chilled. The cooperative has also launched into Predicato wines, to make a pure Sangiovese sold under the name of Coltifredi, the name of the vineyard at Mercatale. It spends six to eight months in *barriques* and the 1985 vintage, which I tasted in June 1988, was still redolent of new oak. Best of all was the Sant'Angiolo Vico l'Abate. The 1985 was a substantial mouthful of fruit and tannin, which promised well, with balance and flavour.

Despite their insistence upon a very careful selection of grapes and the practice of *vendemmia verde*, the cutting off of bunches of green grapes before the vintage in order to reduce the crop, the wines of the cooperative failed to really excite me. They do these regional selections only in the best years, and only since 1985. Their standard label is Castelgreve for everyday Chianti Classico, with a label depicting the lily of Florence, which flowers in colourful abundance in May. They are trying hard to improve their wines and deserve to succeed.

Isole e Olena

Isole e Olena is the home of one of Tuscany's leading winemakers, for there is no doubt that Paolo de Marchi, who comes originally from Turin, is achieving great things for his estate and for Chianti Classico. His family bought this attractive property in the 1950s and Paolo himself came here in 1976, after studying agriculture in Turin and broadening his horizons with six months in California. This experience has given him a perspective that stretches far beyond the hills of Chianti. He is aware of tradition, which he respects, but also brings a spirit of innovation to winemaking.

De Marchi recognises the qualities of the Sangiovese grape, and also its limitations. Much of his innovative work has been directed towards improving that grape variety. As soon as he arrived at Isole e Olena he began working with Sangiovese on its own and he is very pleased with the results, as tasted in Cepparello; this alternative wine is made instead of a Chianti *riserva*, taking its name from a nearby stream. The wine is aged for twelve to fourteen months in Bordeaux barrels of Allier or Nevers oak, a third of which are replaced each year. The bungs are kept on the side so that there is no need to

Paolo de Marchi of Isole e Olena.

top them up. The results are delicious; de Marchi has produced a series of vintages of Cepparello with rich berry flavours, balanced with oak and tannin. These are wines that develop with bottle age. They do much to redeem the tattered reputation of Chianti.

In good years Sangiovese makes excellent wine, but in an average vintage it can lack body and length; in a bad year it ripens too late and is liable to rot, which may lead to a lack of colour. Ideally de Marchi would like to give support and structure to the Sangiovese, but without changing its taste, or that of his Chianti. Cabernet Sauvignon is a popular option on other estates, but he does not consider it suitable for Chianti. A blend of 15 per cent Cabernet Sauvignon with Sangiovese would not taste of Chianti and would still make a bad Sangiovese. So after talking to Guigal from the Côte Rôtie in the northern Rhône valley, he has planted Syrah. Just one and half hectares came into production in 1985. He was pleased with the results, but overcropped the vines, a mistake that he attributes to lack of experience. In 1986 a little Syrah went into his Chianti *normale*, giving it an attractive hint of pepper. The 1988 vintage of pure Syrah, which I tasted

in September 1989 was a superb example of the grape variety, with the flavour of rich blackcurrant-gum fruit.

De Marchi has also grafted some Cabernet Sauvignon, partly because everyone else has it. He does not want to miss out on the experience of vinifying this grape variety. He produced a pure varietal for the first time in 1985. I tasted the 1986, which had a rich oaky nose, with some powerful cassis and herbal flavours in the mouth. It was very successful, but de Marchi still believes that it is better for an area to keep to its traditional framework, so he really prefers to concentrate his energies on Sangiovese. Another idea is a Sangiovese, Cabernet and Syrah blend. Ideas are certainly not lacking, only the time to carry them out.

His Chianti is made mainly from Sangiovese, with a little Canaiolo and a drop of white wine. He is looking at the ageing of it. This is one of the few estates to retain some old chestnut barrels; approximately a third of his Chianti will be aged in small 500-litre barrels, rather than in large *botti*; another third will be in *barriques* and the last third in vat, with about four to six months in wood altogether. The chestnut barrels retain some of the original taste of Chianti, but they need to be old, as the flavours are too green from new ones. Barrel ageing is good if the wine is intended to be bottled young, but it requires a longer period in bottle before sale. Essentially de Marchi sees two styles of Chianti, a young wine with fresh fruit that would compete with, say Beaujolais for early drinking; and a *riserva* that is intended for ageing, as a *vino da meditazione*. For him this is Cepparello. The taste of Chianti *normale* from Isole e Olena is good, a wine that is ready to drink early, but with an immediately appealing fruitiness counterbalanced with good structure.

White wine has not escaped the attention of de Marchi's enquiring mind either. He has succumbed to Chardonnay, which he ferments in medium-toasted 500-litre oak barrels, to give the wine more complexity. The 1988 wine tasted of tropical fruit, lychees and pineapple, with a richness reminiscent of Australia and a firm toasted flavour on the finish. It is still very experimental, with plans to ferment the 1989 vintage in one-year-old barrels. De Marchi would also like to try Sauvignon Blanc or Vermentino, maybe even Müller Thurgau. He considers that Trebbiano provides a satisfactory natural base, with good acidity, and could be successfully blended with other grape varieties. His Malvasia is used for Vin Santo.

As an agronomist de Marchi is very aware of the importance of work in the vineyard. Yields have been reduced and the pruning adapted to give earlier ripening grapes. Essentially wine is produced in the vineyard and merely adjusted in the cellar, by for example blending grapes. The less you do in the cellar, the better the wine. There is no doubt that Paolo de Marchi with his youthful enthusiasm and talent as a winemaker will continue to achieve great things for Chianti Classico, and for Isole e Olena in particular.

Olena is in fact a nearby hamlet, while Isole is an attractive old house. Here we sat and chatted in the courtyard. The white hound Napa, named after the valley in California, chased a cockerel that had the impertinence to venture within. The sun was shin-

ing and the Cepparello tasted delicious. This is what the wines of Tuscany are all about.

Lamole di Lamole

There is just one estate in the tiny hamlet of Lamole up in the hills above Greve, Lamole di Lamole. The name is repeated for emphasis. Anyone else with vineyards sells his grapes or sends them to the cooperative of Castelpesa. Lamole is one of four estates belonging to a company called Antiche Fattorie Fiorentine. The others are Salcetino, further down the dirt track towards Panzano, Poggio il Pino, an estate in the Val d'Arno making Chianti Putto, and finally another estate in the Val d'Arno that does not produce wine at all. The owners are a Milanese family, with the surname Toscano.

The vineyards of Lamole are amongst the highest in Chianti Classico, between 400 and 500 metres. The soil is *galestro*. Wines here start off quite hard. They never have a very deep colour and need ageing, for they only develop perfume and fruit after their second year. I liked what I tasted. A 1985 *riserva*, in practice made only from Sangiovese, had an element of austerity, as though it had been aged in a *barrique*, but in fact had been only in larger casks. The austerity was balanced with some good rounded, perfumed fruit. A second 1985 *riserva* containing 10 per cent of Cabernet Sauvignon had a hint of cassis on the nose and even more blackcurrant fruit on the palate. They were planning to keep it in wood for five years altogether. However in normal vintages a *riserva* will only spend three years in wood and the *normale* eighteen months. The wines seemed both hard and soft at the same time, with some deliciously ripe, almost sweet fruit, balanced with a good tannic structure.

The wines from the estate of Salcetino are more experimental. The property includes seven hectares of Chardonnay and Pinot Bianco, from which they make a table wine, Messer Bianco, with equal proportions of each grape variety. The Pinot Bianco softens the Chardonnay, so that the wine tasted lighter than a pure Chardonnay, with slight overtones of bitter almonds. Its red counterpart, Messer Rosso, is mainly Sangiovese with 10 per cent Cabernet Sauvignon, so not unlike the second 1985 Lamole *riserva* that I tasted.

Fattoria delle Lodoline

The romantic story behind this estate is that the present incumbent, Hugh Hamilton was parachuted here during the Second World War. Breaking a leg on landing, he was hidden from the Germans by the daughter of the house; then after the war they married. Mr. Hamilton, now a distinguished man in his sixties, dismisses this as more fiction than fact. However, he admits that while the villa was used as the local SS headquarters, escaped British prisoners of war were hidden in what is now the *vinsanteria*; the Free French were lurking in another villa across the valley. His wife, the Countess Maria Radicati di Brozolo, had buried her jewellery in the garden at Le Lodoline. The Countess has made her name as the Italian champion for show jumping side saddle.

Lodoline means 'little lark' and the name comes from the painted ceiling of a sixteenth-century loggia, which is decorated with a flock of tiny birds. The estate is in the southern part of Chianti Classico, just outside the village of Vagliagli. Altogether they have twenty hectares of vines, which have gradually been converted from *cultura promiscua* since 1967. Methods here are quite traditional. Mr. Hamilton says that he learnt from the farmers when he first arrived. He asked questions and did courses. Although he employs a consultant oenologist, he makes the wine himself. He comments that the problems of winemaking have changed over the last thirty years; when he first came to Chianti, one tried to make wines that were ready to drink early; but today one makes wines to last. Wine used to be kept in wood much longer, whereas today people prefer to age it in bottle. This is a measure of the revolution in Tuscan winemaking. Mr. Hamilton keeps his wine in concrete vats for at least a year, after which it usually spends three years in wood; but four or more if it is destined to be a *riserva*.

I liked his wines. The 1983 was warm and mature, a pleasant glass of Chianti with good fruit and the typical astringency of Sangiovese on the finish. The 1980 was smooth and balanced.

Lilliano

The villa of Lilliano, near Castellina, is approached along an alleyway of lime trees, which flower in June, giving off a rich scent in warm sunshine. There was once a fortified abbey on this site. Lilliano has endured a somewhat chequered history, successive buildings having been destroyed three times during the conflict between the Florentines and Sienese, and again in the Second World War. Only the cellar underneath the villa dates back to the Middle Ages.

Today it is the property of Eleonora Berlingieri, and her sons Giulio and Pietro Ruspoli. Altogether there are 450 hectares on the estate, with forty-five of vines, of which twenty are kept as *promiscua*, 'for the landscape'. As well as the old cellars under the villa, there is a more modern warehouse with stainless steel vinification vats. Part of the Chianti *normale* goes into wood, while the *riserva* spends at least a year in small *botti*. We tasted the 1986 *riserva* from cask, which had a good deep colour, a hint of oak on the nose, with some rounded fruit and a dry long finish. There was still some 1981 Chianti in wood, which had a lovely mature flavour not unlike the cedarwood of St. Julien in Bordeaux. The 1985 was closed but showed some ageing potential.

Their alternative wine, made for the first time in 1985, is called Anagallis, the name of a wild flower. It is composed of equal amounts of Sangiovese and Colorino, which is unusual; but they have a twenty-year-old Colorino vineyard, which gives wine with more substance than is usual for that grape variety. For the moment Anagallis is aged in thirty-hectolitre *botti* of Allier oak for seven or eight months, but they are considering trying *barriques*. We tasted the 1986 vintage, which had a peppery nose, reminiscent of blackcurrant gums, with a drier palate and firm structure.

La Madonnina

La Madonnina lies on a hill outside Chiocchio, on the northern edge of Chianti Classico. Officially the area is called La Puglia, as a family arrived here from southern Italy some 500 years ago. However since 1969, when the abandoned estate was bought by a Swiss company Fratelli Triacca, it has been called La Madonnina, after a small chapel on the site, to avoid confusion with the wines of Apulia. The investment has been considerable, with new functional cellars equipped with a forest of stainless steel vats for both fermentation and storage, and *botti* and *barriques* too.

Altogether they have seventy hectares of vines, which are managed by Oliviera Masini, who has been involved with the estate since 1970. Apart from the name La Madonnina, one can find their wine under other labels, including Il Colombaio, which is a farm on the estate, Villa Franchi after some previous owners, and Ponte Vecchio.

The vineyards lie at 300 metres. The soil is poor, mainly chalk with some clay. In very hot years the grapes can become too ripe, making for particularly alcoholic wines. Certainly the 1985 *riserva* that I tasted had a warm Rhônish quality about it, attractive but not classic Chianti. The 1986 was more typical, while their alternative wine Il Mandorlo, meaning an almond, is made from equal parts of Cabernet Sauvignon and Sangiovese, aged for eighteen months in *barriques* after separate fermentations. It was not yet quite knit together in 1989. There was some rich cassis fruit, but it needed more time in bottle.

Melini and Serristori

Immediate impressions of Melini are of size and anonymity. The estate is part of the Gruppo Italiano Vini, which in turn is part of Winefood, a public company with interests all over Italy. They have 220 hectares of vines, in the Colli Senesi as well as in Chianti Classico, and also deal in Vernaccia di San Gimignano and Vino Nobile di Montepulciano. They own the Fattoria di Terrarossa near Castellina, the Fattoria di Selvanella near Radda and the Fattoria di Granaio, in the immediate vicinity of their cellars near Poggibonsi. Total production is somewhere between five and six million bottles a year, which places them third in the hierarchy of size after Ruffino and Antinori. Their cellars, which are just inside the Chianti Classico zone, boast a capacity of 100,000 hectolitres, including 12,000 in wood and 60,000 in stainless steel. The rest is accounted for by concrete vats.

Some 70 per cent of their Chianti requirements are met from their own vineyards, while they buy in more wine between January and June. They use the *governo* method for their Chianti *normale*, but not for the *riserva* wines. Fermentations are carefully controlled and vinifications conducted as befits a well-run modern cellar. As well as Slavonic oak barrels, they have some old large Limousin oak casks from France, in which their *riservas* are aged for three years. Their Chianti *normale* does not usually go into wood at all. In addition they have a few *barriques* for their *vino da tavola* I Coltri, which is made mainly from Sangiovese, with a little Cabernet Sauvignon. These are blended together after fermentation and spend six to eight months in *barriques*. The first vintage of I Coltri was 1980. Perhaps surprisingly they do not make Galestro, but prefer to sell a white table wine made from Trebbiano and Malvasia, called Lacrima d'Arno.

Melini also has associations with the Serristori company, another part of the Gruppo Italiano Vini, which sells its Chianti under the name of Machiavelli. It has an eighteen hectare estate at Sant' Andrea in Percussina, which once belonged to the family of Niccolò Machiavelli. Exiled from Florence, he spent a few months here in 1512–13 and this is where he wrote *The Prince*. The Machiavelli family died out in the eighteenth century, when the remaining daughter married a Count Serristori. Then the Serristori family sold the estate about fifty years ago. The house is now a museum, for it is the only surviving building in which Machiavelli is known to have lived. The architecture is sombre, with the solid walls and high win-

Norman Bain of Le Masse di San Leolino, with pickers.

dows typical of the fifteenth century. There is an Italian garden, a labyrinth of hedges, created by the Serristori family. Machiavelli's old cellar is used to age *riservas*, while the wines are vinified at Poggibonsi. The cellar still has the original cobbled floor, typical of Tuscany. Next door is the 'tavernetta', mentioned by Machiavelli in a letter, and now run as a bar by Melini.

The Serristori range of wines includes what they call a *bianco da uve nere*, or a white wine from red grapes, mainly Canaiolo. This is sold under the name of Monna Primavera, Machiavelli's sister, as a Vino da Tavola di Sant'Andrea in Percussina. Then there is a red wine with the same geographical indication, called Albergaccio, principally from Canaiolo and destined for early drinking. The Serristori *riserva* is called Machiavelli, while Ser Niccolò is the *vino da tavola*, made from Sangiovese with a little Cabernet Sauvignon and aged, like I Coltri, in *barriques*.

Le Masse di San Leolino

This small winery just outside Panzano is owned by Norman Bain, an immediately likeable Scot and General Manager of Shell Europe in a previous existence. Since retirement he has spent his time making delicious Chianti, with the help of his oenologist Franco Bernabei. He has just three hectares of vines. Although these adjoin those of Fontodi, there are differences in the microclimate. The soil is a mixture of clay with lots of stones and some schist, which provides good drainage.

A careful selection in the vineyard is all important. Mr. Bain has a competent team of pickers who know what they are doing, selecting the best grapes for the *riserva* and the worst for an ordinary *vino da tavola*. His Chianti comes from 90 per cent Sangiovese and 10 per cent Canaiolo, with no white

View from the balcony at Vignamaggio in Chianti Classico. Leonardo da Vinci painted the Mona Lisa here.

Fattoria Le Calvane, in Colli Fiorentini.

grapes any more. Sangiovese has been grafted on to the Trebbiano and Malvasia.

Vinifications take place in a small, neat cellar. There are small *botti* of twenty-five hectolitres. The *riserva* wines, which in a good vintage such as 1985 may account for half the crop, alternate between six months in these and six months in stainless steel vats, with three years of ageing altogether. Bottle ageing is important too, causing Franco Bernabei to comment: 'The wine matures in the cellar, but I age it in the bottle, which sounds better in Italian as "In cantina matura il vino; in bottiglia lo invecchio".' Mr. Bain is sceptical about what he calls '*barrique* mania'. We tasted some vintages from the 1980s. Fruity tastes of sour cherries and dry raspberries were the predominant impressions and the good, long flavours of wines with structure and balance.

Monsanto

Monsanto is down a dirt track from Isole e Olena, on the edge of Chianti Classico, towards Poggibonsi. From the terrace there are wonderful views of the towers of San Gimignano. The estate belongs to Fabrizio Bianchi, whose father bought it in 1962. He reorganised the vineyards so that they now have thirty hectares of Chianti Classico and twenty of Colli Senesi. There is a difference in altitude between the two, the Chianti Classico vineyards lying at 300 metres and those of the Colli Senesi at 250 metres. The soil is different too, with more clay in the Colli Senesi and more *galestro* in Chianti Classico, making wines that last longer.

The family business is textiles, but wine is much more than a hobby for Fabrizio Bianchi; it is an absorbing passion. He bubbles with enthusiasm about everything to do with Monsanto. They make a variety of wines, in the modern functional cellar. A sparkling champagne method wine, called Bianco dei Bianchi, is made from pure Trebbiano that spends three years on the lees. The taste was full and fat.

They too have joined in the craze for Cabernet Sauvignon, first planting some in 1974. Tinscvil, an Etruscan word meaning

sacrificial offering, consists of 25 per cent Cabernet Sauvignon and 75 per cent Sangiovese. It was made for the first time in 1979. The Cabernet Sauvignon is kept in new *barriques*, whereas the Sangiovese is aged in Slavonic oak; they consider that the *barriques* give too much tannin for the Tuscan grape. The two varieties are then blended and aged for a year in bottle before sale. The taste was smooth and rich, with tannin and fruit. Since my visit a pure Cabernet Sauvignon has been introduced, called Nemo, and also an oak-aged Chardonnay, Il Gotha.

Their Chianti *riserva* is called Il Poggio, after a hilltop vineyard on the estate, planted with their own particular clone of Sangiovese. It is a much longer-lived wine than the Monsanto *normale*, with concentrated flavours, even after five years in wood. The 1983 will be ready to drink sometime after 1990. When it was only three years old, Fabrizio Bianchi commented: 'c'è stoffa, ma ha bisogno di fare l'abito', or in other words, the basic elements of a fine wine are there, but it needs to mellow a little. The Chianti Colli Senesi of Monsanto is sold under the name of Valdigallo.

I liked the wines of Monsanto. They had an old-fashioned feel about them, but in the very best sense of the word. In a wine like Il Poggio I felt that Fabrizio Bianchi was combining the best traditions of Chianti Classico, while producing a wine with good structure and soft but complex flavours of great length.

Montagliari

If there is any uncertainty as to the ageing potential of Chianti, the wines of Montagliari will allay all doubts. Minuccio Cappelli is one of the most congenial and generous hosts in the whole region and he treated me to four vintages, tasted when the youngest was eighteen years old (1971) and the oldest over thirty (1958). The colours were those of mature Burgundy, not a deep red, but a gentle brick-orange red. On the nose the 1971 was reminiscent of the cedarwood of the Médoc, very elegant with a lovely long finish. Even though 1964 was not a great vintage, the fruit

*Opposite
Barberino Val
d'Elsa, in Colli
Fiorentini: cellars
here are used by the
Pasolini dall'Onda
estate.*

had lasted, with a lightly minty herbaceous character on the nose and a sweet finish. The 1962 was deeper in colour, more youthful, with the elegance of a St. Julien, redolent of cedarwood and pencil shavings, and a dry finish. 1958 was a very good year and this wine, labelled Vino Vecchio, had a concentrated dry raisiny character on the nose, with similar herbaceous minty overtones. Even with as much as 20 per cent of white grapes, the staying power was there.

Montagliari is a very traditional estate and yet it was one of the first to make a so-called alternative wine. The pure Sangiovese Brunesco di San Lorenzo was produced as early as the 1770s by Francesco Bernardino Cappelli, when he wanted a wine for a special occasion. It was he who gave the wine its name and it was made until 1917, when the spread of phylloxera reduced the vineyards of the estate to just two hectares. Then in 1980 Minuccio Cappelli began making Brunesco again 'according to the old recipe'. The grapes are *passiti* or dried for fifteen days and then fermented in the normal way, spending about eight to ten days on the skins, with three *remontagi* per day. A small quantity of *governato* grapes is added, to increase the alcohol level slightly. First the wine is kept in large barrels and then on San Lorenzo's day, 10th August, it is transferred to Slavonic oak *barriques*, in which it spends four to eight months, depending on the age of the *barriques*. After this it is all blended and the wine is bottled. However it needs some bottle age before it shows its best. In 1989, the 1981 vintage was rich and smoky, almost raisiny on the nose, with rich, almost sweet fruit in the mouth, with flavours of vanilla and cinnamon. Tasted at the same time, the 1985 still had more obvious oak on the nose and palate and, with plenty of soft tannin and rich fruit, promised well for the future. Brunesco di San Lorenzo has been made only in the better years, particularly in 1988, 1985 and 1983. None at all was produced in 1989, 1987 or 1984. The longevity of the older vintages was proved when a bottle of 1854 was recorked in 1985. It was apparently still very good, even after a remarkable 130 years.

The Cappelli family has been at Montagliari, outside Panzano, since 1730. The land originally belonged to the church. Minuccio Cappelli's father replanted the vineyards after the phylloxera crisis, when others abandoned their vines. He even exported his produce to the United States in 1932, when Prohibition was at its height, as sacramental wine. Today there are thirty-eight hectares of vines for wine sold under the Montagliari label. They are also responsible for the La Quercia label, for which they buy in grapes from surrounding small farmers.

The wines of Montagliari are fermented in *botti* and a *riserva* may stay for several years in wood. In 1989 Minuccio Cappelli still had some 1977 in cask. However a five to seven year ageing period is more usual and for the *normale* he allows twelve to eighteen months. He continues to practise the *governo* method, with just 3 per cent of grapes to give extra vivacity and alcohol to the wine, and he still includes 5 per cent of Malvasia, but no Trebbiano in his blend. I asked him about Cabernet Sauvignon and the reply was a very definite 'absolutely not. Chianti Classico was born like this and that is the way it should remain'. He agrees with the Master of Wine, Kit Stevens who has described Cabernet Sauvignon as 'the cuckoo of Chianti'.

Cappelli is one of the few who continue to use the label Bianco della Lega, which is for a well-made but unexciting Tuscan white table wine. Vin Santo is another speciality of the estate. It is made in the traditional way and aged for at least seven years in *caratelli*. Winston Churchill was given some by Minuccio Cappelli's father during the Allied advance in 1944.

An evening in the *trattoria* of Montagliari presents perhaps the epitome of Tuscan wine and food. Cappelli welcomes you with a twinkle in his eye and a smile. When you protest that you are not feeling terribly hungry, as you have been well entertained for lunch by another enthusiastic wine grower, he insists indignantly that you cannot possibly drink his wine with a salad. On the basis of the French proverb, that the appetite comes with eating, you find yourself enjoying delicious *crostini*, with chicken livers, and olive paste; ravioli, accompanied by a *pesto* sauce based on walnuts rather than basil, and then perhaps a *bistecca alla fiorentina*, cooked on the open fire in the rustic restaurant. Good Chianti goes with the essentials of Tuscan cooking. Any astringency is countered by olive oil and the warm fruit complements the flavours in the pasta and meat. And with a glass of Brunesco in your hand, or even a young vintage of Montagliari, all seems very right with the world.

Montecchio

Montecchio is an elegant eighteenth-century villa, near San Donato, with thirty hectares of vineyards. It was bought in the early 1970s by Ivo Nuti, a wealthy industrialist from Pisa, as his hobby. The villa was built by the Tuscan Torregiani family, which has since died out; their coat of arms remains on the old *orci* for storing olive oil. At one time oil was as important as wine at Montecchio. Until the end of the 1960s there was even a kiln here for making the terracotta pots.

The thirty-hectare vineyard is planted mainly for Chianti Classico, but in common with most other estates, there is also an alternative wine, called La Papessa. They make a white wine, from Trebbiano, Malvasia and 50 per cent Chardonnay, called Vilucchio, the Tuscan name for columbine, which grows prolifically in the fields. They have two hectares of Chardonnay. Each grape variety is fermented separately and then blended together for bottling, so that the wine spends no time in wood; nor does it undergo a malolactic fermentation. It is intended for early drinking and the 1988 vintage, which I tried when it was a year old, was fresh, with hints of butter and apples, and almonds on the finish.

The 1987 Chianti Classico *normale* was a good example for the vintage. It had spent only seven or eight months in wood and had some meaty fruit, with overtones of berries and a good firm finish. The soil outside San Donato is very stony and, with vineyards at 400 metres, there is quite a lot of wind, so that the vines are well ventilated and rot is not a problem.

La Papessa, which is the name of the best vineyard on the estate, is made from 95 per cent Sangiovese Grosso, and 5 per cent Cabernet, which was grafted in another vineyard in 1983. They are fermented together and then spend eighteen months in wood. The first vintage was in 1985, which I tasted. It needed more bottle age, for there was sweet oak and dry tannin which needed to soften and mellow, as well as a good mouthful of fruit, with a long finish.

Montemaggio

Montemaggio is hard to find. Taking a bumpy dirt track north of Radda, the road twists, turns and gently climbs, leaving behind all habitation. Finally you arrive at an isolated estate, with wonderful views over the valley. The remains of a fourteenth-century watchtower are incorporated into the house, for this is the boundary between Florence and Siena. The castle of Radda used to stand close by, but nearly all vestiges have disappeared. The name remains as the second label of Montemaggio.

Montemaggio is the property of Giampaolo Bonechi and his friendly wife Giovanna Magi, who run a successful publishing house in Florence. They bought Montemaggio in 1974, when it was a ruin. There were no cellars and just a few vines, so they started from scratch, planting, restoring and building. Today the wine is made with the help of Vittorio Fiore. They have seven hectares planted with the usual grape varieties for Chianti Classico, as well as half a hectare of Cabernet Sauvignon. The vineyards lie at 520 metres, on stony *galestro* soil, and face southwest. Sunshine abounds and there is some cooling wind too. A little white wine is made from Malvasia, but they concentrate on Chianti and on a *vino da tavola* called Granvino di Montemaggio.

Their Chianti *normale* is kept in wood for a year, after fermentation in stainless steel vats, and the *riserva* is given at least three years' wood ageing, as well as some bottle age. I liked the 1986 *normale*, which had firm cherry fruit. We also tasted the 1983 Granvino, made purely from Sangiovese, which had spent three years in Limousin *barriques*. To my tastebuds this was too much, as the oak drowned the fruit, and the wine seemed very tannic and ungiving. Maybe it will age. A wine for the future is their pure Cabernet Sauvignon, produced for the first time in 1988.

Montevertine

Montevertine is a small estate in the hills behind Radda. Bought in 1966 as a hobby by a steel industrialist, Sergio Manetti, over the last twenty years or so it has been transformed into a serious winery. It is now Manetti's German son-in-law, Klaus Reimitz, who runs the estate and makes the wine. He came to Montevertine in 1981 after studying philosophy and Italian literature.

The seven and a half hectares of vines are planted with Sangiovese, Canaiolo, Malvasia, Trebbiano and an experimental thirty ares of Colorino. It is perhaps a surprise that a winery with a reputation for nonconformity should not have any Cabernet Sauvignon, but they are adamant that the future lies with Sangiovese. Although most of their wines would conform more or less to the DOCG regulations of Chianti Classico, they have chosen to go their own way, selling them with the geographical indication of Radda. But that is a detail on the label. In fact, they make some of the most expensive wines to come from the Chianti Classico area.

There is the same serious approach to white wine as to red, and the same adherence to the traditional grapes of Tuscany. Montevertine Bianco is made from equal measures of Trebbiano and Malvasia, which are fermented together after a night of skin contact and spend seven months in wood before bottling. The Trebbiano is picked after the red grapes, so that it is really ripe. This is the process that you might expect for Chardonnay and it works with Trebbiano, too. The nose is fragrant, almost buttery, with a good balance of oak, fruit and acidity. If comparisons are to be made, the taste was not unlike that of a good white Bordeaux, suggesting the weight and flavour of the Sémillon grape.

The 1986 Montevertine *riserva*, which spends two years in twenty-three hectolitre *botti*, is made from Sangiovese with 20 per cent Canaiolo, to soften the dominant grape. It was drinking very well in 1989, a rounded harmonious glass of wine, balanced with rich smooth cherry fruit. Il Sodaccio, named after a vineyard, comes from 88 per cent Sangiovese, with Canaiolo. It too is aged for two years, but in smaller, eight to sixteen-hectolitre casks. The 1986 was similar to the *riserva* of the same vintage, but more closed on both nose and palate, with stronger tannin and some rich plummy fruit.

Finally there is Le Pergole Torte, with its stylish labels. The artist Alberto Manfredi designs a new one for each vintage. This is pure Sangiovese aged for twenty months in small *botti* of varying sizes, and also for three or four months in Limousin *barriques*. It spends two or three days longer on the skins than the other red wines. The 1986 was tough and concentrated when it was three years old, a serious, stylish wine needing considerably more bottle age.

Another attraction at Montevertine is their small museum, which is open to the public by special arrangement. It is devoted not just to wine, but to all aspects of country living. There are old tools, a painted carriage, old *fiaschi* and all kinds of artefacts associated with a farmer's life on a *mezzadria* in Tuscany. The origins of Montevertine go back to the middle of the eleventh century. The hill was used as a beacon, from which to send messages, and at one time the property belonged to the Archbishop of Fiesole. Today it is among the leading estates of central Tuscany.

Pagliarese

This estate takes its name from its medieval owners, for it belonged to the Pagliarese family of Siena from 1242 until 1480. Neri Pagliarese played a part in papal history and contributed to the poetic literature of the thirteenth century. Another member of the family was a chamberlain, or *camerlengo*, which explains the choice of name for the estate's alternative wine.

The Sanguinetti family bought the property in 1965 and it is the friendly Signora Alma Sanguinetti who runs the estate, with the help of her children, Antonio and Alessandro. Altogether there are thirty hectares of vines, close to Castelnuovo Berardenga, in the south-eastern corner of Chianti Classico, only twenty-five kilometres from Montalcino. This explains why they also have Sangiovese Grosso in their vineyards, which is used for Camerlengo. Their Chianti comes from a different Sangiovese, blended with 5 per cent Cabernet Sauvignon and Franc, as well as some Malvasia and Trebbiano, but no Canaiolo. Their methods are traditional, with fermentation in concrete and stainless steel vats, no *governo* as they have always deemed it unnecessary, and ageing in *botti*; two years for their Chianti *normale* and three years for the *riserva*. Part of Camerlengo is kept in *barriques* for a few months.

Their vineyards also come within the DOC of Bianco Val d'Arbia, which must comprise the traditional Tuscan grapes varieties, 85 per cent Trebbiano with some Malvasia. Theirs is well made, fresh and slightly nutty. Signora Sanguinetti then gave me a marvellous vertical tasting of vintages from 1985 back to 1965, which was the first year that the new vineyards came into production. Her favourite and also the highlight for me was the 1977 vintage, which in 1986 was a wonderfully elegant wine, on both nose and palate. There were flavours of raspberries, with hints of wood and the wine was well balanced, with just the right touch of astringency on the finish. The 1972 was another very good vintage, with a lovely warm mature flavour that was long and lingering; the 1974 was beginning to dry out and the most disappointing of the range.

Il Palazzino

It all began as a hobby for Alessandro and Andrea Sderci, when they inherited this small estate outside the village of Monti, close to the Castello di Cacchiano. There were already a few vines, just for family use, but they began planting specialised vineyards, really without considering just what they were undertaking.

They now have five hectares of vines, from which they make a little white wine, some Chianti and a pure Sangiovese called Grosso Sanese, after a coin issued by the Sienese republic. The idea of a pure Sangiovese aged in *barriques* has considerable appeal to them. They have one particular vineyard with an excellent aspect, where the vines often suffer from drought – in 1988 there was no rain from June to September – and the stony soil does not retain water. Sometimes Sangiovese fades quickly, making it unsuitable for lengthy ageing in oak; but from this particular vineyard they obtain well structured wine, which they keep in *barriques* for twelve months. After that it is given at least another two years' ageing in bottle before sale. It was first made in 1981 and so far they have only missed the 1984 vintage. I tasted the 1987, which in June 1989 still had a very pronounced nose of vanilla and oak, with plenty of fruit on the palate. It was long and rich, but needed more bottle age for the oak to mellow.

Alessandro Sderci is a self-taught oenologist. He has not studied, but has learnt from practical experience. His Chianti is good. The 1987 *normale* had some warm flavours a little reminiscent of the Rhône valley, with good structure and tannin and a slightly herbaceous note on the nose. The 1985 *riserva* had a pronounced cedarwood character, both on nose and palate, which may come from the occasional use of *barriques*. Sderci would like to experiment with Cabernet too, and has planted small quantities of both Cabernet Sauvignon and Cabernet Franc, as well as some Merlot. However they will not be in production until 1991.

I liked the white wine from Il Palazzino as well. Made mainly from Malvasia, it was quite fragrant on the nose, softer and with more flavour than the usual Trebbiano. After the tasting, I admired a beautiful collection of violins of different sizes, made by Alessandro Sderci's grandfather and uncle.

Poggio al Sole

Poggio al Sole is the property of Aldo Torrini, who owns an exclusive jewellery shop in

Florence. Wine is his hobby. He bought the estate some twenty years ago, when there were just a few old vines planted in *cultura promiscua* and a farmhouse, bearing the date 1729. It was once the property of the nearby abbey, Badia a Passignano. There are now seven hectares of vineyards, around the house, between Greve and Tavarnelle, on south-facing slopes at an altitude of 450 to 500 metres.

Although Signor Torrini employs someone to make his wine for him, he remains very involved and always has the final say. The bottom line is, quite rightly, that he has to like it. The first of his two white wines comes mainly from Malvasia and Trebbiano, with a drop of Gewürztraminer. It tasted quite fresh and perfumed, with a slightly bitter finish. More unusual was the Vino della Signora, a pure Gewürztraminer, with some varietal character. Signor Torrini explained that he did not really care for white wine, but that his wife did; so this wine was made, for the first time back in 1972, especially for her, hence its name. Gewürztraminer, rather than any other grape variety, was chosen for its spicy flavour.

As for his Chianti, it comes from 80 per cent Sangiovese, with some Trebbiano and Malvasia, as well as Canaiolo, and a drop of Mammolo, Ciliegiolo and Colorino. He uses the *governo* method and the wines are kept for a year in vat and a year in cask, of either Slavonic oak or chestnut, with no fining and hardly any filtration. The flavours were fruity and light, of soft attractive Chianti. Finally there was what Signor Torrini used to call a Vino di Primavera, now called simply Vinrosso; the original name became a little confusing once the autumn had arrived. It is vinified in the same way as his Chianti, but from grapes that are harvested earlier. They are therefore not so ripe, so that the wine has less alcohol and more acidity, and does not require ageing. The taste was fresh and fruity, just the thing for a lunchtime plate of pasta.

Il Poggiolino

Il Poggiolino is a small estate outside San Donato, on the western edge of Chianti Classico. It is run by Maria Grazia Pacini.

Ten years ago she knew nothing about wine, to the extent of being a teetotaller. Then her husband, who runs a textile business, bought her a wine estate. Although there were vines at Il Poggiolino, the grapes were sent to the cooperative. Essentially Signora Pacini started from scratch, replanting the vineyards, building a small cellar and learning how to make wine with the help of her oenologist, Andrea Mazzoni.

Altogether she has nine hectares of vines, eight for Chianti Classico and one for *vino da tavola*. There is an aura of sobriety about the place, with a meticulously run cellar, equipped with stainless steel fermentation vats, and oak and chestnut *botti*. She makes a little red and pink table wine, but concentrates above all on her red wine. Chianti Classico is made mainly from Sangiovese, with hardly any white grapes. I tasted the 1986, which was still very young and firm when it was three years old, with some dry cherries and a slightly smoky taste on the finish. It was a wine to age.

Le Balze, meaning 'terraced vineyards', comes from Sangiovese, Trebbiano, Canaiolo and some other grapes, the details of which Signora Pacini refused to divulge, but including some Cabernet Sauvignon. This wine was first made in 1982. I tasted the 1985, which had been bottled six months earlier in January 1989. It had been aged in oak *botti* and was a solid mouthful, with a lot of tannin, still very closed with dry fruit and a long, firm finish.

Finally there was Roncaia, which is a Tuscan word for *roncolo*, meaning a pruning hook. This is 90 per cent Sangiovese. For the other 10 per cent she has grafted some old Sangiovese vines with other old grape varieties, the names of which she firmly maintained were a secret. The 1985 was the first vintage of Roncaia, of which just 6,000 bottles were made, aged in *barriques*, of Tronçais, Allier and a little Slavonic oak. The taste was an elegant balance of tannin and fruit, with an underlying richness.

Castello di Querceto

The Castello di Querceto in the north-east corner of Chianti Classico, close to the village of Dudda, has belonged to the François family for the last 100 years or so. The origins of the estate are medieval. The François family arrived in Tuscany some 200 years ago, from Lorraine, with the Grand Duke of Tuscany. The present incumbent, Alessandro François settled here as recently as 1980, having spent twenty years as a chemical engineer, 'spoiling the world', he says. 'Now I am atoning for it'. Like many people who come to a new career late in life, he has an objective view of the Tuscan wine scene and has expanded the activity of the estate, building new cellars and planting vineyards.

My tour of the estate was diverted by a family of peacocks strutting round the courtyard, and a peahen nursing one-day-old chicks. There are now forty-five hectares of vineyards at Querceto, at the relatively high altitude of 500 metres, as well as 120 hectares of oak trees. The name in fact means a forest of oak trees, the Italian for an oak being *quercia*. This is an estate that has progressed considerably in the last few years, under Signor François' direction. They make some serious Chianti Classico from Sangiovese, with 10 per cent Canaiolo, a drop of Malvasia and Trebbiano, and the same of other local grapes such as Ciliegiolo, Mammolo and Colorino. They also produce various *crus* and a wine called Querciatino, which is their answer to Sarmento.

Two hectares of Chardonnay have been planted, for which the first vintage was 1988. For the moment they also make a traditional white wine, but may discontinue it, depending on the success of the Chardonnay. There is a sparkling wine too, called François I, made for them by the Charmat method. However their production of white wine is not very serious and there is infinitely more scope in their red wines.

Querciatino is intended as a young wine for summer drinking. It is not a *vino novello*, for Signor François is adamantly against them, saying quite rightly that they appear at the coldest time of the year, when you should really be drinking more substantial full-bodied wines. Instead Querciatino is released in the late spring, like Sarmento. A quarter of the grapes are vinified by carbonic maceration, which gives a slightly peppery, instantly fruity wine.

La Corte is a single vineyard wine, or *cru*, made only from Sangiovese, which now spends at least eight months in *barriques* and about a year in bottle before sale. The first vintage was 1978 and I tasted the 1983, which was very rich, with vanilla and nougat on the nose, and packed with fruit on the palate. Then there is Querciolaia, a Predicato di Biturica, with 70 per cent Sangiovese and 30 per cent Cabernet Sauvignon. Each grape variety is aged separately in wood, the Sangiovese for seven to eight months, while the Cabernet Sauvignon, which needs longer in wood, spends as much as fourteen months in Allier or Tronçais *barriques*. In the blend the Cabernet gives the intensity of colour and some austerity, to complement the softer character of the Sangiovese. Merlot has been planted too, for which the plan is a 90 per cent Cabernet Sauvignon, 10 per cent Merlot blend. The first vintage of this to appear will be the 1986.

Fermentations at Querceto tend to be quite long, lasting as much as fifteen days, in order to extract the maximum amount of colour, with two or three *remontagi* a day. The Chianti *normale* of Querceto is sold after two years and the *riserva* after three. It comes from vines that are thirty to forty years old and is aged in *barriques*, whereas the *normale* rarely goes into *barriques*, as the structure of the wine is not suitable. Signor François observes rather cynically that *barriques* are a fashion and that if a bad wine goes into *barriques*, it only gets worse. He also makes a second wine, rather like some Bordeaux châteaux, from younger vines that are less than twelve years old. The wine is called Capanne and the *normale* is sold after a year, without any ageing at all in wood.

The 1985 Chianti Classico, which had spent six months in *barriques*, was rounded with a rich flavour of strawberries and enough tannin to make for long-lasting. The soil and microclimate of this corner of Chianti give very perfumed wine, balanced with a lot of body. The climate here is milder than in Florence. Winters are never very cold, nor summers very hot. There is not much rain, but a lot of underground water in the valley means that the vines never suffer from drought.

Although the Castello di Querceto only began bottling seriously ten years ago, there are bottles dating back to the beginning of the century. Two bottles of 1904 were opened for Signor François' father's eightieth birthday in 1984 and they were still very good. Wine from that period was exported as far as Argentina, winning a prize there in 1910.

Quercetorta

The small estate of Quercetorta outside Castellina is really a hobby for Monique and André Verwoort, but that does not prevent them from making some quite delicious Chianti. He is an investment banker and she is mad about gardens. Her own was looking quite spectacularly beautiful in June. They arrived here from Holland in 1975 and planted four and a half hectares of vines, Sangiovese and a little Canaiolo. There are no white grapes in their Chianti, though they do make a little white wine for friends. Their first vintage was 1980.

The vineyards are part of the hilltop village of Pietrafitta and their cellar is under the castle, which has its origins in the tenth century. The *riservas* spend time both in wood and in vat, so that the 1985 will not be bottled until 1990. In 1989 they were still selling the 1983 vintage and that was what I tasted. It had a lovely warm mature nose, with ripe fruit and an almost Burgundian softness on the palate. André Verwoort makes a very careful selection of his grapes. He produced no wine at all in 1984, as a hailstorm damaged part of his vineyard and a herd of thirsty wild boar demolished the remaining grapes. He was not pleased with 1987 either and sold off his wine in bulk. However the 1985 is very good, and already bespoken, mainly in Holland and the United States; 1988 will be as good, if not better.

Castello dei Rampolla

The Castello dei Rampolla dates back to the fourteenth century. The oldest remaining

parts are the cellar and the main drawing-room, where our tasting took place. In later centuries, subsequent owners have added a room there or a wing here to produce an architectural hotchpotch. There is a tiny church and this particular part of the *commune* of Panzano is called Santa Lucia in Faulia. Faulia is a more poetic word for a *campo di fave*, or a field of beans. Finding my way from Panzano was not easy, for the castle is very isolated, along bumpy dirt tracks, without any reassuring signposts.

The estate was bought by the grandfather of the present incumbent, Alceo di Napoli, in 1973. A young man, tall and distinguished, Alceo himself has been involved with the estate since 1976. He has followed no formal training in winemaking, but his attention to detail and quest for perfection are overriding considerations in his work. He is very much one of the rebels in Chianti Classico, not belonging to the Consorzio, which he dislikes for its inhibiting bureaucracy. He not only makes a *vino da tavola* with a considerable proportion of Cabernet Sauvignon, but also includes it in his Chianti Classico.

The vineyards, thirty-four hectares in all, lie around the castle, at an altitude of about 400 metres, half in the province of Siena and half in that of Florence, separated by the river Pesa. The soil is different. On the Siena side of the river there is less clay and the grapes ripen earlier, so that the wine has more colour and structure, while *galestro* is the predominant soil on the Florentine side.

Alceo di Napoli makes his Chianti from Sangiovese, with about 5 per cent Cabernet Sauvignon, no white grapes and no Canaiolo, a variety which has not adapted well to specialised vineyards. The proportion of Cabernet Sauvignon rises for the *riserva*, made from a careful selection of the best grapes. He has never used the *governo* method, as he firmly believes that it ages the wine prematurely. Nor does he believe in the use of concentrated must, preferring a careful selection of the grapes at harvest time, with two, if not three pickings, only when the grapes are fully ripe. After eight or nine months in vat, the wine is transferred into Slavonic oak casks for further ageing.

New barrels of Nevers oak are used for Sammarco, named after Alceo's dead brother Marco. It is a blend of one quarter Sangiovese and three quarters Cabernet Sauvignon, which spends less than two years in *barriques*, after a year in vat. The 1980 was the first vintage. Cabernet Sauvignon was grafted on to useless Trebbiano, Canaiolo and Malvasia vines. Alceo di Napoli recognises that his enthusiasm for Cabernet Sauvignon was inspired by Antinori's Tignanello. He finds the grape easy to grow, as it is resistant to disease. However he admits that too many people may plant Cabernet Sauvignon, and that not enough are cultivating Sangiovese properly, with the correct pruning to give small yields. I tasted the 1982 Sammarco, which in the spring of 1986 was just being bottled. It had a deep colour, with a rich blackcurrant nose, redolent of Cabernet Sauvignon and new wood. On the palate it had backbone and structure, with some solid tannins and full rich fruit that was not overwhelmed by the oak. It will need time to show its best.

The Chiantis of Castello dei Rampolla, both *normale* and *riserva*, are in a class of their own, for these are not Chiantis to drink in early youth, but wines that develop with a few years of bottle age. That is di Napoli's objective. He wants his wine to stand out from other Chiantis. The hint of Cabernet Sauvignon in the *normale* gives the wine a firm structure, and a flavour that is not really Italian. The *riserva* is a rich complex wine with masses of potential.

Next in Alceo di Napoli's repertoire is a white wine, Trebianco, so called for the simple reason that it is made from three different grape varieties, none of which is traditional to Tuscany; namely a large proportion of Chardonnay, with Gewürztraminer and Sauvignon. All three are fermented together. I tasted the 1984, which in 1986 had benefited from some bottle age, and had the pronounced flavour of Alsace with some spicy fruit. Di Napoli thought that there was too much and would also like to give the wine a hint of wood.

Like most Tuscan estates, they make Vin Santo too, from Malvasia, in the traditional way. The quantities are tiny, just 25 litres in 1985. It reminded me of Bual Madeira, having a similar yellow-green rim and taste, with the same high acidity. It was very distinctive and a wonderful way to finish the visit, the flavours lingering until my next appointment.

Giorgio Regni

The name of the owner, Giorgio Regni, is displayed in much greater prominence on the label than the estate name of the Fattoria Valtellina. Signor Regni owns just four hectares of vineyards, forming an amphitheatre around his house, close to the Castello di Meleto, by the viewpoint of Monte Luco. He arrived in 1977 from Rome, following a successful career in rubber, as an executive for Pirelli.

I liked his approach to his wine. Everything is on a small scale, with an immaculate cellar adjoining the house. Great attention is paid to every detail, with small yields of grapes entailing a very careful selection at the vintage. There are stainless steel vats for the fermentation and for keeping the Chianti *normale*, while the *riserva* spends six to twelve months in wood, depending on the vintage. He also makes a white wine, Tusco Bianco, mainly from Trebbiano and Malvasia, but including 20 per cent of Cortese that is bought in Piedmont. The taste was quite attractive, slightly nutty and appley, with some fresh acidity.

Then there is Convivio, meaning simply convivial, in the sense used by Dante, which of course is what wine should be. It has Merlot and Cabernet Sauvignon, as well as Sangiovese and spends three or four months in *barriques*, and then a couple of months in *botti*. The 1986 Convivio was rich and spicy, with good fruit and tannin. The 1985 Chianti *riserva* proved a lovely taste on which to finish a week in Chianti Classico, with a youthful fruitiness of sour cherries, hints of wood and tannin, and a long finish.

Castello di Rencine

The Castello di Rencine is one of those delightfully old fashioned Chianti estates that

Giorgio Regni in the vineyard.

time seems to have passed by. In Ireland it might have been the setting for a Molly Keane novel. The castle, or more accurately the fortified village, was a Florentine outpost, across the valley from Sienese Monteriggioni, and was destroyed in 1478 by Aragonese troops fighting for the Sienese. Vestiges of walls remain and a medieval chapel with a façade dating back to the thirteenth century. You are right on the edge of Chianti Classico here, with the Staggia stream separating it from the Colli Senesi.

Rencine has been in the hands of the Brandini Marcolini family since the early nineteenth century. Today three brothers live on the estate. Riccardo Brandini Marcolini showed me round. He explained that they have twenty-four hectares of Chianti Classico vines, with an average age of fifteen years. They do not believe in making *vino da tavola*, as they consider that it detracts from their Chianti. They have been bottling their own since 1968, but still only their best wine. The rest is sold to merchants. Methods are rather rustic, although they no longer use the *governo* method. Temperature control

seemed somewhat erratic and some of their wines are kept in *botti* for several years. In 1989 they still had some 1978 in wood. There are the standard concrete vats and the remark was made that they are 'ugly outside, but good inside'. This is not a cellar for tourists.

I have preferred older vintages of Rencine to younger ones, which seem a little coarse; the older wines soften and mellow. There is an old fashioned feel about them. Surprisingly good was the family *spumante*, made from Trebbiano and Malvasia, with the second fermentation taking place in small demijohns. There is no attempt to remove the sediment. The wine is simply decanted from bottle into carafe. It proved refreshingly soft and fruity, going very well with the delicious egg and anchovy *crostini* that Signora Brandini Marcolini kindly provided.

Riecine

This tiny estate close to Gaiole is the creation of an Englishman, John Dunkley, and his Italian wife, Palmina Abbagnano. He tired of life as a successful advertising executive in

Sandro Caramelli at Fattoria La Ripa.

London and bought Riecine, then with a few *cultura promiscua* vines, in 1971. The first vintage in 1972 was not a good one, neither for Riecine nor for Chianti Classico. They made a small amount of rather bad wine and learnt an enormous amount in the process. In 1973 they planted more vines in specialised vineyards and have not looked back since.

The wine at Riecine is made in a neat little cellar under the Dunkleys' house. Methods are classic and rational. The *governo* was abandoned several years ago. Very few white vines remain and no white grapes are used for their *riserva*. Chianti *normale* is aged for at least fifteen months in *botti*, while the *riserva*, which is almost pure Sangiovese, may spend as much as three years in wood. It all depends on how the wine develops.

Reluctantly, Dunkley has followed the trend of making a *vino da tavola*, although he feels that it is really public suicide to make a wine that is more expensive than your

Chianti. It reduces Chianti Classico to the status of a second wine and reduces its quality by using up the best grapes, drawing attention to just 5 or 10 per cent of the estate's production. La Gioia di Riecine spends two years in *botti* and a year in Allier *barriques*. Essentially it is the same wine as Riecine *riserva*, with a little Canaiolo. Dunkley is very concerned to maintain the typical characteristics of Chianti. He does not want any of the vanilla flavours associated with new oak in his wine, commenting that vanilla is best kept for ice-cream. Too much tannin is not typical of Chianti either.

Dunkley's meticulous methods come over in the quality of his wine. There are flavours of red fruit, sour cherries above all, with a good backbone of body and a long elegant finish.

Fattoria La Ripa

For those seeking live lobsters in the heart of Chianti Classico, miles from the sea, La Ripa is the place to go; as well as vines they have a large tank farm of fresh lobsters. This part of the estate's activity seemed rather more organised than the winemaking.

Sandro Caramelli's father bought the estate, between Castellina and San Donato, before the Second World War and there are now twenty hectares of vines, fifteen of which produce Chianti Classico and five Cabernet Sauvignon and Chardonnay; for which the first vintages were 1986 and 1987 respectively. The Cabernet Sauvignon is blended with the same amount of Sangiovese and aged in *barriques* for about a year. It is called Santa Brigida, after another farm near Pontassieve. The Chardonnay is added to Trebbiano, 30 per cent to 70 per cent respectively, making a fresh white wine to accompany the lobsters, sold under the Bianco della Lega label.

I tasted two or three vintages of Chianti, which seemed to have good structure, flavours of dry cherries and some length. In contrast Santa Brigida was sweeter and more perfumed.

Rocca delle Macie

Rocca delle Macie is the brain child of Italo Zingarelli, better known as a director of spaghetti westerns such as *I'm for the Hippos* and *They Call me Trinity*. His initial purchase of land was from a member of the Capponi family, a different branch from the owners of Calcinaia, and he has gradually extended the estate, so that it now consists of some 150 hectares of vineyards. In addition a further fifty hectares of land is rented in Chianti Classico and twenty hectares in the Colli Senesi. The company also buys in grapes and wine, as needed, which makes them merchants, as well as producers.

The cellars, built in 1974 and subsequently expanded, form a modern complex in a valley outside Castellina, on the edge of Chianti Classico. Seen from above, from the village of La Leccia it is something of an eyesore, although it cannot rival the cement works in Castellina for sheer ugliness. The cellars are modern and functional, and the winemaking methods efficient. The fermentation on the skins for their Chianti takes six days, with

computer-programmed *remontagi*, and no *governo* anymore. They have their own equipment for making concentrated must. Chiantis for early drinking spend no more than six months in oak, while the *riserva* wines stay between eighteen months and two years in wood. They are anxious not to overdo the wood and certainly will not consider using *barriques* for their Chianti. However when I saw them in 1986, they were experimenting with Sangiovese and Cabernet Sauvignon from the 1985 vintage for a *barricato* wine. This has subsequently been released as Ser Gioveto. Everything will be very carefully considered, for they are adamant that they will not make 'a copy of a Chianti ruined by wood'.

Generally Rocca delle Macie Chianti is light, fruity and easy to drink, without the depth or complexity that you find in other estates. Their wines are intended for early drinking, not for ageing. Rubizzo, which they consider one of their best, is made from the grapes that have ripened first and therefore have quite a low acidity. It is bottled in the spring following the vintage. They said it was the result of a special type of vinification, entailing a variation on the *governo* method, as they added extra must and yeast to the fermenting juice. The taste was rich and raisiny. In complete contrast, the 1980 *riserva* was soft and chewy, with a dry finish. They also make Galestro, from Trebbiano, with up to 20 per cent Chardonnay, following the standard procedures of a well controlled cool fermentation. The taste was clean, fresh and as nondescript as Galestro usually is. A glass of Rocca delle Macie Chianti may never excite, but it is unlikely to disappoint.

I. L. Ruffino

The house of Ruffino was founded in 1877 by two cousins, Ilario and Leopoldo Ruffino. Curiously, neither was a dynamic businessman. On the contrary, Ilario read mathematics at the University of Florence and remained there as a lecturer; but he was also a keen oenologist. Although little is known about Leopoldo, he too enjoyed an academic life. In fact the cousins were more like brothers, living together on the estate of Villa Branco-lano outside Florence. Wine was made, bought and sold with some success, until financial difficulties caused partly by bad vintages and partly by bad debts, forced them into liquidation in 1912. The estate was bought by the Folinari family the following year. The Folinaris were already well established in the wine trade, but not in Tuscany. They had vineyards in both northern and southern Italy, with their activity concentrated on the distribution of bulk wine. Their aim, with the purchase of I. L. Ruffino, was the upgrading of their image.

Today I. L. Ruffino is owned by two families of Folinari cousins. I met Ambrogio Folinari, who is responsible for the production side of the business, with his technical director Dott. Orsoni. They are the largest vineyard owners in the whole of Chianti Classico, with eighty-five hectares at Fattoria di Nozzole, north of Greve, and 300 hectares scattered elsewhere. These are mainly in Chianti Classico, including an estate called Zano on the north-western edge of the area, and another near Castellina, called Santa-dama, purchased in 1988. In addition to running vineyards, they buy grapes, must and wine, as necessary, usually on the basis of long-term contracts with grape growers. They also have a share in a vineyard in San Gimignano, Tenuta dei Castelvecchia and rent the Montalcino estate of Il Greppone, of which more on p. 143.

The best known wine is undoubtedly their traditional Chianti Classico Riserva Ducale, but in recent years they have begun to concentrate on numerous alternatives, both red and white. Their range is impressive. For white, they have two vineyards, Casa di Sala, near Panzano, and another estate near Rignana, where they have planted Pinot Grigio and Sauvignon, which are not yet in production. At Casa di Sala they make a pure Chardonnay, called Cabreo, labelled with the vineyard name Vigneto la Pietra. This is fermented in vat and kept in new Allier barrels for eight to ten months, as Predicato del Muschio, with the intention of appealing to the international market. I found it quite fat, solid and not too oaky, but preferred the palate to the nose, which was a little clumsy.

The second category of white wines has the typical Tuscan flavours of Malvasia and Trebbiano, such as Bianco di Ruffino, which is a clean vinification of Trebbiano, and Galestro, which comes from Trebbiano, Chardonnay and Vernaccia. Libaio is a blend of 90 per cent Chardonnay and 10 per cent Sauvignon, to which they will probably add some Pinot Grigio from the 1989 vintage. The Sauvignon gives acidity and structure to the Chardonnay, while the Pinot Grigio will add body. I liked it, finding it more elegant and buttery than the Cabreo.

As for red wine, as well as the Riserva Ducale they have other traditional reds, called Aziano and Torgaio, which are both unassuming Chianti. Then there are what they prefer to call 'parallel wines', rather than alternative wines, a Cabreo Rosso, made from 70 per cent Sangiovese and 30 per cent Cabernet Sauvignon, and Nero del Tondo which is a pure Pinot Noir. I found the 1985 Cabreo, Vigneto Il Borgo to be still dominated by oak in 1989, after fourteen months in Limousin *barriques*. The 1985 Pinot Noir had more varietal character than some of the wines that emerge from Burgundy, but it had not yet acquired the quintessential elegance of the grape variety.

Ruffino has been one of the leaders in the innovative movements within Tuscan winemaking. Founder members of the associations for Predicato, Sarmento and Galestro, they are also a member of the Istituto di Vino Novello. However they have withdrawn from the Chianti Classico Consorzio, considering that their interests were divergent. A comprehensive tasting left an impression of enormous effort concentrated with some success into the new wine. On the other hand, a number of the traditional wines were a little on the dull side and failed to excite. However there is no doubt that this is a company that is making a great effort to improve its quality image, and it may well succeed with Libaio or Cabreo.

San Felice

The pretty medieval hilltop village of San Felice is the home of one of Chianti's larger wine estates. Geraniums and hydrangeas provide brilliant splashes of colour in large terracotta pots. The village was the property of the Grisaldi del Taia family until the late 1960s. Then in 1978 it was bought by its current owners, the large insurance company, RAS. Within that framework there are three smaller estates, Villa la Paglaia, with forty hectares of vines close to Castelnuovo Berardenga; San Vito, which has been absorbed into San Felice, and Poggio Rosso, the wine from which is sold as a single vineyard wine or *cru* of San Felice. Altogether they own 120 hectares in Chianti Classico, as well as the twenty-hectare estate of Campogiovanni in Montalcino. They insist that they are an Azienda Agricola, not a Casa Vinicola. In other words, they deal only in the wine of their own vineyards.

Their new vinification plant is streamlined and efficient, providing the right basis for experiments in both vineyard and cellar. They are concentrating their energies on producing good traditional Chianti, as well as some alternative wines. Rosato di Canaiolo is a Vino da Tavola di Castelnuovo Berardenga, for which the juice is run off the skins after twenty-four hours, so that the wine is fresh and fruity. Bianco Val d'Arbia is fragrant, well made white wine.

However more exciting are their red wines. Il Grigio is their most characteristic Chianti, aged in *botti* for two years, with the firm fruit of sour cherries. Usually a *normale* spends eight to twelve months in wood, the decision as to whether the wine has sufficient body to be aged for a *riserva* being taken after the malolactic fermentation.

Vigorello was one of the very first wines in Chianti to be made just from red grapes, namely Sangiovese and Canaiolo, back in 1967, by the general manager Enzo Morgante. Since then Cabernet Sauvignon has been planted and Vigorello now consists of 15 per cent Cabernet Sauvignon, 50 per cent Sangiovese from Chianti, and 35 per cent Sangiovese Grosso. It is aged like a Chianti *riserva* in Slavonic oak, as well as spending four months in *barriques*. On tasting it proved firm and concentrated, a good example of the success that can be achieved by blending

these two grape varieties. With the experimental work that is taking place in the vineyards of San Felice, this estate is contributing to the rosy future of Chianti Classico in the twenty-first century.

San Giusto a Rentennano

Rentennano is an Etruscan name in origin. The history of the estate goes back to the early Middle Ages. In the thirteenth century there was a Cistercian monastery here, San Giusto. The now rather dilapidated villa was built in the fifteenth century, although the cellars date back to about 1000. The present owners are the Martini di Cigala family. I met young Francesco Martini di Cigala, who came here in the mid-1970s. He has gradually transformed the estate into a producer of serious Chianti. In fact they only began bottling their wine in 1981 and still sell a substantial part of the production of their twenty hectares in bulk, to Ricasoli. Other improvements have included the elimination of most of the white grapes and the introduction of a *vino da tavola*.

San Giusto is in the southernmost part of Chianti Classico, near the village of Monti, where the soil is either the classic *galestro* of Chianti, with limestone; or alternatively limestone with volcanic tufo, which is damper and therefore unsuitable for Cabernet Sauvignon. The microclimate gives little rain and with its position of the edge of the Chianti hills, there is very good ventilation, resulting in few problems with disease or rot.

The *governo* method is used for both *normale* and *riserva* Chianti, as Signor Martini di Cigala is convinced that it adds something extra to the wine. After a year in vat, the *normale* will spend six months in *botti* and the *riserva* twelve to eighteen months. The wines have the flavour of sour cherries, with good structure and tannin, and all the firmness of Chianti Classico from the south.

Percarlo, named after a friend who was killed in a car accident, is made from a selection of Sangiovese, with a very small amount of Cabernet Sauvignon. It spends about a year in *barriques*, of Limousin and Allier oak. The 1983 was the first vintage.

We tasted the 1985, which had a very deep colour and smelt of new wood, but with a rich concentration of fruit and tannin, and hints of blackberries.

Francesco Martini di Cigala is also very enthusiastic about Vin Santo and makes a small amount by the traditional method, with great care. The taste is of liquid biscuits and almonds, and quite delicious. Production is tiny, less than 500 bottles each year.

San Polo in Rosso

San Polo in Rosso stands on a hill to the south of Castellina, so that you can see the town's tower in the distance. The origins of this fortified church go back to the eleventh century, when it stood on the much disputed boundary between Florence and Siena. Today the estate is owned by the Canessa family. They bought the property in 1973, but their first vintage was not until 1977. A new cellar was constructed in the following year and Maurizio Castelli began to supervise the wines, so that today they bear the hallmark of his talent and creativity.

There are twenty hectares of vineyards altogether, in two parts, one close to the castle and the second a kilometre away, but they are both very similar in soil and microclimate, lying at 380 metres, with a mixture of chalk and clay. After a quick visit to the cellar to admire the shining stainless steel fermentation vats and pristine *botti*, we adjourned to a large sitting-room, furnished in impeccable Italian style, for a comprehensive tasting.

First was Bianco dell'Erta. The 1988 vintage consisted mainly of Trebbiano, as Malvasia suffered from *coulure* that year. It had been gently pressed, with a cool fermentation and no fining or refrigeration, but a light filtration before bottling. The flavour was very dry, with a firm fruitiness and plenty of acidity, which is typical of Trebbiano if it is picked before the red grapes. The *rosato* is made only from Sangiovese, which spends twelve hours on the skins. It had a mouth-filling fresh raspberry flavour, with an attractive acidity; but as Castelli pointed out, pink wine does not go with Tuscan food.

Then we moved on to Chianti. The 1986 *normale* is made from pure Sangiovese to all intents and purposes. Castelli said jokingly that there was just one white grape. There is no *governo* either and the taste had overtones of cedarwood, with some astringency on the finish. The 1985 *normale* was richer, with the same cedarwood character. Castelli considers 1986 to be the finer vintage, producing better balanced wines, as 1985 was too dry and hot. However in 1989 I preferred the 1985. The *riserva* was even better, with a rich, smoky tobacco nose and yet more cedarwood on the palate, with balancing tannin and length.

Cetinaia is their alternative wine, named after a farm on the estate. It is pure Sangiovese, chosen at the vintage, but aged differently from the Chianti, for 65 per cent of the wine spends one year in *botticelli*, 500-litre barrels of different French oak, Tronçais, Nevers and Limousin, while the rest of the wine is aged in the traditional and larger *botti*. Castelli believes that the mixture of oak gives the wine greater harmony. In June 1989 the 1985 vintage was still very closed and much too young. It had the cedarwood structure of the Chianti *riserva*, but even more so, needing bottle age. It promised well for the future. The 1982 vintage had begun to open out with some lovely ripe fruit and considerable elegance.

Castelli is not someone who is content to concentrate on purely Tuscan grape varieties. At San Polo in Rosso he has planted Sauvignon in vineyards where it is too cool for red grapes, and also Sémillon. He considers the chalk soil to be particularly suitable for Sauvignon, of which 1989 was the first vintage. Next he would like to try Grechetto and Verdicchio, as grape varieties typical of central Italy, but of Umbria rather than Tuscany. Nothing stands still at San Polo in Rosso.

Savignola Paolina

The estate of Savignola Paolina is a delightful spot in the hills just outside Greve. When I was there in May, the wistaria was flowering in a brilliant display of colour. Savignola is the name of the farm and Paolina is the Christian name of Signora Fabbri, in whose family this property has been since 1780. I met Signora Fabbri just before her eightieth birthday in 1986. She is a small, stout lady, very bright and alert, exuding an energy that belies her years.

The farm consists of just six hectares, including one and a half of specialised vineyards. Signora Fabbri said that she preferred the old system of *cultura promiscua* as it provided better aeration for the vines. Everything has remained delightfully old fashioned. Although she has given up using the *governo* method, there is no electricity in her cellar under the house, so the wooden manual press is still used. There are old barrels and all the wonderfully evocative atmosphere of a small wine cellar. She has an oenologist to help, but has her own ideas about winemaking. She pays particular attention to the phases of the moon, filtering and bottling only during the last quarter when the wine is calm. Signora Fabbri began bottling her wine in 1973, but otherwise thinks that little has changed. Before there were fewer machines and more people. Her wines are intended to be aged, with a firm backbone of tannin and some good solid fruit.

Castello di Tizzano

The Castello di Tizzano stands on the very northern edge of Chianti Classico. It is approached along a row of imposing cypress trees and from the terrace one can see the towers of Florence. The oldest part of the castle is reported to date back to the ninth century, when it was of strategic importance. In subsequent centuries it was transformed into a more habitable villa and the estate now belongs to the Pandolfini family. I met Roberto Pandolfini. However his father Count Filippo Pandolfini, who is nearly as old as the century, still maintains a firm hold on the running of the vineyards and appears to veto any attempt at modernisation. In consequence everything is still very old fashioned here.

Only a small amount of their wine is sold in bottle and it seems to remain in *botti* for rather longer than is necessary. The cellars under the villa are 500 or 600 years old and full of elderly *botti*, mainly of chestnut. There is just one new oak one. They do have some stainless steel fermentation vats, as a concession to the twentieth century. The taste of the 1981, bottled in 1986, was very much that of an old style Chianti, made with the *governo* method, with at least 15 per cent of white grapes. It was raisiny on the nose and dry on the palate. I was left with a rather sad impression of gentle decay.

Castello di Uzzano

The Castello di Uzzano, outside Greve, belongs to the Count Briano Castelbarco. His appearance is somewhat reminiscent of an Oxford don; he would not look out of place on high table at Balliol or Merton. The person who runs Uzzano is Marion de Jacobert, who has arrived like a gust of fresh air to inject new energy into this rather sleepy estate. When I visited it, in May 1986, the cellars were in the middle of considerable restoration work. New fermentation vats were being installed and the 200-year-old chestnut barrels were being cleaned. They have oak casks too, which are considered to be better. However all their wine spends at least three years in wood, or longer. In 1986 there were still casks of 1977 waiting to be bottled, in the way of old-style Chianti.

The original castle of Uzzano goes back to the eleventh century. The cellars were built in 1050, with walls nine metres thick. Then in the sixteenth century a more elegant villa was built on top; this has some delightful gardens, which have been renovated recently. They have forty-five hectares of vineyards of traditional Tuscan grape varieties in production. However Marion de Jacobert is full of projects for the future. She is planning a second label, called Niccolò da Uzzano, after a man who lived here in the fourteenth century and opposed the Medicis. The wine will come from their oldest Sangiovese vines, and will be aged in wood and bottle for longer than their ordinary *riserva*. She would also like to revive a white wine that used to be made here, from an unusual blend of Gewürztraminer, Chardonnay and Pinot Bianco. In 1986 eleven bottles of this wine remained and they were thirty-five years old.

As for winemaking techniques, Marion de Jacobert emphasised their adherence to what was natural and traditional. They do not use any chemical fertilisers in the vineyard and in the cellar there is no need to fine the wines, as they spend so long in barrel. They still usually practise the *governo* method. The vintages I tasted were rather light, with some astringency on the finish; in other words, sound but not exciting Chianti.

Vecchie Terre di Montefili

I have always had a soft spot for the wines of Vecchie Terre di Montefili. I first visited the estate in 1984, not long after the Acuti family had bought the property. Things were already beginning to change. A few *barriques* had appeared in the cellars and there were other signs of improvement. Returning four years later, the changes were even more spectacular. New cellars were under construction, new vineyards were in production and one of Tuscany's outstanding oenologists, Vittorio Fiore was in charge of the winemaking. There were new wines too, and more were promised.

Altogether there are eight hectares of vines in the hills between Panzano and Greve. This is one of the lost estates of Chianti Classico. Even my friend from the Consorzio took a wrong turning or two. Winemaking methods are meticulous. There is a careful selection of the grapes at harvest time, those for the *governo* and those for the *riserva*. Unlike many producers, they do believe in the validity of the *governo* method. Chianti *normale* spends ten to twelve months in thirty-hecto-litre barrels, both old and new, while *barriques* are used for the Chianti *riserva* and their *vino da tavola*, Bruno di Rocca. This is a blend of two-thirds Sangiovese to one third Cabernet Sauvignon. Both wines spend twelve to fourteen months in *barriques*, which are renewed every three years. They are then given some bottle age before sale, four months for Chianti *normale*, to as much as ten months for Bruno di Rocca.

As for white wines, 2 per cent of Trebbiano and Malvasia remain, 'to recall the past', but they are now concentrating on Chardonnay, Sauvignon and a little Pinot Grigio. They plan a wine made from all three grape varieties, entailing the separate fermentation of the Chardonnay in *barriques*. Unfortunately, it was not yet available for tasting at the time of my visit.

The red wines that I tasted were delicious. Perfume is the characteristic of the wines of Panzano. They do not have the firm structure of wines from further south, but a delicate bouquet and some delicious fruit. This was borne out by the flavours of the wines of Vecchie Terre di Montefili. I thought the 1985 *normale* smelt of raspberries — Vittorio Fiore called them *frutti di bosco*, or fruits of the woods, in other words tiny wild strawberries — as well as nutmeg and dried roses. The flavour was long and elegant. The 1982 *riserva* had hints of cedarwood, associated with the *barriques*, with some spicy overtones and good mellow, ripe fruit. The 1983 Bruno di Rocca, which was the first vintage of this wine, had a firmer structure and hints of vanilla. For Vittorio Fiore the Cabernet Sauvignon gives finesse and delicacy, while the Sangiovese contributes structure, what he calls 'shoulders'. Cabernet Sauvignon also makes for a wine with greater attraction to the international consumer. I thought the wines of Vecchie Terre di Montefili had enormous appeal.

Castello di Verrazzano

This estate takes its name from Giovanni di Verrazzano, who was born here in 1485. He played a part in the history of America by discovering the mouth of the Hudson river. The Verrazzano bridge in New York, the largest suspension bridge in the world, is named after him. The Verrazzano family built the castle in the early fifteenth century, but the line died out in 1820. Today the estate is the property of Luigi Cappellini and, in his absence, is managed by Alberto Napoleone.

There are fifty-four hectares of specialised vineyards on the hill around the castle outside Greve, planted mainly with Sangiovese, but also with a little Cabernet Sauvignon, which was introduced in 1980 in answer to market demand. Their Chianti is made of Sangiovese with as much as 20 per cent Canaiolo and just 2 per cent Colorino, but no white grapes. For the moment 30 per cent Cabernet Sauvignon is blended with 70 per cent of Sangiovese to make a barrel-aged alternative wine, which they call Sassello, the Tuscan name for a thrush. There are indeed a lot of thrushes in the surrounding woods and they are happy to eat the ripe grapes. For Sassello both Sangiovese and Cabernet Sauvignon are aged together in Limousin oak barrels, for six to twelve months. They may even consider including Cabernet Sauvignon in the blend for their Chianti.

Their Chiantis have a traditional flavour. They use concentrated must, which is added at the end of the fermentation, instead of the dried grapes of the *governo* method. They said it had the same effect. The fermentation takes about fifteen days, with regular *remontagi*, in cement vats. Their Chianti *normale* spends two years in Yugoslav casks; the *riserva* up to four years. The *normale* had some good fruit and a little astringency, while the *riserva* was fuller and more rounded.

Castello di Vicchiomaggio

One can see the imposing tower of Vicchiomaggio in the distance from the road to Greve (see illustration on p. 107). For me that is when I feel that I have arrived in the heart of Chianti Classico. The origins of Vicchiomaggio go back to the ninth century; 'Vicchio-' describes a Lombard village. The place was transformed into a Renaissance villa by the Medicis and the name changed to Vicchiomaggio, after the month of May, for it was then used as a summer residence by wealthy Florentines. Today it belongs to an Anglo-Italian, John Matta, a young man who fits with ease into either nationality. His father was one of the first people to import Italian wines into England after the Second World War, founding the company of F. S. Matta. It was he who bought the rundown estate of Vicchiomaggio in the mid-1960s, which John Matta has subsequently inherited.

In 1966 there were just two hectares of vines in production. Today there are twenty-five, planted with the traditional Chianti grape varieties, as well as a little Chardonnay to improve the flavour of the white wine and some experimental Cabernet Sauvignon. Matta views the current craze for that grape variety with a certain amount of scepticism and firmly believes that the best and most expensive wine of an estate should be a Chianti Classico, not an experimental table wine. His one concession to fashion is the use of new Burgundian barrels for the ageing of Prima Vigna, his best wine, which is made from the grapes of the original vineyard. Otherwise John Matta's winemaking methods are quite traditional.

The fermentation takes place in cement vats and the wine is then transferred into large Slavonic oak casks. The Chianti *normale*, from the San Jacopo vineyard, will spend three to six months in wood and the *riserva*, labelled Vigna Petri and made in most years, six to nine months. Prima Vigna is made only in the very best years, such as 1988 and 1985. It is kept for three to five months in small barrels as well as some months in larger casks. The 1977 was the first vintage of Prima Vigna and I remember my first taste of it in 1982, wonderfully rich and concentrated, with a depth of flavour quite unlike any Chianti I had hitherto encountered. In common with several other estates, Matta has worked to improve the quality of his white wine, adding a little Chardonnay to enliven the traditional flavours of Trebbiano and Malvasia.

Vicchiomaggio was one of the very first Chianti estates I ever visited, at the beginning of my love affair with Tuscany, but long before I thought of writing this book. Its wines have contributed to my appreciation of good Chianti Classico. They are quite traditional, in the softer style of Greve, wines that will develop over seven or eight years before they begin to fade. I particularly remember the 1977, with some wonderful rich flavours, and also the 1971. The first vintage of Vicchiomaggio to be bottled was the 1969.

Vignamaggio

Vignamaggio lies in the hills above Greve, towards Lamole. For me it is one of the most

Gianni Nunziante with the oenologist Franco Bernabei at Vignamaggio.

have been restored to reveal red-brick arches and vaulting.

The fermentation of both red and white wine has taken place in stainless steel vats since 1985. Bernabei is in favour of the *governo* method, believing that it gives more extract and colour to his wines. He also likes to use a variety of different oaks, to give more complexity to the flavour. For the moment he is concentrating on Sangiovese at Vignamaggio, although there is just one hectare of old Cabernet Sauvignon vines, brought back from France by the former owner. These are vinified separately and added to the *riserva speciale*, sold under the name of Mona Lisa in Italy.

Altogether there are thirty-two hectares of vines, including some very old plants of forty years and more. They are mostly at an altitude between 250 and 350 metres, on stony *galestro* and clay soil. A white wine is made from Trebbiano with a hint of Chardonnay and there are plans to plant Sauvignon, which may go better with their Trebbiano grapes.

The older vintages of Vignamaggio have tended to fade, but since 1985 with the more sophisticated fermentation equipment there has been a marked improvement in the wines. They have concentration and depth. The *normale* spends time in *botti*, while a proportion of the *riserva* is aged in *barriques*, alternating six months in wood and six months in vat. Then it is given some bottle age to allow the vanilla and oak flavours to mellow and the fruit to develop. Gherardino is made of pure Sangiovese, which spends fifteen days on the skins and is aged in *barriques* for twelve months. In 1989 the 1985 tasted very concentrated and still very tough, but it promised well for drinking in around the year 2000.

beautiful spots in the whole of Chianti. This is where Leonardo da Vinci painted the Mona Lisa. The Renaissance villa was the birthplace of Mona Lisa Gherardini, who married Francesco di Zanobi del Giocondo, hence the other name of the famous portrait *La Gioconda*. Today the soft pink stone villa stands in a formal Italian garden, with statues and box hedges. I suspect that the view from the terrace, with haunting cypress trees on the skyline, has scarcely changed since Leonardo painted here (see colour illustration opposite p. 84).

Vignamaggio is one of the rising stars of Chianti Classico. It used to belong to the Sanminiatelli family. Bino Sanminiatelli who bought the estate in 1929 was a man of letters, known for a biography of Michelangelo, for his diaries and for *La Vita in Campagna*, a book about life in the Tuscan countryside. Then in 1987 the estate was bought by Gianni Nunziante, a Roman lawyer. He is now investing a considerable amount of money and energy in the property. Franco Bernabei has been the consultant oenologist since 1982, but since the arrival of Nunziante he has been given *carte blanche* to renovate the cellars. *Botti* have been cleaned and *barriques* purchased. The cellars, excavated out of rock,

Fattoria Vignale

The cellars of the Fattoria Vignale are right in the village of Radda, adjoining the rather smart hotel of the same name (see illustration on p. 33). The owner is Leonardo Rossetto, an industrialist from Rome who bought the estate in 1980 and formed a company to manage both winery and hotel. Vignale has a historical claim to fame as the seat of the Consorzio of the Gallo Nero, which was founded here in 1924.

An initial attempt to visit the cellars was sabotaged by a power cut, but once the electricity had been restored, it was possible to wander through a labyrinth of large *botti*, including some century-old chestnut ones. There are seventeen hectares of vines in production, with another four planted, in two separate vineyards near Radda. The soil here is very stony, which gives wines that age slowly, with tannin and acidity. A *riserva* will spend four years in cask, as opposed to two years for a *normale*, followed by a minimum of a year's bottle age. They also make an alternative wine called Le Macie del Ponte alla Granchiaia, from a vineyard near Gaiole. It comes mainly from Sangiovese with 10 per cent of Cabernet Sauvignon and is kept in *barriques* of Limousin oak for two years.

The tasting took place in the hotel courtyard. First there was a white wine from Trebbiano and Malvasia with between 5 and 10 per cent Chardonnay, which was quite fresh and fragrant with some good acidity. They do not have enough Chardonnay to vinify it separately. The 1985 Chianti *normale* had hints of violets on the nose and was a fleshy wine with firm tannin and some rich fruit. In contrast the 1983 *riserva* was more austere with a closed nose, a rugged wine with a mouthful of tannin that demanded more bottle age. Finally Le Macie had the perfumed nose of new oak, with vanilla and blackcurrants on the palate and a firm mouthful of fruit.

Vignavecchia

Vignavecchia has belonged to the Beccari family for over a hundred years, something that is quite rare in Chianti, with the considerable changes in landownership following the abandonment of the *mezzadria* system. Franco Beccari's grandfather was an explorer, whose portrait features on Vignavecchia labels, and his great-grandfather acquired

Vignavecchia by marriage.

The cellars are in the centre of Radda, excavated out from under the hill, and the vineyards, twenty-four hectares of them, are close to the village. The soil here is loose and stony, with good drainage. The old fashioned cellars are gradually being modernised, as old vats are replaced with stainless steel tanks. Even so, an atmosphere of traditional wine-making remains and Franco Beccari continues to run his estate in much the same way that he always has done. His Chianti *normale* spends twelve to fifteen months in wood, and the *riserva* two years, sometimes including a few months in *barriques* of Slavonic oak. Dott. Beccari lamented the cost of new oak barrels. A forty-hectolitre *botte* costs an astronomical-sounding 5 million lire, while *barriques* are somewhat more modest at 450,000 lire apiece. The flavours of Vignavecchia are those of good old-style Chianti, full and rounded, not wines with a great deal of weight, but soft and easy to drink, even when relatively young.

Like everyone else, Dott. Beccari has followed the fashion for alternative wines. His is called Canvalle, the name of a farm on the estate. It comes from 20 per cent Cabernet Sauvignon and 80 per cent Sangiovese. I tasted the 1983, which had spent a year in wood and a further four years in vat; it had only just been bottled in the summer of 1989. It had quite a pronounced vanilla nose, with tannin and some sweet fruit on the palate, and at 14° was full-bodied and high in alcohol. I preferred their Chianti.

Vistarenni

My first glimpse of Vistarenni was of an elegantly ornate villa, overlooking the valley between Radda and Gaiole (see illustration). The name appears in archives as 'Fisterinne' back in 1033 and a Renaissance villa was built here by the Strozzi family at the beginning of the sixteenth century. In 1895 the property was bought by the Baron Giorgio Sonnino, who restored many of the original features of the villa with the help of the architect Luigi Fortini. Today it is the property of the Tognana family, industrialists from Treviso.

The villa and vineyards of Vistarenni.

Elizabetta Tognana runs the estate. This represents something of a change in lifestyle, for her first career was as a successful racing driver.

The vineyards of Vistarenni are at some 500 metres and total forty-six hectares. Underneath the villa are the traditional red-brick cellars, with fine arches, that house the *botti* for ageing their Chianti. Assòlo is a second Chianti, made from specially selected Sangiovese grapes, as well as a little Canaiolo, Malvasia and Trebbiano. A third is aged in *barriques*, rather than *botti*, for twelve to fourteen months. They also make a satisfactory Bianco Val d'Arbia and an alternative wine called Codirosso, which is a selection of Sangiovese, including Sangiovese Grosso, aged for about a year in *barriques* and for three months in *botti*. The first vintage of this was 1985. Vistarenni may well be an estate to watch, for with the influence of the dynamic Elizabetta Tognana, what was bought as a holiday home, has become a serious commitment.

Viticcio

Ludovico Landini is a friendly hospitable man. He owns the twenty-hectare estate of Viticcio, just outside Greve, jointly with his brother. There are views of the town from the terrace of their house and a compact modern cellar is next door, with vineyards all around. These are planted with Sangiovese and Canaiolo, while some Sangiovese Grosso and Cabernet Sauvignon have been grafted on to Trebbiano and Malvasia. Officially the prerequisite 2 per cent of white grapes remains in the vineyards, for there is the odd vine mixed up in the rows, but essentially Viticcio Chianti is made from Sangiovese and Canaiolo.

The fermentation of the two grape varieties begins separately and finishes together. The *normale* spends a year and a half in *botti* and the *riserva* three years. There is also a table wine, made from Sangiovese Grosso, as in Montalcino, which is aged in *barriques* for at least a year. It is called Prunaio. *Pruno* is the Italian for a thorn and *prunaio* describes very poor land where nothing but thistles will grow. We tasted the 1985, which had a firm smell of new oak, with some good blackcurrant fruit and soft tannins on the finish. As for his Cabernet Sauvignon, of which the first harvest was 1988, Signor Landini had yet to decide what to do with it. We finished the tasting with a 1981 Viticcio, which was soft and mellow, without much body, and characteristic of the wines of Greve.

Castello di Volpaia

Castello is a misnomer in this case. In fact Volpaia is a fortified village, on the top of a hill, not far from Radda. A cellar visit entails a wander through a labyrinth of passages and basements, crammed with *botti* and *barriques*, scattered through the village, including some in a deconsecrated church. Once the village belonged to three families, each with their own small church. Today it is the property of the elegant Giovannella Stianti, who has married Carlo Mascheroni, a Milanese industrialist. However it is Maurizio Castelli who makes the wine and he is the guiding light through the numerous experimental projects of the estate.

There are thirty-six hectares of vineyards altogether, all around the village, including some of the highest in Chianti at 720 metres. A vineyard tour was conducted in Castelli's open-topped Volkswagen Beetle. There is a hectare of Pinot Nero planted quite densely for Chianti with 6,600 plants per hectare; the norm on the Côte d'Or would be even denser with 9,000 to 10,000 plants. There is also Chardonnay, just one and half hectares; as well as 500 plants of Müller Thurgau, an experiment destined to enliven their Bianco Val d'Arbia. It is not yet allowed in the DOC, but could have potential for improving the flavour. One snag: the wild boar love its ripe juicy berries. Cabernet Sauvignon was first grafted on to Canaiolo in 1980, and with subsequent plantings there are now five hectares. Merlot was planted as recently as 1988. There are even two rows of Nebbiolo, which may go well with Sangiovese, not to mention some Sauvignon and a hectare of Sémillon.

Maurizio Castelli explained the microclimate of Volpaia. There is an enormous variation in altitude, between 420 and 650 metres. During the day the temperature may reach as high as 37°C in summer, while cool air currents can cause the temperature to drop at night to 15°C. This sharp contrast helps to give perfumed flavours to the Chiantis of Volpaia. In the higher vineyards the harvest is sometimes as much as ten days later than in other parts of Chianti Classico. Generally the *riserva* wines come from the highest vineyards, *normale* from the middle and the *vini da tavola* from the lower slopes.

The cellar may consist of a maze of small rooms, but the vinification techniques are well controlled and carefully programmed. Each grape variety is fermented separately, with baby stainless steel vats for microvinifications. Fermentation times vary, depending on the wine. The *normale* will spend ten days on the skins, the *riserva* up to fifteen days, and the *cru*, called Coltassala, which is pure Sangiovese, as much as twenty days. The *governo* method no longer has a place in Castelli's winemaking. Coltassala is aged for several months in *barriques* and the Chianti in *botti*. A comprehensive tasting of the wines of Volpaia demonstrated the wonderful potential of this estate.

Their basic white wine is a Bianco Val d'Arbia, with a good base of Trebbiano, a little Malvasia and as much as 30 per cent Chardonnay. It had some gentle buttery fruit and was dry without being acidic. However Castelli plans to try more aromatic grapes, such as Pinot Bianco and Müller Thurgau.

Next came a pure Sauvignon, called Torniello, rather than Predicato del Selvante. Castelli is not convinced by the Predicato wines, saying that in his view a wine should stand on its own merits. The 1987 was fermented in *barriques* and spent a further four months in wood. There were hints of apricots, with some spice, an oily character more reminiscent of Gewürztraminer and the still quite overpowering flavour of new wood. The 1986 Sauvignon which had spent eight months in wood, had some grassy character, but tasted slightly stewed. Somehow it confirmed a prejudice that Sancerre is the best place for Sauvignon.

The 1985 Chianti Classico *normale* was elegant. It had the lovely dry cherry flavour of southern Chianti, with some fruit and tannin. The 1983 *riserva* was richer and fuller with a long finish. In contrast the 1981, with as much as 10 per cent of white grapes was lighter and softer, with less bite and backbone.

Then we went on to Coltassala, which was made for the first time in 1981 from pure Sangiovese. The 1985 had spent fifteen

The Castello di Vicchiomaggio.

months in *barriques* and had a deep colour, with a rich berry nose and ripe rounded blackcurrant fruit on the palate, with balance and length. The 1983 had more the character of cedarwood. The 1982, with a very small percentage of Mammolo, again had cedarwood on the nose, and masses of fruit on the palate. It was rich and elegant at the same time, very concentrated and complete. The 1981 was even better, a lovely mature wine, with ripe cedarwood and delicious fruit.

Finally we tasted 1985 Balifico, a blend of 70 per cent Sangiovese, 10 per cent Cabernet Sauvignon and 20 per cent Cabernet Franc. Merlot will be added to it, when it comes into production. The taste was of rich blackcurrants and new wood, very perfumed, with considerable length and concentration. As Castelli says, these wines were born out of the crisis in Chianti, to show just what can be achieved from the vineyards in the hills of central Tuscany.

Rufina

Rufina is the most distinctive of all the zones of Chianti, outside Chianti Classico. The small town of the same name stands on the river Sieve to the north-east of Florence and the vineyards cover the parishes of Rufina and Pelago, as well as parts of Dicomano, Londa and Pontassieve. Pontassieve is where Rufina meets the Colli Fiorentini. The dividing line is marked by a change in soil. Within the parish of Rufina is the tiny DOC of Pomino, one of the few Tuscan DOCs that allow non-Tuscan grape varieties, of which further details are given in that chapter (see p. 178). Rufina is the smallest of the sub-zones of Chianti, representing just 5 per cent of the total, but it makes some of the region's most distinguished and long-lived wines. Producers include Frescobaldi, Selvapiana, Villa di Vetrice and the Fattoria Travignoli.

The regulations for the production of Rufina are similar to those for Chianti Classico, in that they require lower yields, 80 quintals per hectare, than all other Chianti sub-zones apart from Colli Fiorentini. In practice the yields are often even lower than for Chianti Classico. Rufina and Colli Fiorentini are released for sale at the beginning of June, as Chianti Classico used to be, rather than on 1st March, which is the date for other Chianti. The use of concentrated must from outside the zone is not permitted. The minimum alcohol level for Rufina is slightly lower than for Chianti Classico, 11° for a *normale* and 11.5° for a *riserva*, as opposed to 11.5 and 12°. In the same way as Chianti Classico, Rufina would also like its own separate DOCG, for the producers consider their wines to be better than many from the other zones. Occasionally Rufina is likened to the Colli Fiorentini, but although some of the wines from the hills closest to Rufina are similar in quality, that region is too amorphous to merit comparison.

Parallels with Chianti Classico are inevitable. The vineyards of Rufina lie on the foothills of the Apennines, on steep south-facing slopes, at between 230 and 550 metres. The average temperatures tend to be slightly lower than in Chianti Classico, with cool air coming from the mountains. This difference will result ultimately in wines with higher acidity. The soil is very varied, very stony with clay and limestone. Clay makes for damp soil, so that drought is not a problem and, in fact, the best wine is made in drier years. Maybe the wines of Rufina are a little more elegant, taken overall, than those from some parts of Chianti Classico. The wines always have a considerable amount of tannin and acidity, and need ageing. They can last for many years. I drank a bottle of 1958 Selvapiana when it was thirty-one years old and it was still delicious.

Castello di Nipozzano

Best known of all the producers of Rufina is the Frescobaldi family, at Castello di Nipozzano. Unlike the other large producers of Chianti, they have very little land in Chianti Classico. Their main production plant is at Pontassieve, almost in the suburbs of Florence. The Frescobaldi family first came to Tuscany in the tenth century. They became successful bankers in Florence and even opened a bank in London in the first half of the thirteenth century, during the reign of Henry III. As merchants they dealt in silk and wine, but gradually over the years shifted their interests and activity to the land. Records of their involvement with wine go back to 1346. The Castello di Nipozzano came to them as part of a dowry in the nineteenth century, when Leonia degli Albizi married Angiolo de' Frescobaldi. The same dowry brought their estate in Pomino.

Today the Frescobaldis have large holdings of vineyards, produce wine only from their own grapes and are one of the largest family companies of Tuscan viticulture. They were among the founders of the association for the Predicato wines, and of Galestro. They also manage the estate of Castelgiocondo in Montalcino, own vineyards in the Colli Fiorentini and have a small holding in Chianti Classico, but their reputation is based upon the Castello di Nipozzano, and on the wines of Pomino.

The origins of Nipozzano go back to the tenth century, when it was a fortress guarding the strategic approach to Florence, on a hill overlooking two valleys; it continued to form part of the defence system of the Florentine republic during the Middle Ages. Today one can enjoy wonderful views from the terrace, especially in June when the irises are in flower. There are 124 hectares of vines altogether, including nineteen hectares planted with Cabernet Sauvignon and an individual vineyard or *cru*, called Montesodi, which gives its name to the flagship of the Frescobaldi wines. The vineyard has a particularly favourable site, on the highest part of the estate, with vines that are at least thirty-five to forty years old.

The Frescobaldis attribute the quality of the wines of Nipozzano to the particular clones of Sangiovese and Canaiolo found on the estate. These have been identified and are used for new plantings. Both Castello di Nipozzano and Montesodi contain some Cabernet Sauvignon, only 5 per cent for the first, but as much as 10 per cent for the latter. Another difference lies in the fermentation; for Montesodi this is always in wood, with a longer period on the skins. The ageing may include as much as twenty months in *barriques* and possibly no time at all in the large casks, whereas the wine for the Nipozzano label will spend time in *botti* and maybe only a short time in *barriques* (see colour illustration opposite p. 72). The large barrels are seen simply as containers, which soften the wine but do not give any extra flavour or aroma, whereas the *barriques* give structure and complexity. Both are stylish wines, but Montesodi undoubtedly has greater depth and will last longer. It also costs three times as much. Cabernet Sauvignon is also grown at Nipozzano in the Mormoreto vineyard, not only for Chianti, but also towards blending with Sangiovese for a Predicato di Biturica.

Fattoria di Selvapiana

The Fattoria di Selvapiana is one of the traditional estates of Rufina. It is owned by Dott. Francesco Giuntini, a charming, enthusiastic and mildly eccentric bachelor. He explained how his ancestor Michele Giuntini, a successful banker in the last century, had used his wealth to buy estates all over Tuscany, namely Selvapiana, Badia a Coltibuono and La Parrina. Today there are still family ties between the properties. Dott. Giuntini is related through his mother to the Antinori family.

There are twenty-nine hectares of vines at Selvapiana, from which they make a Chianti *normale*, a *riserva* and a *cru* called Vigneto Bucerchiale, after a vineyard that is steeper and stonier than the others. There are also two white wines and a pink. The simplest white is called by the local geographical indication, Bianco della Val di Sieve, as is the pink. It is made from pure Trebbiano. The better white, called Borro Lastricato after another vineyard, includes 60 per cent Pinot Bianco, which was planted in 1982 and only came into production in 1987. In 1988 they experimented with some skin contact.

As for the Chianti, some white grapes may be used for concentrated must, if the vintage necessitates it, but otherwise the *normale* includes 10 per cent Canaiolo and the *riserva* 5 per cent, while the *cru* is pure Sangiovese. I liked the wines of Selvapiana. The 1986 *normale*, tasted in the spring of 1989 had a full cherry-flavoured nose and palate, while the 1985 was rather firmer, more austere and elegant, with plenty of potential. The 1985 Vigneto Bucerchiale was more concentrated and substantial than the *riserva*, requiring longer bottle ageing. The 1983 Selvapiana *riserva* had begun to develop, showing some fruit in the form of rich cherries, but with an elegant austerity, while the 1977 had overtones of mature fruitcake and was long and elegant. It was delicious. Then we compared the 1968 and 1965 vintages. The younger wine had hints of farmyards on the nose, with some herbal flavours mixed with cedarwood on the palate. The 1965 was not so rich, with a lovely mature nose and some elegant fruit, combining walnuts and herbs. However it was the 1977 that we drank with dinner.

The cellars at Selvapiana are delightfully old fashioned. There are some chestnut casks, as that is the traditional wood of the region. Their wine may spend anything between six months and three years in wood, depending on the acidity level; the more acidity, the longer in cask. There were reserves of old bottles going back many years, and *barrili* (an old measure of barrel) stamped with the family coat of arms. Olive oil is an important product here too and there are numerous *orci*, the traditional amphorae for storing oil, including one that is dated 1827 and bearing the family crest.

Fattoria Travignoli

The Fattoria Travignoli, owned by the young Count Giovanni Busi, is a more innovative

estate than Selvapiana, for they have planted Cabernet Sauvignon and Chardonnay in order to make Predicato wines, as well as Chianti Rufina. The estate has belonged to the Busi family since the eighteenth century. Before that it was the property of the beautiful Florentine church of Santa Maria Novella. There is a reference to Travignoli in some twelfth-century archives and Etruscan artefacts have been found on the land, which are now housed in a museum in Florence.

We went for a bumpy ride in the vineyards in the spring sunshine. They adjoin those of Nipozzano and there are views over the Colli Fiorentini. Most of the vines were planted about fifteen years ago, so they are still relatively young. Next came a cellar visit, where there were stainless steel tanks for the fermentation and casks for ageing the wine. A *riserva* will spend two years in these, followed by a year in bottle. The decision to make a *riserva* is taken at the fermentation. In 1988 as much as 30 per cent of the crop was deemed to be of *riserva* quality; in 1985 about 20 per cent, while none was made in 1980, 1981, 1984 or 1986.

There are a few *barriques*, for experimentation with Cabernet Sauvignon and Sangiovese. They intend to keep each in wood for six months, from March to September, and then maybe to blend the two grape varieties together .

I liked the wines I tasted at Travignoli. The 1987 smelt of cherries and strawberries, with some fruit and tannin. The 1985 had developed an elegant nose reminiscent of cedarwood, with some herbal overtones on the palate. It was rich but stylish, with good ageing potential.

Fattoria di Grignano

The Fattoria di Grignano looks across the valley to Selvapiana. The villa was originally built in the fifteenth century, but underwent considerable alterations during the eighteenth. Today it is painted in yellow ochre, with attractive gardens and rather disorganised cellars. Until 1974 it belonged to the Marchesi Gondi. Then it was bought by Avvocato Fabio Inghirami, who began to bottle and export the wine, which until then had been sold to merchants. Avv. Inghirami is much better known for a make of shirt, as advertised on Italian television, the factories for which are all round the world.

He has replanted the vineyards and, as well as the standard Chianti grape varieties, there is Merlot, which is included in the Chianti to give the wine a little more colour. Franco Bernabei supervises the winemaking, but methods remain quite traditional. I was mildly disappointed with what I tasted. Much more delicious were some sage leaves fried in batter by the *fattore's* wife, and the estate's olive oil.

Villa di Vetrice

The Grati family own four estates altogether in Rufina, making them one of the principal producers, with seventy-two hectares of vineyards. Vetrice and Galiga are their principal properties, but there are also the smaller estates of Fattoria di Monte and Fattoria di Prunatelli. In addition to making Rufina from their own vineyards, they buy grapes or wine to sell as basic *vino da tavola*, or as Chianti without any mention of a sub-zone. Like many Tuscan merchants, they also deal in Orvieto, the white wine of Umbria. The parish church in Rufina records the name Grati in the fifteenth century, but the family only became involved with wine four generations ago, around 1900, at a time when numerous merchants were beginning to sell Rufina and establish a reputation for it. Many of them have long since disappeared and Rufina faded from view, until recent years.

Villa di Vetrice is the best known estate of the Grati family and I was treated to a comprehensive tasting, first from bottles over lunch and then from cask in the cellars.

Our tasting went back to 1972, which they considered to be a very good vintage in Rufina, unlike the rest of Tuscany. This wine certainly had a lovely mature flavour, but it was beginning to fade. The 1974 showed well too, but best of all was the 1977, with some cedarwood fruit and herbal overtones, and a dry finish on the palate. The 1978 was more Burgundian in character, while the 1985 was a solid mouthful of fruit and tannin that promised to turn into a fine bottle. They still have wines from these older vintages in cask, partly to save the expense of keeping it in bottle, as it is easier to store this way. However I wonder whether a little more fruit might not remain if the wine were bottled earlier. Production methods are quite traditional, without any non-Tuscan grape varieties, and the *governo* method is practised if necessary.

Rufina: The Future

Unlike some of the peripheral Chianti areas, you can earn a living from making Rufina, provided that you put your wine in bottle. There is no profit to be made from selling it *sfuso* to a merchant. There is also no doubt that of all the Chianti areas outside Chianti Classico Rufina has the most optimistic future. The producers share a common cause, all agreeing to work for their own DOCG. The town of Rufina has bought the old villa of Poggio Reale, which once belonged to the Spaletti family, who were large producers of wine; and this will be used as an *enoteca* to promote Chianti Rufina. There are plans to open a wine museum too. The people who make Rufina are proud to use the name on their labels, which is more than can be said for the producers of the other Chianti zones.

Colli Fiorentini

The Colli Fiorentini district covers quite a large area around Florence, touching both Rufina and Chianti Classico. The region meets Rufina at Pontassieve and then extends south, almost mixed up with the suburbs of Florence, to the northern edge of Chianti Classico at Strada-in-Chianti. Then it continues round the western edge of Chianti Classico to Tavarnelle Val di Pesa and Barberino Val d'Elsa. To the west it is separated from simple Chianti by the river Pesa, but in reality the distinctions are blurred as producers here tend simply to call their wine Chianti. Some of the estates described in this chapter are, therefore, not part of the Colli Fiorentini, but in practice there is little difference between them and their neighbours who are.

The Colli Fiorentini produces a wide range of quality and styles. I spent a couple of days exploring and encountered some long-lived *riserva* wines from the northern hills near Rufina and some deliciously fruity youthful Chiantis around Tavarnelle and Castelfiorentino. The attention to quality varies too, from the committed producer who has invested in modernising his cellar, to the family for whom winemaking is overshadowed by more profitable *agriturismo*, with a neglected cellar in urgent need of renovation.

Pasolini dall'Onda

One of the better known estates of the Colli Fiorentini is Pasolini dall'Onda at Barberino Val d'Elsa. This is the family property of Count Pier Maria Pasolini. The estate came to him through his mother, who was a Borghese, and there are records of wine being made here in 1573. He also has an estate in Romagna, from his father's family. Count Pasolini has had a successful career as an international lawyer, but although his vineyards are a secondary activity, he cares about them passionately and is an enthusiastic promoter of his wine.

The cellars are right in the village of Barberino, running under houses by one of the old city gates (see colour illustration opposite p. 85). He has fifty-eight hectares of vineyards, situated not only in the Colli Fiorentini, but also in Chianti Classico and elsewhere in Chianti. To simplify a potential bureaucratic muddle, he calls it all plain Chianti, with a vineyard name, but no mention of a particular zone. In addition he makes Sarmento and some table wines. After a walk round the cellars, which have cement fermentation vats and some large casks, we settled down to a comprehensive tasting. First there were two white table wines, Terre del Palazzo and Montepetri. Terre del Palazzo comes mainly from Trebbiano with 10 per cent Chardonnay. It had a hint of butteriness from that grape variety on the nose, but the typical bitter almonds of Trebbiano dominated the taste. It is intended to be an inexpensive wine and so the percentage of Chardonnay will not be increased. Montepetri is more interesting, as a blend of 50 per cent Trebbiano, 40 per cent Chardonnay and 10 per cent Malvasia, with a grassy herbaceous nose and some buttery fruit.

As for reds, we began with Terre del Palazzo, again an inexpensive table wine, made from Sangiovese with 10 per cent Cabernet Sauvignon. It was quite raisiny on the nose, with a hint of blackcurrants. The 1986 Chianti Drove had the bite of bitter cherries; the 1983 Chianti Montoli, which is considered a Chianti *riserva*, was more

The fortress of Torre a Decima.

at Montevarchi south-east of Florence.

There are large cement fermentation vats, a cellar of *botti* and a tiny cellar of new Allier barrels. In September 1988 they were filled with fermenting Chardonnay, which was singing gently through the glass bungs that allow the carbon dioxide to escape. Although they first planted Chardonnay in 1978, this was the first time that they had used *barriques* and they were envisaging keeping the wine in wood until it was ready to bottle. They also grow some Pinot Grigio and Rhine Riesling, which the Italians call Riesling Renano, with which to make a wine called Dolce Amore. The base is Trebbiano, blended with Chardonnay, Pinot Grigio and Riesling, to give some extra flavour. Certainly there were hints of apricots from the Riesling on both nose and palate. A second white wine called La Contessa della Torre is made principally from Pinot Grigio with 10 per cent Chardonnay. I found the somewhat mushroomy flavour of the Pinot Grigio in the 1986 vintage rather unattractive and much preferred the fresher 1987. The Dolce Amore was even better.

They planted Cabernet Sauvignon as early as 1972 and it does well on the poor stony soil here. There is usually a small amount in their Chianti and they are also planning a Sangiovese–Cabernet Sauvignon blend of equal proportions. The length of time that they keep their Chianti in cask before bottling depends very much on the character of the vintage. Generally the soil gives wines that do not have a lot of body and are slow to mature. In 1988 they still had the 1981 vintage in wood, while all the 1983 had been bottled after three years in *botti*. I tasted the 1981 from cask. It was substantial, full and round, but in Signor Viliani's opinion not yet ready. The 1985 Chianti, which was bottled in July 1988, was full of sour cherries, with good fruit and structure. The Rosso della Torre 1986, which had 50 per cent Cabernet Sauvignon with some Canaiolo, Malvasia Nera and a substantial amount of Sangiovese was more ready to drink, with softer fruit, making a full-flavoured mouthful of wine. Best of all I liked the 1983 *riserva* with its mature, spicy nose and herbal fruit.

mellow, with some soft mature fruit. Then just to prove that wine from this part of Tuscany does age, I was treated to a 1959 Chianti. It had some lovely mature fruit, with slightly herbal overtones, and was long and delicate, an elegant glass of wine.

Torre a Decima

Next I went to the northern part of the Colli Fiorentini, to Torre a Decima, near Pontassieve, which is the property of a certain Signora Bianchini, whose grandfather, a Signor Biondi, bought the estate about sixty years ago. However it was the very well informed *fattore*, Signor Viliani who showed me around. He explained that Torre a Decima had been a fortress defending the city of Florence in the thirteenth century, and that since 1300 it had belonged to only three families, the Pazzi, the Salterelli and now the Biondi, from Lombardy (see illustration). The cellars are rather newer, for they were built in 1974, and are well organised to vinify the production of 160 hectares of vines. As well as 60 hectares of Chianti at Torre a Decima, they own 100 hectares for basic table wine

Unusually for this region, there is a long tradition of bottling at Torre a Decima, with a room containing bottles going back to 1927. They keep 120 bottles of each vintage irrespective of quality. I was given a bottle of the 1975 to take home, which was drunk in January 1990. It was delicious, a rich concentrated glass of wine, with cedarwood and cherry fruit.

Fattoria di Lilliano

It is easy to become lost finding the Fattoria di Lilliano near Antella, in the suburbs of Florence. This is not to be confused with the property of the same name in Chianti Classico, outside Castellina-in-Chianti. The estate, once owned by the Grand Duke of Tuscany, was bought by the Malenchini family at the end of the last century. There is a lookout tower from the Middle Ages and the villa was restored by one of the Medici, Cardinal Francesco. There is a small opulently Baroque chapel and a salon with Chinese paintings covering the walls. The cellars are rather delightfully old fashioned, with elderly *botti* and old terracotta *orci* for oil. As for the wine, we tasted the 1985 vintage, which had some attractive fruit and the typical touch of astringency.

Fattoria Oliveto

The Fattoria Oliveto near Castelfiorentino is rich in history. It is an imposing building, built as a fortress in a strategic position during the Florentine–Sienese wars, then transformed in more peaceful times into a country villa. Until 1850 it belonged to the Pucci family, whose portraits adorn the magnificent salon. The painted ceiling shows the coat of arms of the family. Three popes came here – I saw the bedroom of Paul III – and also Vittorio Emanuele III, the last King of Italy. The estate is now run as a private company, which is, I suspect, more interested in *agriturismo* than in wine production.

They explained that they were rationalising their vineyards, reducing them to twenty hectares from the current twenty-seven, and insisted that they wanted to make a Chianti that would age, rather than the traditional Chianti for early drinking. There has been some renovation in the cellars underneath the castle. They have refrigeration equipment for their white and pink wines, and have given up using the *governo* method. However they admitted that, as their wine is not very deep in colour, they 'improve' it with 3 or 4 per cent of Sangiovese from Emilia Romagna. The 1988 Chianti was a fruity glass of wine, but nothing special. I preferred their sparkling white, made from Trebbiano, plus some Chardonnay and Pinot Grigio, bought from the Oltrepò Pavese in northern Italy. They use the champagne method and the wine spends two years on the lees of the second fermentation. It had an attractive yeasty, nutty flavour. They have planted some Vermentino for it and are also considering Roussanne. Their motive is a desire to do something new.

The Parri Family

The Parri family have three estates, all close to Montespertoli, namely Tenuta Monte, Tenuta Ribaldaccio and Tenuta Corfecciano Urbano. As well as making wine from their own estates, they buy in wine as merchants for their branded Chianti, Santa Lucia. The name comes from a tiny chapel on their property, where a mass is held annually for Santa Lucia on 23rd December. None of their vineyards is within the Colli Fiorentini, as the dividing line comes just after Montespertoli, on the river Virgineo. However there is little difference between their vineyards and those of the nearby zone. They would like another Chianti zone to be recognised as Colli Montespertoli.

They gave me a friendly welcome and we tasted a variety of wines, not just Chianti, but also experiments with Chardonnay and Cabernet Sauvignon. A Chardonnay from Ribaldaccio was light and buttery. The Cabernet Sauvignon, which first came into production in 1986 and is kept in new *barriques*, was rich and smoky, with flavours of cassis and new oak. There were Chiantis of varying ages and styles, some lighter and fruitier, others more tannic and closed. A 1985 *riserva* was balanced with fruit and tannin, while a 1968 simple Chianti *normale* had some lovely delicate mature fruit. It may have been fading gently, but it was quite delicious.

San Vito in Fior di Selva

From there I went to San Vito in Fior di Selva, which looks across the valley of the Arno to Artimino in Carmignano. The estate belongs to the Drighi family, who are establishing a reputation for organic viticulture. As well as the customary grapes for Chianti, they have planted others which are not yet all in production, namely Chardonnay, Pinot Grigio, Sauvignon, Verdicchio, Gamay for a *vino novello*, Cabernet Franc and Cabernet Sauvignon. Up to 10 per cent of Cabernet may be added to their Chianti, when it comes into production, replacing Canaiolo in the blend. They still retain the white grapes, as they believe that they give their Chianti a certain vivacity and flavour. They also make two white wines, a Trebbiano–Malvasia blend, labelled Vino da Tavola di San Vito in Fior di Selva, which is a geographical indication, and a pure Verdicchio called Verdiglia. It is rare to find Verdicchio in Tuscany. It is much better known in the Marches, notably the wines of the same name from the hills near Ancona. The taste was quite attractive, slightly bitter, without a great deal of character. As for their Chianti, it could be called Colli Fiorentini, but they prefer simply Chianti. This gives them the commercial advantage of selling it earlier in the year, in March rather than June. The taste was rich and fruity, full of sour cherries.

They are one of the largest organic estates in Tuscany and have followed this method of viticulture since 1981. Controls for organic viticulture as yet have no legal backing or government recognition in Italy, with the result that there are numerous private associations, but no national organisation. At San Vito they belong to two: Suole e Salute, which was the pioneer association, founded thirty years ago by a Turin professor, Garofono; and since 1985, a newer organisation Coordinamento Toscano di Prodottori Biologichi, which is more politically involved with green issues. They began to transform the vineyard at San Vito in 1978, a process that can take several years. Fortunately their land had not been treated too heavily with chemicals, so that they were able to join Suole e Salute in 1981. They use the traditional copper sulphate sprays in the vineyard and a product called *propoli*, which is based on seaweed. In the cellars they rely upon physical methods, avoiding sulphur dioxide as far as possible.

Le Calvane

From San Vito I drove in a heavy rainstorm to Le Calvane, near Montagnana Val di Pesa. This estate has absentee owners from Brescia and Vittorio Fiore supervises the winemaking. Their sixteen hectares include Chardonnay and also some Cabernet Sauvignon, which is not yet in production. They make Chianti (not all their vineyards are in the Colli Fiorentini), Chianti Colli Fiorentini, Sarmento and Sorbino, a white wine from Trebbiano with 30 per cent Chardonnay. The run-down estate was bought six years ago and in 1987 Vittorio Fiore was asked 'to perform a miracle'. He suggested grafting to change the composition of the vineyard, concentrating on Sangiovese, Chardonnay and Cabernet Sauvignon. When the Cabernet comes into production, they will buy some *barriques* and in the meantime the cellars have been renovated, with the installation of efficient refrigeration equipment and new stainless steel vats. The combination of Vittorio Fiore's expertise and financial investment is beginning to show results. The 1988 Il Quercione delle Calvane, their basic Chianti, provided a good, honest glass of wine, with some attractive cherry fruit.

Fattoria dell'Ugo

The Fattoria dell'Ugo outside Tavarnelle belongs to Franco Amici Grossi. There is a fifteenth-century villa with an attractive pink façade covered with creeper, and a courtyard decorated with pots of lemon trees and

The Azienda
Sammontana.

brightly coloured geraniums. Signor Grossi takes a hard view of the position of the Chianti Putto. He could but does not choose to make Chianti Colli Fiorentini, as he feels that this imposes a commercial limitation on when he can sell his wine. His is intended for early drinking and is ready in March. He considers that a Chianti for ageing is the exception. He also laments that Chianti has lost its character, that the consumer does not know what Chianti means, as it covers such a wide area. The price of Chianti has fallen way behind that of Chianti Classico. A few years ago the difference was accounted for by the larger yield, but now Chianti Classico is three times more expensive. The only way to recoup is to create a reputation for your wine in bottle, although he complains that the price of Chianti has remained virtually static for the last three years.

Methods in the cellars at Fattoria dell'Ugo are pretty unsophisticated and, like the villa, the cellars exude an air of gentle dilapidation. Signor Grossi practises the *governo* method and is in favour of white grapes, arguing that

otherwise the wine is too heavy. There is one cask dated 1892, but that is just for show. None of the casks is used. The 1988 vintage was a good example of what Signor Grossi would like his wine to be, fruity and fresh, with a lively bite. He has also succumbed to an alternative wine, but I suspect rather tongue in cheek, treating his *barriques* for a Vino da Tavola di Tavarnelle, called Rugo, as something of a joke. It is mainly Sangiovese, with 15 per cent Cabernet Sauvignon, and was made for the first time in 1986.

Azienda Sammontana

The village of Sammontana to the west of Florence, near Montelupo, is much better known in Italy for ice-cream than for wine. The Azienda Sammontana is the property of Andrea Dzieduszycki, the president of the Società del Putto (see illustration). His family came from Poland at the beginning of the century and his father was one of the first producers in the area to put his wine in bottle. He sent *fiaschi* of Chianti to Milan as

early as 1937. Sammontana is outside the
Colli Fiorentini, separated from it by the river
Pesa, but there is little difference, as the soil
is very similar. I tasted the 1988 Chianti in
the spring of 1989, which was everything that
a young Chianti should be. Made with the
governo method, it was rich and fruity,
redolent of almost sweet cherries, with the
typical dry finish that complements olive oil
so well. There is also Cabernet Sauvignon,
which first came into production in 1987 for
a blend with Sangiovese. Some Chardonnay
is blended with Trebbiano.

Castello di Poppiano

The Castello di Poppiano near Tavarnelle
has belonged since the middle of the eleventh
century to the Guicciardini family, who are
cousins of the Guicciardini Strozzis in San
Gimignano. I talked to Fernando Guicciardini, who is a consultant engineer in Milan,
dealing with irrigation for Third World countries. He only comes to this lovely old castle,
with its palatial rooms and magnificent
watchtower at weekends. He explained what
were for him the characteristics of the Colli
Fiorentini, comparing the region with Chianti
Classico and nearby Montalbano. He thought
the wines had more acidity and perfume than
the other zones, and that they matured more
slowly than the other Chianti Putto.

At Poppiano they have eighty-one hectares
of vines, mainly for Chianti, but including an
enormous mixture of others such as Cabernet,
Merlot, Verdicchio, and even Nebbiolo and
Barbera, all of which were planted in the
mid-1970s. When I was there in 1986, they
were planning an alternative wine made from
60 per cent Merlot and Barbera, and 40 per
cent Cabernet and Nebbiolo, all fermented

together and then aged in Yugoslav oak,
rather than *barriques*. Poppiano Bianco contains not only Trebbiano and Malvasia, but
also a substantial proportion of Verdicchio,
which is considered to give the wine more
flavour. Their Chianti is traditional, with a
fermentation in cement vats and the addition
of *governato* grapes, so that the taste is full
and fruity.

Fattoria Il Corno and Other Growers

Fattoria Il Corno at San Pancrazio is another
estate with some potential. They have planted
Cabernet Sauvignon and Chardonnay and
Sauvignon for their white table wine. They
have invested in new stainless steel vats and
are even experimenting with ageing their
Chianti in *barriques*. They make both simple
Chianti and Colli Fiorentini, which spends
longer in wood. We compared the 1986
Chianti, which was rounded with sour cherry
fruit, with the 1985 Colli Fiorentini, which
was drier and more substantial.

At Fattoria la Querce it seems that the
wines suffer from the common fault of being
kept too long in wood. The 1988 from the
cask was a delicious glass of fruity wine in
September 1989, but the 1985 *riserva* had
become rather dry and tired. As for the
Castello di Montegufoni, the Pasarelli family
are much more interested in *agriturismo* and
their cellars are disorganised and neglected.
The estate once belonged to Osbert Sitwell
and we tasted in the room where he used to
write. Much more interesting than the wines
was Osbert Sitwell's library; but that is one
of the surprises of wine visits in Tuscany.
You never know what else you may see.

Colline Pisane

Amongst the various zones of Chianti, after Rufina the Colline Pisane has the most coherent individual identity. While the others are limited by the boundaries of the provinces of Arezzo or Siena, the Colline Pisane comprises a group of hills to the south-east of Pisa. They are not to be confused with the Monte Pisano, which lies to north and east of the city of the leaning tower and the magical Piazza dei Miracoli.

None of these gentle hills rises much above 200 metres, in sharp contrast to the higher altitudes of Chianti Classico. This is softer, more peaceful countryside, with scattered villages and hamlets. It is very much a backwater, on the way to nowhere, with few passing tourists. The centre is the village of Terricciola, with an *enoteca* in an old cellar where you can taste the various wines of the region. Casciana Terme is larger, and as its name implies, a spa town, noted for its cures for rheumatism. Fauglia, Lari and Crespina are the other important wine villages. I stayed in Soiana, a hilltop village with the vestiges of a castle destroyed in the wars between the Florentines and the Pisans during the late Middle Ages. In fact the vineyards of the Colline Pisane are closer to those of Montescudaio than to Chianti Classico. However for better or for worse, history and tradition have thrown them into the millpond of Chianti.

There are similarities with other Chiantis. Sangiovese is of course the principal grape variety. The *governo* method is still practised extensively, while it is unknown in Montescudaio. However you find grape varieties here that are rarely grown elsewhere, notably Vermentino from Liguria and the Cinque Terre. It does well here, for they say that it likes salt, which blows in on the sea breezes. It can be included in Bianco di San Torpè, the white wine of the region, and also makes a successful varietal wine, with its slightly nutty, fragrant flavour. Ciliegiolo, too seems more popular here than in the heart of Tuscany, while a little Cabernet Sauvignon and Chardonnay are gently encroaching upon the region. However there is no doubt that the growers of Colline Pisane are way behind their colleagues in Chianti Classico in terms of innovation and experimentation.

Bruno Moos at Soiana

Bruno Moos of Soiana is the region's most articulate advocate. He is new to the area, coming originally from Switzerland, by way of New York City, Long Island, Argentina and Montreal. In the Colline Pisane, he discovered what he calls with some justification 'his paradise' and gave up architecture for wine. His first vintage was the disastrous 1984. He makes his wine in what were once the cellars of the castle of Soiana. He has small oak barrels and a few *barriques* in a long gallery. A pure Vermentino was attractively nutty, while his 1988 Chianti *riserva* showed great promise in the autumn of 1989, with some lovely sweet cherry fruit, with balance and good structure, coming from the wood ageing. Fontestina is made principally from Sangiovese with 15 per cent Ciliegiolo, and

In quality it is an area of contrasts. There is good innovative, serious winemaking and there is careless winemaking, perpetrating all the crimes for which Italian wines are criticised. One can see extremes in a day in the Colline Pisane. In between, many growers are making the first tentative steps towards improvement, breaking away from tradition, buying some *barriques*, or planting some Cabernet Sauvignon.

Tenuta di Ghizzano

The most impressive innovatory wine comes from the Tenuta di Ghizzano, which belongs to the Count Pierfrancesco Veneroso Pecciolini. His family have been at Ghizzano since 1370. The villa is rather austerely decorated with heavy furniture, but there are views from the tower over the formal gardens and the village. The painter Annigoni was a friend of the Count's father, and there is a room of family portraits and other work by him.

Until a few years ago they simply sold a little wine to merchants, without making any attempt to promote it. The Count rightly decided that it was not worth having vines at all if the wine fetched such a low price. He sought advice and decided to produce something really worthwhile to sell for more, and so Veneroso was born. Cabernet Sauvignon was grafted on to old vines in 1982 and contributed to the first vintage in 1985. The blend is of Sangiovese with 35 per cent Cabernet Sauvignon and 10 per cent Malvasia Nera, aged for twelve months in Allier *barriques*. Each grape variety is fermented and aged separately and blended before bottling, after which the wine is given twelve months bottle age. I tasted the 1986 Veneroso, which in the autumn of 1989 had some herbal overtones on the nose, with good rounded fruit and tannin, and a lingering finish of cedarwood. It is a shining example of what can be done if you are prepared to spend money wisely in the vineyard and cellar. The Count is working on his Chianti too, eliminating the Trebbiano and giving up the *governo* method. The 1988 was an attractive glass of fruity sour-cherried Chianti.

Bruno Moos of Soiana.

is a lighter, fruitier wine. Ciliegiolo ripens early and gives good colour, fruit and body. For Moos it is the secret of the wines of the Colline Pisane.

They also take their character from their relative proximity to the sea. The climate is milder than in the heart of Chianti, a maritime climate, without great extremes of temperature and no spring frosts. It rains less than in Chianti Classico, as the hills here are lower and the clouds pass over them. The wines are softer and lighter, and generally considered not to age particularly well. However there are exceptions to every rule. One such proved to be 1983 *riserva* from Tenuta Belvedere, which was a meaty, spicy glass of wine when it was five years old, still with plenty of life in it.

The soil is very varied. Once this area was under the sea and one can still find fossilised shells. There is sand and clay, minerals and iron. Yields here are higher than in Chianti Classico, as much as seventy-five hectolitres a hectare, which Bruno Moos is convinced is too high. He obtains fifty hectolitres per hectare at the most.

Fattoria Gaslini

The other extreme is represented by the Fattoria Gaslini, which is owned by a wealthy Genoese businessman. He can afford to buy Etruscan antiques, but has spent little money on his cellar in recent years. The old *fattore* is, I suspect, left very much to his own devices and continues to make wine in the same way that he always has done. The tasting left me distinctly unimpressed, as my host lit up a cigar, and although the bottles were opened with an antique silver corkscrew, the glasses left much to be desired; so did the wine.

Fattoria di Sant'Ermo

The Fattoria di Sant'Ermo is benefiting from new ownership in the form of an anonymous corporation, which is obviously using it as a tax loss, spending money to renovate the cellars and improve the vineyards. The original motive for the purchase was the seventeenth-century villa, once an old convent, but the vines came with it. They have bought some *barriques* and planted some Chardonnay, which is not officially allowed in the Colline Pisane; but no one seems to mind. They have made a *vino novello* and a Galestro lookalike. The investment promises well, but for the moment I prefer their olive oil, which can only be described as utterly delicious, rich and opulent.

Other Growers

Smaller independent growers are also trying hard within their limited means to improve their wines, such as Paolo Tognacchi at Fattoria Scopicci in Fauglia. He studied oenology at Pisa University and bought this estate in 1985, with fifteen hectares of vines. He has planted some Cabernet Sauvignon and makes a *vino novello*, as well as a white wine from the Colline Pisane, and of course some Chianti. The *riserva* is aged experimentally in *barriques*. Lauro Lulli, also at Fauglia has planted other grape varieties, Pinot Nero, Pinot Bianco, Sauvignon and Cabernet. These people give the impression that they are keen and motivated, working hard against considerable odds.

Colline Pisane: The Future

In spite of its geographical coherence, the overriding problem with the Colline Pisane is that the name has no prestige. Larger growers prefer to call their wines simply Chianti, with perhaps the Putto symbol. Probably it is unfair even to call the Colline Pisane Chianti, for the region is bound to be compared with Chianti Classico. However as Bruno Moos aptly points out, the zone is now where Chianti Classico was fifteen years ago; and look where Chianti Classico is today.

Montalbano

Since the creation of a separate DOC for Carmignano in 1975, Chianti Montalbano has been overshadowed by its much more prestigious neighbour, which is discussed below (see p. 159). The vineyards of Carmignano were originally incorporated into Chianti Montalbano, so the overall area has been substantially reduced.

This zone takes its name from the Monte Albano, which dominates the skyline of the Arno valley west of Florence. The vineyards of Carmignano are virtually limited to the parish of the same name on the eastern slopes of the mountain. Those of Montalbano are more spread out on the western slopes, around the little town of Vinci, where the great Renaissance painter was born. There is a slight difference between the soils on the two sides of the mountain, which helps to differentiate between the wines, quite apart from the obvious inclusion of Cabernet Sauvignon in Carmignano.

Nearly every producer of Carmignano makes Chianti Montalbano too, but they consider it very much as their second wine. Equally there is no significant producer of Chianti Montalbano who does not also have vineyards in Carmignano. Any experimentation or innovation is concentrated in Carmignano, therefore. Chianti Montalbano remains a lightly fruity, youthful wine, in the shadow of its grander neighbour.

Colli Senesi

The Colli Senesi is the largest of all the Chianti sub-zones, in that it covers most of the vineyards in the province of Siena, except those in Chianti Classico. However Chianti usually takes second place here to more prestigious wine, notably Vino Nobile in the vineyards of Montepulciano and Brunello in Montalcino. More attention is paid to it in San Gimignano, where it is the red wine to complement the white Vernaccia; and also among the estates on the southern edge of Chianti Classico, near Castelnuovo Berardenga, such as Chigi Saracini and Villa Sestano, where the only red wine is Chianti. Generally however, it is very much the second string in the repertoire.

As the name implies, the vineyards are on the Siena hills, on hillsides going towards San Gimignano and stretching south-east towards Montepulciano and Montalcino along the southern edge of Chianti Classico. The most interesting wines of the Colli Senesi come from San Gimignano. The majority of Vernaccia producers make some red wine, with varying degrees of enthusiasm. Sometimes they prefer to produce an alternative wine rather than a Chianti, such as Paretaio, the pure Sangiovese from Falchini; or Sòdole from Guicciardini Strozzi, or the Sangiovese *crus* from Il Paradiso. Chianti from San Gimignano is usually in the young fruity style, probably fermented in a cement vat and not aged in wood. One of the most enjoyable Chiantis from the Colli Senesi that I have tasted was made by the Fattoria Il Paradiso. It was a deliciously fruity wine with no pretensions. I also liked the spicy flavours in the Chianti from Pietraserena (see p. 173).

In Montepulciano there are people with vineyards not suitable for Vino Nobile, who make Chianti. At Poliziano for instance they have fifty hectares of Chianti to twenty-five of Vino Nobile; but the fame of an estate is based firmly upon Vino Nobile. Historically Chianti from Montepulciano has had a good reputation and was sold, and still is sold *sfuso* to the large merchants. There is little profit to be made from bottling it. Il Cerro make perfectly acceptable Chianti, for which they use a different Sangiovese than the Prugnolo of Vino Nobile. The wine spends eight months in *botti* and has attractive raspberry fruit and a typically astringent finish. Fassati too have vineyards for Chianti outside the zone of Montepulciano; as merchants they also buy more wine, to blend and sell. The Vecchia Cantina di Montepulciano has quite a large production of Chianti among its members and the better wine is aged in *botti* for three or four months. Further details of growers are given in the chapters on Vino Nobile di Montepulciano and Vernaccia di San Gimignano (see pp. 149, 166). Chianti Colli Senesi remains singularly anonymous and more often than not is just called plain Chianti on the bottle.

Colli Aretini

The Colli Aretini is the region with the least identity of all the zones of Chianti. It has the most easterly vineyards, covering the hills around Arezzo, and limited by the provincial boundaries of Florence and Siena, so that it abuts the Colli Fiorentini, Colli Senesi and Chianti Classico. Close to Arezzo the vineyards are mixed up with the suburbs of this sprawling birthplace of Petrarch, whose inhabitants are considered by other Tuscans to be quite the worst drivers in the region. Arezzo is better known for its enchanting frescos by Piero della Francesca than for its wine. The Colli Aretini includes a handful of estates of interest, as well as a large cooperative, the Cantina dei Vini Tipici dell'Aretini, which produces perfectly acceptable but unexciting Chianti Colli Aretini. The Chianti of the Colli Aretini tends to be light and fruity, without much depth or length.

Villa Cilnia

The most interesting estate of all is Villa Cilnia, also known as Podere Cignano, which is just outside Arezzo at Pieve di Bagnoro and belongs to Giovanni Bianchi. However Chianti is far from being his main concern. He settled here in 1974 and since then has devoted his energy to making an exciting and original range of alternative wines. He is enthusiastic, inventive and very self-opinionated. A meeting and tasting with Giovanni Bianchi is certainly a stimulating occasion for the wealth of ideas that he puts forward. He is an outsider to Tuscany, coming from northern Italy.

Altogether he has thirty-five hectares, from which he makes as many as ten different wines, mainly *vini da tavola* including Predicato wines and a *vino novello* called Privilegio. There is also some very good Chianti. For Giovanni Bianchi the characteristics of the Colli Aretini are fruity, soft wines with some glycerine and the perfume of violets. Essentially they are wines to drink young, but with a careful choice of grapes, Bianchi argues that you can make *riserva* wines, as well. The vineyards here lie at about 300 metres, on *galestro* soil, combined with a little sand and clay.

Bianchi is the most fervent believer in the quality and potential of Tuscany. He is adamant that Tuscany should be the first wine-producing region of Italy, for white as well as red wine, and that Italy, not France, should be the world's number one wine country. It is much better suited to the production of grapes, as there is not enough sunshine in France. However Tuscan growers need to plant the right grape varieties and to lose the peasant mentality which equates quality with quantity.

First we walked round the cellars, which were small and well organised, with *barriques* of Allier and Nevers oak for white wine, and Limousin for red. The Chianti is put into *botti*. However you can also make a good Chianti *riserva* in stainless steel vats, he argues, for you do not need any taste of wood in Chianti; and certainly not that of small barrels. Although he makes fine Chianti, he has no intention of conforming to what he calls the 'formule antipatiche' of DOCG.

Then we tasted. First there was Poggio Garbato, a Chardonnay and Müller Thurgau blend. Müller Thurgau, which is unusual in Tuscany, was planted about seven years ago and blends surprisingly well with Chardonnay. Neither grape dominated the flavour and there was some elegantly fruity acidity.

Campo del Sasso is a Chardonnay and Malvasia Nera blend (which is vinified off the skins), fermented in *barriques*. This had good buttery fruit and grassy Chardonnay overtones, and was elegant, without any obvious wood influence. Bianchi also makes a pure barrel-fermented Chardonnay, sold as Predicato del Muschio.

Next came 1987 Vocato, made of Sangiovese with 20 per cent Cabernet Sauvignon, fermented together, with several months of ageing in *barriques*. The nose smelt of cassis and on the palate there was a strong taste of blackcurrants with new wood. The flavour was concentrated, with very good fruit and balance. Le Vignacce is a blend of equal parts of Sangiovese, Cabernet Sauvignon and Montepulciano d'Abruzzo, which are blended after fermentation; partly because Montepulciano ripens after the other two grape varieties. It spends twelve to eighteen months in *barriques*, followed by a year's bottle ageing before sale. The 1982 was the first vintage. I tasted the 1986 soon after it had been bottled and found that the Cabernet dominated the flavour, while Bianchi could taste the Montepulciano too. The Sangiovese softens them both, but in any case it was a well balanced wine, with some tannin and blackcurrant fruit and a long finish.

One of his most original wines is Sassolato, made from dried grapes, like the *recioto* of northern Italy. The blend is 40 per cent each of Malvasia Bianca and Chardonnay, and 20 per cent Trebbiano. Half of the grapes are pressed and half are left to develop just a little noble rot, which can be artificially induced with a humidifier and a ventilator; to give a *velutino di muffatino*, 'a hint of noble rot'. Those grapes are then pressed and blended with the other juice, before the combination is put into *barriques*, for at least a year. There was none available for tasting, but it smelt delicious from the *barriques*.

Giovanni Bianchi is yet another newcomer to Tuscany who has brought ideas from outside the region to the great benefit of its reputation. He has a healthy disrespect for Italian bureaucracy and for organisations like the Chianti Putto. He concentrates his energy on wine and nothing else, to great effect.

Men such as this are capable of hauling the peripheral zones of Chianti into the mainstream of Tuscan viticulture.

Fattoria di San Fabiano

In contrast the Fattoria di San Fabiano was a much more typical Chianti estate. It is owned by an industrialist from Milan, Count Borghini Baldovinelli and has been in his family for many generations. The Count is an absentee landowner, but his family have long associations with Arezzo, for they commissioned the Piero della Francesca frescos. Vincenzio Borghini oversaw the building of the baptistery in Pisa and was responsible for the reform of Florentine law under the Medicis. The villa is dominated by a watchtower. There was a battle here in 1272, when the Aretini defeated the Florentines. The first floor of the house was built in the more peaceful early seventeenth century and another storey was added in the early nineteenth century. Everything was very sombre, as in a house that is more often closed than lived in, with an enormous collection of weapons that had been amassed by the Count's father. Horses were evidently another enthusiasm for there were numerous hunting trophies.

Armaiolo di San Fabiano therefore seemed an appropriate name for their Predicato wine, for an *armaiolo* is someone who makes weapons; they know that there was an armoury somewhere closeby in the Middle Ages. The blend is of Sangiovese and Cabernet Sauvignon in equal parts and the 1985 vintage, the first year of production, which I tasted in 1989 seemed surprisingly ready, soft and rounded with plenty of fruit. It had spent twelve months in *barriques*. Slavonic oak *botti* are used for Chianti, with six months of ageing for the *normale* and two years for the *riserva*.

However only a small part of their Chianti production is actually bottled; as much as 70 per cent is sold to merchants. This is typical of much of the Colli Aretini. Only about ten estates put their wine in bottle, as the price for it is far from remunerative. To make some profit, a bottle should sell for 4,000 lire,

whereas in reality it may make 3,500, and
even as little as 2,800. On the other hand,
Armaiolo fetches 17,000 lire, so the attraction
of the alternative wine is obvious. The 1988
Chianti had just been bottled. It was a
solid but soft mouthful of fruit, without the
astringency of some wines. They practise the
governo in years when the grapes are free
from rot, as they believe it sustains a youthful
lively character, which is the essence of the
Colli Aretini.

Other Chianti

Other estates come within the broad delimitation of Chianti, but not within a defined zone, or even close to one. Many are working hard to improve their wines.

The Fattoria Sassolo.

Fattoria Sassolo

I enjoyed my visit to the Fattoria Sassolo outside San Miniato. This is very close to the Colline Pisane, but not within the delimited area. Guido Bianco's great-grandfather bought the estate, including a fine old villa, in 1920 when he came here from Bergamo (see illustration). Until a few years ago, little was done with the vines. There were fields of cereal, sunflowers and olive groves. Then

Guido Bianco began to take an interest in his wine and, in bottling it as well, he attempted to develop an image for it. Today he makes Chianti and Vin Santo, as well as Bianco di San Torpè, for his vineyards come within that DOC. He is convinced of the great future for Tuscan wines, and not just for the best areas, but the others too. Gradually they are learning new techniques.

There is nothing particular about the vinification methods for his Chianti. The 1987 was a glass of eminently drinkable young wine, while Aquabona, named after a farm on the estate, is made from pure Sangiovese. The first vintage was 1988 and I tasted it two days after it had been bottled in September 1989. There was some spicy fruit and youthful astringency. It needed bottle age, but tasted good, as did the Vin Santo.

Azienda Agricola Montellori

Across the Arno in the suburbs of Fucecchio, I found the Azienda Agricola Montellori, which is owned by the Neri family. Here experimentation seems to be the order of the day, for although they make perfectly agreeable fruity Chianti, that is far from all. Altogether they have sixty hectares of vines, which allows for both traditional and experimental grape varieties. First in the tasting was a typical white Tuscan wine, made of pure Trebbiano, which tasted much as you would expect. Next came Bianco della Villa. Trebbiano was the base, but enlivened with Chardonnay and Pinot Bianco, planted on the slopes of the Monte Albano, in the midst of Chianti vineyards. Alessandro Neri is considering trying Grechetto too; the oenology school of San Michele all'Adige is offering advice. He intends this wine to come within the parameters of a new DOC, which has been agreed for the 1990 vintage, called Bianco dell'Empolesi. The new regulations confirm Trebbiano as the base, at 80 per cent minimum, but complemented by any of the experimental grape varieties allowed in the region, such as Chardonnay, Pinot Bianco and so on. Malvasia is limited to 8 per cent. The vineyards are on either side of the valley of the Arno, around the towns of Empoli, Fucecchio, Vinci and Montelupo Fiorentino. As for the wine, it was slightly buttery on the nose, with some almond overtones and a mildly herbal flavour.

Chardonnay has been in production since 1985 and provides two wines, one that only goes into stainless steel, called Vigneto della Rosa, and a barrique-aged version called Castelrapita. Sixty per cent of it is fermented in wood and spends a further three months in barriques, before being put into vat and bottled in May. I preferred the barricato wine. The Vigneto della Rosa left plenty of room for improvement, possibly because the vines are still rather young, but the Castelrapita had a subtle oak character on the nose and toasted buttery flavours in the mouth. There are plans for a riserva Chardonnay, which would spend even longer in wood.

They make sparkling wine too, by the champagne method, mainly from Chardonnay, but with a little Sangiovese, which they explained was a substitute for Pinot Noir. I tasted the 1984 Brut and the 1983 riserva, which had spent a minimum of three years on the lees. I liked them both. The Brut was light and creamy, while the riserva was fuller and more yeasty, but well balanced. A pink wine is made from Sangiovese.

As for red wine, there is a vino novello of Sangiovese, with some carbonic maceration, but only for 20 per cent of the grapes. If there is too much, it takes away the intrinsic character of Tuscany, tasting rather of France. As for Chianti, there are plans for a riserva, with six months of barrique ageing to give the wine more structure. They consider that even a basic Chianti need not be a wine for early drinking, if it comes of low yields, with the minimum amount of white grapes. If a red wine spends a little time in wood, it will have more character, enabling it to last longer.

Their experimental red wine is also called Castelrapita, from Sangiovese and a maximum of 30 per cent Cabernet, which spends about twelve months in new Vosges and Tronçais barriques. The 1985 was the first vintage. I tasted the 1987, which when it was two years old still had a lot of oak on the nose and in the mouth. Maybe more bottle age would improve it. There are plans for a Cabernet–Merlot blend, for Merlot was planted in 1987, again on the slopes of Monte Albano; as well as some Sauvignon, which is not yet in production.

This is a fascinating example of what can be achieved, not just in Chianti Classico, but in simple Chianti, with money and time to invest. The potential is enormous.

MAP OF THE MONTALCINO REGION

Buonconvento

River Ombrone

Altesino
Caparzo

Castiglion del Bosco

Montosoli

Val di Suga

Paradiso

Montalcino

Castelgiocondo

Villa Greppo

Barbi

Case Basse

La Chiesa di
Santa Restituta

Sant' Antimo

Camigliano

Sant' Angelo
in Colle

Monte Antico

Castello Banfi

Argiano

River Orcia

Col d'Orcia

Brunello di Montalcino

In 1988 the wine growers of Montalcino celebrated a centenary, a hundred years of Brunello di Montalcino. In some ways the date was rather arbitrary, for it just happens that 1888 is the vintage of the oldest existing bottles. It was appropriate, however, that they should belong to the Biondi Santi family, who have done so much to make Brunello the wine we know today.

A great excuse for a celebration, it was an occasion to which Montalcino rose in style. There were processions of medieval pageantry in the narrow streets of the hilltop town, with fanfares of trumpets in the brilliant sunshine, and the church bells rang. Italians can never resist a speech and this was no exception. It seemed as if the whole town had gathered for an aperitif in the main square, and there followed a copious and delicious lunch. The Biondi Santi family held their own private celebration the following day.

Montalcino is attractive. Much remains of the city walls and the old gates, as well as the fourteenth-century fortress, which now houses an *enoteca*. The tower of the Palazzo Comunale dominates the central square, which contains the Caffé Fiaschetteria, a delightful bar that has retained its Art Nouveau décor. There is an unassuming atmosphere about the place. You would not realise that you were in the home of one of Tuscany's, and also one of Italy's, finest wines. There is the occasional wine shop, but nothing ostentatious or showy, just a quiet leisurely charm and a colourful flower market.

The first written reference to Montalcino goes back to 814, when it was called 'Monte Lucini'. Throughout the Middle Ages the fortunes of the town were closely linked with those of the Sienese, who valued Montalcino for its strategic importance, in their struggles against the Florentines. Montalcino attempted to establish its own independence and the town even had its own mint for a time, but in 1559 it finally came under Medici rule.

There is no doubt that viticulture has always been an important activity in Montalcino, along with the cultivation of olives, but it is surprising that the earliest references describe a white wine, not a red wine. In the sixteenth century, Leandro Alberti in his *Descrittione di tutta l'Italia* wrote that Montalcino was known for 'the good wines that came from those agreeable hills'. Francesco Redi writing in 1685 waxed lyrical about the charms of 'the divine Moscadelletto di Montalcino'.

The first mention of red wine is in an apocryphal story. During the siege of Montalcino in 1553 the French Marshal in command reputedly smeared red wine on his face to camouflage his pallor after the deprivations of the siege.

There is evidence that red wine from Montalcino was drunk by William III of England. In the winter of 1696 Sir Lambert Blackwell wrote to the Secretary of State that the wine of Montalcino for His Majesty was not yet quite ready, but would be so in time for a boat that was sailing in twenty-five days time. In the spring of 1698 Blackwell came to Tuscany, too late to buy wine from the previous year, but in time to make a contract for the next vintage. He wrote 'I have made a contract for the very best wine of the next vintage, of the kind enjoyed by His Majesty, from Montalcino'.

So far there is no mention of Brunello, and that is where the Biondi Santi family come in. In his monograph about them, written for the centenary, Burton Anderson traces the part that they played in the recognition and development of the particular variety of Sangiovese which has come to be called Brunello. It all began with Ferruccio Biondi Santi. The family already had a reputation for their wines. In the eighteenth century the naturalist Giorgio Santi wrote of his estates in Montalcino, and their 'exquisite fruits, much and above all, rich wine'. His nephew and Ferruccio Biondi Santi's maternal grandfather Clemente Santi won a prize at a local fair for his 'Vin rosso scelto (brunello) 1865'. It was also recognised at international exhibitions in Paris and London. Clemente Santi favoured this particular variety of Sangiovese, called Sangiovese Grosso, as opposed to the Sangiovese Piccolo or Sangioveto that is more common in Chianti. In fact the grapes of Sangiovese Grosso are not particularly big, but Sangioveto produces small berries by comparison. When Sangiovese Grosso ripens, the grapes take on a dark dusky colour, described as *brunello*; hence the name given to this particular sub-variety of Sangiovese. Clemente Santi had already planted it on his estate of Il Greppo.

Ferruccio Biondi Santi was a courageous young man, who fought with Garibaldi's troops at the battle of Bezzecca in 1866. His interest in oenology grew when he took over his grandfather's cellar. It was a difficult time. Oidium and peronospora had affected the vineyards of Montalcino. The white Moscadello vines suffered particularly from these diseases, but Sangiovese seemed to fare rather better. So Ferruccio set to work to isolate this particular variety of Sangiovese and to replant all his vineyards with it. He took cuttings from the vines that were already there, carefully selecting the best plants. This was some of the earliest work on clonal selection.

Ferruccio Biondi Santi's work was particularly innovatory, for at that time, not only was the wine of Montalcino still predominantly white, but such red wine as was produced, was made in the style of young Chianti; from a mixture of grape varieties, including white grapes, and with the use of the *governo* method to make a fruity wine for early drinking. Ferruccio Biondi Santi set out to make a wine from Sangiovese alone, anticipating, as Burton Anderson says, by nearly a century the vogue among contemporary Tuscan winemakers. He limited the yields from his vines, selecting only the best. He gave up using the *governo* method and left the juice in contact with the skins for a long fermentation period. The wine was then aged, as it is today, in large Slavonic oak casks. Naturally all this attracted attention, for the wines were good, notably the 1888 and 1891. The most appropriate analogy appeared in an Italian wine magazine *Civiltà del Bere*, where the grapes were compared to the marble of the Apuanian Alps. Craftsmen had worked this for years, but it took Michelangelo to create masterpieces from it. This is what Ferruccio Biondi Santi did for the Brunello variety of Sangiovese.

Ferruccio's son Tancredi continued his father's work and he really deserves the credit for establishing the international reputation of the family and its wine. He took over the running of the estate after his return from the First World War, following an agreement with his brother Gontrano to divide their inheritance. In this way Tancredi retained Il Greppo. He maintained an active interest in everything to do with Montalcino, as well as his own estate, until his death in 1970. In 1925 he founded a cellar known as Biondi Santi & C. Cantina Sociale, inviting other producers to join and encouraging them to plant more vineyards.

An early story about the stature of Biondi Santi Brunello relates to a dinner of Tuscan wine producers, hosted by Biondi Santi, which included Baron Luigi Ricasoli from the Castello di Brolio, one of the leading estates of Chianti Classico. The story goes that when the Baron tasted the 1888 and 1891 Brunellos, he simply admitted, 'Well, I can't achieve this!'

In 1963 Tancredi Biondi Santi was consulted about the new regulations for the DOC. His last act as a winemaker, just four months before he died in 1970, was to assist at a recorking ceremony of the bottles of the great vintages, 1945, 1925, 1891 and 1888. It was a fitting end to a notable career. According to Mario Soldati, who describes the occasion in *Vino al vino*, Tancredi attributed the longevity of Brunello to the cork, which had been changed every twenty-five years; for eventually every cork shrinks and lets in air which will harm the wine.

Franco Biondi Santi began to help his father with the running of the Il Greppo estate in the early 1950s. By that time Brunello di Montalcino was no longer the sole preserve of his family. They have continued to play a part, but their current activities will be described later. Others were also coming to the fore, to the extent that the Biondi Santis regretted they had not registered Brunello as a trademark. At the first exhibition of *vini tipici* in Siena in 1933, there were Brunellos from three other producers: namely from the estates of Montosoli and Castelgiocondo of Guido Angelini, the Fattoria dei Barbi dei Colombini and the Fattoria di Sant'Angelo in Colle belonging to Roberto Franceschi. All of these still exist today, if not in the same form. Two other exhibitors, but for Chianti rather than Brunello, were Poggio alle Mura and Argiano, which later established reputations for their Brunello.

Phylloxera decimated the vineyards of Montalcino during the 1930s and production declined still further during the Second World War and its aftermath. It was not until 1980 that the vineyard area of Montalcino returned to that of 1929. However already in the 1950s several estates had begun to sell Brunello too, notably the Colombini, but also the Lisini, Franceschi, Costanti, Lovatelli, Mastropaolo, Camigliano, Casale del Bosco, Castiglion del Bosco and others. The reputation of Brunello di Montalcino was established, so that it became one of the earliest DOCs, even before Chianti.

The DOC regulations of 1966 laid down the outlines for the production of Brunello di Montalcino, with some particularly restrictive rules, under the guidance of Tancredi Biondi Santi. The area of production was defined, so that the vines could only be grown in specific types of soil at no higher than 600 metres. The maximum yield could not exceed 100 quintals of grapes per hectare, with a yield of 70 per cent in juice, in other words equating to seventy hectolitres per hectare. The DOC regulations confirmed the four-year period of ageing in cask, which is longer than for any other Italian wine, except Barolo. Wine that was sold before four years ageing could be called Vino Rosso dai Vigneti di Brunello, although this was opposed by Tancredi Biondi Santi, who consequently withdrew from the growers' association. This was the future Rosso di Montalcino. With five years of ageing, not necessarily in wood, but also in bottle or tank, the wine was eligible for the additional qualification of *riserva*.

The DOC gave a definite impetus to the production of Brunello di Montalcino. The sharecropping system had been dismantled and the 1970s saw the development of many small estates, as well as considerable outside investment by industrialists from northern Italy and wine companies from elsewhere in Tuscany, Italy and overseas.

A further boost was given in 1980 when Brunello di Montalcino became one of the very first Italian wines to be given the extra status of *garantita*. This was an opportunity for a modification in the regulations. The yield was reduced from 100 to 80 quintals per hectare, still with a 70 per cent yield of juice, making 56 hectolitres per hectare. The obligatory ageing period in wood was reduced to three and a half years, from 1st April following the vintage. The DOC for Montalcino had allowed the inclusion of a corrective maximum of 10 per cent of must or wine from elsewhere, but that possibility was happily forbidden by the new DOCG regulations.

As well as Brunello di Montalcino, most growers make a second red wine, Rosso di Montalcino, which became a DOC in 1985 and replaces the former Vino Rosso dai Vigneti di Brunello, which did not have any legal standing. Rosso di Montalcino is made from exactly the same grapes as Brunello di Montalcino. Nor is there any difference in the vineyard area. What the DOC of Rosso di Montalcino allows is a selection of grapes and vineyards, so that any wine unsuitable for the obligatory three and a half years of ageing can be bottled after a year; it does not even have to be in wood. Sometimes the decision is made in the vineyard, as it can already be apparent at the vintage which grapes will be suitable for Rosso di Montalcino and which will make wine requiring longer ageing. Sometimes the decision is postponed until the wine has spent a year in cask, when it is more obvious which will survive a further two and a half years in wood. Rosso di Montalcino is a remarkably successful wine, in that it has some of the flavours of Brunello, but without the weight or structure. Nevertheless a good Rosso di Montalcino offers excellent value, at a third of the price of a Brunello di Montalcino.

The third wine of Montalcino is the Moscadello di Montalcino, which takes up the medieval tradition of sweet white wine in the region, the Moscadelletto that was praised by Francesco Redi. In fact few people make it and the prime instigator of its resurrection in the twentieth century has been Banfi Vintners. As we shall see, their success has been limited.

The vineyards of Brunello di Montalcino are confined to the parish of Montalcino, which is bordered by three rivers, the Orcia, Ombrone and Asso. There are vineyards all over the parish, but the greatest concentration is close to Montalcino itself, and around the village of Sant'Angelo in Colle and the nearby abbey of Sant'Antimo. This monastery dates back to the time of Charlemagne, with a wonderfully simple stark grey stone church. The map of Montalcino comprises a thirty-kilometre square outline of hilly terrain, while Tuscany's highest mountain, Monte Amiata is off to the south-east (see p. 128).

There are variations in climate, with a hot and dry microclimate to the south, where the warm winds of the Tyrrhenian Sea blow across the Maremma. The vineyards lying to the north-west are cooler. Altitude plays a part too, with vines usually planted at between 300 and 500 metres, and certainly no higher than 600 metres. Monte Amiata helps to protect Montalcino from extremes of climate, such as hail. Most rain falls during the autumn months of October and November, and in May. Frost is not a problem and the mild climate with gentle breezes makes for healthy ripe grapes in most years.

The geology of Montalcino is complicated too. Around Montalcino itself and to the south-west there is a lot of limestone, with marl, while in the north towards Castiglion del Bosco, *galestro*, as found in Chianti Classico, is the main soil type, with some clay. In the outlying vineyards a mixture of clay and limestone is most usual. It is possible to divide up Montalcino into three broad districts, with the most elegant Brunellos coming from the north-east of the town of Montalcino. The smallest area, which extends south-east towards Castelnuovo, is protected by Monte Amiata and is considered to be the best, including the estates of Biondi Santi and Colombini, amongst others. The third zone, to the south-west includes Camigliano, Sant' Angelo in Colle and Sant' Angelo in Scala, and is said to produce the most robust Brunellos, including Il Poggione and Case Basse.

The potential total area of Brunello di Montalcino is about 1,000 hectares. There has been a steady increase over the last few years, so that in 1989 there were over 910 hectares of vineyards, cultivated by about 130 growers, of whom just over 80 now put their wine into bottle. This represents a complete recovery from the ravages of phylloxera. The vineyard area reached its lowest point in 1969, when there were just 56 hectares of vineyards. By 1979 this figure had risen to nearly 628. More figures appear in Appendix II.

Banfi Vintners

The Mariani brothers, John and Harry, the owners of the large American wine company, Banfi Vintners have made a phenomenal investment in Montalcino. They were largely responsible for the terrific success in the United States of Lambrusco, from the cooperative Riunite, and were looking for a white equivalent. Ten years ago there was land to be bought in Montalcino. Initially they purchased vineyards from Argiano and Poggio alle Mura, in 1977 and 1978; then the castle and remaining land of the estate of Poggio alle Mura in 1983 (see colour illustration opposite p. 156). The last wine made under that label was 1979. Banfi now owns a total estate of some 3,000 hectares, including 850 hectares of vineyards, which they began planting in 1978, starting completely from scratch, pulling up any existing vines. The whole operation was masterminded by Ezio Rivella, the head oenologist and general manager of Banfi in Italy. It is probably no exaggeration to say that what is now called the Castello Banfi is his dream and brainchild.

I expected a man who had spent $100 million to be rather intimidating, but I was mistaken. Ezio Rivella is stocky, friendly and relaxed. When I met him, he was dressed in jeans, a leather jacket and a large hat, which would have been more in place in Australia's Hunter Valley or on a Texan cattle ranch. Certainly this was not my idea of a business tycoon. Rivella comes from Piedmont, which is generally considered to be the other great wine region of Italy. With perhaps an element of local chauvinism, he admitted that he had thought the reputation of Brunello di Montalcino to be exaggerated; but that he had changed his mind when he came to Montalcino to see for himself. He explained that the Mariani brothers had wanted to sell something better than Lambrusco. After trying out various importers, they decided to make their own wine. Rivella attempted to dissuade them, arguing that it would be expensive and that the returns would be low; alternatively, he said, they must do something on a vast scale. They looked in France, Spain, Australia and in California too, but Italy was already familiar, for they were not only importers of Lambrusco, but producers of Moscato d'Asti and other Piedmontese wine at their cellars in Strevi. There was land available at Montalcino. However they had underestimated the cost of planting vineyards, for the initial projected cost of $50 million soon doubled. Happily the exchange rate worked in their favour.

They re-landscaped the hillsides to plant hectares of vineyards, completely changing the terrain. Gone were the steep sharper hills. They were levelled and contoured by armies of bulldozers. Small valleys were removed to make larger slopes. Drainage channels were built before the vineyards were even planted, as there is a high percentage of clay in the soil. They have adopted the *casata* system of Friuli, with vines trained high for mechanisation, at 1.6 metres and planted in wide rows 3.5 metres apart, with 2.8 metres between the rows. However Rivella admitted that they had made a vital miscalculation in deciding to plant Moscato. The financial success of Moscadello di Montalcino depended upon the possibility of mechanical harvesting to cut their labour costs. It transpires, however, that the Moscato grape does not adapt to this. The skins of the grapes are too soft and the machines simply reduce the grapes to a pulpy mush.

The production of Moscadello di Montalcino also requires expensive technology. The grapes are pressed; the juice is cleaned in a centrifuge, chilled to freezing point and kept in a refrigerated warehouse until it is needed. The essence of Moscadello is a fresh, grapy taste, but Moscato does not age well, hence the need to keep the juice until it is required, rather than turning it into wine. They use cultured yeasts for a cool fermentation in pressurised stainless steel tanks so that the carbon dioxide from the fermentation is retained, leaving two atmospheres in the wine. The fermentation is stopped by chilling, so that 5° of sugar still remains, with 7° alcohol. It is then pasteurised, so that the sugar is stable, and filtered under pressure. The resulting wine is very similar to Asti Spumante, though slightly less fizzy, *frizzante* rather than *spumante*. Moscadello can also be a still wine, which Banfi do not make.

Banfi also produce a Moscadello *passito*, a version that is included in the DOC regulations. The grapes are left in the vineyard until they are overripe and then put in a prune oven for a few hours to concentrate the sugar. Next they are pressed and the juice fermented very slowly. The wine is aged in a kind of solera system, in *barriques* with a five-year rotation, so that the final wine consists of 70 per cent of one year and 30 per cent of the previous five years. This is their answer to Vin Santo, with a flavour of bitter-sweet oranges, reminiscent of good home-made marmalade. They suggest that it would go well with Gorgonzola, or any other blue cheese.

Banfi in Montalcino must be one of the most modern wineries not just in Europe but anywhere in the world (see illustration). It was built in 1982, in time for their first vintage at Montalcino and is described by Rivella as a unique combination of technology and the grand scale. This is certainly true. The impression is breathtaking. Quite simply the grapes arrive at one end of the streamlined vinification plant and emerge in a bottle at the other, without ever being exposed to anything that might have a detrimental effect on the ultimate flavour of the wine. A forest of stainless steel pipes connects all the tanks, which are programmed by computer. Everything is shining, spotlessly clean, allowing for the minimum use of sulphur dioxide in their winemaking. They insist that they prefer physical methods to chemical means. Their bottle store is insulated and their barrel cellar is immediately underneath the refrigeration cellar (see illustration on p. 48). It seems that the human hand is almost unnecessary; everything is done by machine. Certainly on the two occasions that I have visited Banfi, I have found this enormous winery almost entirely empty of people.

This is one of a couple of estates to try ageing Brunello di Montalcino in *barriques*. They would like more flexibility over the ageing, preferring three years to four years in wood, and consider three and a half as a compromise that really means four. After all, what do you put in your barrels for the remaining six months? The taste of the *barr-*

Modern computer-controlled horizontal presses, at Villa Banfi.

ique-aged Brunello was good, but it was not true Brunello.

The *barriques* they now keep for one of a range of other wines, which they call Castello Banfi. This is composed of 20 per cent Pinot Noir and equal parts of Cabernet Sauvignon and Sangiovese. The three grape varieties are blended together after nine months of separate ageing and then kept in wood for a further nine months. When I tasted the 1986 vintage shortly before it was bottled, Cabernet Sauvignon was the dominant grape variety and the wood was still obvious. However that should tone down after two or three years in bottle.

As well as Cabernet Sauvignon and Pinot Noir, they have planted Chardonnay and Pinot Grigio, both of which are vinified as varietal wines. Chardonnay, sold as Fontanelle, has an appeal to the international market and spends four months in new Tronçais barrels, to give it a lightly buttery nose, with a fatter and richer flavour. The grapes are usually ripe in the second week in August. The Pinot Grigio is picked around

20th August, in order to obtain some crisp acidity. At present this is the only example of a Tuscan varietal Pinot Grigio. It is more Italian in style than the Chardonnay, with its international flavour.

Banfi also make a pure Cabernet Sauvignon, which spends about twelve months in *barriques* that are changed every five years. I tasted the 1984 vintage in 1988. It had hints of cedarwood on the nose and was still very tannic on the palate, with some dry cedarwood and a hint of blackcurrants. Varietal versions of Pinot Noir and Sauvignon Blanc are still both at an experimental stage, and have not yet been released on to the market. Like several other big Tuscan producers they have joined the *vino novello* market, with a pure Sangiovese made by carbonic maceration, called Santa Costanza.

The arrival of Banfi in Montalcino was viewed with a certain amount of unease and suspicion by the more conservative members of the winemaking community. Banfi have a reputation for cheap table wine and they do indeed buy in grapes to make a considerable quantity of basic branded table wine, such as Bell'Agio and Entrée, that are destined for the United States. However they have agreed with the local producers that these should not have any reference to Montalcino on the label. As for their Brunello di Montalcino, there is no doubt that the quality is excellent. Made with great technical expertise, it has the traditional flavours of Sangiovese and is equal to many of the longer established names of the area. If the Biondi Santi family brought international acclaim to Montalcino in the last century, Banfi have done so in this one, bringing the wines of this small town in southern Tuscany to an international audience. Certainly Dott. Rivella is optimistic about the future of this enterprise. He can look upon the future with a smile, for he has realised a dream.

La Casa and Caparzo

Several other newcomers have contributed to the reputation of Brunello di Montalcino. Often they have been industrialists from northern Italy with money to invest in a wine estate. Those at Caparzo, Altesino, Val di Suga and Case Basse are notable examples. At Caparzo the estate is administered by Nuccio Turone, while Vittorio Fiore masterminds the winemaking. In fact there are two separate vineyards, Caparzo and La Casa. It all began in 1968, when four friends from Milan decided to buy a house in Tuscany. What started as a quest for a holiday home, turned into a serious company, with twelve shareholders. The first vintage at Caparzo was 1970.

La Casa (there is a ruined house adjoining the vineyard) is a six and a half hectare vineyard. Two and a half hectares consist of old vines, while four more have been planted where the olive trees died in the frost of 1985, mainly for experimental purposes. Instead of using the customary wide planting system, with three metres between rows and 1.4 metres between the vines, to give 2,700 plants per hectare, they have increased the number of vines to 4,000, and included five different clones of Sangiovese Grosso, to see which performs best. Different rootstocks have been

used, to find out whether this has any effect on the yield. The soil at La Casa is a mixture of stones and *galestro*, whereas there is more clay at Caparzo.

At Caparzo they have thirteen hectares of Sangiovese, three and half of Chardonnay and one and half of Cabernet Sauvignon. In contrast to Banfi they have no interest in Moscadello, but for a note of frivolity they are experimenting with a pink sparkling wine. There is a little innovation in the vinification of their Brunello di Montalcino, in that they have not only traditional large casks but also smaller 350-litre barrels. These are all of oak. Chestnut casks are allowed in the regulations and used to be quite common, but are now considered less suitable. They would not consider ageing Brunello in *barriques*, as they believe that there is already enough tannin in the wine. Smaller barrels are also more demanding to use. Their Brunello is fermented in cement vats, spending ten or twelve days on the skins, at a maximum temperature of 30°C, with two *remontagi* a day.

The Brunello of Caparzo is one of the more elegant wines of the area. The estate is somewhat isolated from the others, lying in the northern part of Montalcino. I liked the wine's spicy flavours, with overtones of liquorice and a hint of farmyards, with a good balance of tannin. The Rosso di Montalcino was good too, with a slightly herbal nose and some smoky fruit on the palate. Then there is a red *vino da tavola* called Ca' del Pazzo, a blend of equal parts of Sangiovese and Cabernet Sauvignon, which was planted in 1980. The first gives strength to the wine and the second finesse, which makes a successful combination. The 1982 was the first serious vintage of Ca' del Pazzo. Each grape variety is vinified separately and then blended together in April for eight to twelve months of ageing in Limousin *barriques*, which are changed every three years. In May 1988 the 1985 vintage was still showing a lot of new wood on both nose and palate, but the 1982 had developed more complexity, with a herbal cedarwood quality and some smoky tobacco fruit.

As for white wine, Le Grance is a barrel-fermented Chardonnay, which stays in new or two-year-old Allier or Tronçais barrels until the following May. I tasted the 1987 vintage from the barrel, which had a good balance of oak and fruit, while the 1986 was full and buttery, but lacked acidity, even though the grapes had been picked at the end of August. They first planted Chardonnay in 1982, as they had become convinced that it was almost impossible to make a decent white wine from Trebbiano. They now have three and a half hectares of Chardonnay. Their objective is to create a white wine that will develop with age.

Altesino

Neighbouring Altesino is also the creation of a Milanese, one Giulio Consonno, who bought a ruined house here in 1970, with land but no vines. He now has sixteen hectares of vineyards, eleven at Altesino itself and five on Montosoli, on the hill opposite, as well as stables for eleven race horses. There are quite distinct differences between the two sites, so he, or rather his manager Antonio Cassisi makes two separate wines. Montosoli is higher at 390 metres and, with very stony chalky soils, the yields are low. The vineyards of Altesino lie between 250 and 300 metres and are less stony, with a mixture of clay and limestone so that there are higher yields. Each vineyard gives its particular character to the final wine. The first vintage at Altesino was in 1975, which, with the ageing requirements for Brunello, was not released until 1980.

In addition to some deliciously smoky Brunello di Montalcino, they make two alternative wines, Palazzo Altesi and Alte d'Altesi. Palazzo Altesi is pure Sangiovese, half of which is rather unexpectedly vinified by carbonic maceration, while the rest is fermented in the classic way. The two wines are blended afterwards and aged in *barriques* for between eight to twelve months, depending on the vintage. The 1980 was the first vintage. They had wanted to develop a new wine and were aiming for something with a Burgundian taste. The label even says 'sistema borgogna', but I was not convinced. The 1982 had hints of liquorice, with slightly rubbery overtones.

I suppose that those are characteristics of Burgundy, but there was not a whiff of the farmyards associated with Pinot Noir, nor for that matter the distinctive nose of carbonic maceration.

More successful was Alte d'Altesi, a blend of approximately 70 per cent Sangiovese and 30 per cent Cabernet Sauvignon – the exact proportions may vary from year to year – which are fermented together in the traditional way and aged in new *barriques* for about twelve to fifteen months. They have an insulated cellar for their barrels, which they call a *barricaia*. They do not age their Brunello in *barriques*, for they consider that it would no longer be Brunello di Montakino, but after two years in large casks of 130 hectolitres, the wine is usually transferred into smaller ones of thirty hectolitres.

Their Bianco di Montosoli is a blend of 90 per cent Trebbiano with 10 per cent overripe Malvasia, which is picked in the middle of October, when it has more flavour. The two grape varieties are blended together after fermentation and bottled in April for early drinking. To my tastebuds, almonds was the dominant flavour. At Altesino too, they are following the fashion for Chardonnay, grafting some on to Trebbiano vines. They are also experimenting with Moscadello Passito, from just half a hectare. The grapes are dried, fermented and will be aged in barrel, for at least three years they expect. So far no conclusions or tastings have been forthcoming, as 1985 was the first vintage, with just one small barrel.

But why so many different wines? They replied that they wanted more modern products, not just Brunello di Montalcino. They recognised that while the *barrique* was the modern fashion, it might not be the answer for the future. They wish to keep an open mind, in a spirit of innovation that promises well for the estate.

Case Basse

Gianfranco Soldera at Case Basse made his first wine at Montalcino in 1975. He is an insurance broker from Treviso in northern Italy. Back in 1972, he was looking for somewhere to plant vines. He had tried Piedmont and the Veneto, but neither was quite right. When he came to Montalcino, he fell in love with it. 'It was too beautiful'. He bought Case Basse in June 1972 and by November had planted a vineyard of six hectares. This was something that he particularly wanted to do himself, rather than buying one, to ensure that everything would be right. The soil is *galestro*, very poor and stony, and his land is at an altitude of about 300 metres, with a good aspect and microclimate. He has had to build a cellar too. It is small and neat, with Slavonic oak casks that were bought new for his first vintage.

He is probably the only producer of Brunello still to ferment his wine in cask, for he is convinced that good wine should be fermented in wood. He maintains that temperature control is not necessary; 'Nature is much better than me, while the others think they can do better than Nature. Man should not intervene in a natural process, as he will only make the wrong choice. If the grapes are healthy in the first place and Nature has done her job, the wine will be good'. Soldera believes in what he calls homoeopathic oenology and practises organic viticulture, with no anti-rot sprays, only Bordeaux mixture. Any fertiliser is made from horse manure. He uses natural yeast and runs the juice over the skins frequently, so that all the goodness is extracted.

We tasted our way through the casks in his cellar. In May 1988 the 1987, which had already been racked three times and had just finished its malolactic fermentation, was tannic with some firm fruit. The 1987 will be a fine vintage, as will the 1986, which had a nose of bitter cherries and was beginning to develop some good fruit. For Soldera the two most important things in a wine are elegance and harmony, which should be combined. The wine must be living in the mouth. 1984 was a more difficult year, but he was pleased with what he had achieved, a wine with a lightly smoky character on both nose and palate, with elegance and tannin, but quite lightweight. The 1985 will be a great year. It had an attractive smoky character and cedarwood on the palate, with structure,

length and balance. The 1983 had developed even more character, with tobacco overtones and some good fruit, with body and balance; this too will be a great year.

Val di Suga

Val di Suga is the property of Lionello Marchese, another newcomer to Montalcino. He also owns Trerose in Montepulciano and has recently bought San Leonino, a run-down estate in Chianti Classico near Castellina. He has a full-time occupation running factories that produce car accessories, such as seat belts and wing mirrors. Wine is a hobby and in his absence Val di Suga is run by Stefano Barzotte.

The estate was bought in 1985, three years after Trerose. There were already the rudiments of a cellar and some vineyards, including one of the oldest in Montalcino, planted in 1937. More vineyards have now been planted, with cuttings taken from their existing plants, and the cellar has been enlarged and modernised. The vineyards are in two different places, just outside Montalcino, facing north-east to north-west at 300 metres, and to the south of the town near Col d'Orcia, where the soil is decomposed schist. Here it is hotter and the vines face south-west, so that they have on average an hour and a half more sunshine a day. With such a variety within their vineyards, they can make a considerable selection of the grapes. Those from the warmer vineyard make wine suitable for ageing into mature Brunello, while those from the cooler place are more likely to be destined for Rosso di Montalcino. A third possibility, for grapes that are not good enough for either, is Quercianello, their *vino novello*, made by carbonic maceration.

In the cellar they are replacing cement vats with stainless steel ones and gradually renewing the old casks. They are also buying *barriques* of Vosges and Tronçais oak for the final ageing of their Brunello *riserva*, in which the wine will spend just four or five months. An insulated bottle store has been built too. The overall impression is one of competent efficiency, and the wine is well made. The

1985 Rosso di Montalcino had some young cherry fruit, with a touch of wood, while the 1982 Brunello had a smoky nose, with hints of cigar boxes and an attractive smoky flavour, with tannin and fruit. In 1988 it was still very youthful.

La Chiesa di Santa Restituta

Roberto Bellini came to Montalcino and La Chiesa di Santa Restituta in 1972, at a time when Brunello was really not very well known. There were few estates and these had tended to rest on the laurels of their former reputation. The tiny fifteenth-century church of Santa Restituta – she was a martyr in the third century, who suffered under the Roman persecutions – belonged to the bishopric of Siena and badly needed restoration; but the church was not prepared to spend the necessary money and preferred to sell the land. Roberto Bellini seized the opportunity. There were vines, but no specialised vineyards, so Bellini started from scratch, planting Sangiovese, as well as Trebbiano and Malvasia for white wine and Vin Santo.

The church remains plain and simple, with a beautiful peal of three bells. Opposite are the new cellars. Altogether Bellini has planted twelve hectares of Sangiovese and he rents five further hectares on a second farm, Brizio. His aim is not so much to increase the production of Brunello, as to give himself a greater choice of grapes, so that he can make more Rosso di Montalcino. There is an initial selection at the vintage, although both wines are vinified in the same way, spending fifteen days on the skins, and then a second selection six months later. The Rosso di Montalcino spends six months in wood and the Brunello usually four years. The *riserva* is chosen during the third year, from the best two or three casks, and bottled as such.

Bellini has also planted a little Cabernet Sauvignon, which is not yet in production. Experiments with *barriques* are for the moment confined to the white wine, Bianco del Vescovo. This is one of the few estates in Montalcino to produce Vin Santo, although it is really just a hobby, as it is very difficult indeed to make money from this wine. When the grapes are pressed, the result is more like pulp than juice and there should not be too many lees or too much *madre* in the barrel, just a little to start the fermentation. The flavour was delicious, an amber-coloured wine, tasting of orange marmalade and madeira cake, very rounded, with no sharp edges. We drank it with *recciarelli*, the Sienese almond biscuits.

Podere Colombaio di Montosoli

Podere Colombaio di Montosoli is the property of Signor Baricci, an elderly man, who told me how he had been born a wine-grower. He helped his father as a small boy and they lived on a farm that was part of a *mezzadria* until he was thirty-five. He explained how small the returns were. Half went to the landowner and half to the *contadini*. When the Italian government offered advantageous loans to encourage people to buy their own land, he came here in 1956. There were vines and olive trees mixed up together, and it was not until 1968 that he began planting specialised vineyards, of which he now has four hectares.

Baricci began bottling his wine in 1968, first as Rosso dai Vigneti di Brunello and then in 1971 as Brunello di Montalcino. His small neat cellar is equipped with cement vats and *botti*. He checks his fermentation temperatures, but if the wine gets too hot, he just opens the door and windows. Methods are pretty unsophisticated, but I thought that the two wines I tasted from the 1983 and 1985 vintages were delicious. The 1983 had a lovely smoky tobacco flavour, with some concentrated fruit. Baricci reckoned it would need at least another five years, before it was at all ready to drink. The 1985 had a similar concentration of flavour.

The Costanti

The Costanti are one of the old Montalcinese families, for they can trace their antecedents back to the fifteenth century. I talked to Andrea Costanti, although his uncle's name, Emilio, is on their label. They have five hectares of vines, quite close to the town of

Montalcino, from which they make not only Rosso and Brunello di Montalcino, but also a table wine, called Vermiglio, which is something of a family tradition. It comes from Sangiovese too, but spends three years in chestnut barrels, which give a stronger flavour to the wine than oak. I found the taste of the 1983 rather meaty and chewy, reminiscent of smoky bacon.

In common with all serious producers, Costanti carries out a strict selection of grapes at the harvest and follows the evolution of the wine very carefully. The fermentation usually takes between seven and ten days, and they may let the temperature rise as high as 35 °C. In hotter years, everything happens faster. We tasted from cask and bottle. The overall impression was one of immense elegance. A 1983 *riserva*, which will have spent five years in wood, was both concentrated and elegant, with good balance and fruit. A 1980 Brunello was quite closed on the nose, with excellent fruit on the palate and some oaky vanilla, while a 1981 *riserva*, bottled in March 1987, had vegetal hints on the nose. It was not as robust as the 1983, but my tasting notes include smoky, velvet and a little tannin, while Andrea Costanti talked of leather and what he called 'sotto bosco' or undergrowth.

Ironically the centenary celebrations could have taken place twenty-three years earlier, for the Costanti family have a record that Tito Costanti bottled some of the 1865 vintage for an exhibition in 1867. Sadly there are no bottles left. This was among the earlier estates to begin regular bottling, as long ago as the 1950s.

Azienda Agricoli Pertimali

I found Azienda Agricola Pertimali a kilometre or two outside Montalcino, at the bottom of a steep hill, leading down from the old city gate. Livio Sassetti is a friendly man, a talkative, ruddy faced farmer, full of old fashioned country wisdom and proverbs. We went into the tiny cellar under his house. 'At church and in a wine cellar one talks quietly'. There were large hams and salamis hanging from the beams. It was all very simple and

traditional. Sassetti explained that he let his wine ferment for about eight to ten days and that he cooled the juice by regular *remontagi*, passing the juice over the cap of skins, before the wine spent the prerequisite period in wood. There is no fining or filtration. Philosophically he observed, 'wine is made in the vineyard; in the cellar it is kept.'

He is one of the very few to make traditional Moscadello, for he has half a hectare of Moscato vines, as well as three and a half of Sangiovese. The Moscato grapes ripen early, but should be picked late, when they are very sweet. The fermentation is stopped in the traditional way, by running the juice through a muslin bag, five times to remove the remaining yeast. On tasting, the flavour was not so much sweet, as deliciously grapy. His Brunello had an attractive blackcurrant flavour, with smoky undertones and masses of tannin, a meaty wine, with considerable ageing potential. We concluded with a taste of honey liqueur, made according to a secret family recipe. It was pure liquid honey and quite delicious.

Poggio Antico

Poggio Antico is one of the new estates in Montalcino. The manager Signor Albanese pointed to the vineyards outside the cellars and explained that twenty years ago this had been a field of sheep. The change reflected the boom in Brunello di Montalcino, when the traditional estates created a reputation for the wine, which attracted investment from elsewhere. At Poggio Antico they do not want to make a wine that is unapproachable and this is also part of the new trend in Montalcino. Previously Brunello had the cachet of a collector's item that no one could afford to drink. The old fashioned Brunello was also made with higher fermentation temperatures, which resulted in harder wines with more body and alcohol, needing a long period of ageing. At Poggio Antico they would like it to be more easily available, even if it remains a wine for a special occasion. They would also like it to be ready to drink earlier; for it to have reached its plateau after four years in wood and twelve months in bottle. Of course once on that plateau, it should not fall away quickly; on the contrary.

There are modern efficient cellars, with fermentation tanks outside, so that they can run water over them for cooling if necessary. Fermentation may last as long as twenty to twenty-five days for Brunello, compared to twelve or thirteen days for Rosso di Montalcino. Ripe, healthy grapes are essential. Then Brunello is not difficult to make. It is high up here – *poggio* means a hill – at 450 to 500 metres, so there are no problems with humidity. Altogether they have twenty hectares all planted with Sangiovese Grosso. They also make a *vino da tavola* called Altero, from Sangiovese, but this spends less time in wood. As they pointed out, the French *appellation* regulations rarely stipulate a minimum length of time in wood and they believe that the minimum of three and a half years for Brunello can be too long. Therefore they have conducted an experiment with the 1983 vintage, ageing some wine for just two years in the same casks that they use for Brunello, after which the wine is kept in vat for twelve to eighteen months before bottling. The wine is regularly racked, two or three times a year during the first couple of years and once in the third year, when there are fewer lees. On tasting Altero seemed more ready than the Brunello, as there was less tannin from the wood in the wine. The 1983 vintage was very smooth and velvety, but with a good structure and some lovely fruit. The 1981 Brunello had hints of cedarwood, with some elegance, while the 1979 was drinking deliciously, with a slightly smoky nose, a good balance of tannin on the palate and a long finish.

Castelgiocondo

The estate of Castelgiocondo is one of the oldest in Montalcino, for it belonged to the Angelini family, who were among the growers to present their wine at the 1933 Mostra di Vini Tipici Senesi. It now belongs to a Milanese financial group MITEL and is managed for them by the Frescobaldi family. The seventeenth-century villa had been abandoned and they bought barren land in 1974 to plant vineyards. It required bulldozers and dynamite, so the cost of preparing the soil was considerable. The vines are trained for mechanisation, with the *cordone speronata* system. There was a large mechanical harvester in the courtyard when I arrived, but apparently it is only used after they have hand picked the best grapes.

They now have a total of 220 hectares of vines, including 160 for Brunello di Montalcino, which makes them the largest producer, and twenty-three hectares for Chianti Colli Senesi. The rest is planted with Cabernet Sauvignon and Sauvignon for Predicato wines or *vini da tavola*. The Sauvignon was unexpected, in this hot climate. The manager, Signor Cosci, who has supervised the estate from the beginning, explained that the vineyard, on the top of a hill, was particularly suitable, for the soil was very dry and sandy, with a different microclimate from their Brunello vineyards.

A new modern cellar, or rather warehouse, has been built, equipped with stainless steel fermentation vats and 8,000 hectolitres of casks from Conegliano. It is all very streamlined and efficient. Cosci explained that they vinify their Rosso di Montalcino and their Brunello in the same way, seeing how the different vats develop. Thus they can change their mind after the initial decision. They do not bother with *riserva* wines, as they do not consider that an extra year's ageing in wood contributes anything worthwhile. We tasted the 1982 Castelgiocondo, which had a vegetal nose, reminiscent of Merlot and was quite soft and drinking very well in 1988. The Cabernet Sauvignon goes into a wine called Giardinello, a *vino da tavola* with 10 per cent Cabernet blended with Sangiovese, all aged for eighteen months in *barriques*. It was soft and chewy, with a little tannin. The 1986 Vergena, called after a vineyard, is a Predicato del Selvante and had a few months in oak, so that it was full and rounded, but with little obvious varietal character of Sauvignon. It was what the Americans might call a Fumé Blanc style, but not a Sauvignon. They consider that the Sauvignon here gives 'fabulous results'. I have to admit that I was less convinced.

Camigliano

Camigliano is a pretty little hamlet. Its origins are Roman and the church dates back to the fourteenth century. At the beginning of this century there were 350 inhabitants. Today there are barely thirty, such is the rural depopulation following the end of the share-cropping system. The 900-hectare estate is owned by the Gezzi family from Milan and managed for them by Corrado Pecchiari, who comes from Alba, in the heart of Barolo. They have forty-seven hectares of Brunello, with plans to plant another twenty-eight, and just three hectares of Trebbiano and Malvasia. There are also cows and olive trees and large expanses of woodland. We went on an exceedingly bumpy ride through the vineyards, during which Signor Pecchiari explained that their vines were trained in the *guyot* system, which is unusual for Montalcino. The vineyards here are at 180 to 300 metres, which is lower than in other parts of the region, and the soil is very red with a high proportion of clay.

They have a large cellar of oak barrels. There is just one of chestnut, a reminder that fifty years ago all Brunello was aged in chestnut. This changed when it was realised that oak gives a better flavour; chestnut is too tannic. Vinification methods seemed traditional, and the taste of the Brunello was quite austere. Even the Rosso di Montalcino was quite firm and solid. However they have abandoned tradition to experiment with *barriques*. A wine that would otherwise be Rosso di Montalcino spends seven months in new wood and is sold under the vineyard name Vigna di Fontevecchio. The oak was quite obvious in the flavour, with some firm fruit. Pecchiari explained that because it had been *barricato*, it would command a price nearly twice as high as ordinary Rosso di Montalcino, without costing anywhere near double to produce. Such is the marketing power of the *barrique*.

Il Poggione and Talenti

Il Poggione, in the village of Sant'Angelo in Colle, is one of the oldest estates, belonging to the Franceschi brothers, Roberto and Clemente, in whose family the estate has been for over a century. Originally it was part of a larger estate called Sant'Angelo, but some years ago this was divided into Il Poggione, after the nearby hill, and Col d'Orcia. The property is run for the brothers by the very competent and likeable Piero Talenti, who also has his own tiny Brunello estate, just outside the village, called Talenti Podere Pian di Conte.

Il Poggione is one of the larger estates of Montalcino, with eighty hectares of vines. They also rent the Azienda Agricola Casello, but make and bottle the two wines separately. There is nothing exceptional about their vinification methods. They usually go through the vineyards twice at harvest time, choosing the best grapes for Brunello. In addition to red wine, they produce Moscadello, a Bianco di Sant'Angelo from Malvasia, Trebbiano and a little Chardonnay, and Vin Santo. The fermentation of the red wine takes about ten days, at 27–28°C, with a couple of *remontagi* per day. They have heat exchangers to control the fermentation temperature and used to have smaller open vats, as well, which automatically remained cooler. Large closed vats will inevitably result in higher temperatures.

Talenti explained that he had been making Moscadello at Il Poggione since the mid-1960s, long before Banfi. It was his wine that provided the model for the DOC. Old vines of Moscato di Canelli, which is a more aromatic grape variety than simple Moscato Bianco, were found in Montalcino. The grapes are picked in mid-September, when they are quite golden in colour. The fermentation begins on the skins for twenty-four hours, in order to obtain the maximum flavour, and continues until there is 5° to 6° of alcohol. It is then stopped by chilling, so that the yeasts 'fall asleep'. The second fermentation takes place in a pressurised tank, to obtain two atmospheres of pressure in the wine, with an alcohol level of 7° to 8.5°. Moscadello is made three times a year, in December, April and June so that the wine is always very fresh. It tasted lightly grapy and quite deliciously refreshing. However it is an expensive procedure to keep unfermented must in this way.

We tasted our way through several vintages of both Il Poggione and Talenti, beginning with the Bianco di San Angelo, which is a blend of 50 per cent Trebbiano, with equal parts of Malvasia and Chardonnay. The Chardonnay was planted in about 1981 to give the wine a little more flavour. They wanted to improve it, but not to change the taste completely. The nose certainly had a hint of Chardonnay, with a dry nutty finish on the palate and the flatness typical of Trebbiano. As the Chardonnay ripens ten days earlier than the others, it is fermented separately and the two wines blended afterwards. There is no malolactic fermentation, nor any skin contact, as that would give too much flavour to the wine.

I liked Talenti's red wines enormously. The 1985 Il Poggione Rosso di Montalcino, which had spent six months in wood, had a rich nose, with good body and fruit. His own Rosso di Montalcino of the same vintage was more closed and youthful. He attributed the difference to altitude. His vineyards are at 350 metres, whereas those of Il Poggione lie between 150 and 300 metres; there can be quite a wide variation of altitude over 80 hectares of vines. Then we compared Brunellos. Again the 1983 Il Poggione was softer than the 1983 Talenti. It had a smoky nose and was less rigid in the mouth, with softer fruit; the Talenti wine was meatier, with herbal overtones, good fruit and a firm finish. We concluded with a 1969, which was by no means a great vintage, just an average year, but it proved a magnificent demonstration of how well Brunello di Montalcino can develop in bottle. It was long and elegant, with flavours of cedarwood and a herbal quality on the finish. A wine like this justifies the reputation of Brunello di Montalcino.

Lisini

Lisini is another old estate, the property of a Sienese family of the same name. Until the 1950s, the production of olive oil was more important than wine. The estate is close to the village of Sant'Angelo in Colle and across

the valley you can see an attractive cluster of houses and the old church tower. The vineyards have developed from just five hectares in 1963 to eighteen in 1988, of which however only ten are specialised. They are gradually transforming the old *promiscua* vineyards and still have some pre-phylloxera vines, seventy or eighty years old, the wine from which is vinified separately as an experiment. The cellars at Lisini are very simple and quite old fashioned.

We compared the 1982 and 1981 vintages of Brunello. In May 1988 the 1982 had some herbal, cedarwood qualities and was still very tannic, although it promised well. The 1981, a lighter year, was more meaty on the nose, but with the same herbal character on the palate. It was more mature and less tannic, so that the style of Lisini seemed to me to be a successful combination of tannin and elegance.

Il Greppone

The estate of Il Greppone belongs to the Socini family, who have rented it for fifteen years to Ruffino, one of the largest wine producers in Tuscany. They will have the option of buying the estate in 1999. Ruffino, as has already been mentioned (see p. 97), are a major producer in Chianti and wanted to expand their interests. They were attracted by the prestige attached to Brunello di Montalcino and now they are applying their technical competence to it.

Il Greppone adjoins the Biondi Santi estate of Il Greppo and is also close to the Fattoria dei Barbi. There is an old villa, with an attractive courtyard, filled with lemon trees in terracotta pots. They have eight hectares of vines surrounding the villa, on poor stony soil. The cellars are small. As well as large casks, they have some experimental *barriques*. These were first used in 1984, but the vintage was poor and the 1985 was a more serious test.

We compared the two wines, from *barriques* and *botti*. The *barrique*-aged Montalcino seemed softer and more rounded, with some hints of vanilla, while, as you would expect, there was a less obvious taste of wood in the wine from *botti*. The type of wood is also important, for you would not obtain the same results from a *barrique* made of Slavonic oak. They consider that Brunello has the right structure to withstand ageing in such small wood casks, but it remains to be seen whether it is really appropriate to the wine.

They do not make a Rosso di Montalcino, but prefer to produce a *vino novello*, which was made for the first time in 1987. Their vinification methods are rational, with a fifteen-day period on the skins, depending of course on the vintage. The temperature is never allowed to exceed 32°C. The picking time is important. They begin taking samples from the grapes in mid-August, but do not usually pick until mid-October and then only in the morning, beginning after the nocturnal humidity has evaporated and stopping as soon as the grapes become too hot. Their 1985 Brunello seemed to have good potential. The nose was young and closed, reminiscent of soft red fruit, and on the palate there was good structure and balance.

Fattoria dei Barbi

Fattoria dei Barbi is another of the old Montalcino estates. It first belonged to the Tamante and Padelletti families, who came to Montalcino some 400 years ago. Now it is the property of the Colombini, who arrived in Montalcino in the 1550s with the Medici troops. Sometime about 1850 two Colombini brothers married the Padelletti and Tamante daughters. Today the head of the family is Signora Francesca Colombini. Her two children, Donatella Cinelli and Stefano Colombini share in the running of the estate. In fact there are two estates, Fattoria dei Barbi near Montalcino and Fattoria del Casato, near Altesino, totalling thirty-four hectares in all, under only one label. The two estates produce quite different styles of wines, which complement each other in the final blend. At Barbi the wine is firm and requires a long period of ageing, while that from Casato is fuller and matures faster.

Fattoria dei Barbi is a traditional Tuscan estate, for not only do they make wine, but they also have olive trees, pasture for sheep

(providing milk for *pecorino* cheese), fields for wheat and large expanses of woodland. They rear pigs for salami and ham. So as well as visiting the cellars and tasting their wines, I saw ham being smoked, salamis being made and *pecorino* cheeses in various stages of maturity. All this home produce can be tasted at the cheerful restaurant which is attached to the farm.

There is a series of small cellars, rather like a rabbit warren, containing numerous old barrels and even a billiard-table in one room. Donatella Cinelli explained that the particular variety of Brunello on their estate was called Brunellino, which gives very small grapes, as the name implies, smaller than those of Sangiovese Grosso or Brunello. In the past every estate renewed its vineyards by taking cuttings from its own vines. Then at one point it became easier to buy plants from nurseries. Now there is a reaction against this and growers again prefer to take cuttings from their own vines.

As well as traditional Brunello di Montalcino, an alternative wine is made, called Brusco dei Barbi. Unlike most alternative wines, this was not created in the last five years, but rather was first made by Donatella's grandfather, Giovanni Colombini. It is made mainly from Sangiovese Grosso, with some Canaiolo and Trebbiano. The fermentation takes longer than for Brunello and in November they add some *governato* grapes, so that the wine remains in a closed vat until Christmas. It is then put into wood for six months. The object is a rustic wine to go with rustic food, a rugged wine for the rugged countryside. I tasted the 1985 and 1986 vintages, which could be described as substantial and full-flavoured, with spicy liquorice overtones and rich fruit.

I was also given a selection of classic Brunello di Montalcino to taste. Some were good, while some I found slightly clumsy and austere. The 1983 was elegant, while the 1982 was richer and meatier. Very good was their *riserva* wine, labelled Vigna del Fiore after a vineyard that was first planted in 1592. The 1982 Vigna del Fiore was more elegant than the Brunello of the same vintage. The 1981 had overtones of vanilla on nose and palate, and was long and dry on the finish. Best of all was the 1975 Brunello, with an elegant herbal nose and a similar herbal quality on the palate.

Col d'Orcia and Argiano

The two estates of Col d'Orcia and Argiano were until recently run by Dott. Enzio Tiezzi, president of the growers' association, for the large drinks company Cinzano. They bought Col d'Orcia in 1973 and Argiano in 1980, another example of an outsider taking interest in a prestigious wine. Col d'Orcia was originally the property of the Franceschi brothers. There are now seventy hectares of vines on the estate, roughly fifty of Brunello and twenty of Chianti Colli Senesi. They make some Moscadello, which was called Moscadello della Toscana before it became DOC, and also a *vino novello*, made partially by carbonic maceration, called Novembrino, appropriately, as it is released in November. The Chianti is not very important, as Brunello is very much more remunerative. Everything at Col d'Orcia is rather rustic, as though Cinzano have not yet put much into their investment. Apparently they are concentrating on the vineyards first.

Argiano is an attractive sixteenth-century villa, approached along an alley of cypresses. It was designed by a Sienese architect, who also built in Siena and in Rome. There is jasmine in the courtyard and the cellars have wonderful vaulted ceilings, with arches in soft red brick. Again the equipment is rather unsophisticated. We tasted wines from different vats and the flavours were good. The wines of Argiano, where the vineyards are on a high plain, tend to be a little tougher than those of Col d'Orcia, where the vineyards are more varied in altitude and the wines more rounded, with more body. Best of all was the 1981 Col d'Orcia with a lovely, rounded fruity nose and on the palate, a lovely lingering finish.

Fattoria Il Paradiso

A chance bottle in a restaurant in Siena led me to Fattoria Il Paradiso, where Florio Guerrieri makes some of the best Brunello di Montalcino that I have tasted. There was a friendly welcome, not only from Florio, but also from his wife Rosella, from her mother whose family property this is – her husband Manfredi Martini planted the vines twenty years ago – and their four-year-old daughter Gioia, who helped with the tasting. They have just one hectare of vines, in two plots close to their house, just outside Montalcino. It is a lovely spot that deserves its name, especially in the peaceful evening sunshine. Guerrieri keeps an impeccable cellar underneath the house. He is a school bursar by profession, but wine is his passion. He pays meticulous attention to every detail. In his spotless cellar there is just one cask for each vintage, for he produces only eighty quintals of grapes a year, controlling the quantity very strictly, cutting off any excess bunches after the flowering. Anything that is not up to scratch becomes Rosso di Montalcino and he still sells spare wine to friends and neighbours. Guerrieri explained that the casks represented a considerable investment. At six million lire a piece, they cost the *lire di Dio*, but he still wants to renew them regularly. His wines have fruit, elegance and balance, with a harmony of flavours of cedarwood and blackcurrants. His first bottling was in 1986, of the 1981 vintage, which was the wine I drank at his cousin's restaurant in Siena. It was elegant but rich, with balanced acidity and tannin, all in all a very impressive bottle. This will be an estate to watch for the future.

Biondi Santi

Finally let us return to Biondi Santi, the estate that started it all. In November 1988, 60 per cent was bought by a Sienese lawyer Calogero Cali, who also owns the estate of Rocca di Castagnoli in Chianti Classico. Franco Biondi Santi, who retains the other 40 per cent and is the present incumbent of Il Greppo is elegant, charming and distinguished. He explained that they now have eleven hectares of vines, half at Il Greppo close to the town of Montalcino and half on the north-east side of the town. We walked round the cellars, which have remained somewhat old fashioned. They bought cooling equipment as recently as 1983. They make two styles of Brunello, what they call Brunello *annata* from ten to twenty-five-year-old vines, and a *riserva* from vines that are more than twenty-five years old. A couple of small plots of vines are as much as fifty years old. The vinification process is the same for both wines; the difference lies in the age of the grapes. They now make a Rosso di Montalcino, replacing the former Rosso dai Vigneti di Brunello. The name Il Greppo means a small, but steep hill and describes the terrain. The soil here is *galestro* and limestone. The vineyards are at an altitude of 550 metres, where average temperatures are cooler than lower down, so that the grapes are slower to ripen, making a wine with more structure.

Biondi Santi Brunello *annata* will last fifteen to twenty-five years, while a *riserva* may live for fifty. The great vintages have been 1888, 1891, 1925, 1945, 1955, 1964 and 1975.

Maybe 1985 and 1988 will come into that category too. I was privileged to drink the 1955 at the centenary celebrations and it was undoubtedly one of the best glasses of red wine that I have ever tasted, a wine with a wonderful depth of complexity, smoky overtones and hints of cedarwood, all in balance, and a flavour that seemed to go on for ever. However I must admit to reservations about some of the more recent vintages. On the same occasion, the 1981 and 1982 were infinitely less exciting and I could not see them having such a long life. When I asked Dott. Biondi Santi why his Brunello was the most expensive of all, he replied quite simply, 'because it is the best'. That may well have been so thirty years ago, but I am not sure that this is still the case. However there is no doubt that without the Biondi Santi family, Brunello di Montalcino would not be the fine wine that we know today, meriting a place amongst the great red wines of the world.

*The Piazza Grande
in Montepulciano
with the Palazzo
Comunale.*

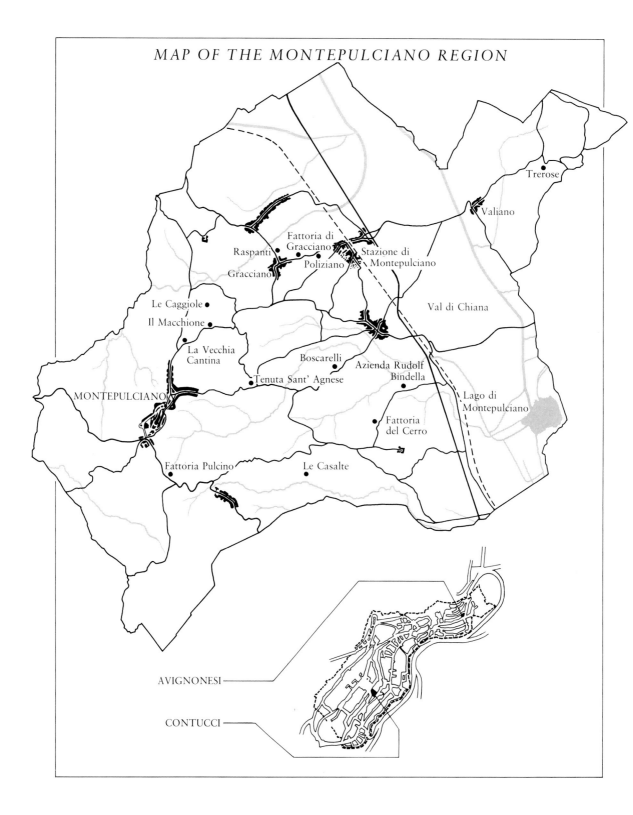

MAP OF THE MONTEPULCIANO REGION

Trerose

Valiano

Fattoria di
Gracciano

Raspanti

Gracciano

Poliziano

Stazione di
Montepulciano

Val di Chiana

Le Caggiole

Il Macchione

La Vecchia
Cantina

Boscarelli

Azienda Rudolf
Bindella

MONTEPULCIANO

Tenuta Sant' Agnese

Lago di
Montepulciano

Fattoria
del Cerro

Fattoria Pulcino

Le Casalte

AVIGNONESI

CONTUCCI

Vino Nobile di Montepulciano

The first question to answer is: 'why noble?' Montepulciano can produce fine wine, but without the individuality of Montalcino, for the grape varieties are virtually identical to those of Chianti. Cynics might therefore say that it is nothing more than a superior Chianti; or worse still, an inferior one, for Montepulciano has certainly not always produced wines to justify its epithet. Happily however, there have been improvements in recent years, with an influx of new producers.

Two hypotheses have been put forward to explain the name, both quite simple and applicable to virtually any other wine with any reputation. One is that the vineyards belonged to noble families, who selected the best grapes for their wines. The other is that this was the wine drunk by the nobility. According to Emanuele Pellucci, the first written reference to the 'nobility' of the wines of Montepulciano comes in a note written by one Giovan Filippo Neri as recently as the middle of the eighteenth century, in which he describes wine bought from Monte Pulciano, as *vino nobile*. However the word is used as a description, not as a name. Perhaps Francesco Redi should take some of the responsibility, for as publicity brochures about the wines of Montepulciano never cease to explain, it was he who described Montepulciano in his poem of 1685 as 'the king of all wines' – 'Montepulciano d'ogni vino è rè'.

The oldest labels say simply Rosso Scelto di Montepulciano. It was Adamo Fanetti, the father of the present owner of the estate of Sant'Agnese, who first used the word *nobile* on the label, after the success of his wine at the Siena wine fair of 1933; where he shared a stand with his friend Tancredi Biondi Santi. He should probably take more credit than anyone for the modern reputation of Vino Nobile di Montepulciano. His success at Siena encouraged other producers to participate in a second fair a couple of years later and in 1937 his Vino Nobile won a gold medal in Paris.

Winemaking in Montepulciano goes back at least 1,200 years. The earliest document providing written evidence of vineyards records a donation of land to the church in 789 AD, including a vineyard at 'castello pulciani' on a hill known as Mons Pulciano. Other documents, with mentions of vineyards as gifts or sales, date from the early ninth century.

The reputation of Montepulciano flourished during the Middle Ages. In 1350 one Bertoldo di Guglielmo del Pecora made a trading agreement to sell his wines to a certain Jacopo da Santa Fiora. Sante Lancerio, who had been the wine steward to Pope Paul III, recorded the pontiff's oenological likes and dislikes in wine in a book entitled *Della Natura dei Vini e dei Viaggi di Papa Paolo III* (1549). He says: 'The wine of Montepulciano is absolutely perfect, as much in winter as in summer. Such wines as these have aroma, colour and flavour and His Holiness drinks them gladly, not so much in Rome where they were delivered in *fiaschi*, but more so in Perugia.'

In 1596 Andrea Bacci, a professor of botany in Rome and doctor to Pope Sextus V, published a detailed study of the vineyards of Italy. He mentions the wines of Montepulciano, both red and white, as being among the most famous in Tuscany, perfumed but always vigorous. The poet Gabriello Chiabrera claims in his *Vendemmie di Parnaso* (1561) that Montepulciano reigns over all and we have already encountered Francesco Redi, extolling the virtues of Montepulciano as the best wine of Tuscany. Montepulciano appears as a red wine on a wine list printed in Naples in 1634 and in 1689 it was sent, along with Moscadello from Montalcino, to the court of William III of England. Describing his Grand Tour, Boswell recalls that he regaled himself in Siena with delicious Montepulciano. When Henry Vizetelly described the wines of Tuscany at the International Exhibition of Vienna in 1873, however, it seems that the single sample of Montepulciano at the Exhibition was not up to scratch.

The town of Montepulciano dominates the skyline from the vineyards, which are on the surrounding hillsides (see colour illustration opposite p. 157). It is a rather sombre place. You climb the main street, past the Palazzo Avignonesi and the Palazzo Contucci, to the Piazza Grande, the square at the top of the hill, where stand the cathedral and the town hall, both dating back to the sixteenth century. Montepulciano's most famous son was the poet Angelo Ambrogini, otherwise known as Il Poliziano. He was born here in 1454 and his birthplace still stands. While tutor to the sons of Lorenzo the Magnificent, he wrote the *Canzoni a Ballo*, the *Rispetti* and the *Stanze* and then later in Mantua, *Orfeo*, which is one of the first stage representations of a secular subject in Italian literature. The inhabitants of Montepulciano are to this day called *poliziani* in his memory. The other landmark of Montepulciano is the church of San Biagio, which stands outside the walls. This simple edifice with its elegant dome, built during the fifteenth century, is a work of the architect Antonio da Sangallo, the Elder.

Vino Nobile di Montepulciano was recognised as a DOC in 1966. The regulations defined the vineyard area, grape varieties and methods of production. As mentioned above, the varieties are in fact little different from those for Chianti. Sangiovese is the dominant grape, but in Montepulciano it is called Prugnolo Gentile. As in Chianti, the complementary grape varieties are Canaiolo Nero, Trebbiano Toscano, Malvasia del Chianti and Mammolo. One that does not feature at all in the regulations for Chianti is Pulcinculo, a local name for Grechetto, a white grape variety that is more common in Umbria. The area of production is limited to the *commune* or parish of Montepulciano, excluding the flat valley of the Val di Chiana, which is fertile land for grazing cattle.

As for ageing requirements, the DOC regulations stipulated two years in wood from the first of January following the vintage, while three years of ageing, not necessarily in wood, made a *riserva*, and four years a *riserva speciale*; but that is rarely found. In 1980 elevation to DOCG status brought certain changes and a general tightening of production methods, so that for instance all Vino Nobile grapes must now be vinified and the wine aged, but not necessarily bottled, within the area of production. The permitted yield was reduced from 100 to 80 quintals of grapes per hectare and the minimum alcohol level was increased from 12° to 12.5°. It was no longer possible to correct deficient Vino Nobile with wine or must from elsewhere.

Further improvements were made to the DOCG regulations in 1989, reducing yet further the percentage of white grapes. This now stands at a maximum of 10 per cent, with no minimum, so that several producers include no white grapes at all in their wine. The difference was made up with a greater proportion of Prugnolo Gentile, now set at 60 to 80 per cent, which is the grape variety that gives Vino Nobile its particular character. This is the clone of Sangiovese typical of Montepulciano, in the same way that Brunello is typical of Montalcino. It was apparently identified at the end of the sixteenth century. It has small cylindrical bunches of little grapes, which look rather like tiny plums, hence its name; whereas Brunello is fatter. The Prugnolo gives the wine both body and tannin, good structure, elegance and intensity of flavour. It is also tough and resistant to disease.

Although one can occasionally find Mammolo in Chianti, it is very much more characteristic of Montepulciano. The name means violets, from the aroma it gives to a wine. However it ripens with difficulty, so that it should be picked last. Opinions differ as to its merits. Some growers have given up using it altogether, while others are now replanting it again. Giuseppe Fanetti describes it as the worst grape of all, criticising it for giving very low alcohol levels and saying that it does not contribute anything. He considers that the more grape varieties there are, the better the wine is. For some reason he even has a drop of Gamay in his Vino Nobile, as well as some Ciliegiolo and Malvasia Nera. Although these grape varieties are not specifically mentioned in the DOCG regulations, they are included in the 10 per cent of complementary grape varieties; as would be Cabernet Sauvignon, but so far everyone who grows it uses it for an alternative wine. The customary complement to Sangiovese, Canaiolo can be a little erratic in its yields, as it is sensitive to parasites, but it adds finesse.

The introduction of the DOCG for Vino Nobile di Montepulciano has opened the way for a parallel DOC, as in Montalcino, namely Rosso di Montepulciano, for wines which are not suitable for two years' ageing in wood. The grape varieties are identical and the wine can be sold in the April following the harvest, with effect from the 1989 vintage. Several producers of Vino Nobile also have vineyards of Chianti Colli Senesi, as there is an overlap between the two regions. The white wine of the area is Bianco Vergine Valdichiana, discussed on p. 176.

The soil of Montepulciano is quite varied, with differing proportions of clay and sand. There is some chalk too in the south-west corner of the parish, but few vines grow there. On the alluvial plain of the Chiana valley there are other crops, tobacco, sunflowers and wheat. The vineyards are on the hills, at a permitted altitude of between 250 and 600 metres, though not often over 500 metres. Winters are mild, although it snows occasionally. Spring comes early and during the summer it rains rarely. However it is not too hot and stays warm until October or November bring the autumn. Most rain falls during February and March, or after the vintage at the end of October and in November. In other words it is a very propitious climate for growing grapes.

There is no doubt that the DOC, followed by the DOCG, has given a considerable boost to wine production in Montepulciano. Old established producers are improving their wines and new investment has come from outside, all giving a positive momentum to a wine whose reputation was somewhat tarnished. In 1988 there were 722 hectares of vines in production, cultivated by 190 growers, of whom 36 actually bottled their own wine. Of the others, 114 were members of the cooperative and the rest tiny growers, making wine for family and friends, or selling their grapes to other producers. As Appendix III shows, the area of production of Vino Nobile has gently increased over the last few years.

The Contucci

While the DOCG regulations lay down the broad outline for the production methods of Vino Nobile di Montepulciano, the details vary from grower to grower. Some are experimental in their outlook; others are more conservative. The epitome of the traditional must be the house of Contucci, which is now run by Alamanno Contucci, a cheerful chubby-faced man with a bushy moustache. He is president of the growers' association and comes from an old Montepulciano family, which can trace its origins back to the early twelfth century at least. The Palazzo Contucci was built in 1520 and has belonged to the family since the end of the seventeenth century. Earlier it was the property of the family of Pope Julius III. The rabbit warren of cellars below was built in the thirteenth century and this is where the Contuccis keep

Alamanno Contucci.

their old casks for ageing the Vino Nobile. It is a picturesque showpiece, conforming to the tourist image of romantic wine cellars. More prosaic is their vinification plant outside the town.

They themselves say that methods are traditional. All the grapes are fermented together, as they ripen more or less at the same time, and the fermentation is controlled 'by Nature'. The blend is made up of 70 per cent Prugnolo, 15 per cent Canaiolo, 5 per cent Mammolo and 10 per cent of white grapes. They do not want to give up white grapes altogether. Since 1986 they have made a wine called Rosso di Sansovino, named after one of their ancestors from Montepulciano, a poet. It is made from Sangiovese that has spent twelve months in cask and tastes not unlike a young Chianti, with that fruity astringency characteristic of Sangiovese. Bianco della Contessa is a typical Tuscan white wine from Malvasia and Trebbiano. Contucci's wines are not the most exciting introduction to Vino Nobile, but apparently they have shown improvement in recent years.

The Avignonesi

In contrast are the Avignonesi. Although this is another old Montepulciano family, they have only recently begun to concentrate their energies on wine. The first bottling was of the 1978 vintage. The sixteenth-century Palazzo Avignonesi stands at the bottom of the main street; the cellars below were built in the fifteenth century, incorporating Etruscan remains. I sat in an elegant drawing-room, decorated with eighteenth-century frescos and talked to the two Falvo brothers, who run the company. Ettore Falvo married into the Avignonesi family and he makes the wine, while his brother Eduardo sells it. They have an international perspective, for they do not see the other producers of Vino Nobile as their competitors; rather their competitors are the producers of other fine red and white wines on the international market. They were among the first to plant French grape varieties in Montepulciano and have made a considerable investment in vineyards. They now have three estates, La Selva, near Cortona, outside the zone for Vino Nobile, and Il Poggetti and Le Capezzine, where they grow the prerequisite grape varieties for Vino Nobile. There are also three hectares of Cabernet Franc at Il Poggetti. At La Selva they grow mainly Chardonnay, as well as small quantities of Sauvignon, Merlot, Cabernet Sauvignon, Pinot Noir and Grechetto.

Besides the usual Vino Nobile di Montepulciano, Chianti Colli Senesi and Bianco Vergine Valdichiana, they make three more innovative wines, called Il Terre di Cortona, Il Marzocco and Grifi. With further experimental grape varieties coming into production, there will be others to follow. The first vintage of Merlot was only in 1988. Maybe they will blend it into Grifi, which is currently made of 85 per cent Prugnolo and 15 per cent Cabernet Franc; or perhaps it will go with the Cabernet Sauvignon, or even be vinified as a varietal wine. The Cabernet Sauvignon, which came into production in 1987, will probably be aged for one year in *barriques* and one or two years in *botti*, before being sold as a varietal wine. In any case each grape variety is vinified separately and blended as required, before ageing in wood.

Terre di Cortona and Il Marzocco are both pure Chardonnay. The first is fermented in stainless steel and does not touch a stave of oak, while in complete contrast Il Marzocco is both fermented and aged in oak. It takes its name from the lion on the coat of arms of Montepulciano, which is also to be seen on a column opposite the Palazzo Avignonesi. The juice is chilled to 3°C and left for a week so that it falls clear, after which the clean must is put in the *barriques* for fermentation. These are left at cellar temperature, while the juice gently ferments at about 16°C. Then after racking the wine spends a further six months in wood, on the fine lees, which are stirred up from time to time. The *barriques* are always new and always French, but of

different oaks. Il Marzocco is intended for some bottle age, with its smart presentation in a dark glass bottle. There are gentle overtones of oak and some rich, buttery Chardonnay fruit. In contrast Terre di Cortona has a more leafy flavour.

Grifi smells of wood and fruit, with lots of tannin, and is again a wine to age. The Avignonesi Vino Nobile has considerable substance, with a bouquet of leather and firm fruit in the mouth. In 1988 they reckoned that the 1983 needed another three years to reach its peak. They also make the most fabulous Vin Santo, red as well as white, which is unusual, in the smallest quantities. This not the kind in which to dunk your *biscotti di Prato*. It is quite the richest and smoothest Vin Santo I have ever tasted, with wonderfully concentrated flavours of apricots and orange peel.

Poliziano

Poliziano is another relative newcomer to winemaking in Montepulciano. Since 1981 the estate has been run by the friendly, hospitable Federico Carletti, whose father is a shareholder in the property. The first vines were planted in 1962 and the cellars built in 1970, but it was not until 1980 that they began to sell wine in bottle. They now have thirty hectares for Vino Nobile and a further fifty for Chianti on lower-lying land near the cellars at Montepulciano Stazione – the station at Montepulciano is a good five miles from the town itself – as well as a couple of hectares for the white wine Bianco Vergine Valdichiana.

In common with the Falvo brothers at Avignonesi, Federico Carletti at Poliziano has a questioning attitude towards the potential of his grape varieties and the limitations of the DOCG regulations. He does not use any white grapes for his Vino Nobile, but 90 per cent Prugnolo, 5 per cent Canaiolo and 5 per cent Mammolo. He makes wines to age, which will have what he calls 'a history in the bottle'. The old concrete vats have been replaced and there are now heat exchangers and refrigeration equipment. Rather than enormous 50-hectolitre casks, he considers that small ones of five or ten hectolitres are better for Sangiovese. He has also bought some new *barriques*, which he uses for his pure Sangiovese and also for Le Stanze, which is mainly Cabernet Sauvignon with just 5 per cent Cabernet Franc. The first vintage was 1987 and his Chardonnay came into production in 1988.

However it is on Sangiovese that he really concentrates his efforts. His alternative wine is called Elegia, continuing the poetic theme of the name of the estate, and is made from a selection of the best Sangiovese grapes. It spends twelve months in *barriques* of Limousin or Nevers oak and the taste is rich and concentrated, with a structure comparable to good Brunello. Vigna Asinone is a *cru*, the wine of the best vineyard on the estate, which has been aged in 500-litre barrels of Allier oak.

As for Chianti, he no longer bottles it himself, but sells the wine in bulk. Montepulciano has always had a good reputation for Chianti, but in the current commercial climate, there is little profit to be made from selling it in bottle, when a full bottle of wine makes only the price of an empty one. Carletti is an agronomist, so that working in the vineyard and cellar is his enthusiasm, rather than commercial considerations. He has reservations about DOCG, but thought that in the long run it should improve the image of Vino Nobile and motivate the producer.

Fattoria di Gracciano

Dott. Franco Mazzucchelli, aged eighty-three, at the Fattoria di Gracciano is one of the characters of the region. His mother was Scottish and he has a cousin with the good Scottish name of Jock Stuart. He regaled me with stories about his experiences as a prisoner of war in Kenya and of a lifetime spent growing bananas in Somaliland. He came back to Montepulciano twenty years ago, when he inherited this estate from his aunt. I do not think that much has changed since. We wandered round the cellars, followed by a shaggy poodle and a black cat, while Dott. Mazzucchelli affirmed that 'we are traditional here, not industrial'. They

were certainly unsophisticated cellars, with a muddle of cement vats and old casks.

He has seventeen hectares of vines, six of Vino Nobile. From the rest he makes Chianti and some basic table wine. We tasted three vintages of his Vino Nobile, unfortunately in a room where the furniture had just been polished, but despite the smell of wax, the 1983 came through as a rich rounded mouthful of flavour, with tannin and raspberries.

Trerose

Trerose is under the same ownership as Val di Suga in Montalcino. Here one is right on the edge of the vineyard area of Vino Nobile, near Valiano and almost into Umbria. Everything is brand new and this certainly ranks among the more experimental estates of Montepulciano. The 1985 was the first vintage. Adjoining the modern cellars is a sombre yellow-ochre villa, built in the fifteenth century, when it belonged to the Cardinal Paserini. It is surrounded by tall cypress trees and the old cellars, with their wide arches, are used for storing *barriques*. They make a striking contrast to the modern vinification plant.

Altogether they have twenty-nine hectares of Prugnolo, with a little Trebbiano, Malvasia, Canaiolo and Mammolo for Vino Nobile. All the grape varieties are fermented together for eight to ten days. They also have a little Chardonnay, which is not yet in production; so that for their white wine, they are currently buying Chardonnay grapes from Friuli and blending them with 80 per cent Trebbiano. The wine is labelled Furfantino. In Tuscany, a *furfano* is someone who stirs things up. Both grape varieties are fermented together and the wine tastes more of Trebbiano, with a slightly bitter finish on the palate, although it has the buttery character of Chardonnay on the nose.

They have also planted some Sauvignon and, under the guidance of their oenologist Vittorio Fiore, are making a wine from Sauvignon, Trebbiano and Malvasia that has spent eight months in small barrels. It is quite experimental, the precise method of production remaining Fiore's closely guarded secret. I liked it with its full rich flavour. There was some oak influence, but not too much. It is called Saltero. What they call their 'Sauternes experiment' is made from Malvasia and Trebbiano grapes, left to dry in the vineyards and then fermented and kept in *barriques* for eighteen months. It is a dessert wine to match Vin Santo, and smelt and tasted of marmalade, rich, orangy and unctuous.

As for their Vino Nobile, the 1985 *normale* had some good blackberry fruit with tannin, elegance and length. The 1985 *riserva* had spent between six and twelve months in *barriques*. There was a rich nose of black-berries, with the firm flavour of new wood, balanced with some good fruit. Both wines will have a long life.

Fattoria del Cerro

The Saiagricola, at the Fattoria del Cerro, with its second label Baiocchi, named after an earlier owner of the estate, is one of the largest producers of Vino Nobile. Altogether they have 120 hectares of vineyards, which were planted about 1970, fifty-seven of Vino Nobile, forty-six of Chianti and the rest for white wine. Saiagricola is an insurance company that has invested in land, with other farms in Umbria and near Pisa. As well as vines they grow soya, sunflowers and wheat on the flat, fertile land of the Val di Chiana.

The new cellars were ready for the vintage of 1987. No expense has been spared here and they say that they have spent billions of lire. There are sparkling stainless steel vats and an enormous insulated cellar of *botti*. Some *barriques* have been ordered too, though probably not for Vino Nobile. Some grafted Chardonnay and Cabernet Sauvignon came into production in 1989, for which the *barriques* are particularly destined.

This is also the only estate in Montepulci-ano to use a mechanical harvester. They believe that it works well with Sangiovese. They can regulate how hard the machine shakes the vines, so that the unripe fruit remain. In the cellar stainless steel vats with glycol blankets are used for computer-con-trolled fermentations, which last about twelve

to fifteen days, with regular *remontagi* for Vino Nobile. The malolactic fermentation takes place after racking into yet more stain-less steel vats, so that they put absolutely clean wine into *botti*, which are in turn racked at least twice a year. A gentle filtration with albumen before bottling removes any harsh tannins. In May 1988 I found the 1985 Vino Nobile to be still rather tough.

Their Bianco Toscano is made chiefly from Trebbiano, which in 1987 as an experiment, was given twenty-four hours of skin contact, before fermentation at a cool temperature. The taste was of bitter almonds on both nose and palate, with some acidity and substance and a gentle fragrance. Their Chianti is made from ordinary Sangiovese, not Prugnolo. It spends eight months in *botti* and has hints of raspberry, with the astringency typical of young Chianti.

Azienda Rudolf Bindella

The Azienda Rudolf Bindella is a company of Swiss origin, with its first vintage as recently as 1985. In Switzerland Bindella is known as a major wine importer and also owns vineyards there. However the company wanted vineyards in Italy too and thought that Vino Nobile was not as well known as it deserved to be. They have been helped by Pablo Härri, the Swiss oenologist from Banfi. They intend to concentrate on Vino Nobile, with no Chianti or white wine, but they cannot resist making an alternative wine, called Vallocaia, after a farm on the estate. It is made only in the best years and based on old Prugnolo vines that were planted in 1953. From these they obtain a very low yield indeed, just 40 quintales of grapes from two hectares. Vallocaia is aged in *barriques* for a few months. They are also trying *barriques* for a Vino Nobile *riserva*.

The Bindella Vino Nobile comes from 85 per cent Prugnolo, 10 per cent Canaiolo and just 1 per cent of Mammolo. The rest is Trebbiano and Malvasia. Their quality selec-tion is very strict and anything that is not suitable for Vino Nobile can of course be sold as Rosso di Montepulciano. 'We came here to make silk shirts,' they say, 'not cotton ones and we are responsible for our wine from the vine to the glass.' The cellars may be modern, but they use the traditional method of fining their wines, namely with real egg whites, the yolks going to the pastry shop. They believe that filtration takes too much out of a wine. Certainly the 1985 Vino Nobile that I tasted was excellent, well structured, with a good fruit and tannin balance. The 1985 Vallocaia was fuller, with a more perfumed nose and a stronger effect of new wood from the *barriques*.

Fassati

Fassati is one of the longer established names associated with Vino Nobile. The company was started in 1913 at Gaiole-in-Chianti. Since 1969 they have been under the same ownership as the Verdicchio company, Fazi Battaglia. They first bought vineyards in Montepulciano in 1974, just ten hectares initially, which they augmented in 1988 with another thirty-six hectares. All associations with Gaiole have long since gone, although they do still make Chianti, from the Colli Senesi. As well as vinifying the production of their own vineyards, they also buy grapes from their neighbours, from people who are not members of the cooperative. They used to buy in grapes for Chianti too, but found that the price was too high; so instead they buy wine that is five or six months old, and just blend and bottle it. Increasingly they are concentrating their activities upon Vino Nobile and have just built a brand new cellar outside the town of Montepulciano. They age their Vino Nobile in small *botti* of fifty or seventy hectolitres and consider that *barriques* would hasten the ageing of their wine too much. Nor do they believe in the term *riserva*, for they hold that all Vino Nobile should be of *riserva* quality. The 1985 was a firm, solid mouthful of tannin and raspberry fruit, with ageing potential.

Tenuta Sant' Agnese

The Fanetti family at Tenuta Sant' Agnese did much for the reputation of Vino Nobile earlier in this century. Adamo Fanetti was the first to bottle Vino Nobile in the *pulcinella* flask of Orvieto in 1931. Others followed his example, but their names have since disappeared, with the exception of Baiocchi. Today Giuseppe Fanetti has placed himself outside the mainstream of wine activity in Montepulciano. He is no longer a member of the growers' association, as he disagrees with their policies, preferring to remain in splendid isolation.

As well as Vino Nobile, he makes Vin Santo; a wine called Principesco, from the same grape varieties as Vino Nobile but aged in mulberry wood; and Vino del Sasso, a pure Cabernet Sauvignon made for the first time in 1983 and aged for eight months in *barriques*. The blend of grape varieties for his Vino Nobile comprises 70 per cent Sangiovese, 20 per cent Canaiolo and 5 per cent Malvasia, Trebbiano and Grechetto. The remaining 5 per cent is made up of Gamay, Malvasia Nera and Ciliegiolo, but no Mammolo. Fanetti has fifteen hectares of vines, all beautifully tended, in fourteen different plots. I also visited the *vinsanteria*, in the attic of an old farmhouse. Everything was very rustic, with barrels that had belonged to his grandfather. The taste was pretty rustic too, leaving me with a strong impression of individuality, if not eccentricity.

La Vecchia Cantina di Montepulciano

The cooperative of Montepulciano, La Vecchia Cantina di Montepulciano, was founded in 1937, making it one of the earliest wine cooperatives in Tuscany. It was considered revolutionary at the time, to form a 'communist' association, when the Fascist movement was at its height. It had small beginnings, with just fifteen grape growers who joined forces to make and sell their wine. The vineyards were neglected during the Second World War, and then given fresh impetus with the moves towards DOC, so that a new cellar was built at the end of the 1960s, with a capacity of 10,000 hectolitres of barrel ageing. Today there are 330 members, who cultivate 700 hectares of vines, not just in Montepulciano, but also in the surrounding

*Villa Banfi, in
Montalcino.*

*The hilltop town of
Montepulciano.*

parishes. The membership accounts for about three quarters of the vineyards of Vino Nobile. They also produce Bianco Vergine Valdichiana, Chianti and other red and white table wine.

At harvest time there are eight reception lines for the grapes, allowing for different qualities of Vino Nobile, of which the best is ultimately destined to be a *riserva*, two lines for Chianti, one for Bianco Vergine, and one each for red and white table wine. There is a strong incentive to produce the best possible fruit, as the price for Vino Nobile grapes is much higher than that for the others. Prugnolo accounts for 80 per cent of the blend, Canaiolo 10 per cent, Mammolo 5 per cent and the white grapes 5 per cent. In comparison Chianti is made from ordinary Sangiovese, with 10 per cent or more of Canaiolo, no Mammolo and 10 per cent of Malvasia and Trebbiano, with no Grechetto. The Vino Nobile ferments in smaller vats, entailing a better control of temperature, while their Chianti is vinified in larger ones.

In comparison on the palate, the Chianti had flavours of raspberries and pepper, while the Vino Nobile was a more solid, substantial wine. Usually about 20 per cent of each vintage of Vino Nobile is made into a *riserva*. The decision is taken after two years of ageing in wood, when the wine is either bottled, or transferred back into tank for a further year's ageing. With the tighter controls brought in with DOCG, the cooperative bottles Vino Nobile for Tuscan merchant houses, such as Melini, under their own label.

Podere Macchione

The Podere Il Macchione belongs to the anonymous limited company of Francavilla Agricola. The wine is made for them by the competent, but inarticulate manager of the estate. It is a beautiful spot. The old farmhouse or *casa colonica* has been restored. There are vineyards and olive trees all around, with pots of colourful geraniums, cypress trees and a view of the skyline of Montepulciano in the distance. The addition of *-one* to an Italian noun implies largeness, so *macchione* is a large *macchia*, describing the

maquis or scrubland found more often in the south of France than in Tuscany.

The first bottling of Il Macchione was of the 1978 vintage. They make Chianti as well as Vino Nobile, in a neat little cellar with cement vats and some small oak casks of just fifteen hectolitres. The 1985 Vino Nobile, tasted about a month after it had been bottled in May 1988, had some berry fruit on the nose, with the flavours of full dry cherries on the palate, and plenty of body and tannin.

Fattoria le Casalte

It seemed as though the Fattoria le Casalte was in the middle of nowhere, an old farmhouse owned by a Roman banker, with a friendly *fattore* to run the estate for him. There are eight hectares of vines altogether. We walked in the vineyards in the spring sunshine, followed by a white cat with a tabby tail. Instead of roses, there were artichokes at the end of the rows, so that they too could benefit from any treatment given to the vines. They make a Vino Nobile comprising 80 per cent Prugnolo, 10 per cent Malvasia and Trebbiano, 10 per cent Canaiolo and the smallest drop of Mammolo. All are fermented together in cement vats for about eight days, with two *remontagi* a day. Then the wine goes into wood. The cellar is tiny. There are *botti* of every size squeezed into the available space, with just two new *barriques*, as an experiment for a Swiss customer. There are even little *caratelli* of Vin Santo, in a delightful organised chaos. The wine from the *barriques* was very perfumed in flavour, but was not really characteristic of Vino Nobile. The more conventional wine was a solid mouthful of fruit and tannin, with plenty of promise.

Fattoria Pulcino

The Fattoria Pulcino is owned by Sergio Ercolani, whose first vintage there was only in 1985. As well as a wine estate, he also runs a restaurant, serving simple homely fare, like *bruschetta* and *pici*. The sixteenth-century cellars were part of an old friary, with arches and a barrel in each alcove. A wonderful

Etruscan stone carving, dating back to 200 BC, shows the face of Silenus, the father of Bacchus. When I visited the Fattoria Pulcino in May 1988, the cellars had not yet been modernised. Old wooden fermentation vats and an old fashioned press remained, but there were plans afoot for renovation.

Cav. Raspanti Giuseppe

Cav. Raspanti Giuseppe & Figli is a small family estate. Giuseppe Raspanti's father bought land in 1960 and planted specialised vineyards for Vino Nobile, Chianti and ordinary table wine. Surprisingly out of his fifty hectares, only three are for Vino Nobile and most of his production is Chianti, which he sells in bulk to a large Chianti house. It all comes down to money. If he were to make more Vino Nobile, he would need more ageing facilities, which he cannot afford to build; he can also sell the Chianti very much earlier, with a quicker return. His cellars are modern and functional, but lack any systematic means of controlling fermentation temperatures. He depends upon the night-time temperature, cooling his fermentations by leaving the cellar doors open; in October the nights are long and cool. Nature takes over. The 1985 Vino Nobile had an attractive herbal character, with overtones of new wood from his new *botti*. In contrast the Chianti was light and fruity.

Boscarelli

Boscarelli is a small estate, with a good reputation, belonging to Paola Corradi de Ferrari, who spends most of her time in Genoa, leaving Maurizio Castelli in charge of the winemaking. There are eight hectares of vines, from which they make Chianti, Vino Nobile and Rosso Boscarelli, which comes from the same grape varieties as the Vino Nobile, but is aged in *barriques* for eighteen months. They have just planted some Chardonnay too. The first vintage and bottling at Boscarelli was in 1966, which makes it a more established estate than many of the other newcomers to Montepulciano. I liked their wines. We compared the 1986 Vino Nobile with the Rosso Boscarelli of the same vintage. The Vino Nobile was a rich mouthful of fruit, with hints of cedarwood and some soft tannins, while the Rosso Boscarelli had more obvious tannin, with flavours of new wood and vanilla. Both promised well.

Le Caggiole di Mezzo

Le Caggiole di Mezzo is a small estate, bought by Gianni Giordano as recently as 1984. A young man, he used to work as a lawyer in Milan but tired of the Milanese rat race. He came to Montepulciano quite by chance, but here he has stayed. He has just four and a half hectares of Vino Nobile, and that is all he wants, preferring to concentrate on quality. He reckons he is still learning how to make wine, following the advice of his oenologist. 'You have to take great care of your wine, just like a child.' His first harvest was in 1984, but only for a basic table wine, so that 1985 was his first proper vintage. It was rounded, complete and balanced, with a flavour of rich cherries – an enjoyable taste on which to leave Montepulciano.

Carmignano

Carmignano lies to the west of Florence, on a hillside overlooking the Arno valley and the plain of Pistoia (see colour illustration opposite p. 168). It is ironic that although the reputation of the region goes back to the Etruscans and that the wine was appreciated by the Medici Dukes of Florence, Carmignano was not recognised as a DOC and separated from Chianti until 1975. It has long been distinguished from the surrounding Chianti Montalbano by the inclusion of Cabernet Sauvignon as an essential part of the blend. Unlike other parts of Tuscany, Cabernet has been present in the vineyards of Carmignano probably since the early eighteenth century.

The origins of Carmignano are Etruscan. There are Etruscan remains at Artimino and two Etruscan tombs on the land of the Fattoria della Calavria, which are currently being excavated. One of the earliest references to the wine dates back to the fourteenth century. The Prato merchant Francesco Datini bought it, paying a Florentine *sugello* per *soma*, apparently some four times the price charged for the most prestigious wines of the period. At the same period the chronicler Domenico Bartolini mentions the excellent wines of Carmignano and Artimino. Three centuries later Francesco Redi described Carmignano:

But if I hold a cup in hand
of brilliant Carmignano,
so much pleasure does it bring to my heart
that ambrosia and nectar I do not envy of Jove.

The Medici Dukes of Florence also contributed to its fame. Proximity to the city of Florence made this land convenient for their hunting, so that they built villas and hunting lodges here, which still stand. The villa at Artimino, called La Ferdinanda, with its hundreds of chimneys, was designed by the architect Buontalenti for Ferdinand I at the end of the sixteenth century. His father, Cosimo I, was responsible for the construction of the long stone wall to enclose the Barco Reale, literally 'royal property', as a hunting reserve for the Medici dukes.

Duke Cosimo III issued the famous Bando in 1716. Mentioned above (p. 18), this is considered one of the first attempts to limit a vineyard area and guarantee the authenticity of a wine. Four are mentioned, Chianti, Pomino, the Val d'Arno di Sopra and Carmignano. Wine not produced within the specified areas, could not be sold by that name. Carmignano today covers much the same area as was defined then, that is to say the parish of Carmignano, and part of the adjoining parish of Poggio a Caiano.

Cosimo III also despatched people to France to collect cuttings of different vines. It was at this time that Cabernet Sauvignon was first planted at Carmignano and a few plants have always remained, referred to as *uva francesca*, or French grapes. At one time there were over a hundred different grape varieties grown in the region, nearly all of which have now sadly disappeared.

When the vineyard area of Chianti was delimited in 1932, Carmignano was content to be absorbed into it. No attempt was made to distinguish it from the adjoining Chianti Montalbano until the mid-1960s. At this time more Cabernet Sauvignon was planted in an effort to reinforce the separate identity of the region, for it is the long established use of Cabernet Sauvignon that really differentiates it from Chianti. With the new regulations for Chianti, allowing for the inclusion of Cabernet Sauvignon, the differences are of course less defined; but in 1975 when Carmignano was recognised as a separate DOC, there was very little Cabernet Sauvignon in production elsewhere.

The Monte Albano dominates the skyline of Carmignano and gives its name to the adjoining sub-zone of Chianti. Most of the producers also have vineyards for Chianti. Those of Carmignano are on the eastern slopes of the hill, whereas the vineyards of Montalbano and the village of Vinci, where Leonardo was born, are on the other side. There is a difference in the soil. Montalbano itself has more sandstone, while that of Carmignano is heavier, with limestone, schist and *galestro*, not unlike the soil of Chianti Classico. However there is more rain here than in Chianti Classico. Altogether the DOC area of Carmignano consists of some 100 hectares, with little scope for more planting.

The Bonacossi at Capezzana

There are only a handful of producers of any significance, five members of the Congregazione, as the growers' association is called, and two outside. One of these is the estate that has put Carmignano on the international wine map, for Carmignano is much better known in Britain and the United States than it is in Italy. This is thanks to the efforts of Count Ugo Contini Bonacossi and his family at the Tenuta di Capezzana.

The first written reference to Capezzana goes back to 804. It concerns the granting of the leasehold of part of a property in a place called Capezzana, inhabited by the farmer Petruccio, with the house, its buildings and land, the courtyard, the gardens, the vineyards, the woods, the olive orchards and so on. Already at the beginning of the ninth century, Capezzana produced wine and olive oil, as it does today. The place name may derive from Capitus, one of the veterans to whom Caesar gave lands between the Arno and the Ombrone Pistoiese. The villa that stands on the estate today was built by the Medicis in the fourteenth and fifteenth centuries, with further additions in the seventeenth century (see illustration). After various

changes of ownership, it was bought by Ugo Bonacossi's grandfather.

The present estate consists of some one hundred hectares of vines, forty-four of Carmignano, twenty-two of Chianti Montalbano and the rest for table wine, such as Bianco di Toscana, or Vin Santo. Included in the estate is the Villa di Trefiano, a three and a half hectare vineyard belonging to Vittorio Bonacossi, Ugo's son, who now makes the wine at Capezzana. He trained at Conegliano, so his technical expertise is above reproach. The wine for Villa di Trefiano, of which the first vintage was 1979, comes solely from that vineyard, while the wine for Villa di Capezzana is made from the best grapes of the vintage. In some years it is Villa di Trefiano that makes the better wine, but in very hot summers the grapes can be too ripe, as the vineyard is on an exposed site.

Count Bonacossi began planting more Cabernet Sauvignon about 1965 in an effort to emphasise the difference between Carmignano and Chianti, and now the DOC regulations include a maximum of 10 per cent Cabernet Sauvignon. In addition to a substantial proportion of Sangiovese and some Canaiolo, other grapes such as Occhio Pernice, Mammolo and Montepulciano d'Ab-

The Contini Bonacossi family at Capezzana.

ruzzo can also be included in the blend, in tiny proportions. There may too be an argument for increasing the percentage of Cabernet Sauvignon, as the general feeling is that it complements the Sangiovese so well.

Ugo and his wife Lisa are amongst the most welcoming people in Tuscany. Ugo was brought up by an English nanny and speaks English with an old-world aristocratic charm. A meal at Capezzana is a feast, with Lisa's wonderful cooking, from home-grown ingredients. The shaggy white Maremma sheepdogs give you a noisy welcome too. The cellars are even older than the villa. At the door there is a granite stone carved with the words:

Della tua bontà
Abbiamo ricevuto questo vino
Frutta della vita
E del lavoro dell'uomo.

This sums up Ugo Bonacossi's personal philosophy about his winemaking, that the result is both a gift of God and the result of man's hard work.

Winemaking techniques at Capezzana reflect Vittorio's experience at Conegliano.

Most of their Carmignano is fermented in closed wooden vats. They have a powerful heat exchanger to cool the temperature if necessary, by passing the wine through the heat exchanger and over the top of the cap; the problem with thick wooden vats is that they do not allow the heat to escape. The juice spends several days in contact with the grape skins to obtain the maximum amount of flavour and extract, for these are wines that will age for several years, as a tasting of 1931 and 1937 vintages illustrated. The 1937 had a certain farmyard character, reminiscent of old Burgundy, which faded very quickly, while the 1931 had more staying power, with some delicate dry nutty fruit. Vittorio thought it was reminiscent of old leather. Normally a Carmignano of a good vintage, like 1985 or 1988, will need about eight to ten years to reach its plateau, on which it should remain for several years.

Carmignano spends a minimum of two years in wood, in the large casks typical of central Italy, while a *riserva*, which is not made every year, will be kept for about three years in wood. Each year there is a considerable selection of the grapes, depending on the character of the vintage and the quality of the fruit. For instance no *riserva* was made in 1986 and only a little in 1987. The older casks are shaved inside in order to renew some of the wood effect. Bottle ageing is important too and they have invested an enormous amount of money in building an insulated warehouse, with a sophisticated control of temperature and humidity. As well as Carmignano and Chianti Montalbano, since 1979 they have made a *vino da tavola* called Ghiaie della Furba, which is a blend of Cabernet and Merlot. It is aged in *barriques* of Nevers or Vosges oak, which are changed on a three-yearly rotation.

Two other wines are traditional to Carmignano. The first is a *vino da tavola* called Barco Reale, which is Carmignano that has only been aged for one year. When Carmignano becomes a DOCG, it may eventually become a DOC in its own right. The second is Vin Ruspo, a more colourful name for what the DOC regulations call Rosato di Carmignano. This is a recent addition to the DOC, dating only from 1982. Vin Ruspo translates literally as 'stolen wine'. In the days of the sharecropping system, when peasant farmers took the grapes to their landlord's cellar to be pressed, the last picking of the afternoon was not usually delivered until the next morning. This allowed for some of the juice to be run off, which was then fermented without the skins in the peasant's own cellar. Modern Vin Ruspo is still made in a similar way, from juice that is run off from a vat of fermenting red wine after a few hours. The vinification then continues in the standard way for a cool fermentation. Vin Ruspo demonstrates how good Sangiovese can be for the making of Rosato, making wines with both colour and fruit, that are dry without too much acidity.

In common with many forward-thinking Tuscan producers the Bonacossi family has planted Chardonnay, and experimented with ageing it in oak barrels, for the 1985 and 1986 vintages. However they have found that it does not last well and they now obtain a much more interesting wine, with good varietal character, by fermenting in stainless steel vats. The wine is bottled in June to be ready

for drinking the following Christmas. Ugo Bonacossi is also convinced that they should be working on the true Tuscan varieties. He gave me a tasting of Trebbiano, which I might almost have confused with Chardonnay, so rich was it. The secret lies in skin contact, for most of the flavour of Trebbiano is in the skins. If there is no skin contact at all, you lose the flavour. Instead with twelve hours maceration at 6–7°C, followed by a gentle pressing, the results proved much better.

They also perform a new technique of saturating the must with oxygen, which enables them to use a minimum amount of sulphur dioxide in their winemaking. Initially the must turns dark brown, like an apple exposed to air, but as the yeast eats up the oxygen during the fermentation, the pale colour returns. The results were certainly very good, nutty and buttery. The problem with Trebbiano is that it has a bad name, because it is grown on less favourable sites and often so poorly vinified. Very little work has been done on the clonal selection of Trebbiano, although there are numerous different clones. At Capezzana they select vines that produce small grapes in loose bunches.

A champagne-method sparkling wine is the other item on the menu at Capezzana. This is made from equal parts of Trebbiano and Chardonnay, and spends three years on the lees of the second fermentation. On tasting, it had a lovely creamy nose, but was a little green on the palate, with a strong yeasty character. They would like to age the base wine in *barriques*, which could be an interesting experiment.

Artimino

Artimino is a small hamlet, a *frazione* of Carmignano, with some ninety inhabitants and with wine cellars scattered in several buildings round the village. It is dominated by the Medici villa. In fine weather there are magnificent views from the top floor, looking towards Montalbano and over the undulating hills of Carmignano, towards Pistoia or the urban sprawl of Florence. What was the pages' house, the *paggeria*, has been turned into a smart hotel, with an elegant dining-room.

The estate has been run by an anonymous limited company since 1970, with, out of a total of 730 hectares of land, eighty hectares of vineyards. The rest is woodland and olive groves. The vineyards include forty hectares for Carmignano, twenty for Chianti Montalbano and the remainder for white wine, a *vino novello* and other *vini da tavola*. The rather solemn manager, Signor Poggi, is the fourth generation of his family to run the estate. His father saw the transition from the sharecropping system.

We wandered through a maze of cellars, escaping the drizzle, passing numerous large casks of indeterminate age. The Carmignano of Artimino consists of 75 per cent Sangiovese, 15 per cent Canaiolo and 10 per cent Cabernet Sauvignon. Poggi explained that those were the percentages in the vineyard, but his Cabernet Sauvignon is grown on a hillside where the soil is particularly stony, so that it produces very small bunches and a low yield of only about twenty-five hectolitres per hectare. Therefore there is usually less than 10 per cent of Cabernet Sauvignon in his wine. The DOC regulations do permit a maximum of 10 per cent of white grapes, but as there is no minimum quantity, he prefers to make a white *vino da tavola*. In 1988 his Cabernet vines produced a little more wine than usual, so a small amount has been vinified separately and may be aged in a *barrique*.

However his is the traditional style of Carmignano. He keeps his wine in cask for between three to five years, so that in the spring of 1989 he still had some 1983 in wood. He thinks that he is probably the only producer of Carmignano to age his wine for so long. I found his basic Carmignano, which had been in wood for a couple of years, rather unexciting and austere, but there was a definite quality leap in our tasting when we reached the 1983 Riserva del Granduca. Even better was the Riserva Villa Medicea, which he described as a *riserva* of a *riserva*, in other words a selection of his very best grapes. The 1983 had spent four years in wood and had a solid flavour, with a good fruit and tannin

balance. It was long and rich.

Poggi explains that the Sangiovese which he uses for his Carmignano is different from that for the Chianti Montalbano. Carmignano is made from the Sangiovese Grosso, the tiny berries of which give more colour and concentrated juice, whereas the Chianti comes from Sangiovese Piccolo or Sangioveto. He has traditional views and does not believe in Chardonnay, nor in *barriques*. However he does make a *vino novello* called San Leonardo, and a Rosso dei Comignoli, after the numerous chimneys of the Medici villa (*comignolo* is the Italian for a chimney stack), which comes principally from Canaiolo with 10 per cent Sangiovese. This is his answer to Sarmento and it was certainly very fruity and easy to drink. Perhaps it was the 1971 Artimino that showed the true potential of Carmignano. It was the colour of mature Burgundy, with the vegetal farmyard nose most commonly associated with old Pinot Noir. On the palate there were similar flavours, but with the dry bite of Sangiovese on the finish.

Fattoria di Baccheretto

The Fattoria di Baccheretto is run by the lively Signora Rosella Bencini, whose family estate it is. The villa was a Medici hunting lodge, at the foot of the Monte Albano. The Barco Reale ran nearby and a few vestiges still remain. They have fourteen hectares for Chianti and four and a half for Carmignano, which they hope to increase a little. Unlike the other producers of Carmignano, they make not a *riserva*, but what they call a *cru*, Le Vigne di Santuaria, from the very best of the Carmignano grapes. A third of the wine for Le Vigne di Santuaria spends five months in French *barriques*. The first vintage was produced in 1985.

We sat in the drawing-room, which was decorated with frescos painted in the last century and illustrating scenes from Italian history, including the Genoese Christopher Columbus discovering America. We began our tasting with Vin Ruspo. The juice had been in contact with the skins for twenty-four hours and the wine had some delicious raspberry fruit. It went very well with the *risotto di vin ruspo* that I ate later for lunch in the village restaurant, in a house once owned by the family of Leonardo. The 1987 Chianti Montalbano is made with the *governo* method, using hardly any white grapes, and has the astringent sour-cherry flavour of young Chianti. After a year in wood the 1986 Barco Reale proved fuller with more fruit, while the Carmignano 1986 was slightly herbal in flavour, with good structure. The Vigne di Santuaria of the same vintage was more closed in comparison. Best of all was the 1982 Carmignano, with flavours of cherries and cedarwood.

Fattoria della Calavria

The Fattoria della Calavria is a traditional estate, belonging to Count Michon Pecori, an elderly aristocratic Italian. He explained that the Pecoris were a Florentine family, who had been here since the 1500s. The Michons came from Savoy. The place is called Calavria after settlers from Calabria. When the postal system was started up in the 1870s, the name was changed to Calavria, to avoid confusion.

The wine is kept in wood for two or three years. There are still some old chestnut barrels from Arezzo, as well as some newer post-war oak casks in his cellars. All the grapes, about 80 per cent Sangiovese, 10 per cent Canaiolo, 7 per cent Cabernet Sauvignon, and a little Malvasia and Trebbiano are fermented together. The wine is put into wood immediately afterwards. The cellars seemed very unsophisticated. People were arriving on Saturday morning to buy wine to take away in assorted containers. A family of black and white cats scuttled behind the barrels. The wines had an old fashioned feel about them, but were none the worse for that. The 1985 Carmignano had some good cedarwood fruit and the 1982 was a solid, meaty mouthful.

Il Poggiolo

The other estate of any size is Il Poggiolo, which is owned by Giovanni Cianchi. He has

thirty hectares of vines: nine for Carmignano, which he may increase by planting some more Cabernet Sauvignon, eleven for Chianti and the rest to make *vino da tavola*. He ferments his wine outside in stainless steel vats for ten to twelve days, after which it goes into cement vats for the malolactic fermentation. It is then put into cask, or in some instances, small *botti* or *botticelli*, as they are quaintly called. These of course age the wine faster. Usually Cianchi's Carmignano is made of 10 per cent Cabernet, 70 per cent Sangiovese and 10 to 14 per cent Canaiolo, with a drop of Colorino, Occhio di Pernice, Malvasia and Trebbiano. He does not bottle his wine every year, but only if the vintage is good enough. I enjoyed his 1985, which promised well, with a slightly herbal nose, some cedarwood fruit and a good structure.

Fattoria di Ambra

I was particularly impressed by the wines of the five-hectare estate of Fattoria di Ambra, which is the family property of Giuseppe Rigoli, an immediately likeable, friendly young man. He makes Carmignano, Barco Reale, and just a little old fashioned white wine, but no pink wine and no Chianti. For the Carmignano he gives the grapes a traditional vinification of twenty to twenty-five days on the skins. They comprise 75 per cent Sangiovese, some Cabernet, Canaiolo and Colorino, but no white grapes. The best vats are kept for a *riserva* wine, the precise amount of which will depend on the quality of the vintage, usually 30 per cent in a good year; but in 1988, which Rigoli described as 'un annata stupenda', half his wine will be *riserva*. Since 1985 he has matured about 40 per cent of his *riserva* wine in *barriques*, for just four or five months. His wines have a rich, smoky quality, with cedarwood and cassis. They are well balanced, the wood-ageing filling out the structure of the *riservas*, to produce wines of great length.

Lo Locco

The smallest producer is Lorenzo Pratesi at Lo Locco, who has just eighty ares of

Carmignano. He works in the cellar and his brother looks after the vines, which were planted fifteen years ago on land inherited from their grandfather. Pratesi has a neat little cellar under the house, the keys to which he called 'the keys to paradise'. When I asked him about vinification methods, he said that that was his secret, but that his wine spent six or seven months in chestnut barrels, followed by five or six months in oak. He does not make any *riserva*, for the simple reason that he does not have enough space, nor will his cash flow permit it. The 1987 tasted from vat had a good deep colour, with a firm nose and flavours of sour cherries, with lots of body.

The DOCG of Carmignano

Carmignano will soon be elevated to the status of DOCG, all that is needed being the President's signature on the decree. There have been some mixed feelings about this amongst the producers. Some believe that it will help the reputation of their wine, while others say that the additional 'G' will not improve anything. As it is, since 1971 Carmignano has organised an annual tasting, similar to that necessary for DOCG, so that any wine which is not up to scratch is sold as *vino da tavola*. The overall quality of the wines of Carmignano is very good and the presence of Cabernet Sauvignon arguably gives them the edge on neighbouring Chiantis.

Vernaccia di San Gimignano

San Gimignano is visible in the distance long before you reach it. The high medieval towers loom out of the haze, making a dramatic skyline, which someone once described as a Tuscan Manhattan (see colour illustration opposite p. 169). The towers were built by local families as a measure of defence during the struggles between the Guelphs and Ghibellines; the higher the tower, the more important the family. Today only thirteen remain from the original seventy. Once inside the gates of the old town, you are in a bustling street, which climbs to the attractive cathedral square. San Gimignano is on the tourist route and the main street is lined with shops offering souvenirs, interspersed with the occasional wine shop run by a local producer. Thursday is market day, when the town really comes to life and the Piazza della Cisterna is filled with stalls. Perhaps San Gimignano is at its best in early evening, as I saw it one September, when the tourists had left, the sun was setting and swallows were wheeling round the square.

The origins of San Gimignano are Etruscan. The first written reference to the town dates back to 991, when it is recorded that Marchese Ugo di Provenza donated a farm that he owned at San Gimignano to the cathedral of Volterra. The place owed its importance to its position on the Via Francigena, which ran through the valley of the Elsa, linking Rome with northern Italy and the rest of Europe. In the Middle Ages grain, wine and saffron were the principal crops of the region, and Vernaccia di San Gimignano began to establish a reputation for itself. It was enjoyed by several popes. Sante Lancerio, the cellarmaster of Paul III, records that Vernacciuole or Vernaccia was much drunk by His Holiness. Martin IV was also a great consumer, for which he is placed by Dante in the sixth circle of Purgatory, where he 'purged through fasting the eels of Bolsena and the Vernaccia wine.' Vernaccia also travelled. In the wine shops of medieval London it was known as vernage.

There are poetic references to Vernaccia. Gabriello Chiabrera wrote:

Its clusters make
a happy harvest,
where in Tuscany Gimignano pleases.

More famous is the line from Michelangelo Buonarroti the Younger, written in 1643, that Vernaccia 'kisses, licks, bites, slaps and stings.' No Tuscan wine of any note escapes mention in Francesco Redi's poem of 1685, *Bacchus in Tuscany* and Vernaccia di San Gimignano is no exception. He condemns all those who do not appreciate it, particularly the Vernaccia of Pietrafitta (still a reputable estate today), to drink inferior wines, to be crowned with beetroot and to be whipped by a satyr!

No one is quite certain of the origins of the Vernaccia grape, or can explain why it is that Vernaccia is grown in the vineyards of San Gimignano, when Trebbiano and Malvasia are the dominant grape varieties for most of the other white wines of Tuscany. There are other Vernaccias in Italy, but they are quite different. Vernaccia di Serrapetrona, from the Marche near Pescara, is a red wine, while Vernaccia di Oristano is a dessert wine from Sardinia. Neither bears any resemblance to the dry white wine of San Gimignano. One theory is that the word derives from the same root as 'vernacular', or the Latin *vernaculus*, and therefore that it may have been a way of describing the native or local wine. This would explain why it describes several wines of completely different taste and colour.

The first written reference to the grape variety in San Gimignano dates back to 1276, when the Ordinamenti di Gabelle or tax list of the town established that the tax for a *soma*, a medieval measure of about seventy-six litres, was two *soldi* for Greco wine and three *soldi* for Vernaccia. Obviously Vernaccia was the more highly regarded.

A seventeenth-century authority, Vincenzo Coppi, records that the first vines were brought from Greece by Messer Perone Peroni. However he omits to say when. Another view, put forward in the nineteenth century, on uncertain grounds, is that one Messer Veiri de' Bardi brought Vernaccia di Corniglia from Portovenere in Liguria in the later fourteenth century. This wine was also made in the adjoining area of Vernazza, so it is suggested that Vernaccia might be a corruption of Vernazza. In fact there is little evidence to support this idea, as the wines must have been quite different in taste. Vernaccia di San Gimignano is a table wine, while Vernaccia di Corniglia was a fortified wine, which is no longer made. Whatever the origins, there is no doubt that Vernaccia is a grape variety with a long history in the region.

During the Middle Ages references were also made to Greco in San Gimignano. In 1489 Lorenzo the Magnificent requested that 500 shoots of Greco should be sent to him, so that he could plant them on his estates. A document of 1525 announces a sale of land that was planted partly with Greco vines, and partly with Vernaccia. Since then Vin Greco has gradually disappeared. Today Vernaccia is the principal grape variety of Tuscany's most famous white wine. The DOC regulations allow for 10 per cent of a complementary grape variety, but Vernaccia remains the backbone of the vineyards of San Gimignano.

Modern Vernaccia di San Gimignano is in a state of transformation. It was the very first Italian wine to become a DOC, as early as May 1966, but since then it has tended to rest upon its laurels. Now there are moves afoot for a DOCG, but this elevation in status may be jeopardised by local political machinations. Optimistic producers are hoping for a DOCG for the 1990 vintage, but the more realistic consider that differences between the growers need to be settled first; a DOCG requires the support of all the members of a growers' association. The problem is that about a quarter of San Gimignano is marketed by people who do not own vineyards there, such as Antinori, Ricasoli and Melini. Their objectives are simply not the same as those of the small growers. Bureaucracy in Rome complicates their differences and the procedure.

As with other new DOCGs, a corresponding DOC has been proposed to take up a tradition for what is called Vin Brusco. This is made from Trebbiano, Grechetto and other white grapes grown in the valleys around San Gimignano, as far as Certaldo in the Val d'Elsa. However for the moment this is no more than talk.

At present the DOC regulations for Vernaccia di San Gimignano allow for a production of 110 quintals per hectolitre, which with a 70 per cent yield gives 77 hectolitres of juice. In 1988 there were 577 hectares of Vernaccia di San Gimignano in production, giving a total annual average production of 40,000 hectolitres. For the moment any substantial increase in the vineyard area is blocked by EEC restrictions. It is however possible to change the composition of existing vineyards. This is happening in some instances, with the replacement of vines for Chianti with those for Vernaccia.

Vernaccia is a marginally more interesting grape variety than either Malvasia or Trebbiano. Some people feel that it might benefit from blending with Chardonnay, Pinot Bianco or perhaps Riesling, although others think that Chardonnay would add too much flavour. As the regulations stand at the moment, a corrective 10 per cent of another grape variety is allowed. However most people prefer to make their wine from Vernaccia alone, or to supplement it with Trebbiano. Hardly anyone makes only white wine, for the vineyards of San Gimignano come within the Chianti zone of Colli Senesi.

The soil of the vineyards accounts for the dominance of white wine in the area. Tufo or yellow sandstone, sometimes mixed with clay, is the predominant component, which the Vernaccia enjoys in preference to heavier soil with a higher proportion of clay. In the vineyard Vernaccia produces small tight bunches of grapes, which can be susceptible to rot. When they are ripe, they turn a golden yellow colour. The preferred method of pruning is either the *guyot*, or more recently the *cordone speronata*. The vines are planted in wide rows, three metres apart to allow for the easy use of tractors. Within the rows the vines are usually 1.2 metres apart. The minimum number of plants should be 3,000 per hectare, whereas at the moment many vineyards have only 2,200, which is considered far too few.

The climate is favourable to viticulture. Rainfall varies between 550 and 800 millimetres a year, with the most in the autumn between September and December.

At its simplest Vernaccia di San Gimignano undergoes the standard, classic white wine vinification. The grapes are pressed, the juice is chilled, so that it clarifies overnight, and the fermentation is controlled at between 15°C to 20°C. The malolactic fermentation is sometimes avoided on the grounds that it removes fruit from the wine, but others prefer this second fermentation to occur, considering that it gives a rounder fuller flavour. Bottling takes place about nine months after the vintage, following fining with bentonite and filtration. A *riserva* quality requires an extra year of ageing. Generally Vernaccia di San Gimignano is a dry white wine, destined for relatively early drinking, although it can develop in bottle, as it has a firm streak of acidity which enables it to age. The dominant flavour is a dry nuttiness, reminiscent of almonds.

In San Gimignano Chardonnay is usually destined for a Predicato del Muschio, or for inclusion in a sparkling wine. At Fattoria di Cusona they planted nearly two hectares of Chardonnay in 1983, which only came into production in 1987. They intend it for a Predicato del Muschio, with 20 per cent Vernaccia. They are also convinced that it will give more flavour to their sparkling wine, which for the moment is pure Vernaccia, made by the Charmat method. They are considering changing to the champagne method and including 25 per cent Chardonnay in the blend. As yet the regulations for Vernaccia di San Gimignano do not include a sparkling version, but as more people are making one, there is a move afoot for it to be included in the new DOCG regulations.

*The town of
Carmignano.*

At Azienda Agricola Casale, where they began making sparkling wine in 1979, they include with the Vernaccia 40 per cent Pinot Bianco, which is bought in the Oltrepo Pavese. The wine spends three years on the lees of the second fermentation. For their Predicato del Muschio they add just 5 per cent of Riesling to the Chardonnay, to give it an extra hint of flavour, like adding pepper or garlic to a sauce. The Chardonnay is fermented in stainless steel vats and then spends about six months in new and one-year-old barrels. The 1987 Predicato del Muschio had a lovely buttery nose and palate; the oak was still obvious, but the wine had rich overtones and a good dry, nutty finish.

People are also working on vinification methods, in an attempt to extract more flavour from the Vernaccia grape. Views differ on the merit of giving the juice skin contact. It can be a difficult process, as the skins of the Vernaccia grape are very soft, with a high polyphenolic content, so that the wine tends to oxidise very quickly if the juice is not cleaned properly. At Fattoria di Cusona they make three qualities of Vernaccia di San Gimignano, which demonstrate the varying potential of the wine. The basic one comes of a standard white-wine vinification. A second wine, from their best vineyard site, is given some skin contact, which they consider contributes more body and flavour. Their *riserva* is the result of a selection of grapes, the ripest from all over the estate, which are given forty-eight hours of skin contact at 5°C. The wine is then aged for a year, spending four months in *barriques* after the fermentation. Their first experiment with this was in 1982, but the wine was much too oaky and had to be toned down. The first vintage offered for sale was the 1983.

Enrico Teruzzi's best quality of Vernaccia, Terre di Tufo, is aged in new *barriques* of Allier oak for four months. There is no doubt that this wine takes on a different flavour when aged in oak, especially new oak, although the grape can be overwhelmed by the vanilla character of the wood. However my first taste of Terre di Tufo in one of Florence's grander restaurants, the Enoteca Pinchiorri, was a veritable eye opener as to the potential of Vernaccia di San Gimignano. In contrast, the Baroncini family do not consider that either oak ageing or skin contact improves the flavour. For them Vernaccia is a white wine that is best drunk young.

Fattoria di Cusona

My first visit in San Gimignano was to the Fattoria di Cusona, belonging to the Guicciardini Strozzi family. This is a historic estate, owned by two distinguished families, related through marriage. The Guicciardinis are of German origin and came to Italy with the Emperor Frederick I in the twelfth century. Their name is derived from *guardia di caccia* or, gamekeeper, so they have hunting horns on their coat of arms. The Strozzis came originally from Fiesole. There is an elegant fifteenth-century yellow sandstone villa with a large courtyard, lined by cedars on one side and gardens that were laid out in the early 1800s. The cellars were built in the eighteenth century and remain rather old fashioned. However the estate advanced considerably in just two years, between my first and second visits there. Between 1986 and 1988 experiments had come to fruition, so that they now, as mentioned above, make three styles of Vernaccia di San Gimignano, a basic wine, a wine called San Biagio, which is the name of the farm, and a *riserva*.

The 1987 Vernaccia di San Gimignano was light yellow in colour, with hints of almonds and bananas on the nose, with rounded, nutty fruit, balanced by some acidity. The San Biagio was noticeably different, a fatter, fuller wine. Although it was more substantial on

Opposite
One of the towers of San Gimignano, overlooking the square.

the palate, it was also more elegant, with better structure, while the *barrique*-aged *riserva* had a dry oaky nose, with oak and fruit flavours on the palate. It was quite successful, in that the oak was not too overwhelming, but I liked the San Biagio best. Their sparkling wine had banana overtones, and was fresh and not too acidic.

Altogether they have sixty-five hectares of vines, of which only thirty-two are planted with Vernaccia. In addition there is Chardonnay, as well as the classic grape varieties for Chianti Colli Senesi, namely Sangiovese, Canaiolo, Trebbiano and Malvasia. Their Chianti is cheerful and fruity, destined for early drinking after spending a few months in large old casks. At this age they are storage containers and do not contribute any wood influence to the wine. More serious is their red *vino da tavola*, a pure Sangiovese, made from the best grapes – the rest are used for their Chianti – called Sòdole. It spends six to eight months in wood and undergoes a year's bottle ageing before sale. The 1983 vintage had the pronounced flavour of ripe cherries, but was still relatively undeveloped in the spring of 1988. Asked why they were not trying Cabernet Sauvignon, in the same way as everyone else, the reply was: 'It's too easy'. However they are in favour of the concept of the Predicato wines.

Fattoria Ponte a Rondolino

One of the most imaginative producers is Enrico Teruzzi of Teruzzi e Puthod at Fattoria Ponte a Rondolino, just outside the town of San Gimignano. He has the open-minded attitude of a newcomer to wine, after an immensely varied career, mainly in sport, but also a brief spell in industry. He has raced horses, sailed yachts in the Mediterranean and taught skiing in the Dolomites. His wife Carmen Puthod was a prima ballerina at La Scala in Milan. A chance advertisement in the *Corriere della Sera* of an estate for sale in Tuscany brought them to San Gimignano. They came and liked what they saw, bought the estate and arrived here on 1st October 1974, just in time for the vintage. There was no cellar; this was not built until the following

year, so their first wine had to be made in the old stable.

Teruzzi now has thirty-eight hectares of vines, mainly on steep slopes around the cellars, which are at the bottom of a valley. They are amongst the most modern in San Gimignano. Everything is controlled by computer, which responds to the slightest fluctuation in the temperature of the stainless steel vats. The wine is fermented very slowly at a cool temperature, possibly taking as long as thirty to forty days. The wines for early consumption will be bottled the following March, while others will be aged in *barriques*. The star of Teruzzi's repertoire is undoubtedly the *barrique*-aged Terre di Tufo, which takes its name from the soil of San Gimignano. He was the first grower to use these barrels in San Gimignano and several others have followed his example. He was also one of the first to experiment with sparkling wine, as early as 1976. He made his first true champagne-method wine in 1981, from pure Vernaccia, which is sold under the name of Sarpinello. Nothing stands still at Ponte a Rondolino. There are plans for a new Vernaccia di San Gimignano, to be called Carmen, and a project to improve upon Galestro. As for red wine, Vigna Peperino is a blend of Sangiovese, with 20 per cent Montepulciano d'Abruzzo. Three or four rows of Cabernet Sauvignon vines have been planted by way of an experiment.

Azienda Agricola Casale

Riccardo Falchini at the Azienda Agricola Casale is one of the more energetic producers in the region. He has a healthy contempt for the bureaucracy that besets Italian wine laws and has doubts about the merits of creating a new DOCG. He feels that no one really knows what the essential characteristics of Vernaccia di San Gimignano are. This does not stop him from caring passionately about his wine. He exudes energy and enthusiasm, pleading the cause of San Gimignano with the articulate awareness of an outsider. He arrived in 1974 from the industrial town of Prato. Knowing nothing about winemaking, he proceeded to break all the rules. He criticises the Italian wine trade for its lack of professionalism and for encouraging bad winemakers to concentrate on high yields. He believes that the fault lies in the structure of the trade, rather than with the individual winemakers. Now people are working to escape from the poor Italian image for cheap wine, which he says is one of the reasons for the Predicato wines.

Altogether he has thirty-three hectares of vines, which include twenty-six of Vernaccia, one of Cabernet Sauvignon, one and a half of Chardonnay, half a hectare of Riesling and four hectares, planted mainly with Sangiovese, but including a smattering of the complementary grapes for Chianti. In fact he makes very little Chianti Colli Senesi and prefers to produce a pure Sangiovese, called Paretaio, which is aged in *barriques* for twelve months. He says that it is not a Predicato wine, as it is cheaper. As mentioned earlier, he does make a Predicato del Muschio from Chardonnay, from grafted vines, including a drop of Riesling on the advice of Dott. Tachis. This was produced for the first time in 1986.

His Vernaccia di San Gimignano depends upon a selection of grapes. There is a basic wine and a *cru* from a single vineyard called Vigna Solatio. Sometimes he makes a *riserva* from that vineyard, as well. His Vernaccia spends six hours on the skins, followed by a cool fermentation and sometimes a malolactic fermentation. He would also like to try ageing his Vernaccia in wood, but that is a project for the future. The taste was good, with the firm flavour of bitter almonds, while the Chardonnay in contrast was more buttery.

Falchini is very enthusiastic about Cabernet Sauvignon, describing it as 'una bomba'. I tasted the 1985 vintage, which was his first experiment with *barriques*. It consisted of 94 per cent Cabernet Sauvignon, with a splash of Sangiovese. The colour was deep, with a closed nose and on the palate some ripe blackcurrants and the sweet vanilla overtones of new wood. It promised well for the future. He has just bought twelve hectares of old Sangiovese vines and says that he is now going to learn how to make red wine.

The Baroncini

The family firm of Baroncini are perhaps better known as merchants than as producers, although they have always owned a small farm, called Torreterza. This has a couple of hectares of Vernaccia and slightly less of Sangiovese. Since the death of Jaurès Baroncini in 1982, the company has been run by his daughter Bruna. As merchants the firm aims to present the whole range of Tuscan wines for the export market, including Vino Nobile di Montepulciano and Brunello di Montalcino, as well as Orvieto, which is a traditional item on a Tuscan wine merchant's list; Gaio, which is their answer to Galestro; and a sparkling wine made from pure Vernaccia, for which they buy in the grapes.

From their own vineyards they make two qualities of Vernaccia di San Gimignano. The basic wine is dry and nutty, with firm acidity and quite a full finish. Vernaccia should not be too acid. They do not believe in a Vernaccia di San Gimignano *riserva*, as they are convinced that it is a wine to be drunk young. Instead they sell a better quality wine called after the particular vineyard Piaggia dell'Olmo. The almond character is more pronounced, as the juice is left on the skins overnight before fermentation.

La Quercia di Racciano

Walter Gassino runs the estate of La Quercia di Racciano and there is indeed a 450-year-old oak tree on the property, under the wide branches of which we sat and talked. Walter Gassino explained that his father, who came from Piedmont, had bought the estate in 1964. He was one of the outsiders who arrived in the area when the sharecropping system ended. Altogether he has sixteen hectares of vines, eleven of Vernaccia and the rest for Chianti. His vinification methods are quite simple. He bought a refrigeration machine in 1985, uses selected yeast and controls his fermentation temperatures carefully at 18°C. The wine undergoes a malolactic fermentation and is usually bottled at the beginning of March. As yet he has not tried making a *riserva*, although he reckons that Vernaccia di San Gimignano can age, as he has bottles from 1972 which are still drinking well. He would also like to try using *barriques*.

I enjoyed his wine. We tasted the 1987 vintage, which had a deeper colour than other Vernaccia di San Gimignano that I had tried. Gassino attributed this to the fact that he was not equipped to give all his must a cold clarification; some is left to fall clear naturally overnight. The wine was full, with masses of fruit, rich and nutty in flavour, with quite a soft finish. The body in the wine comes from the soil, of volcanic origin, which in the vineyards of La Quercia has a higher percentage of clay than usual.

San Quirico

The estate of San Quirico, on the road to Certaldo, has belonged to the Vecchione family for 120 years. However Andrea Vecchione only began bottling his wine in 1973. Altogether he has twenty-one hectares of Vernaccia, as well as vines to make a little Chianti. The soil is a mixture of clay and tufo, containing fossilised shells.

The vinification methods are standard for white wine, with no skin contact and a controlled fermentation taking about three weeks. The tartrates are precipitated, but there is no malolactic fermentation. Vecchione considers that the wine might be more stable, but that some of the aroma would be lost. There is no fining, but there are three filtrations before bottling in April. Nor does he make a *riserva*, for the simple reason that he does not have enough stock to keep his wine for a year. He does not like *barriques*, believing that they do not suit Vernaccia. As for the wine, it had quite a deep colour, determined by the ripeness of the grapes. The nose was perfumed and more fragrant than some other wines. On the palate the taste was full and soft, with less bitter almonds than usual and a dry finish.

Le Colonne

The tiny estate of Le Colonne is the property of the Picciolini family, the same family that owns Sorbaiano in Montescudaio. They have

just three hectares of Vernaccia and the grapes are vinified with a meticulous attention to detail in a neat modern cellar. They make a *normale* and a *barricata riserva* wine. This spends three or four months in wood, in Allier and Limousin oak, that is renewed every three years. This is an interesting way to add stature to the wine of San Gimignano, but it can also double the price from the cellar door. In this instance, I also had doubts as to whether the taste was really Vernaccia di San Gimignano and much preferred the non-oak-aged wine, with its leafy, honeyed flavours and firm acidity, not unlike a Chablis. In contrast the oaked wine was heavier and fuller, solid and buttery, a little clumsy. The oak was just too obvious, but maybe it will tone down with bottle age.

Il Paradiso

Dott. Vasco Cetti is the president of the growers' association and the owner of the enchantingly named estate Il Paradiso. When I was there in warm September sunshine, the name seemed very fitting. He makes a variety of wines from his seventeen hectares of vineyards, not just Vernaccia di San Gimignano, but also Chianti, two *crus* from Sangiovese and a sparkling wine, as well as some experimental Chardonnay and Cabernet Sauvignon. The Chardonnay is for a *cru* called Docciolo, for which it is blended with Trebbiano. Cetti would never include it in Vernaccia di San Gimignano, as it has too much character; he considers that it would distort the typical flavours of San Gimignano.

I liked Dott. Cetti's Vernaccia. The juice is given eight or nine hours of skin contact, which makes for a longer-lasting wine that will not fade after its first year. It was delicately nutty, with fragrant fruit, and not spoilt by any bitterness. He does not believe in a *riserva* and does not make one. His Chianti was young and fruity and Paterno II, a pure Sangiovese, which had spent five months in *barriques*, had a rich meaty nose, with lots of tannin and fruit on the palate. The grapes for this are picked late, at the end of October, when they are very ripe so that the wine reaches 14° of alcohol. Bottaccio, the other pure Sangiovese *cru*, is kept in cement tanks. It was not available for tasting.

Pietrafitta

Pietrafitta is one of the old estates of San Gimignano, now run by an anonymous company. I met the manager, Signor Valiani, who was young and friendly. The villa, which is approached along an avenue of cypresses, was built in 1580 by the Acciaioli family. Then it was sold to the dal Pozzo family who subsequently married into the Savoia Aosta family, so that it became royal property for about 150 years. The estate was turned into a company in 1950 and, as such, it was one of the first producers to work to develop the wines of San Gimignano.

Altogether there are forty hectares of vines, over half of Vernaccia, but also substantial amounts of Chianti, as well as some *vino da tavola*. They used to keep all their Vernaccia in large casks, in the traditional way. Now they make two qualities, a young wine for early sale and a *riserva* that goes into *botti*, for anything between three and seven months, depending on the size of the cask. They are also experimenting with *barriques*, under the guidance of the oenology school of San Michele all'Adige, but as yet no conclusions have been reached. For this purpose they have Allier, Tronçais, Limousin and Slavonic oak. I preferred the *riserva* that had been aged in cask to that aged in *barriques*. It had a gently nutty flavour and was delicately rounded on the palate, while the *barricata* wine was too oaky, with a smell of sweet vanilla that camouflaged the taste of the grape. They also make delicious Vin Santo, which tasted like oloroso sherry and sherry trifle, or *zuppa inglese* to the Italians.

Pietraserena

The estate of Pietraserena is the creation of Bruno Arrigoni. He came here from Lucca in 1966 and now has twenty hectares of vines, from which he makes Vernaccia di San Gimignano and Chianti, as well as a pink wine and some Charmat sparkling wine, which is made for him. His methods are standard, no skin contact, a controlled fermentation and no wood, nor a *riserva*. For Arrigoni, Vernaccia di San Gimignano is meant to be drunk young, and he does not like the taste of Vernaccia in wood. However he does make two qualities of Vernaccia, a basic one and a wine from his best vineyard under the name of Vigna del Sole, which is vinified separately. I liked its nutty fruit and firm dry finish. The Chianti Colli Senesi, from the vineyard Poggio al Vento, meaning a windy hillside, was very good too. Signor Arrigoni explained that he had always worked with vines. He obviously loves what he does and is very serious and conscientious in his approach. The delicious results are there to taste.

A DOCG for San Gimignano

San Gimignano is a vineyard in transition and one that has already made considerable progress during the last twenty years, along with most of the rest of Tuscany. In the early 1960s the typical glass of Vernaccia was a deep yellow, oxidising wine. Today modern vinification has left its mark, and most wines are fresh and clean. Now there is a move to reassess old fashioned methods, incorporating the best of them. Oak barrels are used, not because that is all there is, but because the oenologist believes that the wine benefits from a controlled period of wood ageing. Forward-looking growers are considering how to improve the taste of their wines. Most people are optimistic that the eventual introduction of DOCG regulations, whatever the bureaucratic problems along the way, will be a further incentive to improve.

The Other White Wines of Central Tuscany

Several of the white DOCs of central Tuscany were born as a result of changes in Chianti. The introduction of DOCG in 1984 enforced a reduction in the percentage of white grapes in the red wine. The regulations reduced the maximum from 30 to 10 per cent, or in the case of Chianti Classico to 5 per cent. Already, serious growers had been decreasing, if not eliminating white grapes completely. There were a lot of superfluous white grapes. The composition of a vineyard cannot be changed overnight and, although hectares of Trebbiano and Malvasia have since been grafted with more desirable grape varieties, or pulled up completely, something had to be done with the enormous quantities that remained. Fortunately the world market enjoys dry white wine, that is clean, fresh and well made. In this instance neutral flavour is a virtue, not a defect.

Galestro and Bianco della Lega

In Chianti Classico white wines under the name of Bianco della Lega began to appear; but they were nothing more than a simple table wine, a Bianco Toscano made from Trebbiano and Malvasia. One can still find the occasional producer of Bianco della Lega, but it has tended to disappear as more exciting white grape varieties have been planted by experimental producers. The current tendency is to plant Chardonnay or another innovative white grape variety and then to give your wine a fancy name.

The solution of the large growers, notably Ruffino, Antinori and Frescobaldi, was to create a wine called Galestro. They formed an association, consisting initially of seven producers, called the Consorzio per la Valorizzazione dei Vini dei Colli della Toscana Centrale, known more simply as Valvito. The first vintage was made in 1979. Inevitably Trebbiano is the principal grape variety, but the regulations imposed by the association allow for 40 per cent of so-called improving grape varieties. These can include Malvasia and Vernaccia, as well as Chardonnay, Pinot Bianco and other white grape varieties found in Tuscany. Unusually for Italian wine regulations, they have set a maximum alcohol level of 10.5°, which is low; more often than not Galestro reaches only 9.5°.

Galestro is named after the typical rocky soil of central Tuscany and its area of production covers what are called the Colli della Toscana Centrale, in other words most of the area that produces Chianti, but omitting the Colline Pisane. As such it is a simple table wine. There is no desire to turn Galestro into a DOC, as that would have a stultifying effect on its regulations, which are currently very flexible. For instance there is a move to turn the proportion of Trebbiano, which at present stands at a minimum of 60 per cent, into a maximum of 60 per cent. If Galestro were a DOC, this would entail a long bureaucratic procedure, rather than a simple agreement between the members of the producers' association.

Today the membership of Valvito has grown to fourteen and includes large merchants, such as Brolio and Cecchi, cooperatives such as the Cantina Leonardo at Vinci and the Agricoltori del Chianti Geografico outside

Gaiole, as well as private producers such as the Castello di Gabbiano near Greve and the Fattoria Ponte a Rondolino in San Gimignano. Members pay a contribution, according to their sales, which goes towards the promotion of Galestro.

There is no doubt that Galestro has had an enormous success in Italy. As a concept, it takes advantage of the improvement in white-wine vinification techniques in Tuscany; one cannot make fresh, dry white wine without a certain amount of equipment, such as stainless steel vats, heat exchangers to cool the juice and precipitate the tartrates, and up-to-date technical expertise. However outside Italy the success of Galestro has been less marked, for it is competing with numerous more interesting dry white wines. The rather bland neutral taste may appeal to the Italian consumer, but international tastebuds often demand more character and flavour.

Galestro was the solution of the large producers. For the smaller estates a solution to the surplus of white grapes lay in the development of smaller, localised DOCs, such as Val d'Arbia Bianco, Bianco Vergine Valdichiana, Bianco della Valdinievole and Bianco Pisano di San Torpè. These give a more precise identity than Bianco Toscano.

Val d'Arbia Bianco

White wine was made in the valley of the river Arbia before it was recognised as a DOC in 1985. The valley covers quite a large area, from where it rises just south of Radda in the heart of Chianti Classico, to where it joins the river Ombrone near the town of Buonconvento, not far from Montalcino. The Arbia featured in the wars between the Florentines and the Sienese. When the Florentines were defeated in the fierce battle of Montaperti in 1260, Dante wrote that it ran red with blood.

The main producers of Val d'Arbia Bianco are within Chianti Classico, San Felice and Vistarenni being among the largest. Brolio and Aiola are important too, and in the Colli Senesi, Chigi Saracini. However for many estates in the southern part of Chianti Clas-

sico, Val d'Arbia Bianco is a secondary product. They tend to concentrate on red wines, *vini da tavola* as well as Chianti. Further south around Monteroni, several small farmers sell their grapes to the large producers of Val d'Arbia Bianco.

Inevitably Trebbiano forms the backbone of Val d'Arbia Bianco, along with some Malvasia, but the DOC regulations recognise the limitations of these traditional Tuscan grape varieties and allow for 15 per cent of other, more aromatic grapes, such as Pinot Bianco and Chardonnay, as well as, unusually Riesling Renano or Italico.

Val d'Arbia Bianco benefits from the improvement in white-wine technology over recent years. At Chigi Sarencini they practise a standard cool fermentation, at 20°C, in stainless steel vats, which lasts four or five days. Part of the wine undergoes a malolactic fermentation and all of it is subjected to cold treatment to induce a precipitation of tartrates. This is a wine for early drinking and is bottled for sale from the April following the vintage.

At San Felice they are paying more attention to their Val d'Arbia Bianco now and considering how it might be improved. They have eighteen hectares of vineyards near Monteroni specifically for it, so that they buy in only a very small proportion of the grapes. Sixty per cent undergo a standard white wine vinification, while the remaining 40 per cent are crushed and the juice given ten or twelve hours of skin contact at a temperature of 10°C. The ensuing fermentation takes about a month, with part of the wine undergoing a malolactic fermentation.

The San Felice Val d'Arbia Bianco has more flavour than most, as it includes 10 per cent of Riesling Renano. This is vinified separately, as it ripens at the beginning of September, much earlier than the Trebbiano. The problem with Riesling is that it loses its aroma if the weather is too hot, so they take great care to shade the grapes by judicious pruning.

At Aiola they have some Pinot Bianco and at Vistarenni they have planted Riesling Italico, in an attempt to enliven the flavour of their Val d'Arbia Bianco. However the dominant taste remains the faintly bitter almonds of Trebbiano.

Bianco Vergine della Valdichiana

Bianco Vergine della Valdichiana, as the name might imply, covers the broad valley of the Chiana river, in the provinces of Arezzo and Siena. The vineyards are concentrated around Cortona, but overlap slightly with the zones of the Chianti Colli Aretini and Vino Nobile di Montepulciano. Producers who concentrate on Bianco Vergine alone tend to be gathered around Cortona. The valley is flat and fertile and there are large expanses of grazing land for the creamy white Chianina cattle, which provide the enormous *bistecca fiorentina*.

According to Pliny the Elder viticulture in this area goes back to the Etruscans. In the fourteenth century Giovanni Serambi, a writer from Lucca, mentions the delightful wines of Cortona, both red and white. In the sixteenth century the cellarmaster of Pope Paul III mentions the white as one of the pontiff's favourites. Unlike Val d'Arbia Bianco, Bianco Vergine della Valdichiana was given its DOC as early as 1972.

Producers of Vino Nobile di Montepulciano often have a hectare or two to complement their production of red wine. It is no surprise that Trebbiano is the mainstay, but Chardonnay and Pinot Bianco are also allowed; so is Grechetto, which is common in Umbria, but rarer in Tuscany. The local name for it is Pulcinculo. It has small grapes and gives low yields, contributing a distinctive nutty taste, which certainly adds flavour to the Trebbiano.

The virginal quality of the wine, embodied in its name, arises because it is made without skin contact, a tradition in this area which was confirmed in the DOC regulations. The wine is made from free-run juice and care is taken to render this as clean as possible before the fermentation. The malolactic fermentation is avoided, as it is considered here that Trebbiano has no structure or taste without malic acid.

One of the best Bianco Vergine della Valdichiana that I tasted came from Villa Farina, a new estate created out of nothing by the Ozzo family, on the edge of Umbria, near Pietraia di Cortona and Lake Trasimeno. They have bought vineyards and built a cellar, and now have a replanting programme to take them well into the 1990s. Their Bianco Vergine is made mainly from Trebbiano, with some Malvasia and a small amount of Grechetto, all fermented together. There are plans for Chardonnay too, maybe for a sparkling wine, and also for experiments with Sauvignon. They are considering Cabernet for a *vino da tavola*, but only have Sangiovese for red wine at the moment.

The new cellar allows for simple, rational winemaking. It is well equipped with stainless steel vats and cooling equipment. The fermentation with cultured yeast is controlled at between 10°C and 16°C. The free-run juice is used for Bianco Vergine, while the pressed juice becomes ordinary table wine. There is careful fining with bentonite or gelatine, a minimal use of sulphur and cold treatment for a tartrate precipitation. The wine is bottled as needed, and the results are clean, fresh and fragrant, but without a great deal of character. Tuscans do not expect their white wines to exude flavour.

The Fattoria di Manzano, near Camucia, also has a good reputation for its Bianco Vergine, although in some ways it is more interesting for its experimental approach and what it promises for the future. It is run as a private company and until 1985 had fifty-seven hectares of vines. Thirty hectares have now been pulled up in order to plant experimental varieties. They have eleven different clones of Chardonnay, as well as Pinot Bianco, Chasan – which is a cross between Chardonnay and Listan, found in the South of France – Chenin Blanc, Cabernet Sauvignon, Merlot and Petit Verdot. They are working closely with the Istituto di San Michele all'Adige, but as yet few of these vines are in production.

As well as Bianco Vergine they make what they called Bianchetto, a lightly sparkling wine from Chardonnay and Pinot Bianco. A red table wine called Il Vescovo, after a particular vineyard, is made from an unusual mixture of Ciliegiolo and Gamay, which was planted in 1979. I liked the youthful peppery fruitiness of this wine, which was not unlike a Beaujolais, reminiscent of maraschino cherries. Somewhat disappointing was the Rosso di Manzano, from grafted Cabernet and Merlot vines. The 1987 vintage tasted hollow and unbalanced. However there is no doubt that this is an interesting estate to watch, as a considerable amount of money and expertise is being invested in its future.

Bianco della Valdinievole

In Italian a *torrente* is a very small river, a little larger than a stream. The torrente Nievole gives its name to one of Tuscany's lesser white wines. I say lesser, for not only is the wine limited in production, it is also insignificant in taste. The zone covers a small area of the valley, mainly around the towns of Massa and Cozzile, near Pescia and Montecatini, which is known above all for its thermal springs. The river ends in what was once the marsh of Fucecchio, drained by Duke Peter Leopold in the late eighteenth century. The DOC was recognised in 1976.

This is a fertile area, where market gardening is more lucrative than growing vines, with the result that the vineyard area is tending to decline in favour of flowers and vegetables. There is only one producer of any significance, the company of Adolfo Giannini at Serravalle Pistoiese, a traditional Tuscan merchant who buys grapes from half a dozen or more growers. Once again Trebbiano forms the backbone, and is blended with Malvasia, Vermentino and Canaiolo Bianco. Pinot Bianco and Pinot Grigio were planted about five years ago and may improve the taste of the wine. However they have the disadvantage of ripening earlier than the traditional Tuscan varieties, so that the vintage is prolonged. This is inconvenient as Giannini prefer to ferment all the different grape varieties together.

Vinification methods are standard. The grapes are pressed and the juice is either centrifuged or cooled to clarify it. The fer-mentation in cement vats takes about forty-five days at 12°C and there is no malolactic fermentation. Then the wine is treated for tartrates and bottled in March for consumption the following summer. I tasted the 1988, which was slightly nutty with some rounded fruit. It was better than neutral, but still not worth the detour.

Bianco Pisano di San Torpè

Bianco Pisano di San Torpè takes its name from a Roman centurion, Turpis or Torpè. who was beheaded in Pisa in 68 AD. His head is still kept in the church named after him in the city, while tradition has it that his body came to rest at Saint Tropez. Along with San Ranieri, he is considered one of the patron saints of Pisa.

The production area of Bianco Pisano di San Torpè coincides with the Chianti delle Colline Pisane and also includes some lower-lying land near the rivers of the Arno, Egola and Elsa. However the principal producers of the wine are the same as those who make Chianti delle Colline Pisane. Although white wine has always been made here, simply called Bianco delle Colline Pisane, the DOC was not created until 1979. The grape varieties are the standard Trebbiano and Malvasia, as well as the more flavoursome Vermentino, commonly found in Liguria and Sardinia.

In fact there is little to distinguish Bianco Pisano di San Torpè from the other white wines of Tuscany. I tasted samples from Sant'Ermo and the Fattoria Sassolo. Both were made according to standard vinification methods. They were quite fresh and fragrant, but did not thrill. More exciting was a pure Vermentino, made by Bruno Moos at Soiana, which after ten hours of skin contact, had a dry nutty nose, and on the palate, some nutty flavours, with a slightly appley finish. Bianco Pisano di San Torpè can certainly be refreshing drinking, but like most of the Trebbiano-based white wines of Tuscany, nothing more memorable.

Pomino

Although the reputation of Pomino extends back several centuries, it was only recognised as a DOC in its own right in 1983. Hitherto it had been grouped with Chianti Rufina; indeed the hamlet of Pomino is a *frazione* of the town of Rufina, in the hills to the east of Florence. However Pomino had enough individuality in the seventeenth century to merit mention by Francesco Redi and in 1716 the Grand Duke Cosimo III laid down boundaries for it that are still recognised today. The eighteenth-century Florentine writer Giovan Cosimo Villifranchi tells us in his *Oenologia Toscana* (1773) that Pomino is 'pulpy and strong, suitable for keeping a long time'; while Repetti explains in his *Dizionario Geografico della Toscana* (1833) that the region is noted for the exquisiteness and goodness of its wines, coming from the fine quality of the grapes grown on slopes of *galestro* soil.

Vittorio degli Albizi was responsible for laying the foundations of Pomino as we know it today. He came from an old Florentine family, but was born in Auxerre in 1827. He returned to Tuscany in 1855 to manage the family's estates outside Florence, including not only the Tenuta di Pomino, but also the Castello di Nipozzano. A few years later, after Vittorio's death, his sister Leonia married Angiolo de' Frescobaldi and the two properties subsequently became part of the Frescobaldi family's considerable landholding.

Vittorio degli Albizi's contribution was to introduce French grape varieties to his estate. When he arrived in Tuscany at the age of twenty-eight, he already had a great knowledge of French wines. Wishing to experiment with French grape varieties on his estate, he brought cuttings of Chardonnay, Pinot Bianco, Pinot Grigio and Cabernet, both Sauvignon and Franc, as well as Merlot, Malbec, Pinot Nero and Syrah. After his premature death, the Frescobaldis continued to grow many of these, so that whereas the Grand Duke's Bando of 1716 related to a white Pomino made from Trebbiano and Malvasia, the current DOC regulations allow Pinot Bianco, Pinot Grigio and Chardonnay, as well as Trebbiano, but no Malvasia. Red Pomino comes from Sangiovese, blended with Cabernet Sauvignon, Cabernet Franc, Merlot and Pinot Nero. As one of the more recent DOCs, the regulations also include Vin Santo.

Some 2,000 hectares are delimited within the DOC, but only about 130 are actually in production, of which the Frescobaldis are responsible for ninety-four on the Tenuta di Pomino. In fact this means that Pomino is virtually synonymous with the Frescobaldi, as little is heard of the other thirty-six hectares. These are some of the highest vineyards in Tuscany, from 300 to 700 metres, on limestone soil.

Frescobaldi produce two contrasting styles of Pomino Bianco, which are different both in blend of grape varieties and in method of vinification. The basic Pomino Bianco is made from 55 per cent Pinot Bianco, 5 per cent Pinot Grigio, 10 per cent Trebbiano and 30 per cent Chardonnay, which are fermented together without any skin contact at a cool temperature. The result is some attractive buttery fruit, which compares favourably with the more traditional Tuscan white wines. On the other hand, with Pomino Il Benefizio the Frescobaldis claim to be the first to have produced a wood-fermented and oak-aged white wine in Italy. It was first made in 1973 and is named after the highest part of the estate, which was once an ecclesiastical land holding or benefice. The blend of this wine is principally Chardonnay, with 15 per cent Pinot Bianco and 5 per cent Pinot Grigio, which are fermented in forty-hectolitre Slavonic oak barrels, after twenty-four hours of skin contact. Subsequently the wine spends four months in *barriques* of Nevers oak and is given several months of bottle age before sale (see colour illustration opposite p. 72). The influence of the oak is quite pronounced on both nose and palate, but there is good firm fruit too, with more complexity than some of the more recent comers to oak ageing in Tuscany, as well as greater potential for ageing in bottle. Pomino Il Benefizio is made only in the better vintages, which are to date 1973, 1975, 1978, 1980, 1982, 1983, 1985 and 1988.

Red Pomino has been somewhat overshadowed by the white, but is also a serious wine in its own right, made from 75 per cent Sangiovese, 10 per cent Cabernet Sauvignon, 5 per cent Canaiolo and 10 per cent Merlot, vinified in wood and then aged in *barriques* for eight to ten months. I tasted the 1985 vintage, which was rich and smooth, with some oaky fruit and a little tannin, making an eminently drinkable glass of wine. We will hear more of Pomino, for French grape varieties have been established here with notable success. All that remains now is for the wine to gain wider acclaim.

Montecarlo and the Colline Lucchesi

The hilltop town of Montecarlo, to the east of Lucca, above the broad valley of the Arno, gives its name to one of the more exciting white wines of Tuscany. It is true that you cannot escape completely from Trebbiano, but in addition to that ubiquitous grape variety, there are vines of Roussanne, Sémillon, Sauvignon, Pinot Bianco and Pinot Grigio. Furthermore these are not just recent plantings, but originated in the middle of the last century, when cuttings were brought from France. Montecarlo is known above all for its white wine, which was recognised as a DOC in 1969; a DOC for the red came much later, in 1985 and more often the white wine of Montecarlo is paired with Rosso delle Colline Lucchesi. The white wine of the Colline Lucchesi is of secondary importance, in the same way as red Montecarlo.

My first visit to Montecarlo coincided with the annual wine fair, at which the producers of the Colline Lucchesi and Montecarlo show their wares, providing a splendid introductory tasting. Normally Montecarlo is a rather sleepy little town, with a single main street, running from one medieval gate to the other. The stark tower of the church of Sant' Andrea Apostolo stands out on the skyline for miles around. Nearby is Collodi, famous as the home of Pinocchio. During the weekend of the fair, Montecarlo is transformed into a hive of bustling activity, with tasting stands lining the street.

Montecarlo has a long viticultural tradition. The earliest written references appear in a document dated 846, when the place is noted for 'the abundant return provided by nature, including a substantial output of pure wine from grapes pressed three times according to the rule, and then racked.' The town's Latin name was Via Vinaia, deriving from the Roman road the Via Vinaria, which crossed the hill of Montecarlo, linking the Via Cassia near Buggiano and the Via Romea near Altopascio. Evidently, even then vineyards were the most significant characteristic of the area.

In the fourteenth and fifteenth centuries the wines of Montecarlo were drunk in Pisa, Florence and Rome. The Prato merchant Francesco Datini, who was known as a wine connoisseur, recommended the wine of Monte Chiaro, as Montecarlo was then called, to a fellow merchant, if he wanted 'a perfectly made and good white wine'. At that time it was more expensive than any other on the Florence market. In 1408 Pope Gregory XII after tasting the wine in Montecarlo, ordered a quantity to be sent to him in Rome. When the town came under Florentine control in the Medici period, they too appreciated its white wine. Francesco Redi sings:

It is truly potable gold
that despatches into exile every irremediable evil

Until about a hundred years ago, Trebbiano was the principal grape variety of Montecarlo. Then local tradition has it that in the middle of the last century someone from the Fattoria Marchi Magnani, one of the older estates, now called the Fattoria Mazzini, went to France, returning with several different grape varieties; Sauvignon, Sémillon and Roussanne. Pinot Grigio and Pinot Bianco may also have been brought, although they were also grown in northern Italy. Vermentino arrived from Liguria. It might have been possible to find Roussanne in Trentino, but Sémillon was certainly not grown anywhere else in Italy then. It was the phylloxera crisis at the end of the century, entailing a considerable replanting of vineyards, that really established the French grape varieties and reduced the amount of Trebbiano. Merlot, Cabernet Sauvignon, Cabernet Franc and Syrah were also introduced to Montecarlo, but they did not have the same impact upon the region's red wine. Earlier this century, Montecarlo Bianco was known as 'lo Chablis di Montecarlo' and in 1933 Marchi Magnani's white wine was described as 'the best and most appreciated in all Italy'. Today the wine of this estate is of little interest.

The vineyards of Montecarlo are mostly on the hillsides immediately around the town, where the soil is of clay mixed with stones. They spread a little into the adjoining parishes of Altopascio, Capannori and Porcari. The DOC regulations for white Montecarlo demand between 60 and 70 per cent Trebbiano, with a choice for the balance of Vermentino, Roussanne, Sauvignon, Sémillon, Pinot Grigio or Pinot Bianco. It is up to the individual grower to choose which grape varieties and in what proportions. Officially Montecarlo Rosso consists entirely of Tuscan grape varieties, namely Sangiovese, Canaiolo, Ciliegiolo, Colorino and Malvasia Nera, of which the first two are the most important, as in Chianti. However when you ask the producers about their grape varieties, Cabernet and Syrah are mentioned too. The production of white Montecarlo outweighs the red by at least three if not four bottles to one, and it is without any doubt with the white wine that the interest lies. The red is usually not unlike a young Chianti, though sometimes with more spicy flavours, whereas the white offers a unique flavour and a complex bouquet.

Fattoria del Buonamico

After tasting my way through the bottles on offer at the wine fair, I headed off to my first appointment at the Fattoria del Buonamico, just outside the town, which is owned by the Grassi family. They have fifteen hectares of vines and, as well as Montecarlo, make a *vino da tavola* Bianco di Cercatoia and, in the best years, a Rosso di Cercatoia. Cercatoia is the name of a small area within the vineyards of Montecarlo, but confusingly, also the name of another Montecarlo producer, who has no connection with this *vino da tavola*.

The principal difference between the two white wines of Fattoria del Buonamico lies in the grape varieties. The *vino da tavola* has only 40 per cent Trebbiano, as opposed to the 60 per cent required for the DOC. They do not have any Roussanne or Vermentino. Life is complicated by the different ripening times of the various grape varieties. Pinot Grigio is ready first and Trebbiano last of all. Usually for Montecarlo they ferment each grape variety separately and blend them immediately afterwards. For the *vino da tavola*, they tend to ferment everything together, so that the Trebbiano is picked a little early. There is no skin contact for either wine, and both are kept in old chestnut barrels for about six months, while they undergo a malolactic fermentation. Chestnut gives a slightly more astringent taste than oak, but the wood effect is really minimal.

In contrast, their red wines spend two years in large oak casks and the *vino da tavola* includes some Cabernet.

Fattoria Michi

Fattoria Michi is a recently created estate, with some eighteen hectares of vines, making several different wines, not just Montecarlo Rosso and Bianco, but also a *vino da tavola* from 90 per cent Roussanne with some Chardonnay, a pure Malvasia Bianco and a champagne-method sparkling wine. The cellars were built in 1970 and their first vintage was in 1972, since when they have established a good reputation. Vinification methods match the modern cellars. The various grape varieties of the white Montecarlo are fermented separately in stainless steel vats, for which they use the free-run juice, without any skin contact. If necessary they add cultured yeast to help the fermentation and the wine undergoes a malolactic fermentation, but it does not usually spend any time in wood. It is bottled in June and benefits from some bottle age.

The red wine spends fifteen days on the skins, with a fermentation temperature maintained at 25°C and two or three *remontagi* a day. It will then spend five or six months in large oak casks. *Barriques* have yet to come to Montecarlo.

I liked what I tasted. Their Montecarlo Bianco consists of 60 per cent Trebbiano and 25 per cent Roussanne, with the balance made up of Sauvignon, Sémillon and Pinot Bianco. These are the percentages in the wine, not in the vineyard; with Trebbiano, 60 per cent in the vineyard gives you 80 per cent in the wine. However the separate fermentation of each grape variety gives better control over the precise percentages. They are also planning to plant a little Pinot Grigio, for although it has small yields, it adds flavour to the wine. The Montecarlo Bianco had some firm acidity, with good structure and flavours of almonds, while the Roussanne and Chardonnay blend was softer, with leafy fruit on the nose and palate, with hints of herbs. Least successful was the pure Malvasia, which had a rather bitter, coarse flavour. The sparkling wine is made largely from Chardonnay, with a little Sauvignon, Sémillon and Roussanne, spending two years on the lees of the second fermentation. Sparkling wine does not feature in the DOC, but that does not seem to matter.

As for red wine, their ordinary Montecarlo Rosso comes from Sangiovese, Canaiolo, Syrah and Merlot. Like Chianti, the regulations permit the addition of a small drop of white wine, but they prefer not to. In 1987 this unusual mixture of grapes gave a light red wine, with a slightly perfumed nose and some acidity, rather than tannin, on the palate. The 1985 vintage had more structure, with more oak influence and some good fruit. They are also planning a *riserva vino da tavola*, from an unusual blend of Cabernet Sauvignon, Pinot Nero and Syrah in equal parts.

Fattoria del Teso and Other Growers

The largest producer of Montecarlo is Fattoria del Teso, with forty-three hectares of white grapes and thirteen of red. Their white wine comes from Trebbiano, Roussanne, Sauvignon and Vermentino, while their red is mainly Sangiovese, with some Canaiolo and a little Ciliegiolo, Colorino and Syrah. Methods seem somewhat empirical. Sometimes they ferment all the grapes together, sometimes not. Usually the Sauvignon is ready to be picked first, followed by the Vermentino, then the Roussanne and finally the Trebbiano. They make two qualities of white wine, a normal Montecarlo Bianco and a *riserva* white called Stella del Teso; I was told, enigmatically that the grape varieties for this were a secret. However it had an attractive smoky character on the nose, some herbal minty flavours on the palate and a good balancing acidity. The final tasting was of an eleven-year-old Vin Santo, which after nine years in wood had flavours redolent of madeira cake.

I enjoyed other wines at the fair, including Giovanni Fuso's wine from the Azienda Agricola Cercatoia, which had an attractive nutty flavour on the palate. Good too was that of Antonio Vettori, including a high percentage of Pinot Bianco and Grigio, which was soft and buttery. Quality was not uniform, for modern vinification techniques have passed Montecarlo by in some instances. Although there is room for improvement, however, the interest and potential of Montecarlo Bianco is considerable.

Montecarlo Rosso does not quite have the stature of the white, for the white is a wine to age, whereas the red is best drunk in relative youth. For red wine it is perhaps better to turn to the Rosso delle Colline Lucchesi. Until Montecarlo Rosso became a DOC, this was the red pair to white Montecarlo, for it was recognised as a DOC as early as 1968. White wine is also included in the DOC of the Colline Lucchesi, but only since 1985 and it remains insignificant.

The Colline Lucchesi

Vines have long been grown on the stunning, beautiful hills behind the walled city of Lucca. The Etruscans were the first to plant them, followed by the Romans, and viticulture continued to flourish into the Middle Ages. In 1334 it was recorded that a total of 168,300 *barili* (the medieval measure of a barrel of wine) was transported to Lucca from the nearby hills. The wine was described as 'clear, bright red, pure and frank', by a vintner called Cinelio. The Datini archives in Prato show that as early as 1300 wine from San Gennaro, today one of the villages of the Colline Lucchesi, was sent to many Italian cities. Pope Paul III, among others, enjoyed the wines of Lucca.

Today the vineyards of the Colline Lucchesi are limited to the parishes of Lucca, Capannori and Porcari, stretching from the village of Forci, through Cappella and Mastiano beyond the river Serchio, to Matraia, Segromigno, Gragnano and San Gennaro. Altogether there are about 145 hectares of vines, 122 red and 23 white, planted on clay and limestone soil. This is a lost corner of Tuscany, off the beaten tourist track, with pretty little villages and hamlets. The climate is quite mild, as it is closer to the sea than the vineyards of central Tuscany. As the vineyards are surrounded by hills, they are protected from many of the prevailing winds.

The grape varieties for the wines of the Colline Lucchesi are not as imaginative as those for neighbouring Montecarlo. The red wine comes mainly from Sangiovese and Canaiolo, including Colorino, Ciliegiolo and in true Tuscan tradition, the white grape varieties, Trebbiano, Malvasia and Vermentino. However it is not obligatory to include white grapes in the red wine. As for the white, the choice is Trebbiano, Malvasia, Vermentino and unusually Grechetto, which is found more commonly on the Umbrian border of Tuscany.

Fattoria di Fubbiano

First I went to the Fattoria di Fubbiano, a tiny hamlet up in the hills behind Lucca, near the village of San Gennaro. It was bought recently by the de Andreis family, who are medical publishers in Milan. In their absence the *fattore*, the third generation of his family here, runs the estate. The eighteenth-century villa has an air of gentle dilapidation, while what was once an elegant wooded park with statues and fountains has become overgrown with neglect. From the terraces there are wonderful views towards Lucca. They have thirteen hectares of vines and also seventeen hectares of olive trees. Their red wine is mainly Sangiovese, with some Canaiolo, about 5 per cent of white grapes and the same of Ciliegiolo, while their white has 25 per cent of Vermentino to dilute the Trebbiano. They would also like to plant some Grechetto.

There is little evidence of recent investment in the cellars but things may change under new ownership. For the moment they have open wooden vats, and some of cement. They use the *governo* method for their red, as they like the way it softens the wine and makes it ready to drink earlier, even though it is expensive. They have no refrigeration equipment, as the small production of white wine does not justify the cost. The DOC regulations do not allow for a *riserva*, but a second red wine is made here from their best vineyard, which contains 300 plants of Cabernet Sauvignon, planted 'by accident'. It is bottled at the end of August, just before the next vintage, as opposed to May or June for the other red wine. Rosso delle Colline Lucchesi is not a wine to age, but to drink in its youth. This was borne out by their basic red wine, which was not unlike a young Chianti, while the *cru* had a little more weight and substance, and the white wine some of the dusty fragrance of Vermentino.

Fattoria Maionchi

No more than ten estates bottle their wine in the Colline Lucchesi. The Fattoria Maionchi in the village of Tofori probably has the best reputation. Signora Maionchi gave me a friendly welcome, as did her spaniel Bostick (because everything sticks to him), but curiously for a winemaker she is teetotal. First we visited the villa, which was built at the end of the seventeenth century. Many of the rooms had the most wonderful frescos, painted in the mid-eighteenth century. Her great-grandfather bought the estate and she now has eleven and half hectares of vines.

She explained how the purchase of stainless steel fermentation vats had involved a considerable financial sacrifice; for the returns on the wine of the Colline Lucchesi are not such as to justify enormous investment. She cannot afford to buy refrigeration equipment, but they do cool their vats with water. I liked her white wine very much, probably because it did not contain any Trebbiano at all. It is called Toforino after the village and comes mainly from Vermentino and Malvasia. It had an attractive perfumed nose and some fragrant, slightly stony fruit on the palate.

Next we tasted a Rubino di Selvata made from the Hamburg Muscat grape, which is more common as a table grape. Although the regulations do not allow for Moscato in the Colline Lucchesi, apparently Moscato has long been grown in these hills. I found the taste of this wine, which included some

governato grapes, to be rather curious, almost bitter-sweet and slightly astringent, which was a surprise after its sweet perfumed nose. The Rosso delle Colline Lucchesi, without any *governato* grapes, was much better, with a lovely bitter-cherry flavour. Signora Maionchi began experimenting with pure Sangiovese in 1987 and was very proud of her two brand-new oak *barriques*. I was left, not for the first time, with the feeling that the DOC regulations were blocking the creativity of the estate.

Fattoria Tre Cancelli

My final visit was to the traditional Fattoria Tre Cancelli, on flatter land closer to Lucca. It is the property of the Count Sardi Giustiani and his wife, and has been in the Countess's family for nearly a hundred years. After a visit to the cellars, with their cement fermentation vats and rows of old oak casks, we adjourned to the garden to taste, accompanied by the dog Lucy and the cat Panna, which means thick cream in Italian and may be a reflection on the cat's taste.

Count Giustiani has always made white wine, as well as red. There are two whites, one of which is kept in wood for six months. This had a fuller, nuttier flavour than his basic white. Temperature control is rather hit and miss; he racks the vat if the temperature rises too high. The hotchpotch of grape varieties, Trebbiano, Grechetto, Vermentino, Malvasia and Colombano is all fermented together.

As for red wine, he sometimes practises the *governo* method and usually includes some white grapes, as the Trebbiano is mixed up with the Sangiovese in the vineyard. I found the taste a little astringent and green. However Rosso delle Colline Lucchesi is not intended to have much body and certainly goes well with a plate of pasta under the city walls of Lucca.

Candia dei Colli Apuani

The vineyards of this little known white wine are in a lost corner of Tuscany, almost into Liguria, in the north-west of the province. In fact Candia dei Colli Apuani has more in common with the wines of La Spezia than with the other white wines of Tuscany.

The landscape is dominated by the Apuanian hills, the foothills of the Apennines which separate Tuscany from northern Italy (see illustration). These hills behind Massa and Carrara are famous for their marble; marble from Carrara was used by Michelangelo and the quarries are still a flourishing industry. The enormous cuts in the mountainside leave great white scars, so that the mountains look snow-capped even in the height of summer.

The DOC of the Candia dei Colli Apuani was created in 1981 and covers vineyards around the three towns of Massa, Carrara and Montignoso. Candia is the name of a tiny vineyard in the hills behind Massa, which belonged to the church of San Lorenzo at the beginning of the sixteenth century; the monks are said to have made a particularly fine wine, at a time when there were few vineyards in the area. Today most of the growers are in Massa. They had originally hoped for a more restricted DOC of Candia di Massa, but bureaucracy decreed otherwise. Production is tiny,

The vineyards of the Colli Apuani.

about 700 hectolitres a year, and only a handful of growers bottle their wine.

The vineyards are dramatic. The vines are planted on steep terraced hillsides, at an altitude of 150 to 200 metres, each vine with a supporting post, with barely a metre between them, and only one row of vines to each narrow terrace. They cluster together more intensely than vineyards in other parts of Tuscany. Before some of the roads were built up into the vineyards, the growers had to use a kind of cable car, to carry equipment and to bring the grapes down to the cellars.

The climate is very much affected by proximity to the sea and the mountains. The Apuanian Alps protect the vines from cold winds from the north in winter, while in the summer they precipitate rainfall from clouds blowing off the Mediterranean. Unusually for Tuscany, Trebbiano is not the mainstay of Candia dei Colli Apuani, but rather Vermentino. This grape variety is said to originate from Sardinia and was brought to Liguria by the Genoese, who also took it to Corsica. From La Spezia, Vermentino has spread into north-western Tuscany. It is distinctive for its slightly nutty flavoured wine and in Candia dei Colli Apuani must account for 70 to 80 per cent of the blend. It is combined with between 10 and 20 per cent Albarolo, which is another Ligurian grape variety and a member of the Trebbiano family; an optional 20 per cent maximum of Trebbiano and a maximum of 5 per cent Malvasia. Some people make their Candia dei Colli Apuani from just Vermentino and Albarolo, with the Albarolo lightening the flavour. It differs from Trebbiano in that it has more compact bunches and is less productive.

I had no idea what to expect from my first taste of Candia dei Colli Apuani and was certainly not prepared for this lightly sparkling, slightly sweet wine. It was surprisingly delicious. The president of the growers' association Cesare della Tommasina explained to me how it was made. The grapes are picked at the end of September and are destalked before pressing. The fermentation begins in medium-sized chestnut barrels and the juice is in contact with the skins for three or four days, before it is run off into fibreglass vats. There is no particular temperature control; the fermentation takes its own course. The wine is then chilled in order to stop the fermentation, retaining a little sugar for an *abboccato* taste. The wine is bottled as and when it is needed and referments a little in bottle, leaving a slight prickle of carbon dioxide. The process is not unlike the *méthode rurale* of France, to be found in traditional Gaillac or Rosé de Cerdon. Signor Tommasina explained that he did not make a dry wine, only an *abboccato*, which became drier after a while in bottle. It was grapy on the nose, with some sweetness and a dry almondy finish.

Apparently the original tradition in Candia dei Colli Apuani was for a sweet wine, which changed to a drier style after the phylloxera crisis at the beginning of this century. Now local taste again prefers a sweeter wine. The DOC regulations do not allow for any distinction on the label and assume a wine that is rounded, not completely dry but certainly not sweet. The slightly sparkling character came about by accident. Federico Lorieri, whose address is appropriately Via dell'Uva, has experimented with the proper champagne method, but with only three and a half hectares of vines, he says he does not have enough wine to continue with this.

Lorieri is a young man whose horizons extend rather further than those of his fellow growers. He has a desire to create an image for Candia dei Colli Apuani beyond Massa and Carrara, but I fear that for the moment he is alone in this ambition. He certainly has a questioning attitude to winemaking. For example, he has reduced the amount of skin contact he gives his wine to between ten and forty hours, depending on the year. It was traditional to keep the juice on the skins for a few days, in order to increase the colour and aroma, which are sometimes a little elusive with the Vermentino grape. He also tries to rack his wine less, for fear of oxidation, and explained that traditional vinification methods can leave the wine a little unstable and unsuitable for travel. His wine did not have the positive bubbles of Tommasina's, but was full-flavoured with a strong nutty finish.

Lorieri also makes red wine, called Scurtarola after the locality, from various little known local grapes like Vermentino Nero, Massareta and Buonamica, combined with Sangiovese. Any red wine is simply a *vino da tavola*, without even a geographical indication. North of Massa, in the hills around Fosdinovo and Pontremole, there is a traditional local red wine called Vino di Lunigiana, made from a diverse selection of grapes, including Schiava, which is rarely seen today.

Montescudaio

The quiet, unassuming hilltop town of Montescudaio gives its name to both a red and a white wine. Seven parishes in the Val di Cecina make up the DOC area, namely Montescudaio, Casale Marittima, Castellina Marittima, Riparbella, Guardistallo and parts of Santa Luce and Montecatini Val di Cecina, not to be confused with the better known Montecatini Terme. In fact, most of the vineyards are close to Montescudaio itself.

Montescudaio was recognised as a DOC in 1977, for red, white and Vin Santo. The nearest neighbouring vineyards are those of the Colline Pisane and there is little to distinguish red Montescudaio from Chianti. The grape varieties are similar, mainly Sangiovese, Canaiolo and some Trebbiano and Malvasia. White Montescudaio is rendered more interesting by the addition of Vermentino to the customary Malvasia and Trebbiano. There are also occasional plantings of Cabernet Sauvignon and Chardonnay, but not for the DOC wine. The vineyards are on gentle hillsides, lying at an altitude of some 300 metres, with stony limestone soil. The sea is nearby, so the vineyards enjoy the tempering influence of the sea breezes, called the *libeccio*.

I saw four producers, out of fifteen in Montescudaio who put their wine into bottle. Each was 'doing his own thing' without reference to the others and there seemed to be no such thing as a typical Montescudaio.

Sorbaiano

My introduction to the region was the estate of Sorbaiano, lying on the edge of the DOC, in the hills close to Montecatini Val di Cecina. There is an imposing seventeenth-century villa, as well as views of the austere alabaster town of Volterra across the valley. The property is owned by the Picciolini family, who also own Le Colonne, a small estate in San Gimignano. The wines of Sorbaiano benefit from the expertise of Vittorio Fiore, one of Tuscany's leading oenologists, and have improved considerably since he became responsible for them in 1987. Fermentation temperatures are now controlled and they have invested in stainless steel vats, as well as *barriques*. Other grape varieties have been planted too, but are not yet in production, including Chardonnay and Riesling Italico. These may help to make white wine with a little more flavour.

They have two white wines. A simple Montescudaio is made from Trebbiano and is fairly neutral in flavour, with hints of almonds. The second wine is still at the experimental stage. In 1987 it spent six months in wood; in 1988 it was also fermented in oak and spent a few months in *barriques*. The blend of grape varieties includes Vermentino. I tasted the 1987, which was quite leafy and rounded in flavour. It is called Lucestraia, after a farm on the estate.

There are also two red wines; red Montescudaio made from Sangiovese, Ciliegiolo and Canaiolo, which was light and fruity, not unlike a simple Chianti; and Rosso delle Miniere, which includes 10 per cent Cabernet and spends five or six months in small oak.

Poggio Gagliardo

It was Walter Surbone at Montescudaio's largest estate, Poggio Gagliardo, who explained that the use of *barriques* was not permitted under the DOC regulations. He too makes an alternative wine, called Malemacchie, which is aged in *barriques* for six months or so, and includes 20 to 25 per cent Cabernet Sauvignon. This was one of the best wines I tasted in Montescudaio and it may be an argument for allowing these reds to be aged in oak. It was rich and full, with a smoky bacon nose, meaty with plenty of fruit and length.

Surbone came to Tuscany from Piedmont in 1965 and he now has fifty hectares of vines, including some outside the DOC area, where he has planted Cabernet Sauvignon and Chardonnay. They are a little lower in altitude and on the wrong side of a stream called the Linaglia. He is also a farmer, raising Chianina cattle for Florentine *bistecca*.

He makes classic red and white Montescudaio. His white includes Canaiolo Bianco, which softens the Trebbiano, some Vermentino and a hint of Sauvignon. It was rather old fashioned, dry and nutty, but with more character than many neutral dry white wines. He considers that his white wine is worth ageing for a year, as a comparison of the 1987 and 1988 vintages showed in the spring of 1989. The 1988 was still rather appley in character, though quite fresh and fruity. The red Montescudaio is kept for a few months in large casks. Cherries was the dominant flavour, making a soft, fruity wine, with hints of spice and a slightly earthy finish.

Morazzano and La Rinserrata

Two brothers, Jacopo and Stefano Savi, run the tiny estate of Morazzano and they have also taken over the better known Montescudaio property of La Rinserrata. Their main interest is not so much in the DOC of Montescudaio, as in the production of organic wine. They are very careful about the amount of sulphur that they use, both in vineyard and cellar. Their cellars are neat and well organised, and their wines attractive; a light fruity pink table wine and two reds, one aged in *botti* and the other in *barriques*. They admitted that they drank most of this wine themselves.

Fattoria San Giovanni

Roberto Moschen is the proprietor of the Fattoria San Giovanni. It seemed rather disorganised, as though he was trying to make too many wines from his twenty odd hectares of vines. He has the traditional Tuscan grape varieties, as well as Chardonnay, Cabernet Sauvignon and Pinot Bianco. He is thinking about planting Sauvignon. He makes a *vino novello* and experiments with Cabernet in *barriques*, both as a varietal and with Sangiovese. It illustrated an enquiring mind, but left me even more confused as to what really constituted a wine of Montescudaio.

Sassicaia and Bolgheri

Bolgheri is a relatively new DOC, dating from 1983, for white and pink wine. Ironically, the more exciting wines of the region are generally red and the most interesting producers remain firmly aloof from the DOC. Bolgheri itself is an attractive little village, a *frazione* of the parish of Castagneto Carducci. The DOC covers most of Castagneto Carducci, apart from the flat coastal land lying to the west of the Rome–Livorno railway line. In the village there is a cheerful little *enoteca*, which also serves as a meeting-place and café for the local inhabitants. One can taste the wine of most of the producers in the DOC of Bolgheri there, while the old men of the village pass the time of day, smoking and playing cards.

It is no surprise that the white Bolgheri should be made from Trebbiano, with a dash of Malvasia and Vermentino. The pink consists of Sangiovese and Canaiolo. There is little to excite within the DOC. Very much better are the wines outside it. The largest estate in the Bolgheri region belongs to Antinori, but they ignore the regulations, as their vineyards are outside. They make a pink *vino da tavola* called Scalabrone. Nearby are the Sassicaia vineyards, Ornellaia, the new creation of Ludovico Antinori, and the estate of Grattamacco, all of which are making exciting wines, with no regard to the DOC. Such are the contradictions of Italian wine law.

Sassicaia

Sassicaia at the Tenuta San Guido set the pace for the so-called alternative wines of Tuscany. The estate is close to the village of Bolgheri. You turn off the frighteningly fast SS Aurelia, which follows the Tuscan coastline, and drive up a magnificent avenue of cypress trees, planted at the end of the eighteenth century. The estate itself is difficult to find. There is no sign at the gate. Once there, however, the Marchese Niccolò Incisa della Rocchetta offers a friendly welcome. His mother was a Gherardesca and her sister is Piero Antinori's mother. The two women divided the Gherardesca inheritance at Bolgheri. The Gherardescas are an old Tuscan family, which features in Dante's *Inferno*; Ugolino Gherardesca was shut up in a tower and made to eat his children.

It was the Marchese Niccolò's father, Mario, who planted the first Cabernet Sauvignon vines here towards the end of the Second World War, on the steep hillside behind the village of Bolgheri. He came from Piedmont and was inspired by an enthusiasm for French wine. As a student in Pisa, he had studied agriculture and farming. There he spent his weekends with friends in the country who had planted Cabernet. For the first twenty years or so the production of his own wine remained unsophisticated, for family and friends. It was the 1968 vintage that made the impact on the international wine market. By then they had begun to collaborate with their Antinori cousins, taking advice on vinification from Dott. Tachis. This experience at Sassicaia gave Tachis a grounding for the innovatory wines which he has created since for Antinori. Sassicaia was also the first Tuscan wine estate to use *barriques* for ageing a red wine.

Today there are twenty-five hectares of vineyards, mainly on low slopes on either side of the cypress-lined drive. The composition of the wine is 80 per cent Cabernet Sauvignon and 20 per cent Cabernet Franc, which are fermented together and then aged in *barriques* for about two years, from the January following the vintage. Initially they used small barrels of Slavonic oak, but have since changed to Allier oak from the Massif Central of France, which are replaced regularly. The wine is given six months of bottle age before sale. The cellar is well equipped. Improvements have been made over the years, so that they now have stainless steel fermentation vats, which can be cooled with cold water, and an insulated barrel cellar.

Sassicaia is a wine that will last, but it is also ready to drink relatively early. Both the 1986 and 1985 vintages provided attractive glasses of wine in the spring of 1989. The 1985 is a more concentrated vintage than the 1986, fuller with more body. The Marchese considers 1985 to be an exceptional vintage, which will require ten years to develop fully. However it is a mistake to make a wine that you have to wait ten years to drink. He sees no point in diversification, preferring to concentrate his energies on just one wine of outstanding quality.

Ornellaia

Sassicaia is the epitome of a well run, serious estate, which more than deserves its reputation. It may have set a trend amongst Tuscan wines, but it has now become an established part of Tuscan viticulture. The next rising star of Bolgheri is the estate of Ornellaia, the brainchild of Piero Antinori's brother, Ludovico. When I was there in April 1989, the winery was still a building site, but you could see that it would be no ordinary winery. Built with the Italian eye for elegance, even in a functional building, it will incorporate a cellar for *barriques* not unlike a Bordelais *chai*, and all the technology of modern vinification.

I talked to the oenologist, Federico Staderini, who has spent time at the University of California at Davis, and in the vineyards there. He explained how Ludovico Antinori had begun to plant vineyards on the hills just behind Bolgheri in 1982, concentrating on Cabernet Sauvignon and Merlot for a red

wine, called Ornellaia; and on Sauvignon, with a touch of Sémillon, for a white wine, which is called Poggio alle Gazze. Yields are low on these rocky hills. However the temperatures are milder than further inland, under the tempering influence of the sea.

It is obvious that Ornellaia is inspired by Sassicaia, but Merlot has been planted rather than Cabernet Franc, as it performs better where there is more clay in the soil. They have tried making pure Merlot, but for Ornellaia the Cabernet and Merlot are blended together after thirteen months of ageing in *barriques*. For the moment they prefer to keep each grape variety separately, as this helps them to understand the character of each plot of vines. Afterwards the wines are given at least a year's bottle age.

There is not a great deal of vintage variation in this part of Tuscany and three vintages of Ornellaia all showed plenty of potential. The 1987 was a cask sample, which had been fined with real egg whites. It was still overpoweringly woody on nose and palate, with some smoky fruit, as well as ripe blackcurrants. The 1986, which had been in bottle for ten months, was more developed than the 1985 and softer, while the preceding vintage had some pronounced pencil shavings and cedarwood on the palate, with some new oak and red fruit on the nose. The vines are still very young and the wines will improve as these age.

White wine accounts for only a fifth of their production. It is perhaps surprising that they planted Sauvignon, rather than the ostensibly more popular Chardonnay. The grapes are picked early, at the end of August, fermented carefully in stainless steel tanks and given no wood ageing at all. The 1987 was the first vintage of Poggio alle Gazze. I tasted the 1988, which was quite simply delicious. It was light and delicate, with excellent varietal character, good crisp acidity and a clean finish. There is in fact a tiny amount of Sémillon to round out the Sauvignon, but I still thought that the wine would compare better with a Sancerre than a white Bordeaux.

In the manner of Bordeaux they also have a second label, for both red and white wine, called Le Serre Nuove. The white includes the remaining Trebbiano, and the red the less successful Cabernet and Merlot.

Grattamacco

The estate of Grattamacco in the hills above Castagneto Carducci is rather less sophisticated in technology, but nonetheless interesting for its range of wines. It is owned by Pier Mario and Paola Meletti Cavallari, who came here from Milan and a wineshop in Bergamo. They were looking for a vineyard somewhere near the sea and had decided upon Tuscany or the Marches. You can see the sea from the vineyards here and even the island of Elba in the distance.

On eight hectares Cavallari is growing all kinds of grape varieties, such as Pinot Nero, Roussanne, Chasan, Chenin Blanc and Cabernet Sauvignon, as well as the more usual varieties of Tuscany like Malvasia, Trebbiano, Vermentino and Sangiovese. Not all of these are in production yet and none of the wines has a DOC, so that they are sold under the estate name, as a geographical indication. Signora Cavallari showed me round as her husband was busy at Vinitaly, accompanied by a pretty little cat who answered to the name of Cleopatre.

The most exceptional thing about the cellars at Grattamacco was the superb 1939 Delage next to the bottling line, for Cavallari is not only a wine enthusiast, but also a lover of veteran cars. More prosaically, there were stainless steel fermentation vats and just twenty-five *barriques*, which they used for the first time in 1982, ageing the red wine for six to eight months. The Grattamacco Bianco is a mixture of grape varieties, including Vermentino. It was perfumed and fruity, with quite high acidity and some herbaceous character. The red wine proved more exciting, a blend of Cabernet Sauvignon and their best Sangiovese. The 1987 had a lovely smoky cedarwood nose, and was rich and balanced with good fruit. It was drinking well in the spring of 1989, while the 1985 tasted more youthful, with tannin and cedarwood, another stylish wine. It was not yet ready for drinking, but illustrated the enormous potential of this region. The DOC of Bolgheri is dwarfed in comparison.

The Maremma

The Maremma covers the coastal region of Tuscany. What the map calls the Maremma Pisana begins somewhere south of Cecina and extends down over the provincial boundary of Grosseto, to become the Maremma Grossetana. The heart of the Maremma is the coastal land made up of the Parco Naturale di Maremma and the Monti dell'Uccellina. However the hills behind are also part of the Maremma, with the vineyards of Scansano and Pitigliano. La Parrina and the vineyards of Capalbio also come within the Maremma, as do the isolated estates of Meleta and Monte Antico. In the north there is a new DOC called the Val di Cornia.

Bianco di Pitigliano

Pitigliano is a dramatic hilltop town, on the edge of Tuscany, almost in Lazio, not far from the Lago di Bolsena. The houses cluster together on a spur, so that there are views of the surrounding countryside from either side of the main square. The Etruscans came here first and in the rocks underneath the town there are numerous Etruscan tombs, some of which have been transformed into wine cellars. There are good views too, of Pitigliano from the distance, perched on top of its sheer cliffs.

Nearby Sorano is an attractive Etruscan town and the birthplace of Pope Gregory VII, who disputed papal supremacy with the Emperor Henry IV in the eleventh century. There was a Jewish community in Pitigliano in the sixteenth century, to the extent that the place was described as 'the little Jerusalem'. Apparently the Jews would have nothing to do with the local wine production, giving rise to a saying in the Middle Ages: 'Wine merchant, poor merchant'. Today the wine cooperative of Pitigliano prides itself on its kosher wine, which is vinified in the same way as the rest, but strictly observes the religious requirements. Viticulture in Pitigliano goes back to the Middle Ages. Ademollo, the medieval equivalent of Veronelli, one of Italy's most respected wine writers today, describes the fresh white wine of Pitigliano and Sorano.

Bianco di Pitigliano was given its DOC as early as 1966 and today the vineyard area covers the parishes of Pitigliano, Scansano, Manciano and Sorano. The soil here is light, rocky and poor, where little will grow except vines and olive trees. It is volcanic tufo in origin, which makes it particularly suitable for white wine. Most of the vineyards are on hillsides at about 300 metres above sea-level. A little red wine is produced in the region, as simple Rosso della Toscana, but is of very limited interest. As for neighbouring wines, there is an overlap with Morellino di Scansano. Pitigliano is also not far from the vineyards around the Lago di Bolsena, including the notorious Est! Est!! Est!!! di Montefiascone, and the best white wine of Umbria, from the town of Orvieto.

January is cold and there are mild springs and warm summers, with very little rain during the summer months. Most of the rain falls during the spring and autumn, so that the vines may suffer from drought while the grapes are ripening. On the other hand this makes for healthy plants, with little rot. Since the sharecropping system came to an end, vines have been replanted in specialised vineyards, suitable for tractors.

Trebbiano, which here is called Procanico, as it is on the island of Elba, accounts for 70 per cent of the blend. Malvasia is the other principal grape variety. In addition there are tiny amounts of Verdello and Greco. Verdello is also found in Umbria, in Orvieto and Torgiano, while Greco is of Greek origin and best known in Greco di Tufo in Campania. It is no relation of the more common Umbrian grape variety, Grechetto.

As well as these traditional Italian grapes, there are now experimental plantings, masterminded by the cooperative of Pitigliano; of Chardonnay, Pinot Bianco, Riesling and Sauvignon, all in the worthy cause of enlivening the flavour of the Tuscan blend. The first vintage of Pinot Bianco was in 1987, with some satisfactory results; the others came into production in 1989. They expect that 5 to 10 per cent of these grape varieties will improve the traditional flavours and hope that they will be incorporated eventually into the DOC. Pinot Bianco has been planted in preference to Pinot Grigio, which is rarely found outside Friuli, as it gives more acidity. Another option would be to work on some of the old grape varieties, such as Grechetto or Ansonica, which have been in danger of disappearing.

The cooperative is the largest producer of Bianco di Pitigliano, as well as the largest cooperative in Tuscany, accounting for 90 per cent of the production, with 900 members responsible for 1,300 of the 1,500 hectares in the DOC. The cooperative at Scansano also makes some wine and there are three or four independent producers.

The cooperative was founded in 1954 and is working well for its DOC. Their oenologist explained their vinification process to me; essentially it is the same as that of any dry white wine. Unlike Orvieto and other central Italian whites, there is no tradition for Pitigliano *abboccato* or *amabile*. It is always firmly dry, with a minimum alcohol of 11.5°. The grapes must reach a natural minimum of 10.5°, which can be increased by one degree with the use of concentrated must. This they have made for them and they are insistent that it comes from local vineyards and not from the south.

All the grape varieties are fermented together, for they grow together in the vineyards. They are destalked and given a gentle pressing. The must is clarified by cooling and then fermented with cultured yeast at 18°C

to 20°C in stainless steel vats in an insulated cellar. There is no skin contact, as that would require special equipment, although they are aware that Trebbiano can benefit from skin contact. However they are considering adding oxygen to the must, in order to precipitate the polyphenols and give cleaner, more stable juice, requiring less sulphur dioxide. They have been equipped with cooling equipment since about 1978, which is advanced for an Italian cooperative. Consequently they are able to treat the wine for tartrates and bottle it in March for early drinking.

There is one independent estate of note making Bianco di Pitigliano, namely La Stellata, near the village of Manciano. Clara Divizia and her husband gave me a friendly welcome. They came here some six years ago, buying a house with four and a half hectares of vines. Although Clara's mother came from the Maremma and her husband from Montalcino, they had no intention of making wine when they bought the land. However wine has become a passion. There are not many alternatives here; sheep are boring and olive trees too difficult. In a very short space of time, with the help of the oenologist Marco Stefanini, they have succeeded in making an outstanding white wine.

In fact they make two white wines. The best is Lunaia, which comes from a gentle pressing. Originally it was made without any skin contact, but in 1988 they experimented with a very light skin contact for part of the wine and have been pleased with the result. It has lessened the acidity typical of Bianco di Pitigiano and given the wine more body. They were intending to repeat the experiment the following year. They do not feel that wood would be appropriate to the taste of Pitigliano. The second white, called Il Doccio is a *vino da tavola*, rather than a Bianco di Pitigliano, and is made from the second pressing of the grapes.

They are against the cooperative's project to change the DOC regulations to include Pinot Bianco, Chardonnay and Riesling, as they fear that this will lead to uniformity. Instead they feel strongly that original grape varieties such as Grechetto and Malvasia should be nurtured and developed. They would also like to grow some Ansonica.

They are experimenting with red wine, using Sangiovese, Canaiolo and Montepulciano d'Abruzzo. We tasted the 1988 vintage, when it was nearly a year old. It was very solid with firm berry fruit and tannin. As for the Bianco di Pitigliano of La Stellata, it was delicately fragrant, an example of what careful winemaking combined with love and talent can achieve, a deliciously grassy wine, not unlike a Chablis.

What Bianco di Pitigliano lacks is a specific personality to distinguish it from the mass of other white, Trebbiano-based Tuscan wines. Pitigliano is also off the beaten track, which is to the wine's disadvantage, for it remains virtually unknown outside the Maremma. The taste has the nutty almond flavours typical of Trebbiano, and is quite fragrant and full, rounded and not too acid, so that it goes well with Tuscan *antipasti*.

Morellino di Scansano

The picturesque-sounding Morellino di Scansano is the red counterpart of Bianco di Pitigliano, although it was not recognised as a DOC until 1978, some twelve years after the white wine.

Scansano is a rather sombre town. Although its origins are Etruscan, it has little claim to historical fame. Apparently Garibaldi asked for some Morellino di Scansano when he was recruiting volunteers, and for this reason there is a statue of him in the main square. Giacomo Barbino, writing in 1884, observed that 'the wines of Magliano, Pereta and Scansano are excellent and in several places the wine produced is even of exquisite quality.' The French came here under Napoleon, bringing their experience in vineyard and cellar, so that viticulture flourished. They remained after the defeat of the Emperor, until a severe attack of peronospera at the end of the nineteenth century caused considerable damage in the vineyards. Viticulture was more developed a hundred years ago than it is today.

Morellino is quite simply the local name for Sangiovese. I was told that their particular variety was very similar to that of Montal-cino. The name Morello is a derivation of *moro*, meaning brown or a deep colour, so the idea behind the name is similar to that behind Brunello. The area of the DOC covers the whole parish of Scansano, as well as parts of the adjoining ones, Manciano, Magliano in Toscana, Grosseto, Campagnatico, Roccalbegna and Semproniano in the hills east of Grosseto, between the Ombrone and Albegna rivers. Altogether there are some 280 hectares of vineyards in production, the local cooperative being responsible for a little over half of them.

The vineyards are usually at an altitude of 300 to 450 metres. The effect of the intense summer sunshine is reduced by the higher altitude and prevailing winds from the sea have a cooling effect. They usually also blow away cloud cover; although on the day that I was there I awoke to find Scansano shrouded in mist. Generally the vintage does not take place until the beginning of October. The soil is very similar to that of Pitigliano and indeed there is a slight overlap between the two DOCs. There is less tufo and more chalk, but no clay.

Small quantities of Canaiolo are grown, as in Chianti, and of Malvasia Nera; one occasionally finds this elsewhere in Tuscany, although it is more common in Apulia. There is Ciliegiolo, which is particularly suitable for a *vino novello* and also, unexpectedly, Alicante, the local name for Grenache, which was brought here by the Spaniards. Originating in Spain, it spread round the Mediterranean coast to Sardinia as Cannonau; this is the only example of it on mainland Italy. It is not really allowed in the DOC regulations, a fact which seems to be generally disregarded.

The cooperative of Scansano was founded in 1977, the year before Morellino di Scansano was recognised as a DOC. Hitherto the wine had been produced by numerous small growers, lacking any cohesion or sense of direction. The founding of the cooperative reassured the bureaucracy in Rome that a new DOC would have credibility.

Today the cooperative is a modern, efficiently run organisation. Several qualities of Morellino di Scansano are made, including a *riserva*, which necessitates a minimum of

Ezio Mantelassi of Magliano.

two years' ageing, including one in wood. This is a recent development and part of their policy to develop a reputation for quality in Morellino. Usually they put the wine into wood the summer following the vintage, first into fifty-hectolitre *botti* and then into twenty-five hectolitre ones. The wine is then given some bottle age before sale. However as the basic quality of Morellino demonstrated upon tasting, it is not a wine for lengthy ageing, but for drinking in relative youth. It had the flavour of ripe cherries, rich and rounded, with the typical astringent finish of the Sangiovese grape, making a fruity mouthful of wine. In contrast the *riserva*, made only from Morellino, had vanilla overtones from the new wood, not unlike a Rioja. The flavours were a combination of vanilla, fruit and tannin. They also make a *vino novello* called Saragiolo, which had an attractive fruity cherry flavour.

Individual growers were even more rewarding to visit. First I went to see Ezio Mantelassi on his family estate near the walled town of Magliano in Toscana. He explained that his Morellino di Scansano was made from 70 per cent Sangiovese, with some Canaiolo, Montepulciano d'Abruzzo and what he called Tinto di Spagna, or Grenache. Unlike Chianti

there have never been any white grapes in Morellino di Scansano. However he does make a white *vino da tavola* from Vermentino and a sparkling wine, which is vinified elsewhere by the Charmat method.

Mantelassi explained that in his grandfather's time the wine had been given a long fermentation, with fifteen days on the skins and stalks. His father bought a destalker and now he ferments for just six days on the skins. The wine goes into cement vats for a year and then into *botti*, before bottling. Part of his *riserva* wine is kept in Limousin *barriques*, probably for only three months, but depending upon the age of the *barriques*. Mantelassi feels that the *barriques* have improved the quality of the wine enormously, making it more elegant and refined. However the most striking feature of his cellars is the row of large hams hanging from the ceiling. He says that his oenologist does not approve, but that the atmosphere is good for them.

The estate of Le Pupille is closer to Scansano itself and is owned by Elizabetta and Augusto Gentile, having belonged first to Augusto's grandmother. The family live in Pisa and treat the estate as a serious hobby. I arrived to find Elizabetta Gentile reprimanding two mischievous Alsatians, who had stolen a salami from the kitchen. There are ten hectares of vines, from which they make some stylish Morellino di Scansano, of Sangiovese, with 15 per cent of Alicante, Malvasia Nera and Ciliegiolo. They have abandoned large casks and their *riserva* wines are given one year in small wood after a year in stainless steel vats, while the *normale* can be sold in the spring following the vintage. They have grafted some Cabernet Sauvignon, which is just coming into production and are planning to use it for an alternative wine. I tasted the 1985 *riserva*, which was delicious, very rich with plenty of fruit.

For me the most exciting producer of Morellino di Scansano is Erik Banti, in the hilltop village of Montemerano. He came here from Rome, where he used to run a travel agency. Beginning with just one and a half hectares of vines for his first vintage in 1981, he has since expanded the estate to eleven and a half.

Banti makes his Morellino di Scansano from 85 per cent Sangiovese, with some Canaiolo, Malvasia Nera and Grenache, in small cellars scattered round the village. He does not believe in making a *riserva*-quality wine, but does produce a *barrique*-aged Morellino as well as a Morellino *normale*. There are also two *crus*, from specific vineyards, Aquilaia and Ciabatta. In such hilly terrain there are a great many different microclimates. Consequently Banti wanted to demonstrate the particular characteristics of his two best vineyards.

The *barricata* wine spends six to nine months in Tronçais oak, after a fermentation lasting ten to twelve days on the skins, as opposed to seven days for the *normale*. He also has some small *botti*, or rather *botticelli*, of Slavonic oak for his other wines. Nothing stands still here. Banti has recently planted just 900 vines each of Pinot Nero and Cabernet Sauvignon. His wines had a depth and concentration that is not always apparent in Morellino di Scansano, with smoky flavours of herbs and spices, reminiscent of the warm Tuscan sunshine. I left Scansano in the most dramatic thunderstorm, with lightning that turned night to day for fleeting seconds.

Parco dell' Uccellina and Capalbio

The National Park of the Maremma was created in 1975 and is run by an association whose principal aim is to protect the natural environment of this part of Tuscany. There are very strict controls on agricultural and viticultural practices, forbidding the use of weedkillers, insecticides and so on. Altogether there are about a hundred hectares of vines in the park, on gentle slopes a few metres above the level of the reclaimed coastal marshland. Most of the vines are tended by small farmers, who give their grapes to the nearby cooperatives. There is only one estate of any size, consisting of ten hectares, owned by Enrico Pratesi.

He comes from Manciano, within the DOC of Morellino di Scansano and has vineyards there too. As well as vines, he has olive trees and a nursery for market gardening. He also rears racehorses. He referred to this vineyard as his hobby. The ten hectares are altogether in one large plot, eight of white and two of red grape varieties, namely Trebbiano, Malvasia, Ciliegiolo and Sangiovese, with plans for some Vermentino and Pinot Bianco.

Pratesi thought that white wines would do better here, almost at sea-level, than on the hillsides further inland. His vines are trained on a tall pergola system, which is deemed better for white wine, as the grapes ripen more slowly. Excess leaves are removed in the summer. Salt may be a problem, but the vines are protected by a slope of olive trees. The white wine is called Rèdola, which is a local word for a little country lane, of the sort typical in the Parco dell'Uccellina. It is made from 60 per cent Trebbiano, with some Malvasia and 15 per cent Ciliegiolo, which is vinified like a white wine, to give extra structure. As yet they do not have refrigeration equipment to control their fermentation temperatures, which would improve this rather dull white wine.

The red was better. It was called Orfeno, after the friendly old cellarman, who runs everything in Pratesi's absence. It is made mainly from Sangiovese with 15 per cent Ciliegiolo and is bottled in the spring without any ageing in wood. I found it fresh and fruity, and very easy to drink.

There is some talk of the area having its own DOC, but for the moment the wine is guaranteed by the park authorities, who issue a certificate confirming its organic nature.

From the Park I went to the Cantina Sociale di Capalbio. Here you are almost in Lazio, right on the southern edge of Tuscany. Capalbio is an attractive hilltop town, which still retains its medieval walls, perched on the first slopes of the Maremma hills. The cellars of the cooperative, which was founded in 1961, are on the low coastal land. Some 470 members have 520 hectares between them, averaging a little over one hectare per member. They are farmers who grow a little of everything. The vineyards are on the surrounding south-facing hillsides, with vines planted in stony, clay soil.

There is Trebbiano, Malvasia and Vermentino for white wine and Sangiovese, Ciliegiolo, Montepulciano d'Abruzzo and the tiniest amount of Barbera for red. They also have Ansonica, a grape variety peculiar to this coastal area, and to the islands of Elba and Giglio. It is said to be related to the Inzolia of Sicily, and to have been brought here by the Spaniards in the early seventeenth century. Two versions of Ansonica are made, both as pure varietals. Traditional Ansonica is fermented on its skins for forty-eight hours to give more colour and body. This is sold *sfuso* to local restaurants, while the bottled version has no skin contact and is lighter in colour and flavour. This was what I tasted. It was quite firm, with a slightly nutty character, but spoilt by a sour finish, which may have been the fault of the winemaking rather than of the grape. The character of Ansonica remained somewhat elusive. However they are hoping for a DOC for Ansonica di Capalbio before too long, which might be a spur to improvement.

The members of the cooperative come from four parishes, not only Capalbio, but also Orbetello, Magnana and Manciano. Grapes from Capalbio are vinified as Vino da Tavola di Capalbio, while the production of other vineyards is called Vino da Tavola della Maremma Toscana. The cooperative seemed to have quite efficient vinification equipment, but was less organised for offering tastings to visitors. Impressions of their wines were distorted by the inadequacies of a plastic beaker. The white was dry with some almond character, while a sparkling wine, made by the Charmat method proved very easy to drink, with a slightly nutty nose. On the palate it was not too acid, with a fragrant dusty finish. The *amabile* version was less successful, but the Rosso di Capalbio proved very fruity and perfumed. I warmed to the Ansonica over what was described in my programme as a 'colazione di lavora molto frugale', in other words a very frugal working lunch. Italian hospitality does not really embrace the concept of frugality. In theory the meal was only *antipasti*, but in practice it was a banquet. I have never seen such an enormous variety of *crostini* of different flavours, not to mention hams, salamis, bresaola from wild boar, olives and so on. It was with immense difficulty that I escaped to the next appointment.

Meleta

A chance mention in the *Guida del Gambero Rosso*, an independent survey of Italian wines, led me to Meleta, a small hamlet near the town of Roccatederighi, with its ruined watchtower. I was on my way to Grosseto, driving from Siena and had spent a leisurely morning exploring the ruined Cistercian abbey of San Galgano. The road led through some wonderful wild countryside.

The estate of Meleta belongs to a Swiss businessman called Max Suter. He bought this abandoned property some ten years ago and planted grape varieties to suit his more international tastebuds. As a successful car dealer, notably in Mercedes and Lancia, one assumes that money was no object. The five-hectare vineyard, soon to become six and a half hectares, contains Cabernet Sauvignon, Merlot, Chardonnay and Italian grape varieties such as Sangiovese, Trebbiano and Ciliegiolo. The vineyards are on hillsides at an altitude of 450 metres, on very stony soil, with a little clay. There are no other vineyards within at least twenty kilometres. As for climate, this is one of the cooler parts of the

Maremma.

Neat well equipped cellars have been built, with stainless steel fermentation tanks, appropriate refrigeration equipment and a separate cellar for wood ageing, with twenty-hectolitre barrels of Allier and Limousin oak. Marco Stefanini is the consultant oenologist here and he must take credit for the success of the wines of Meleta. He is also responsible for helping the new DOC of the Val di Cornia to find its feet.

I had no idea at all what to expect from this estate. The first surprise was quite the best Trebbiano that I have ever tasted. Superlatives are not usually applied to such an unexciting grape variety, but Lucertolo as they call it (meaning a male lizard in Italian), benefits from some wood ageing. The fermentation begins in vat, for four or five days and ends in wood. Subsequently the wine is kept in small *botti* for a further six months. They have low yields and press the grapes very gently, which helps to avoid the bitterness normally associated with this variety. The result is a lovely, light buttery wine, both on nose and palate, which I could have mistaken easily for Chardonnay. They have only half a hectare of Chardonnay at Meleta, which came into production in 1988. It had not yet been released for sale at the time of my visit. It will be called Bianco della Rocca and will spend fourteen months in wood.

The red wines were of the same exciting standard as the whites. Pietrello is almost pure Sangiovese, with a drop of Ciliegiolo, aged for at least eighteen months in wood. Rosso della Rocca is made from equal parts of Sangiovese, Merlot and Cabernet Sauvignon, fermented together and kept for two years in *botti*. A pink wine, Rocchigiano is made half and half from Sangiovese and Ciliegiolo. Even that had spent three months in wood and it was very refreshing, with good acidity and fruit, almost sweet on the finish. A 1988 pure Sangiovese had in September 1989 some spicy fruit, with tannin and concentration, while the 1987 Rosso della Rocca was balanced and elegant, with hints of liquorice, promising well for future drinking. The first vintage at Meleta was as recent as 1982, but already the

results of the commitment and investment are to be seen.

Monte Antico

I had been intrigued by a reference to Monte Antico as an aspiring DOC in Burton Anderson's pocketbook of Italian wine. My curiosity was aroused, partly I suspect by the name, but it turned out to be what the Italians call, not a wild goose chase, but a search for a *primola rossa*, or a red primrose. The wines of Castello di Monte Antico did enjoy a certain reputation in the late 1970s, when they were imported to the United States, but sadly the estate has gone into decline since then. The previous owner Signor Cabella died in 1986 and none of his children was interested in taking over the property. As a result the estate was sold in 1989 to a construction company from Rome, whose main interest, according to the *fattore*, is *agriturismo*. They say however, that they will not neglect the wine, which for the moment is sold locally *sfuso*.

The closest vineyards to Monte Antico are those of Montalcino; the estate is simply the wrong side of the river Ombrone. From the terraces there are views of what is now called the Castello Banfi, the former Castello di Poggio alle Mura. There are thirty hectares of vineyards at the Castello di Monte Antico, planted mainly with Sangiovese. I tasted the 1988 vintage, which had a deep inky colour and was almost port-like on the palate, so concentrated was it and very tannic too. Either it should be blended with a lighter wine, or it will need plenty of time in wood to mellow. It is to be hoped that the new owners realise the potential of Monte Antico, for it would be sad to see the vineyards disappear.

La Parrina

La Parrina is one of the southernmost vineyards of Tuscany, close to Lazio. The vines are in the parish of Orbetello, on gentle hills above the pine forests of the coastal plain, close to the National Park of the Maremma. From the viewpoint above them one can see the island of Giglio and others of the Tuscan archipelago; and to the north Monte Amiata. These are hillsides of scrub, with the scent of wild roses and herbs.

The DOC of La Parrina is virtually synonymous with the estate of La Parrina. There are a handful of other producers, but none bottles their wine regularly. The estate of La Parrina is run by the enthusiastic and articulate Signora Franca Spinola Malfatti, and came by marriage to her great-great-grandfather in 1860. Once they had 2,000 hectares of land, but they lost the coastal plains to cereal and cattle with the Reforma Agraria after the Second World War. Now they concentrate on wine and other fruit, including kiwis and kumquats. Her husband is a politician, while she is a doctor practising in Rome, but this does not prevent her from taking an energetic interest in the estate.

The label of La Parrina proudly proclaims Vino Etrusco, for this is close to the Etruscan site of Tarquinia. There are also the remains of a Roman villa on the estate, but more recent historical links are with Spain. After Philip II of Spain gave up the city of Siena to Cosimo de'Medici, he retained the ports of Orbetello, Porto Ercole, and Porto Santo Stefano as Spanish possessions. *Parra* in Spanish means a pergola of grapes.

Today the interest in La Parrina is local, mainly from tourists. Without Signora Malfatti's energetic promotion of her wine, La Parrina would remain completely unknown to the outside world. As it is, it does not travel far, to the restaurants of Orbetello and Santo Stefano and to a couple of shops in Rome. The DOC was recognised in 1971, initially for red and white wine, but for pink wine in 1986. The white is the most important, made from 70 per cent Trebbiano, with some Malvasia, a drop of Pinot Grigio and some Ansonica. The taste of La Parrina Bianco is quite different from other Tuscan white wine, very firm and almost bitter, with intriguing flavours of herbs. Malfatti is also considering experimenting with Chardonnay and with Pinot Grigio, maybe for a sparkling wine. Otherwise the vinification methods are those standard to white wine, carried out in cellars that date back to the Middle Ages.

The soil and climate of La Parrina are quite particular. The soil is sandy and light, with very good drainage, and fertile, so that the vines 'explode' in the owner's word; the microclimate is influenced by proximity to the hills and the sea. Windbreaks of cypress trees are needed to protect the vines from the sea winds, while the lagoon of Orbetello gives the vineyards a certain luminosity. The summers are hot and dry, with little rain from May until the autumn. However sea breezes bring humidity and the vintage usually starts at the beginning of September to avoid rot.

Red and pink wines are made from Sangiovese, Canaiolo, Malvasia Nera and Morellone, which is an old Tuscan variety. Since 1986 DOC regulations have also allowed for a *riserva*, which spends two years in traditional large wood casks. The pink wine comes from the first gentle pressing of the red grapes and is quite deep in colour, with the flavour of raspberries. As for the red, I tasted the 1982 vintage, which had a distinctive herbal eucalyptus flavour, which might have had something to do with the eucalyptus trees around the vineyard. It was a pleasant glass of wine, but without much staying power.

Val di Cornia

There are isolated pockets of vineyards all over Tuscany, but some with a higher profile than others. I am sorry to say that I very nearly missed the Val di Cornia altogether. It was only a chance mention by a friend in the London wine trade that sent me off into the hills behind Piombino in search of this brand new DOC; I was assured in September 1989 that all that was required was the President's signature.

Until such time as he has signed, the small group of growers in the area make two *vini da tavola*, a Vino da Tavola di Campiglia under the brand name of Corniello and a Vino da Tavola di Suvereto under the brand name of Ghimbergo. The production of Corniello is controlled by the Associazione Vignaiuoli Alta Maremma; Ghimbergo comes under the jurisdiction of the town council of Suvereto and is confined to vineyards of that parish. The new DOC will cover vineyards in the parishes of Piombino, Campiglia Marittima, San Vincenzo, Suvereto, Monteverdi and Sassetta, the villages that the river Cornia passes on its way to the Mediterranean, which it enters near Piombino. The vineyards benefit from sea breezes and are usually no higher than 350 metres in altitude. In practice there are no vineyards at all yet in Sassetta and the greatest concentration of vines is on the hillsides of Campiglia and Suvereto. Both are picturesque hilltop towns where little stirs, with narrow streets and balconies of geraniums. Suvereto has a small *enoteca*, which the growers keep open during the summer for the benefit of passing tourists.

There are numerous small grape farmers, but only fifteen producers who actually bottle their wine. Jacopo Banti was the first to take this step, as long ago as the mid-1950s. He was also the first to buy a destalker, back in 1960. Everyone thought he was mad, for until then the red wine had always been fermented with the stalks. I had a friendly meeting with Signor Banti and two of his colleagues, Giovanni Graziani and Luigi Roncareggi. We sat outside, observed by a cat, a dog and a parrot, who interrupted our tasting with cries of 'Jacopo'.

The grape varieties for white Val di Cornia are mainly Trebbiano and Malvasia, but there is also Vermentino, some Ansonica and Biancone di Portoferraio from Elba. More innovatory grape varieties like Pinot Bianco and Pinot Grigio have also been planted, and are limited to 20 per cent; as well as Clairette, which they call *uva francese*.

Red and pink Val di Cornia may be pure Sangiovese and must include a minimum of 70 per cent, which can be blended with Canaiolo, Ciliegiolo, Cabernet Sauvignon and Merlot, each limited to 15 per cent. In this way the taste can either be typically Tuscan, or have a strong French influence.

The oenologist Marco Stefanini has worked hard to help these growers improve their vinification techniques, which are still fairly rudimentary. I enjoyed the white Corniello, for the wines were fresh and fragrant, with some leafy flavours, and the Vermentino added an extra hint of character. As for the reds, none seemed quite to conform to the anticipated DOC regulations, for there was pure Ciliegiolo, some Montepulciano and also Barbera. As yet only Signor Banti has planted Cabernet Sauvignon and this is not in production. So far the whites seem more interesting, but time will tell.

Elba

I love islands and Elba proved to be no exception. The plane from Pisa, a tiny eight-seater, bounced in the wind, flying at just 500 metres, so that you would have been able to follow the route over land with a road map. Elba is the largest island of the Tuscan archipelago, a collection lying close to the coast, including Giglio, Gorgona, Capraia and Montecristo, best known for its associations with Alexandre Dumas.

Monte Capanne, the highest peak of Elba at just over 1,000 metres, looms into view and the plane flies over the capital Portoferraio, coming to a bumpy halt on the grass runway outside Marina di Campo on the south side of the island. The absence of a large airport is definitely Elba's salvation. This one only functions during the summer months and even then its operation is rather haphazard. The same girl who weighs in the baggage and checks the tickets, operates the *espresso* machine in the airport bar. Coming by car, one takes a ferry from the unprepossessing town of Piombino.

There is something about Elba that reminds me of the Isle of Wight. It has a similar, unrushed feeling, making no attempt to keep pace with the mainland and happy to remain twenty years or more behind. It is an island of attractive hilltop towns, such as Marciana, Capoliveri and Portoferraio itself, built in strong defensive positions. The coast is popular with sun worshippers during the summer months, but still remains relatively unspoilt, compared to parts of the mainland coastline, more accessible to visitors.

Little is known of early Elban winemaking. As in most other parts of Tuscany, the wine was and still is an essential part of the island's agriculture, along with olives. Generally it is too hot and dry for maize or other cereal crops. Pliny made a passing reference to the wines of Elba and the Bolognese Pier de' Cresenzi mentions Aleatico from the island at the beginning of the fourteenth century. The Genoese bought wine from here to blend with the rather lighter wines of the Ligurian coast.

Elba's greatest claim to historical fame lies in having sheltered Napoleon for ten short months from May 1814 until February 1815. He is said to have appreciated the Aleatico, as well as the Procanico, or Trebbiano. One can visit the Villa dei Mulini in the old centre of Portoferraio, a gently decaying town house with oddments of Napoleonic memorabilia. Rather grander is the so-called Villa Napoleone di San Martino in the hills outside the capital. There is a modest villa described as Napoleon's summer residence and a Neo-classical palace, built by Prince Demidoff several years after the Emperor's death, which houses a display of Napoleonic pictures.

Today the island's wine depends on the tourists. In fact rumour has it that the tourists drink very much more than the 6,000 hectolitres which Elba produces each year. The slightly sour white wine that is served liberally by the carafe at many beachside cafés to wash down plates of *fritto misto*, is quaffably palatable when well chilled, but of uncertain provenance. Elba has its own DOC, since 1967 for both red and white, and now also for sparkling wine. As yet pink wine is not included in the DOC and can only be a *vino da tavola*, which may be qualified with some geographical indication, such as Portoferraio.

The DOC covers most of the island, excluding only the less favourable sites, such as valley bottoms, where it is too damp for successful viticulture. The soil is poor, though quite varied. There is granite, which gives acidity to the wines, a lot of clay in places and some sand, but no chalk. Minerals abound, including iron, to the extent that the soil can be quite red. However it is the grape variety, rather than the vineyard site that determines whether or not a wine is DOC, for not all the island's grape varieties are eligible. Altogether there are some 700 hectares of vines.

The grape varieties are those of the rest of Tuscany, mainly Trebbiano and Sangiovese, but with island differences. Elba Bianco comes mainly from Trebbiano, more commonly called Procanico. It is very similar to the Trebbiano Toscano of the mainland, just a slightly different clone, with a thinner skin and a deeper yellow colour; when ripe, it looks transparent and you can see the pips inside. The DOC regulations allow for 10 per cent of other complementary grape varieties, namely Malvasia, Canaiolo Bianco and Biancone di Portoferraio. This last is a purely local grape variety which is generally considered to give better results as a table grape. Someone remarked that the grape pickers eat them all.

A little Ansonica is also grown, but in very limited quantities and I was unable to taste any. As explained earlier, this grape variety may be related to the Inzolia grown on Sicily for Marsala; it is also grown on the island of Giglio and in a few other vineyards in the Maremma. I was told that on Elba it produces large berries with hard skins and that it is rich in pectins, so that you have to use bentonite to clarify it. Occasionally one can find bottles labelled Ansonica di Portoferraio.

Elba Rosso is often made just from Sangiovese, of which in any case there must be a minimum of 75 per cent. It can be complemented with Canaiolo and also white grapes, such as Trebbiano and Biancone, to lighten it.

Much more individual and interesting than Elba Rosso and Bianco are the dessert wines made from Moscato and Aleatico. Production was considered too limited to merit a DOC and few growers continue to make them, as the yields are so small and they are difficult to produce. Aleatico ripens early, in late August, so the grapes are a delight to thirsty birds during the dry summers of Elba. Likewise wild boar looking for a liquid supplement to their diet are prone to quenching their thirst in the vineyard.

Both Aleatico and Moscato are dried, or *passito*, so that one only obtains about fifteen or twenty litres from a quintal of grapes. The drying process, which concentrates the juice, takes about seven to ten days, usually at the beginning of September, when the weather is still very warm and dry. Then the grapes are vinified in the normal way. Sometimes the fermentation is stopped, depending upon how sweet the wine is intended to be.

Methods of vinification and practices in the vineyards are generally unsophisticated. Elba is a long way from mainstream Tuscan viticulture. There is little mechanisation. *Cordone speronata* is the usual method of pruning, although sometimes one finds *guyot*, but with taller vines than in France. There are usually about 3,000 vines per hectare, giving a yield of some ninety quintals, resulting in some seventy hectolitres per hectare of juice.

There are numerous growers on the island, many of whom make wine for the consumption of family, friends and passing tourists. Surprisingly perhaps, Elba has never had a *cantina sociale* or wine cooperative. I was told that the islanders were far too independent for that. There are only about ten people who actually put their wine in bottle, of whom I went to see a handful.

La Chiusa

The most historic estate is La Chiusa, which belongs to Giuliana Foresi. She has returned from living on the mainland to take over the family property. It is a beautiful place, right on the coast opposite Portoferraio. The Medici fortresses dominate the skyline and the impressive gates on the shore are a reminder of the time when wine left directly by sea, rather than by road. The name La Chiusa describes a walled vineyard, like the French Le Clos, and indeed one approaches the house through a walled vineyard along an alleyway of olive trees. A second alley lined with brightly coloured oleanders takes you down to the sea.

Signora Foresi has eight hectares of vines, planted mainly with Sangiovese and Procanico. She also has some Aleatico, a little Ansonica and just twenty plants of Moscato, which she finds to be very fragile and susceptible to disease. Both the Ansonica and the Aleatico are *passito* wines. I tasted the Aleatico, which had a rich perfumed nose, reminiscent of apricots. It was delicious when young and fresh, but can also be aged.

The cellars still have the traditional large, wood fermentation vats for the red wine, which is made only from Sangiovese. It spends a further year and a half or two years in wood. We tasted the 1986 vintage, which had hints of raspberries on the palate and was light, not unlike a northern Pinot Noir. As for the white wine, it ferments in fibreglass vats. A refrigeration machine for controlling fermentation temperatures is an innovation as recent as 1987. Until a couple of years ago the white wine also spent time in wood. Somehow Elban viticulture misses out on the developments of mainland Tuscany. There are no oenologists here.

The Foresi family arrived in the 1870s and in the tasting-room at La Chiusa there are certificates awarded to Signora Foresi's grandparents, a silver medal in 1886 and at an Esposizione Italiana in London in 1888, a *diploma d'onore* for *vini dolci*. Old labels included one for a *vin mousseux*, harking back to a time when the island was popular with the French.

Tenuta Sapere

One of the largest estates is Tenuta Sapere, near Porto Azzurro. As well as vines, the Sapere family have olive trees and other fruit trees. They grow the customary grapes of Elba, Procanico, Sangiovese, Aleatico and a little Moscato and Ansonica, as well as one surprise, Chardonnay, which was planted in 1985 as an experiment. Signor Sapere is the only producer of sparkling wine on the island and he wants Chardonnay for this, to enliven the flavour of Trebbiano. He may also add it to his still wine. The sparkling wine is made by the champagne method, which the Italians call *methodo classico*, with eighteen months on the lees. The bottle we tasted contained no Chardonnay and was rather earthy, with some full yeasty fruit.

Although white wine is the mainstay of Signor Sapere's production, a little red is made from Sangiovese, blended with Canaiolo, Trebbiano and Malvasia. He has some French *barriques* for his red wine, in which it spends six to twelve months. However I found the taste rather astringent and preferred the gentle, stony, almond flavour of his white wine. His wine cartons remind you of Elba's greatest resident with the words: 'Si Napoleone sapeva di Sapere, non ci sarebbe stato Waterloo'. This pun on his name, for *sapere* is also the verb 'to know', translates: 'If Napoleon had known about Sapere, Waterloo would never have taken place'. In other words, he would have remained on the island enjoying Signor Sapere's wines.

Lupi Rocchi

The final visit was to the estate of Lupi Rocchi, which has a reputation for Moscato and Aleatico. This proved to be justified. I tracked the property down in the hamlet of Vallebuia in the south-western corner of the island. The road from the coastal village of Seccheto climbs steeply up to Vallebuia. The landscape changes. It is drier and wilder than the north coast of Elba, stonier and more arid. I was told that it was also hotter, so that once the Moscato and Aleatico grapes are picked, they need to be dried only for three or four days before the juice becomes sufficiently concentrated. Fermentation takes place in cement vats and then the wine is put into wooden barrels for a few months. As well as Moscato, two versions of Aleatico are made, a sweet fortified wine and a dry wine, which has fermented fully and is also fairly high in alcohol. The sweet wine was rich and mellow and a good taste on which to leave the island.

Vin Santo

A book on the wines of Tuscany would not be complete without mention of that most individual of Tuscan wines, Vin Santo. It is true that variations are to be found in other parts of Italy, but nevertheless there is something quintessentially Tuscan about it. In his authoritative book *Il Libro del Vin Santo*, Giacomo Tachis describes it as 'the wine for hospitality and for friendship, the wine for every hour of the day'. It is the wine that every peasant farmer makes for family consumption and to offer to visitors as a token of friendship.

Various theories have been proffered as to the origin of the name, 'holy wine'. A Sienese legend recalls a friar who in 1348 distributed to victims of the plague a wine that was normally used for the Eucharist, which cured the sick who drank it. It has also been suggested that the wine was made at the beginning of November, around All Saints' Day, or that it was bottled during Holy Week.

The Florentines mention a *vino pretto*, a pure wine, for *prette* or priests, which was served at the Ecumenical Council in Florence in 1349. The patriarch of the Greek Orthodox church, Cardinal Bessarion of Nicaea is said to have drunk this and exclaimed, 'But this is the wine of Xantos!' He may have been referring to a Greek island that made a sweet dessert wine, but his description has also been translated as Vin Santo, a reference to the holy quality of the *vino pretto*.

The essential character of Vin Santo comes from the drying of the grapes, a tradition so old that it is even mentioned by Pliny. In France the equivalent is *vin de paille*, or 'straw wine'. Everyone who makes Vin Santo has their own personal recipe. It has been said that there are as many different Vin Santo as there are recipes for chicken-liver *crostini*, the mainstay of Tuscan *antipasti*. The diversity stems partly from the fact that until recently there was almost no legislation to control the production.

The most common grapes for Vin Santo are Trebbiano and Malvasia, but others can be used, depending on the area, such as Canaiolo Bianco, San Colombano, which is considered to be particularly suitable for Vin Santo but not for any table wine, and even Pinot and Chardonnay. Grechetto is favoured by Avignonesi in Montepulciano. Some people even include red grapes.

It is absolutely essential that perfectly healthy grapes should be used. The grapes are left to dry for several weeks, from the harvest in October until January. They must not have a trace of rot and they must be fully ripe, for as they dehydrate, unripe grapes will concentrate acidity rather than sugar. The fruit is then kept in a dry, well ventilated place, either left on straw mats, or hung up from the rafters of an attic (see illustration). A good circulation of air is important, for otherwise the grapes may begin to rot. This drying procedure is very costly and time-consuming.

The length of time that the grapes are left may vary from as little as three weeks, to as long as three or even six months, depending on conditions; such as the health of the grapes, the ambient temperature and the degree of ventilation. If a sweet Vin

Drying the grapes for Vin Santo.

Santo is the object, the grapes are left for longer, for the greater will be the concentration of sugar. If dry Vin Santo is the aim, the grapes are likely to be pressed in December. In any case the grapes are left until they are dried and raisinlike, which the Italians call *passiti*. Unlike most other great dessert wines, the development of noble rot does not play a part in the production of Vin Santo.

When the grapes are suitably *passiti*, they are pressed in the normal way. This is easier said than done. When raisinlike grapes are pressed, they are likely to turn into a pulpy mess, from which it is difficult to extract a relatively clear juice. The juice is put into the traditional barrels, known as *caratelli*, that are used for Vin Santo (see illustration on p. 208). They are much smaller than *barriques*, varying in size from as little as fifty or sixty litres to no more than 200 or 250 litres. Oak or chestnut barrels can be used, and even barrels in which other drinks have matured, such as Marsala, cognac or whisky; these would of course add a different flavour to the wine. However the best wood is usually oak, which does not give too much flavour or colour.

The barrels are sealed, traditionally with wax, but more commonly today, and more prosaically, with cement. They are not filled completely and the amount of air left at the top of the barrel is said to be one of the factors that determines the sweetness of the wine. For a dry wine, leave a large space; a sweeter wine demands a smaller space, so that there is less oxidation. The carbon dioxide from the fermentation escapes between the staves, which is not a problem as the fermentation is very slow. This is partly because some of the yeast has already been eliminated by the drying process. It is in any case very slow to start with, at a cold time of the year, becoming more energetic during the warmer summer months.

Caratelli *for Vin Santo.*

Another factor that is considered significant to the taste of Vin Santo is the use of a *madre*, literally 'mother', the lees of the previous Vin Santo left in the barrel, resembling a muddy sludge. Those who believe in the value of *madre*, consider it essential for the nutrients and yeasts that it contains, which add an extra dimension of flavour. Tachis is diffident; a *madre* can be beneficial, but if it is full of bacteria 'it would be better if the wine were an orphan', he says. However Guido Bianco at Fattoria Sassolo near the Colline Pisane, who makes delicious Vin Santo, considers the *madre* to be the secret of its success.

Traditionally the *caratelli* are left in an attic, in a place that is subject to both the summer heat and the winter cold. Extremes of temperature are generally considered essential for the development of the wine. Tachis believes, on the other hand, that the extremes are of no use and only give the wine a shock. Three years is the minimum period for ageing, but for many producers it may be as long as seven or eight. During this time the barrels remain firmly sealed and the wine is neither topped up nor racked. A considerable amount of evaporation occurs, so that the final quantity of wine is very small. At the same time a gentle oxidation takes place, which contributes to the flavour. Vin Santo should have a natural alcohol level of around 15°. It should not be a fortified wine, although it sometimes is, in which case the label should carry the mention *vino liquoroso*.

The more recent DOCs of Tuscany include Vin Santo in their regulations, such as Pomino, Val d'Arbia, Valdinievole, Carmignano, San Torpè and Montescudaio; so will the new DOC of the Colli dell'Etruria Centrale. This should succeed in bringing some discipline to the great variety of wine. Part of its charm, however, is its individuality, that no wine is quite like another.

It is generally conceded that Avignonesi make the best Vin Santo in Tuscany; but with a price to match. This is the Château d'Yquem of Vin Santo. Avignonesi themselves say that it compares with fine cognac. However you do not want to drink classed growths all the time and there are numerous other friendlier, more approachable wines to sample. Avignonesi's wine rather inhibits that Tuscan habit of dunking *cantuccini* or *biscotti di Prato* in Vin Santo. These delicious hard Tuscan biscuits need to be softened by Vin Santo to avoid breaking your teeth! The best Vin Santo has a taste of liquid *biscotti* or madeira cake, with some delicious sweet nuttiness and a firm dry finish.

Particularly good is the Vin Santo of Isole e Olena. Paolo de Marchi dries his Malvasia grapes until the end of January, with the aim of making a semi-sweet wine, and he leaves the wine in barrel for four years. He is convinced of the part played by the *madre* in the flavour, contributing he believes to a long aftertaste. After four or maybe even five years of ageing, the wine is put into glass demijohns for a year. Then the different barrels are all blended, to even out any variations. Sometimes wine of the previous year, about 20 per cent, may be added to give even more complexity of flavour. Vintages as such are not significant for Vin Santo. What matters is the health of the grapes and the evolution of the wine in the barrel, which can be very uncertain.

Unpredictability is the hazard of Vin Santo. There is a danger of excessive oxidation and of volatile acidity. The carbon dioxide from the fermentation protects the wine to a certain extent, but there is an argument for keeping it at a more constant cellar temperature to avoid such spoiling.

Francesco Martini di Cigala at San Giusto a Rentennano is a fervent enthusiast of Vin Santo. At the moment he uses the traditional chestnut *caratelli*, but has also bought some new oak ones. Malvasia is the main grape variety, with a little Trebbiano. While Vin Santo is a traditional dessert wine, he advocates drinking it with cheese, rather like Sauternes with Roquefort. His white and gold label bears a marked similarity to the d'Yquem label and the wine tasted of liquid almonds, with a good firm bite on the finish.

At Badia a Coltibuono Roberto Stucchi is experimenting, starting the fermentation in tank before transferring the must into barrels, in this case whisky barrels from Glenfiddich. He uses selected yeast in an attempt to obtain a cleaner fermentation and gives his wine four years of ageing. He is looking for more reliable results, as he has had a high percentage of 'off' barrels. Without any lees or *madre*, the results are perhaps more consistent, but also possibly less exciting.

At Brolio they make Vin Santo on a much larger scale and have one of the largest *vinsantaia* in Chianti. The wine is aged for eight years altogether. The fermentation, which lasts about two years, takes place in 600-litre barrels and then the wine is transferred into two to five-hectolitre barrels for four years, after which it will spend a year in one-hectolitre barrels and then a final year in bottle before sale. The idea is gradually to accustom the wine to the smaller size of container.

Other Vin Santo that I have enjoyed include Castello dei Rampolla, with flavours not unlike a rich Bual Madeira, Fattoria Sassolo, Poggio al Sole, Aiola and La Chiesa di Santa Restituta; here Roberto Bellini says that Vin Santo is a hobby. It does not earn money, but he enjoys making it. The taste reminded me of orange marmalade and madeira cake, and we tasted the wine with *ricciarelli*, the soft almond biscuits from Siena. Vin Santo is much less common in Montalcino than in other parts of Tuscany.

There is no doubt that Vin Santo is expensive to produce. The profits are negligible, for the yields are tiny in the first place and the loss of wine through evaporation is significant. Paolo de Marchi reckoned that from 8,000 quintals of grapes, he obtained just 1,200 litres of juice, in other words just one fifteenth of the original yield of grapes. The quantity reduces to approximately one third as the grapes are *passiti* and then by a further 20 per cent or so during the ageing process. People who make a drier Vin Santo, for which there is less initial dehydration, may obtain more wine from the same weight of grapes. However there is still an element of uncertainty in determining the taste of Vin Santo, as aspects of the ageing process are not fully understood. Maybe that is part of its charm. The best Vin Santo is made by the enthusiast for the love of it.

Olive Oil

The olive tree is as essential to the Tuscan countryside as the vine, and as fundamental to the Tuscan way of life, providing one of the main staples of the local diet, olive oil. It has been like that since Roman times. In the fourteenth century a guild of oilmakers was formed in Florence, called the Corporazione Fiorentina degli Oliandoli, from which the modern Corporation of Master Oilmakers has drawn its inspiration. In the days of sharecropping and *cultura promiscua*, olive trees were mixed up with vines, interspersed with other crops without rhyme or reason. Today the olive groves are more organised, planted in ordered rows. They will grow where the soil is too poor even for vineyards.

Although the olive tree flourishes all over southern Italy, it is in Tuscany, or maybe Umbria that the best olive oil is produced. The reason is that, as with wine or any other agricultural produce, the best results are obtained on the climatic edges of successful cultivation. So England has the best apples and strawberries, Bordeaux and Burgundy have some of the world's greatest wines and Tuscany has superb olive oil. The climate of Tuscany allows for the olives to be picked before they are fully ripe, wherein lies the key to the quality of the oil.

Winter temperatures in Tuscany can wreak untold havoc on the olive trees, as they did in the devastating winter frosts of 1985, when the temperatures in January fell to $-25°$C. Very few trees remained unaffected. In some instances the damage was superficial, in that once the dead branches had been cut down and the trees pruned, new shoots began to grow. In other places the damage was more severe and trees have been pulled up and replaced. At San Vito in Fior di Selva, where they would expect to make 10,000 litres of oil before the frost, the crop was reduced to a mere 2,000 litres. At Castellare, they say that the previous owners had noticed which varieties of olive tree survived the last great frost of 1956, and had planted those varieties, so that their crop was relatively unaffected. It was only in 1989 that the olive crop in Tuscany as a whole returned to a satisfactory quantity. There is still a shortage, making Tuscan olive oil often much more expensive than wine.

This luscious green liquid is redolent of Tuscan flavours. It is acidity or rather the lack of it, that is the principal criterion of quality. Unlike grapes, which lose acidity as they ripen, olives gain in oleic acidity. This is why they are picked early in Tuscany, before they are fully ripe, usually in November after the grape harvest. They are unlikely to be ripe until January or February, when they begin to fall off the trees. Oil from unripe olives derives its colour and an attractive spiciness from the chlorophyl in the green fruit.

As with grapes, there are several different varieties of olive, and in the same way as Chianti, a good olive oil is made from at least two, if not three sorts. At Selvapiana in Rufina they grow more Frantoio, which is a late ripener, than the Morraiolo, which is found more commonly in Chianti Classico. Leccino is another popular variety.

A stone mill for olive oil.

Most Chianti estates produce olive oil, although they may not be equipped with a *frantoia*, to press the olives on the estate. Picking is very labour intensive, for it is virtually impossible to mechanise on steep Tuscan hillsides. It is either done by hand, olive by olive; or an instrument that can only be described as an enormous plastic comb is run through the branches, so that the olives fall off on to sheets laid on the ground around the trees.

The olives are then crushed in a stone mill, and pressed (see illustration). An olive press is not unlike a cider press in method. Layers of crushed olives are built up, like pulped apples, on straw mats, called *fischioli*, with the occasional metal disk to give support. This is given one gentle pressing. The result is a mixture of brown oil and water, which is then centrifuged to separate the two. The pressing should be cold. Sadly there is an increasing tendency for warm water to be washed through the pulp, in order to facilitate the extraction of more oil, a practice that is rightly decried by the purists. The paste that is left from the pressing is called *sansa* and this is sold off to an industrial operation for further pressing. The new oil is put into *orci*, large earthenware containers, to fall clear naturally and there it is kept (see illustration). Some of these *orci* are very old. At Selvapiana they carry the family crest and are dated 1827. The aroma of fresh oil in the *orcaia* is one of the most evocative of smells.

The best oil of all is Extra Vergine Olive Oil, which comes from olives that have been pressed, but subjected to no other treatments. The amount of oleic acid determines the precise quality. Extra Vergine oil contains less than 1 per cent of oleic acid; fine Vergine 1.5 to 3 per cent and Vergine 3 to 4 per cent. Beyond these is refined olive oil, obtained from the *sansa* of the first pressing.

As yet there is no law in Italy to control the provenance of olive oil, nor any concept of a denomination, as exists in France, for agricultural products other than

Earthenware orci
for storing olive oil.

wine. With the shortage of oil in Tuscany, some less scrupulous estates have been buying in oil and bottling it with their own small production. The label will say 'bottled by Fattoria X', with the implication that the oil was also produced by Fattoria X. There are moves afoot to rectify this situation, but Italian bureaucracy is slow.

There are as many flavours to olive oil as there are to Chianti. It is wonderful to sample olive oil after a wine tasting, either in a minute glass, or by dipping a finger into an *orci*. That most Tuscan of *antipasti, fettunta* or *bruschetta* is the perfect excuse for it; slices of bread are baked in an oven, rubbed with garlic, and oil is poured liberally over them. Tuscan cooking demands olive oil. The wonderful bread soup *ribolita*, which is thick with vegetables too, is moistened with it, as is *panzanella*, the bread salad flavoured with basil, tomatoes and anchovies. What would the perfect combination of ripe tomatoes and fresh basil be without olive oil? So many pasta sauces too, start with a liberal quantity of olive oil. Above all, the fruity, but astringent finish of Chianti perfectly complements its richness.

Vintages: The Variations of the Last Thirty Years

Vintages do matter in Tuscany. They matter very much indeed, for while we tend to think of warm Tuscan sunshine, year after year, the reality can be quite different. Tuscany may be further south than Bordeaux, but it has as much annual variation in climate, with a significant effect on the quality of the grapes. There can be years of undiluted sunshine and years of unmitigated rain, and every variant in between. For the purposes of vintage assessment, Tuscany may be taken more or less as a whole. There are differences from one region to another, resulting from variations of microclimate and topography, but in general terms a good vintage in Chianti Classico means a good vintage in Montalcino too; while Greve may have fared less well than Radda or better than Montepulciano, these are purely localised differences.

1989

This was one of those years that are saved as the grapes are being picked. In early September, Minuccio Cappelli at Montagliari was making gloomy comparisons with 1984, for after a mixed summer, with more rain than usual. The beginning of September brought indifferent weather, with cool, damp mornings and a general uncertainty as to whether the grapes would ripen or not. I went home on 14th September. It seems that on the 15th the summer returned and the sun shone for the ensuing four weeks. The grapes ripened more or less, and quality will depend upon a careful selection in vineyard and cellar. At the time of writing the wine has hardly finished fermenting and further pro-gnostications would be premature. However there is no doubt that this is a year that could produce good wine, if also some rather bad wine.

1988

The vintage of the century is too sweeping an accolade, but most people agree that it is the best vintage of the decade. Spring came late to Tuscany. May was cool and wet, and June too was wetter and colder than usual –

I was there and I had to buy woollen jumpers in Florence to keep warm – but come July the sun shone, and continued to shine until almost the end of the vintage in mid-October. There was no problem with rot or disease after the initial treatments in the spring. John Dunkley of Riecine describes the vintage as a dream: it didn't get you up in the middle of the night and the fermentation temperatures stayed low. The crop was as much as 30 per cent smaller than usual, owing to uneven weather at the flowering, but the result is plenty of *riserva* wines with lots of colour, extract and fruit, wines that will develop and age for several years.

1987

A year that requires careful selection, for there was hail during the summer and rain at the vintage, which made for a large crop, but of grapes that were in some cases high in acidity. Some attractive wines were made, but they are generally fairly light and fruity, without staying power. It was considered to be a difficult year in Montepulciano too, with some rot, whereas Montalcino fared better. The summer was dry there, but it rained in the middle of the vintage, so that again the wines will require selection. However Gianfranco Soldera at Case Basse says that it was very good. At Capezzana in Carmignano they think it better than 1986, and they have made some *riserva* wines.

1986

Generally overshadowed by the previous vintage, for the summer was not uniformly fine, bringing rain and cooler weather. However it was followed by a warm autumn, so that the grapes were picked in perfect weather conditions. Maurizio Castelli goes so far as to say that he prefers the 1986s to the 1985s, but Piero Antinori is less impressed. Generally the wines are fruity and forward, enjoyable, but without great staying power.

In Carmignano it is considered a rather light vintage and at Capezzana they made no *riserva* wines. In Montalcino they suffered very unusually from spring frosts, which reduced the crop. The wines are good, but more forward than the 1985s. Some good wines were made in Montepulciano too.

1985

In terms of quality this is the year that Chianti should have become a DOCG, for what the gods denied in 1984 they gave in 1985. It was a wonderful hot summer, in some places so hot that the vines suffered from drought. The higher vineyards, where the vines were cooled by the wind and benefited from greater day and night-time variations in temperature, produced better wines. Some spring frost also made for a smaller crop than usual, so that, for example, Castell'in Villa lost a quarter of its average production. The heat at the harvest caused problems for people who were not equipped with refrigeration machines to control their fermentation temperatures; leading to difficulties with volatile acidity, and resulting in rather cooked, baked wines. However the best wines are very good. Raffaele Rossetti at Capannelle on the high vineyards outside Gaiole says that he had water and sunshine at the right time and describes his 1985 as 'his flagship'. Hugh Hamilton at Le Lodoline reckons it is the best wine he has made since 1971 and Paolo de Marchi at

Isole e Olena is very enthusiastic too. Stefano Farkas at Cafaggio and Vittorio Fiore both describe it as exceptional. The one dissenter is Maurizio Castelli who thinks the wines more uniform in 1986, with less cooked flavours. Generally however the wines of the 1985 vintage in Chianti Classico are rich and concentrated, with depth and colour, wines that will age for several years.

Great wines were made in the other parts of Tuscany too. At Montalcino they had a cool spring and a hot summer, with lower than average quantity resulting in what is considered to be a great year. In Montepulciano and Carmignano they are equally enthusiastic. The Marchese Incisa della Rochetta considers it to be one of the most successful Sassicaia vintages, requiring at least ten years before the wine is at its best.

1984

When I think of 1984, a rather depressing picture comes to mind. I was in Greve in September at a meeting of all the producers, held to discuss whether Chianti should become DOCG that year or not. We were within days of picking the grapes and no one knew what they were supposed to be doing. Outside the rain was coming down, as rain in Tuscany does, relentlessly in no half measures. The atmosphere was not only laden with uncertainty as to what should happen to the DOCG, but also with the gloomy knowledge that the grapes were not ripe and that a lot of them were rotten; DOCG or not, the wine would be bad. The omens were inauspicious for turning over a new leaf in Chianti. Then the next day I went to see André and Monique Verwoort at Quercetorta. All I can say is, thank goodness for the phlegmatic Dutch approach to life. They were resigned to making no wine at all that year. Their vineyard had been hit by a freak hailstorm and a herd of thirsty wild boar had eaten such grapes as remained.

The spring had started warm, so that many people sprayed insufficiently to protect their vines from the rot which came with the summer rain. There was bad weather in May and June, and rain in August and September. The Consorzio wisely decided not to allow any *riserva* to be made in Chianti Classico, and indeed no Chianti Classico at all was made under the Montagliari or Monsanto labels. Selection of grapes is the key, however. Good winemakers can make something acceptable under adverse conditions and I have tasted some perfectly agreeable wines from the vintage, light, fruity and enjoyable; but with no staying power and usually boosted by concentrated must.

The story was much the same elsewhere in Tuscany. The summer was better in Montalcino, but September was wet. At Il Paradiso Florio Guerrieri threw away nearly half his crop. A careful selection was essential to make decent wine, and it will certainly not be a Brunello to keep. Biondi Santi did not make a Brunello at all, nor did Avignonesi produce a Vino Nobile.

1983

In some ways this was a better balanced year than 1985, for the lack of rainfall was less extreme, although the sun shone more or less without a break throughout the summer. Initially the 1983s had a considerable amount of tannin, which is now disappearing to make for well balanced, attractive wines. However the view of the vintage is not uniform. Maurizio Castelli likes it; John Matta at Vicchiomaggio describes it as average, and John Dunkley does not think it as good as 1982.

In Montalcino the wines are considered better than 1982, with great elegance, and will last well. Elegance is a characteristic of the vintage in Montepulciano too, and Carmignano also made some lovely ripe, rounded wines.

1982

Opinions vary over the relative merits of 1983 and 1982 Chianti Classico. Hail, both in the spring and again in September, reduced the size of the harvest. Maurizio Castelli thinks it better than 1983; John Dunkley likes it, and so does Paolo de Marchi. Generally it seems that the wines lack the elegance of the '83s, with some harder tannins, so that 1983 is usually considered to be the more successful vintage.

Elegance was missing too in Montalcino and Montepulciano, with wines that have staying power, but may lack charm. In Carmignano 1983 is again considered to have the edge on 1982.

1981

The weather was mixed. March and April were hot and dry, while May was wet, with more rain in June, making for a late flowering. However a warm dry summer followed, resulting in some good wines, that are well balanced but relatively forward. Rufina fared better than Chianti Classico. Some good, but light wines were made in Montalcino, while Montepulciano is considered less successful.

1980

The summer was uncertain, with rain and sun, and a late flowering resulting in a late harvest. Paolo de Marchi did not begin picking his grapes until 20th October, finishing on 7th November. The grapes were high in acidity and initially the wines lacked balance. The better wines of the vintage are drinking well now, but will not last. The first vintage of DOCG for Brunello di Montalcino and Vino Nobile di Montepulciano did not augur well either, for they are light wines, of mixed quality. Carmignano was better.

1979

This was one of the largest of recent vintages. Antinori had to buy extra tanks to house the crop. The summer was fine and rain fell at the vintage, which slightly diluted the wine in some instances. Some attractive Chianti was made, but little with any staying power. Some good wines were made in Montepulciano, and the vintage is well considered in Montalcino and Carmignano too.

1978

Chianti Classico has more tannin and body than the 1979, but the wines are now at their peak. John Matta at Vicchiomaggio described it as a normal vintage, with enough sun and rain, and no exceptional weather conditions. In both Montalcino and Montepulciano the quality was mixed, while Carmignano produced some good wines.

1977

Some very good wine was made, notably in Rufina, rather than Chianti Classico. John Dunkley describes the year as troublesome, for there were problems with uneven ripening of the grapes. Some good wine was also made in Montalcino; Montepulciano is more uneven, and Carmignano is good.

1976

This is the year that we remember in Britain as the great summer, and we did not have another one like it until 1989. In Tuscany they remember it as the year it rained and rained. Numerous producers did not bottle any wine under their own label, such as Monsanto, Montagliari, Biondi Santi and Boscarelli. The wines of 1976 are perhaps best forgotten.

1975

Some good wines were made in Chianti Classico, although there was rain at the vintage, and the wines are now fading. In Montalcino the vintage was small but very good; at Lisini they describe it as 'the flower in their buttonhole'. Vino Nobile was good too, and Carmignano began life as a DOC on an auspicious note.

1974

The summer was hot and dry in Chianti, making for wines with tannin and body, and some staying power. Sometimes they are better than the 1975, but both should now be drunk. Neither Brunello nor Vino Nobile showed any staying power in their youth and they too should be drunk. The same goes for Carmignano.

1973

The spring was mild, the summer warm and dry. Heavy rain at the vintage increased an already large crop. Some good wines were made, perfumed, with little body, and now faded. Vino Nobile fared better than Brunello, but again both are past their best.

1972

The vintage was nearly as bad as 1976 in Chianti Classico, and Brunello and Vino Nobile were no better. It is best forgotten.

1971

Alma Sanguinetti at Pagliarese describes this vintage as 'a gift of God' and John Matta thinks it the best vintage since the mid 1960s. Both spring and summer were dry and sunny, with a little rain in August, so that the grapes were concentrated in flavour, but not overripe. Sadly hail in September caused problems in some vineyards. This was the first vintage of Tignanello and an auspicious start. Good wine was made in Carmignano too, with a 1971 Artimino that in the spring of 1989 had delicious vegetal, almost Burgundian overtones. Some good Brunello di Montalcino was made, but Vino Nobile was generally disappointing.

1970

Good wines were made all over Tuscany. Chianti Classico and Rufina are considered to be very good, but will now be fading. It is also one of the best Brunello vintages of recent years, with some particularly fine wines. Excellent Vino Nobile di Montepulciano was made too.

1969

I have had some delicious bottles from this vintage. Vicchiomaggio made elegant fruity wines, as did Capezzana in Carmignano. The vintage is particularly rated in Carmignano, while in Montalcino it is considered less successful. However a 1969 Brunello from Il Poggione was a lovely mature glass of wine when it was twenty years old, fading yes, but still very fine with some elegant cedarwood fruit. There was some good Vino Nobile, but again it should be drunk.

1968

Some good wines were made in this vintage, but most have now faded, be they from Chianti, Montalcino or Montepulciano. I drank a Selvapiana from Rufina in the summer of 1989 which was delicious, but at its peak.

1967

This is generally considered to be one of the best vintages of the decade, all over Tuscany but the wines are now tending to fade.

1966

A mixed vintage, better in Montepulciano and Montalcino than in Chianti, but by no means great.

1965

The vintage charts write off this vintage over most of Tuscany. However I have had a delicious Pagliarese, when it was twenty years old, and also a lovely Selvapiana, which was said not to be as rich as the 1968. They are, however, exceptions to the rule.

1964

This was considered one of the best vintages of the decade for Chianti, and very good in Montalcino and Montepulciano too. I drank a lovely 1964 Montagliari in September 1989.

1963

A poor vintage all over Tuscany, and best forgotten.

1962

Some very good wines were made in Chianti Classico, such as a lovely bottle from Montagliari drunk in September 1989. Vino Nobile was good too. Montalcino was the exception with generally poor wines.

1961

Frescobaldi liked this vintage; Burton Anderson rates it especially in Montalcino, but I have never had the opportunity to try it.

1960

Generally considered to be a poor vintage.

In earlier decades 1958, 1955 and 1951 produced some excellent wines in Chianti Classico. The 1949 and 1947 are reputed to be good too, and 1937, 1931, 1929 and 1923 are all highly rated. In Montalcino the great vintages were 1955, 1945, 1925, 1891 and the legendary 1888.

Appendices

I: Chianti Classico Production Figures

Year	Hectares (spec.)	Hectares (prom.)	Total	Hectolitres of wine
1964				167,211
1965				165,698
1966				166,737
1967				115,677
1968				132,122
1969	2,032	8,407	10,439	147,988
1970	3,356	7,064	10,420	205,074
1971	3,451	8,015	11,466	169,619
1972	3,914	7,926	11,840	178,157
1973	4,925	7,496	12,421	281,980
1974	5,497	6,922	12,419	323,029
1975				258,027
1976				253,217
1977	6,491	6,273	12,764	302,566
1978				311,765
1979				458,838
1980				348,133
1981				339,745
1982	8,085	4,968	13,053	387,684
1983				378,469
1984	5,902	511	6,413	248,015
1985	6,010	482	6,492	268,612
1986	6,100	338	6,438	297,715
1987	6,182	466	6,648	323,378
1988	6,358	480	6,838	301,499
1989				302,190

Figures supplied by the Consorzio del Gallo Nero.
Spec. = specialised vineyards.
Prom. = vineyards in *cultura promiscua*.

II: Brunello di Montalcino Production Figures

Year	Growers	Hectares of vines	Hectolitres of wine
1967	37	76.53	2,077
1968	41	56.24	1,977
1969	41	56.24	2,302
1970	42	74.84	2,947
1971	45	156.50	3,798
1972	47	193.81	4,730
1973	56	261.89	7,692
1974	59	275.26	10,429
1975	60	306.60	14,629
1976	63	371.47	15,040
1977	74	421.24	17,679
1978	80	506.54	21,330
1979	83	627.54	28,418
1980	93	647.18	30,324
1981	93	728.36	28,353
1982	96	762.17	32,662
1983	106	807.41	35,192
1984	109	808.83	26,193
1985	95	713.20	34,120
1986	104	754.40	39,660
1987	111	773.50	41,604
1988	116	875.60	39,165
1989	129	910.87	39,880

Figures supplied by the Consorzio of Brunello di Montalcino, representing 95 per cent of producers of Brunello.

III: Vino Nobile di Montepulciano Production Figures

Year	Growers	Hectares (spec.)	Hectares (prom.)	Hectolitres of wine
1967	224	23	446	4,085
1968	103	131	283	1,350
1969	103	131	314	4,202
1970	114	148	299	8,001
1971	125	196	294	7,528
1972	135	311	293	5,403
1973	141	397	275	12,571
1974	141	383	236	17,906
1975	153	486	198	20,401
1976	155	487	198	18,213
1977	163	554	185	19,086
1978	167	555	203	12,687
1979	174	609	188	28,496
1980	175	615	143	29,334
1981	159	619	9	18,323
1982	160	633	10	26,683
1983	162	657	10	25,045
1984		689		13,518
1985		684		25,531
1986		709		26,923
1987				23,672
1988	190	722		26,835

Growers include members of the cooperative.
Spec. = specialised vineyards.
Prom. = vineyards in *cultura promiscua*.

IV: Summary of Italian Wine Law

Italian wines divide into four categories, in descending order, Denominazione di Origine Controllata e Garantita or DOCG, Denominazione di Origine Controllata or DOC, *vino da tavola con indicazione geografica*, of which a list of those allowed and proposed for Tuscany follows, and finally *vino da tavola*, of no precise provenance.

The Italian wine law was formulated in 1963, with the subsequent introduction of DOC, which equates to the French *appellation contrôlée*, laying down vineyard area, grape varieties, yields and so on. The first DOCG wines came with the 1980 vintage, of which two were from Tuscany, namely Brunello di Montalcino and Vino Nobile di Montepulciano. Chianti Classico and Chianti followed four years later. The popular misconception is that DOCG means a better wine. This is not necessarily the case; what it does mean is that the origin of the wine is guaranteed, entailing stricter regulations, with tasting and analysis tests.

In theory the category of *vino da tavola* is lower than DOC. In practice, especially in Tuscany this may not be so, as the numerous experimental wines come into this category. They are often more expensive and indeed may be more exciting than the parallel DOC wine. Finally anonymous *vino da tavola* is what it says it is, namely basic plonk.

Tuscan DOCs (1988)

Designated area	Area in hectares	Production in hectolitres
Bianco delle Colline Lucchesi	23	1,074
Bianco della Valdinievole	23	978
Bianco di Pitigliano	455	26,091
Bianco di San Torpè	333	11,325
Bianco Vergine Valdichiana	687	27,920
Bolgheri	48	1,760
Brunello di Montalcino	780	32,368
Candia dei Colli Apuani	18	683
Carmignano	112	3,869
Chianti	9,325	367,216
Chianti Classico	6,342	263,259
Chianti Colli Aretini	627	32,817
Chianti Colli Fiorentini	724	16,180
Chianti Colline Pisane	173	8,019
Chianti Colli Senesi	2,819	127,027
Chianti Montalbano	394	13,628
Chianti Rufina	519	18,958
Elba	148	4,480
Montecarlo Bianco	142	6,715
Montecarlo Rosso	53	2,696
Montescudaio	181	2,747 – white
		2,725 – red
Morellino di Scansano	279	13,373
Moscadello di Montalcino		170
Parrina	79	4,109
Pomino	84	3,812
Rosso delle Colline Lucchesi	122	4,366
Rosso di Montalcino		1,436
Val d'Arbia	163	7,082
Vernaccia di San Gimignano	592	40,435
Vino Nobile di Montepulciano	604	26,835

Figures taken from *Il Corriere Vinicolo*, March 1990.
The proposed new DOCs of Val di Cornia, Colli dell' Etruria Centrale and Bianco dell'
Empolesi will probably come into production in 1990.

List of Tuscan Vini da Tavola con Indicazione Geografica (1989)

Agreed:
Alta Valle della Greve
Bianco di Nugola
Cercatoia
Colli della Toscana Centrale
Colline di Ama
Colline fra Siena e Firenze
Maremma Toscana
Monte Antico
Montecucco
Toscana – for the following grape
   varieties: Aleatico, Alicante,
   Cabernet Sauvignon, Canaiolo,
   Chardonnay, Malvasia, Pinot
   Grigio, Sangiovese, Trebbiano

Provisional:
Abbazia di Monte Oliveto Maggiore
Alberese
Albinia
Aquabona
Artimino
Bagno a Ripoli
Barberino Val d'Elsa
Barco Reale
Bastia
Bibbona
Camigliano
Campiglia
Capalbio
Capezzana
Casciana Alta
Casciana Terme
Castagneto Carducci
Castelfalfi
Castelfiorentino
Castelnuovo Berardenga
Cecina
Cenaia
Cerreto Guidi
Certaldo
Cetona
Chiusi
Cinigiano
Collesalvetti
Colli Toscani
Cartona
Crespina

Cusona
Doccia
Fiesole
Figlini Valdarno
Fonteblanda
Forcoli
Gambassi Terme
Gaville
Grattamacco
Impruneta
Incisa Valdarno
I Selvatici
Isole di Capraia
Lilliano
Lucciano
Marcialla
Mercatale Val di Pesa
Mola
Monsanto
Montaione
Monte Argentario
Montefiridolfi
Montefoscoli
Montelupo Fiorentino
Montepescali
Montespertoli
Montevarchi
Montisi
Morrona
Orciatico
Paizzolo
Panzano – Cabernet Sauvignon,
   Canaiolo Nero, Chardonnay,
   Malvasia, Merlot, Pinot Bianco,
   Sangiovese, Sauvignon, Traminer
   Aromatico (Gewürztraminer),
   Trebbiano
Peccioli
Piombino – Sangiovese, Trebbiano
Piviere di Santo Stefano a Campoli
Poggibonsi
Pomarance
Pontassieve
Pontelungo
Portoferraio – Aleatico, Ansonica,
   Biancone, Sangiovese
Pozzolatico
Provincia di Arezzo

Provincia di Firenze
Provincia di Siena
Pulignano
Rigutano
Romita
Roselle
Rosignano Marittimo
Sammontana – Chardonnay,
   Trebbiano
San Casciano Val di Pesa
San Donnino
San Felice
San Giovanni d'Asso
San Leolino
San Martino
San Miniato
Sant'Andrea in Percussina – Canaiolo
   Bianco, Canaiolo Nero, Malvasia,
   Sangiovese, Trebbiano
Sant'Angelo in Colle
San Vicenzo
San Vito in Fior di Selva
San Vivaldo
Sassetta
Sassicaia
Saturnia
Scarlino
Secchetto
Siena or Senese
Sorano
Sovicille
Stroncoli
Suvereto
Talente
Tavarnelle Val di Pesa
Toscano della Terra del Petrarca
Trequanda
Uccellina
Vagliagli
Valdarno
Valdera
Vetulonia
Vico d'Elsa
Viesca
Vignale
Villa la Selva
Vinci

Glossary of Fantasy Names

The presence of CC after an entry indicates that the producer is within Chianti Classico.

Agrestino *Vino novello* from Brolio. CC

Albergaccio Serristori's answer to Sarmento; almost pure Canaiolo. CC

Alte d'Altesi A 70 per cent Sangiovese/30 per cent Cabernet Sauvignon blend from Altesino in Montalcino, aged in new oak for about a year.

Altero Pure Sangiovese from Poggio Antico in Montalcino, kept in wood for less time than Brunello.

Anagallis Equal parts of Sangiovese and Colorino aged for seven or eight months in *botti* of Allier oak, from Castello di Lilliano. CC

Ania Pure Sangiovese from Castello di Gabbiano. First produced in 1982 and kept in *barriques* for ten months. CC

Aquabona Pure Sangiovese from Fattoria Sassolo, near San Miniato. First vintage 1988.

Aquilaia Vineyard *cru* from Banti in Scansano.

Ariella Pure Chardonnay from Castello di Gabbiano, fermented and kept for four months in Tronçais *barriques*. CC

Armaiolo Predicato di Biturica from San Fabiano in the Colli Aretini, made from equal parts of Sangiovese and Cabernet Sauvignon.

Balifico Stylish *barricato* blend of 70 per cent Sangiovese, 10 per cent Cabernet Sauvignon and 20 per cent Cabernet Franc from Castello di Volpaia. Merlot may be included. CC

Le Balze *Cru* of Il Poggiolino, mainly Sangiovese with a little Trebbiano, Canaiolo and other unidentified grapes,

aged in sixteen-hectolitre *botti*. May include a little Cabernet Sauvignon. CC

Barullo Sangiovese with 15 per cent Cabernet Sauvignon and two years oak ageing, from Le Selvole. CC

Bellavista Castello di Ama vineyard with 80 per cent Sangiovese and 20 per cent Malvasia Nera. CC

Bianco dei Bianchi Pure Trebbiano, champagne-method sparkling wine from Monsanto. CC

Bianco della Contessa White wine from Contucci in Montepulciano.

Bianco della Rocca Chardonnay from Meleta.

Borro Lastricato Name of vineyard at Selvapiana in Rufina, planted with 60 per cent Pinot Bianco/40 per cent Pinot Grigio.

Boscardini Vineyard at Pagliarese for their Chianti Classico *riserva*.

Bottaccio Pure Sangiovese, from vineyard at Il Paradiso estate at San Gimignano.

Brunesco di San Lorenzo Pure Sangiovese from Montagliari, resurrecting a tradition of the 1770s. Aged in small casks. CC

Bruno di Rocca Two parts Sangiovese to one part Cabernet Sauvignon from Vecchie Terre di Montefili. First vintage 1983. Aged in *barriques*. CC

Brusco dei Barbi From Fattoria dei Barbi in Montalcino, made from Sangiovese Grosso with a little Canaiolo and Trebbiano, by a particular vinification process, including the *governo* method.

Cabreo Bianco Chardonnay from Ruffino's La Pietra vineyard, fermented, kept in *barriques* and sold as Predicato del Muschio. CC

Cabreo Rosso Predicato di Biturica from Ruffino's Vigneto Il Borgo; a 30 per cent Cabernet/70 per cent Sangiovese blend aged for fourteen months in Limousin oak. CC

Ca' del Pazzo Equal parts of Cabernet Sauvignon and Sangiovese, aged in *barriques* for eight to twelve months from Caparzo in Montalcino.

Camerlengo Pure Sangiovese Grosso aged in *barriques* from Pagliarese. CC

Campo del Sasso Villa Cilnia white with 45 per cent Chardonnay and 15 per cent Malvasia Nera and Trebbiano, from Colli Aretini.

Canvalle Sangiovese with 20 per cent Cabernet Sauvignon from Vignavecchia. Kept in wood for a year. CC

Casuccia Castello di Ama vineyard with 80 per cent Sangiovese and 20 per cent Merlot. CC

Cepparello *Barrique*-aged pure Sangiovese from Isole e Olena, made in better vintages instead of a Chianti *riserva*. CC

Cetinaia Pure Sangiovese from San Polo in Rosso, aged partly in *barriques* and partly in *botti*. CC

Ciabatta Morellino di Scansano *cru* from Banti.

Citerno Vineyard at Brolio, planted mainly with Pinot Bianco, with some Malvasia. CC

Codirosso Sangiovese from Vistarenni, with about a year of ageing in *barriques*. CC

Coltassala Pure Sangiovese, aged for fifteen months in *barriques*, from Castello di Volpaia. CC

Coltibuono Bianco Equal parts Chardonnay, Trebbiano and Malvasia from Badia a Coltibuono. CC

Coltibuono Rosso Sangiovese Grosso, plus 25 per cent Canaiolo and 7 per cent Cabernet Sauvignon, from Badia a Coltibuono. CC

Coltifredi Pure Sangiovese Biturica di Cardisco from the cooperative of Castelpesa. CC

I Coltri Sangiovese with some Cabernet Sauvignon, aged for six to eight months in *barriques*, from Melini. CC

Concerto A 20 per cent Cabernet Sauvignon/80 per cent Sangiovese blend from Fonterutoli, aged in new *barriques* for seven or eight months. CC

La Contessa della Torre White wine from Torre a Decima in Colli Fiorentini, made from Pinot Grigio with 10 per cent Chardonnay.

Contessa di Radda Label for Agricoltori del Chianti Geografico, for wine made from grapes coming only from Radda. Kept in wood for longer than usual. CC

Convivio Made by Giorgio Regni at Valtellina from Sangiovese and a little Cabernet Sauvignon, aged first in *barriques* and then in Yugoslav casks. Occasionally there is Merlot too. CC

La Corte Pure Sangiovese, aged in *barriques* from Castello di Querceto. CC

Decembrino Not a *vino novello*, but nevertheless intended for early drinking; made from Canaiolo with some Malvasia by Rocca delle Macie. CC

Il Doccio Second wine from La Stellata in Pitigliano.

Docciolo Trebbiano with 15 per cent Chardonnay from Il Paradiso in San Gimignano.

Dolce Amore White wine from Torre a Decima in the Colli Fiorentini, made from approximately 40 per cent Trebbiano, with Riesling, Pinot Grigio and Chardonnay.

Elegia Pure Sangiovese from Poliziano in Montepulciano, aged for twelve months in *barriques*.

Fattoresco Alternative to Chianti from Sant'Ermo in the Colline Pisane, using up excess Canaiolo, Malvasia and Ciliegiolo, as well as Sangiovese. For early drinking.

Flaccianello della Pieve Pure Sangiovese from Fontodi, aged for nine to twelve months in *barriques*. First vintage 1981 and made only in the best years. CC

Fontalloro   Pure Sangiovese *cru* from Felsina Berardenga, *governato* and *barrique*-aged for twelve months. CC

Fontanelle   Chardonnay, aged in wood for four months, from Banfi in Montalcino.

Fontestina   Sangiovese and 15 per cent Ciliegiolo from Bruno Moos in the Collline Pisane.

François I   Charmat method sparkling wine from Castello di Querceto. CC

Furfantino   Trebbiano with 20 per cent Chardonnay from Trerose in Montepulciano.

Gaio   Galestro lookalike from Baroncini in San Gimignano.

Gherardino   Pure Sangiovese from Vignamaggio, aged in *barriques* for twelve months. CC

Ghiaie della Furba   A Cabernet/Merlot blend from Capezzana in Carmignano, aged in *barriques* for twelve months.

Ghiara   Sangiovese plus 10 per cent Cabernet from Scopicci in the Colline Pisane.

Giardinello   Sangiovese with 10 per cent Cabernet Sauvignon from Castelgiocondo in Montalcino.

Ginestrino   Galestro lookalike from Sant' Ermo in the Colline Pisane.

La Gioia di Riecine   Identical to Riecine's *riserva*, except that it is aged in *barriques* for about a year. CC

Il Gotha   Oak-aged Chardonnay from Monsanto. CC

Le Grance   Barrel-fermented Chardonnay from Caparzo in Montalcino. First vintage 1985.

Granvino di Montemaggio   Mainly Sangiovese from Montemaggio, aged for three years in *barriques*. CC

Grifi   Mainly Prugnolo, with 15 per cent Cabernet Franc, from Avignonesi in Montepulciano. Kept in new wood.

Il Grigio   Good quality Chianti Classico from San Felice. CC

Grosso Sanese   Pure Sangiovese from Il Palazzino. *Barrique*-aged for a year. CC

Lacrima d'Arno   Galestro lookalike from Melini. CC

Libaio   White wine from Ruffino, mainly Chardonnay with 10 per cent Sauvignon, and maybe some Pinot Grigio in the future. Fermented in stainless steel for early drinking. CC

Logaiolo   70 per cent Sangiovese to 30 per cent Cabernet Sauvignon, kept in 60-hectolitre chestnut casks, from best vineyard of Aiola. CC

Lucertolo   Pure Trebbiano from Meleta, vinified in oak and quite unlike any other wine of that grape variety.

Lucestraia   Name of farm at Sorbaiano. A Montescudaio Bianco fermented in wood; includes Chardonnay, Vermentino and Italian Riesling.

Le Macie del Ponte alla Granchiaia   Vino da Tavola di Gaiole, produced by Vignale, from 10 per cent Cabernet Sauvignon blended with Sangiovese and aged in Limousin *barriques* for two years. CC

Malemacchie   *Barrique*-aged red including 25 per cent Cabernet Sauvignon from Poggio Gagliardo in Montescudaio.

Il Mandorlo   Equal parts of Cabernet Sauvignon and Sangiovese from La Madonnina; aged in *barriques* for eighteen months. CC

Il Marzocco   Named after the emblem of Montepulciano, barrel-fermented Chardonnay from Avignonesi, with six months of ageing in wood and more in bottle.

Meriggio   Pinot Bianco, with 10 per cent Gewürztraminer and 20 per cent Sauvignon from Fontodi. Spends three months in Tronçais barrels. CC

Messer Bianco   Equal parts of Chardonnay and Pinot Bianco from Salcetino. CC

Messer Rosso   10 per cent Cabernet with Sangiovese, from Salcetino. CC

Mona Lisa   Partly *barrique*-aged Sangiovese with Cabernet Sauvignon from Vignamaggio. CC

Monna Primavera White wine from Serristori, made mainly from Canaiolo, vinified as *in bianco*. CC

Montepetri Trebbiano and Malvasia blend with 40 per cent Chardonnay from Pasolini dall'Onda in Colli Fiorentini.

Montesodi Name of vineyard on the Nipozzano estate in Rufina, producing the best wine of the estate, from forty-year-old vines, aged in *barriques* for twenty months.

Mormoreto Name of vineyard in Rufina's Nipozzano estate, planted with Cabernet Sauvignon for Predicato di Biturica.

Nebbiano Vineyard at Brolio planted approximately 60 per cent Sauvignon to 40 per cent Italian Riesling. CC

Nemo Cabernet from Monsanto. CC

Nero del Tondo Pure Pinot Nero from Ruffino, aged for ten months in *barriques*. First vintage 1985.

Niccolò da Uzzano The best Sangiovese from Castello di Uzzano, sold as a Chianti Classico. CC

Orfeno Red wine from Parco dell'Uccellina.

Ornellaia Cabernet/Merlot blend from Bolgheri.

Palazzo Altesi Pure Sangiovese from Altesino in Montalcino. Half made by traditional vinification and half by carbonic maceration, aged in *barriques* for eight to twelve months.

La Papessa *Barrique*-aged wine from Montecchio, mainly Sangiovese Grosso, with 5 per cent Cabernet Sauvignon. First made 1985. CC

Paretaio Pure Sangiovese, aged in *barriques* for twelve months, from Falchini in San Gimignano.

Paterno II Name of farm on Il Paradiso estate in San Gimignano, producing pure Sangiovese, aged in *barriques* for five months.

Percarlo Pure Sangiovese, occasionally with a tiny amount of Cabernet Sauvignon, kept in *barriques*, from San Giusto a Rentennano. CC

Le Pergole Torte Pure Sangiovese from Montevertine, aged for three or four months in Limousin *barriques* and then about twenty months in *botti* of various sizes. CC

Pietrello Sangiovese with a drop of Ciliegiolo, from Meleta, kept in wood for eighteen months.

Il Poggio Best vineyard at Monsanto. CC

Poggio alle Gazze Sauvignon with a dash of Sémillon from Ornellaia in Bolgheri.

Poggio Cicaleto Pure Sangiovese pink from Villa Cilnia in Colli Aretini.

Poggio Garbato Chardonnay and Müller Thurgau blend from Villa Cilnia.

Prima Vigna A super *riserva* Chianti from Vicchiomaggio, made from wines planted in the 1930s and matured in Burgundian barrels for three to five months. CC

Principesco Tenuta Sant'Agnese Vino Nobile from Montepulciano, but aged in mulberry wood.

Privilegio *Vino novello* from Villa Cilnia in Colli Aretini.

Prunaio Pure Sangiovese Grosso from Viticcio, aged in *barriques* for a year. CC

Quercianello *Vino novello* from Val di Suga in Montalcino.

Querciatino Young wine from Castello di Querceto, made partially by carbonic maceration. CC

Querciolaia Predicato di Biturica from Castello di Querceto. The Cabernet Sauvignon spends fourteen months in wood, as opposed to seven or eight for the Sangiovese. CC

Rancia Vineyard from Felsina Berardenga, planted with pure Sangiovese. *Barrique*-aged for at least twelve months, but without the *governo* method. CC

Rèdola White wine from the Parco dell'Uccellina.

R. e R. A predominantly Cabernet Sauvignon blend with 10 per cent Merlot and 25 to 30 per cent Sangiovese from Castello di Gabbiano. Each grape variety is aged separately for fourteen months before bottling. CC

R.F. From the best vineyard of Castello di Cacchiano. Same blend as for Chianti, but aged for twelve months in *barriques*. CC

Roncaia *Cru* from Il Poggiolino, mainly of Sangiovese, including some grapes from very old vines, grafted with other unspecified grape varieties; aged in *barriques*. First vintage 1985. CC

Rosso della Rocca Equal parts of Sangiovese, Merlot and Cabernet Sauvignon, aged in wood for two years, from Meleta.

Rosso della Torre Red wine from Torre a Decima composed of 50 per cent Cabernet with Sangiovese and some Canaiolo and Malvasia Nera; aged in *botti*. CC

Rosso delle Miniere Sangiovese with 10 per cent Cabernet Sauvignon from Sorbaiano in Montescudaio, aged in *barriques* for six months.

Rosso di Sansovino Pure Prugnolo from Contucci in Montepulciano, kept for only twelve months in *botti*.

Rubizzo Young style Chianti Classico from Rocca delle Macie. CC

Rugo Vino da Tavola di Tavarnelle from Fattoria dell'Ugo in the Colli Fiorentini, made from the best Sangiovese, with 15 per cent Cabernet Sauvignon and aged for a short period in *barriques*.

Saltero Blend of Sauvignon, Trebbiano and Malvasia, aged in *barriques* for eight months from Trerose in Montepulciano.

Sammarco Three parts Cabernet Sauvignon to one part Sangiovese, aged in Nevers *barriques* for nearly two years, from Rampolla. CC.

San Giocondo *Vino novello* from Antinori. CC

Sangioveto Best Sangiovese from the vineyards of Badia a Coltibuono, as well as the local name for Sangiovese in Chianti. Spends one year in *botti* and one in *barriques*. CC

San Lorenzo Castello di Ama vineyard, with 80 per cent Sangiovese and 20 per cent Canaiolo. CC

Santa Brigida Half and half Sangiovese/Cabernet Sauvignon blend, from La Ripa; aged in *barriques*. CC

Santa Costanza *Vino novello* from Banfi in Montalcino.

Santa Cristina Until 1986 a Chianti Classico from the Antinori estate of the same name, but now treated as a brand name for a pure Sangiovese.

Sant'Angiolo Vico l'Abate *Cru* from the cooperative of Castelli del Grevepesa and their best Chianti. CC

Sarpinello Champagne-method pure Vernaccia from Teruzzi e Puthod in San Gimignano.

Sassello A 70 per cent Sangiovese, 30 per cent Cabernet Sauvignon blend aged in *barriques* from Verrazzano. CC

Sassicaia The inspiration for so many of the wines in this list. A blend of Cabernet Sauvignon and Cabernet Franc from Bolgheri.

Sassolato Villa Cilnia's answer to Sauternes, made from dried, rather than nobly rotten grapes and kept for twelve months in *barriques* (Colli Aretini).

Scalabrone Antinori pink wine from Bolgheri.

Seicentenario Made by Antinori to commemorate their 600th anniversary – a blend of Sangiovese and Cabernet. CC

Selvamaggio A Cabernet/Sangiovese blend from La Selva in the Colli Aretini.

Ser Gioveto *Barrique*-aged Sangiovese and Cabernet from Rocca delle Macie. CC

Ser Niccolò Mainly Sangiovese, with some Cabernet Sauvignon from Serristori and aged in *barriques*. CC

Le Serre Nuove Second label of Ornellaia in Bolgheri.

I Sistri Pure Chardonnay from Felsina Berardenga, fermented and then aged in *barriques* for ten months. First vintage 1987. CC

Il Sodaccio 88 per cent Sangiovese, 12 per cent Canaiolo from Montevertine, aged for two years in small *botti*. CC

I Sodi di San Niccolò Sangiovese, with 10 to 20 per cent Malvasia Nera from Castellare, with twelve months ageing in new *barriques*. CC

Sòdole Pure Sangiovese from Guicciardini Strozzi in San Gimignano, kept in new *barriques* for six to eight months.

Solaia Cabernet Sauvignon with some Sangiovese, from Antinori; the reverse proportions to Tignanello. CC

Solatio Basilica Basilica is the name of a farm on the estate of Cafaggio. Made as an extra special Chianti *riserva*, from old vines. CC

Sorbino A white wine from Le Calvane in Colli Fiorentini made from Trebbiano enlivened with 30 per cent Chardonnay.

Spargolo Pure Sangiovese from forty-year-old vines, sold as Predicato di Cardisco by Cecchi; aged in *barriques* and *botti*. CC

Le Stanze Mainly Cabernet Sauvignon from Poliziano in Montepulciano, with 5 per cent Cabernet Franc. First vintage 1987.

Tavernelle Pure Cabernet Sauvignon from Banfi in Montalcino.

Terre del Palazzo Red and white table wine from Pasolini dall'Onda. White is Trebbiano with 10 per cent Chardonnay, and the red Sangiovese with 10 per cent Cabernet Sauvignon. Colli Fiorentini.

Terre di Cortona Unoaked Chardonnay from Avignonesi in Montepulciano.

Terre di Tufo *Barrique*-aged Vernaccia di San Gimignano from Teruzzi e Puthod in San Gimignano.

Tignanello The leader amongst the Supertuscans, from Antinori, comprising Sangiovese, with about 20 per cent Cabernet Sauvignon, aged in *barriques*. CC

Tinscvil Three parts Sangiovese to one part Cabernet, from Monsanto, aged in both Slavonic and French oak. CC

Toforino Malvasia and Vermentino blend from Maionchi in the Colline Lucchesi.

Torniello Pure Sauvignon from Castello di Volpaia, aged for eight months in wood. CC

Torricella Malvasia aged in wood from Brolio. First made in 1928. CC

Tramonto Pure pink Sangiovese from Brolio. CC

Trebianco White wine from Castello dei Rampolla. As the name implies, made from three grape varieties, Gewürztraminer, Sauvignon and Chardonnay. CC

Tusco Bianco Malvasia and Trebbiano enlivened by 20 per cent Cortese from Piedmont, made by Giorgio Regni at Valtellina. CC

Vallocaia Made only in the better vintages by Bindella in Montepulciano, mainly from Prugnolo, part of which is aged in *barriques* for four to six months.

Veneroso Sangiovese with 35 per cent Cabernet and 10 per cent Malvasia, aged in *barriques* for a few months from Ghizzano in the Colline Pisane.

Vergena Sauvignon Predicato del Selvante from Castelgiocondo in Montalcino.

Vermiglio Sangiovese from Costanti in Montalcino, aged for three years in chestnut casks.

Vigna Asinone Best vineyard of Poliziano in Montepulciano, matured in 500-litre barrels.

Le Vignacce A blend of Cabernet Sauvignon, Sangiovese and Montepulciano d'Abruzzo from Villa Cilnia, aged in *barriques* for twelve to eighteen months. Colli Aretini.

Vigna del Fiore Best vineyard of the Barbi estate in Montalcino.

Vigna del Sorbo Twenty-five-year-old Sangiovese vines at Fontodi, blended with 10 per cent Cabernet Sauvignon. Half the wine is aged in *barriques* for twelve months. Only 5,000 bottles made in all. CC

Vigna del Vescovo Name of vineyard at the Fattoria di Manzano, planted half with Gamay and half with Ciliegiolo.

Vigna Elisa *Cru* from the cooperative of Castelgreve, sold as one of their better Chiantis. CC

Vigna Peperino Sangiovese with 20 per cent Montepulciano d'Abruzzo, from Teruzzi e Puthod in San Gimignano.

Vigneto Bucerchiale   *Cru* from Selvapiana in Rufina.

Vigneto della Rosa   Non-oaked Chardonnay from Montellori in Chianti.

Vigorello   One of the earliest Tuscan alternative wines, made initially from Sangiovese and Canaiolo; now containing 15 per cent Cabernet Sauvignon, with 50 per cent Sangiovese and 35 per cent Sangiovese Grosso, aged in *barriques* and Slavonic oak casks from San Felice. CC

Vilucchio   White wine from Montecchio made from 50 per cent Chardonnay, and 50 per cent Trebbiano and Malvasia. CC

Vinattieri   Brainchild of Maurizio Castelli.

The white has nothing to do with Tuscany, but the red is a blend of the best Sangiovese, 60 per cent Sangioveto from Chianti Classico and 40 per cent Sangiovese Grosso from Montalcino, aged in *barriques* for fifteen months.

Vino del Sasso   Pure Cabernet Sauvignon, aged in new *barriques* for eight months, from Fanetti in Montepulciano.

Vino della Signora   Pure Gewürztraminer from Poggio al Sole. CC

Vocato   Sangiovese, blended with 20 per cent Cabernet Sauvignon from Villa Cilnia in Colli Aretini.

Glossary

abboccato   Medium dry.

agriturismo   A popular activity in Tuscany, covering the renting of accommodation on an estate to holidaymakers.

barrique   The Bordeaux barrel of 225 litres, made from French oak.

bâtonnage   For white wine: the mixing of the fine lees at the bottom of a barrel with the wine during the ageing process.

bollino   Seal on the neck of the bottle, substantiating the authenticity of a wine.

botte   Large cask, of unspecified size, traditional to Tuscany, usually made of Slavonic oak.

botticelli   A small *botte*, often 500 litres.

Charmat   A method of making sparkling wine, whereby the second fermentation takes place in a tank, rather than in the bottle, which is the case for the champagne method.

commune   Translates as 'parish' in English.

consorzio   Growers' association.

cordone speronata   A popular method of pruning in Tuscany, and a slight variation on *guyot*, whereby the arm is not replaced every year, but rather the shoots that grow off it.

crostini   The typical Tuscan *antipasto*, usually made from chicken livers, spread on toast.

cru   Although the literal translation from French is 'growth', in Italy it often denotes a specific vineyard that is deemed to be better than the rest.

enoteca   A wine shop, or wine library.

fattore   Manager of a Tuscan estate.

guyot   A type of pruning, leaving a trunk and either one arm or two.

liquoroso   Describes a fortified wine, with added alcohol.

malolactic fermentation   The secondary fermentation whereby the malic acid, as in apples, is converted into lactic acid, as in milk. It should always occur in red wine, but can be prevented in white wine.

normale   The basic DOC wine, as opposed to a *riserva*.

passito   Describes grapes that have been semi-dried before they are pressed, or the wine from those grapes.

pH   Indication of acidity.

polyphenols   Colouring matter in red wine.

quintals   Italian measure for a hundred kilograms. Yields of wine are given in quintalss per hectolitre. In theory one hundred quintalss of grapes will give you a hundred hectolitres of juice; but in practice the DOC regulations restrict the amount of juice allowable, usually to 70 per cent, in other words 70 hectolitres per hectare.

remontagio   For red wine; the pumping of fermenting juice over the cap of skins in order to extract colour and tannin.

riserva   Wine aged for a longer time in barrel and maybe bottle than the basic DOC wine.

sfuso   Wine sold *sfuso* is sold unbottled in bulk.

sparco inglese   A method of grafting, whereby wood from the new vine, rather than a bud, is inserted into the trunk of the existing vine.

T-budding   A way of transforming the variety of the vine, whereby a bud from another variety is grafted into the trunk.

tufo   Or tufa, A volcanic soil.

Bibliography

Burton Anderson, *Vino, the Wines and Winemakers of Italy*, Little Brown & Co.,
    Boston, 1980.
    Biondi Santi, the Family that created Brunello di Montalcino, Union, 1988.
Nicholas Belfrage, *Life beyond Lambrusco*, Sidgwick & Jackson, London, 1985.
Chianti, Ambiente Cultura Itinerari Vini, Edizioni Tecniche Moderne, Milan, 1986.
Raymond Flower, *Chianti, the Land, the People and the Wine*, Croom Helm,
    London, 1978.
A. D. Francis, *The Wine Trade*, A. & C. Black, London, 1972.
David Gleave, *The Wines of Italy*, Salamander Books, London, 1989.
Lega del Chianti, Edizioni il Torchio, Florence, 1983.
Giovanni Righi Parenti, *Guida al Chianti, La Terra, il Vino i Castelli*, Sugar Co
    Edizioni, Milan, 1977.
Lamberto Paronetto, trans. Bruno Roncarati, *Chianti, The History of Florence and
    its Wines*, Wine & Spirit Publications, London, 1970.
Emanuele Pellucci, *Vino Nobile di Montepulciano*, Fiesole, 1985.
    Antinori Vintners in Florence, Vallecchi, Florence, 1981.
    Brunello di Montalcino, Fiesole, 1986.
Corrado Peruzzi, *Guida ai Vini di Montepulciano*, Edagricole, 1978.
Giovanni Piscolla, *San Gimignano and Vernaccia*, Florence, 1986.
Cyril Ray, *Ruffino*, Westerham Press, 1978.
Jancis Robinson, *Vines, Grapes and Wines*, Mitchell Beazley, London, 1986.
I. L. Ruffino 1877–1977, Florence, 1978.
Mario Soldati, *Vino al Vino*, Mondadori, Milan, 1977.
Giacomo Tachis, *Il Libro del Vin Santo*, Bonechi, Florence, 1989.
Sheldon and Pauline Wasserman, *Italy's Noble Red Wines*, New Century Publishers,
    New Jersey, 1985.
Vino e Olio in Toscana, Casa Editrice Il Fiore, Florence, 1988.
Piero Zoi, *Vino Nobile di Montepulciano*, Edizioni Lui, 1987.

Index

Numbers in italic refer to pages with black and white illustrations, or pages opposite colour illustrations